Beyond Journalist

Beyond Journalistic Norms contests and challenges pre-established assumptions about a dominant type of journalism prevailing in different political, economic, and geographical contexts to posit the fluid, and dynamic nature of journalistic roles.

The book brings together scholars from Western and Eastern Europe, North America, Latin America, and Asia, reporting findings based on data collected from democratic, transitional, and non-democratic contexts to produce thematic chapters that address how journalistic cultures vary around the globe, specifically in relation to challenges that journalists face in performing their journalistic roles. The study measures, compares, and analyzes the materialization of the interventionist, the watchdog, the loyal-facilitator, the service, the infotainment, and the civic roles in more than 30,000 print news stories from 18 countries. It also draws from hundreds of surveys with journalists to explain the link between ideals and practices, and the conditions that shape this divide.

This book will be of great relevance to scholars and researchers working in the fields of journalism, journalism practices, philosophy of journalism, sociology of media, and comparative journalism research.

Claudia Mellado is Professor of Journalism in the School of Journalism at the Pontificia Universidad Católica de Valparaíso, Chile. Her research focuses on the study of journalism cultures, journalistic role performance, and comparative studies. She is the principal investigator of the JRP Project (www.journalisticperformance.org). Her work has been extensively published in journals such as *Journal of Communication, International Journal of Press/Politics, Journalism, JMCQ, Journalism Studies, Journalism Practice,* and *Communication Theory.* Her last edited book is *Journalistic Role Performance: Concept, Contexts, and Methods* (Routledge, 2017).

Routledge Research in Journalism

Critical Perspectives on Journalistic Beliefs and Actions
Global Experiences
Edited by Eric Freedman, Robyn S. Goodman, and Elanie Steyn

Economic News
Informing the Inattentive Audience
Arjen van Dalen, Helle Svensson, Anotinus Kalogeropoulos, Erik Albæk, Claes H. de Vreese

Reporting Humanitarian Disasters in a Social Media Age
Glenda Cooper

The Rise of Nonprofit Investigative Journalism in the United States
Bill Birnbauer

Tech Giants, Artificial Intelligence, and the Future of Journalism
Jason Whittaker

Investigative Journalism, Democracy and the Digital Age
Andrea Carson

Understanding Citizen Journalism as Civic Participation
Seungahn Nah and Deborah S. Chung

Newsroom-Classroom Hybrids at Universities
Student Labor and the Journalism Crisis
Gunhild Ring Olsen

Beyond Journalistic Norms
Role Performance and News in Comparative Perspective
Edited by Claudia Mellado

For more information about this series, please visit: www.routledge.com

Beyond Journalistic Norms

Role Performance and News
in Comparative Perspective

Edited by Claudia Mellado

Routledge
Taylor & Francis Group

NEW YORK AND LONDON

First published 2021
by Routledge
52 Vanderbilt Avenue, New York, NY 10017

and by Routledge
2 Park Square, Milton Park, Abingdon, Oxon, OX14 4RN

*Routledge is an imprint of the Taylor & Francis Group, an
informa business*

© 2021 Taylor & Francis

Library of Congress Cataloging-in-Publication Data
A catalog record for this book has been requested

ISBN: 978-1-138-38849-9 (hbk)
ISBN: 978-0-367-56129-1 (pbk)
ISBN: 978-0-429-42550-9 (ebk)

Typeset in Sabon
by Apex CoVantage, LLC

Contents

List of Illustrations   viii
List of Contributors   xi
Foreword   xv
Acknowledgments   xviii

PART I
Professional Roles and Journalistic Performance   1

1 Journalistic Role Performance and the News   3
  CLAUDIA MELLADO

2 Theorizing Journalistic Roles   22
  CLAUDIA MELLADO

3 Assessing Journalistic Role Performance Cross-Nationally:
  Comparative Design and Methodology   46
  CLAUDIA MELLADO, JACQUES MICK, AND MIREYA
  MÁRQUEZ-RAMÍREZ

PART II
**The Manifestation of Journalistic Role Performance
in the News**   65

4 Mapping Professional Roles in News Content
  Across 18 Countries: A Descriptive Overview   67
  CLAUDIA MELLADO, MIREYA MÁRQUEZ-RAMÍREZ, MARÍA
  LUISA HUMANES, ADRIANA AMADO, CORNELIA MOTHES,
  HENRY SILKE, AGNIESZKA STĘPIŃSKA, GABRIELLA SZABÓ,
  SERGEY DAVYDOV, JACQUES MICK, DASNIEL OLIVERA, NIKOS S.
  PANAGIOTOU, SVETLANA PASTI, PATRIC RAEMY, SERGIO ROSES,
  ANNA-MARIA SCHIELICKE, AND EDSON TANDOC JR.

5 Journalistic Voice: The Performance of the
   Interventionist Role   85
   AGNIESZKA STĘPIŃSKA, GABRIELLA SZABÓ, ADRIANA AMADO,
   AND HENRY SILKE

6 Power Relations: The Performance of the
   Watchdog and Loyal-Facilitator Roles   103
   MIREYA MÁRQUEZ-RAMÍREZ, SERGIO ROSES, HENRY SILKE,
   AND DASNIEL OLIVERA

7 Audience Approach: The Performance of the Civic,
   Infotainment, and Service Roles   125
   MARÍA LUISA HUMANES AND SERGIO ROSES

PART III
Explaining Journalistic Role Performance   145

8 Measuring the Link Between Professional Role
   Conceptions, Perceived Role Enactment, and Journalistic
   Role Performance Across Countries   147
   CLAUDIA MELLADO AND CORNELIA MOTHES

9 Journalistic Role Performance: A News-Story-Level
   Approach   167
   EDSON TANDOC JR., PATRIC RAEMY, SVETLANA PASTI, AND
   NIKOS PANAGIOTOU

10 Journalistic Role Performance: An Organizational-Level
   Approach   186
   CORNELIA MOTHES, ANNA-MARIA SCHIELICKE,
   AND PATRIC RAEMY

11 Journalistic Role Performance: A Societal-Level
   Approach   205
   AGNIESZKA STĘPIŃSKA, GABRIELLA SZABÓ, MIREYA
   MÁRQUEZ-RAMÍREZ, SVETLANA PASTI, AND NIKOS
   PANAGIOTOU

12 **Beyond Journalistic Norms: Empirical Lessons on Role Performance in the News** 225
CLAUDIA MELLADO, MIREYA MÁRQUEZ-RAMÍREZ, MARÍA LUISA HUMANES, CORNELIA MOTHES, ADRIANA AMADO, SERGEY DAVYDOV, JACQUES MICK, DASNIEL OLIVERA, NIKOS S. PANAGIOTOU, SVETLANA PASTI, PATRIC RAEMY, SERGIO ROSES, ANNA-MARIA SCHIELICKE, HENRY SILKE, AGNIESZKA STĘPIŃSKA, GABRIELLA SZABÓ, AND EDSON TANDOC JR.

Appendices 245
Index 289

Illustrations

Figures

2.1   Domains, dimensions, and indicators of journalistic roles   38
2.2   Dimensions and sub-dimensions of journalistic roles   39
4.1   Journalistic voice: Interventionist role   72
4.2   Power relations: Watchdog and loyal-facilitator roles   74
4.3   Audience approach: Civic, infotainment, and
      service roles   75
5.1   Content- and style-related indicators of the
      interventionist role (means)   90
5.2   Presence of content-related indicators of the
      interventionist role (percentage)   92
5.3   Presence of style-related indicators of the interventionist
      role (percentage)   92
5.4   Indicators of the interventionist role in briefs and articles
      (combined) across countries   96
6.1   The interventionist and detached orientations of the
      watchdog role across countries (mean)   111
6.2   The interventionist and detached variations of the
      watchdog role across news topics (mean)   112
6.3   The elite-supporting and nation-supporting orientations
      of the loyal-facilitator role across countries (means)   116
6.4   The elite-supporting and nation-supporting orientations
      of the loyal-facilitator role across news topics (means)   117
7.1   The advocate and educational sub-dimensions of the
      civic role across countries (means)   133
7.2   The advocate and educational sub-dimension of the civic
      role across news topics (means)   134
7.3   Elements of infotainment role performance across news
      topics (mean and percentage)   136
7.4   Elements of service role performance across news topics
      (mean and percentage)   139

8.1   Average conception-performance, perception-performance, and conception-perception gaps for six journalistic roles across countries   155

8.2   Country differences in conception-performance gap, perception-performance gap, and conception-perception gap for the interventionist role   156

8.3   Country differences in conception-performance gap, perception-performance gap, and conception-perception gap for the watchdog role   156

8.4   Country differences in conception-performance gap, perception-performance gap, and conception-perception gap for the loyal-facilitator role   157

8.5   Country differences in conception-performance gap, perception-performance gap, and conception-perception gap for the civic role   157

8.6   Country differences in conception-performance gap, perception-performance gap, and conception-perception gap for the infotainment role   158

8.7   Country differences in conception-performance gap, perception-performance gap, and conception-perception gap for the service role   158

Tables

3.1   Sample Distribution by Country, Newspaper, Audience Orientation, and Total Number of Items   48

3.2   Survey Items and Coding Indicators for Measuring Role Conception, Perceived Role Enactment, and Role Performance   53

4.1   The Performance of the Interventionist, Watchdog, Loyal-Facilitator, Civic, Infotainment, and Service Roles in the News Across Countries   71

4.2   Correlations Between the Interventionist Role and Other Journalistic Roles by Country   76

5.1   Presence of Indicators of the Interventionist Role by Regime Type (Percentage)   93

5.2   Presence of Indicators of the Interventionist Role in the Popular and Elite Press (Percentage)   94

5.3   Presence of Style-Related Indicators of the Interventionist Role in the Popular and Elite Press Across Countries (Percentage)   95

5.4   Presence of the Indicators of the Interventionist Role in the News (Percentage, Means, and Standard Deviations)   97

Illustrations

6.1 The Detached Orientation of the Watchdog Role Across
Countries   109
6.2 The Interventionist Orientation of the Watchdog Role
Across Countries   110
6.3 The Elite-Supporting Orientation of the Loyal-
Facilitator Role Across Countries   114
6.4 The Nation-Supporting Orientation to the Loyal-
Facilitator Role Across Countries   115
7.1 Analytical Sub-Dimensions and Indicators of the Civic
Role (Means and Percentages)   132
7.2 Indicators of the Infotainment Role (Percentages)   135
7.3 Indicators of the Service Role (Percentages)   138
8.1 Strength of the Relationship Between Role Conceptions
vs. Perceived Role Enactment and Role Performance
(Unstandardized Regression Coefficients; Standard
Errors in Parentheses)   161
9.1 Topics, Sources, and Geographic Focus   174
9.2 Story-Level Effects on Journalistic Role Performance   179
10.1 Organizational Effects on the Performance of the
Interventionist and Politics-Oriented Journalistic Roles   196
10.2 Organizational Effects on the Performance of
Audience-Oriented Journalistic Roles   197
11.1 Linear Correlations Between Close-Context Societal
Variables and Journalistic Role Performance
Across Countries   211
11.2 Linear Correlations Between Broad-Context Societal
Variables and Journalistic Role Performance
Across Countries   213
11.3 Societal-Level Effects on Journalistic Role Performance:
Interventionist, Watchdog, and Loyal-Facilitator   217
11.4 Societal-Level Effects on Journalistic Role Performance:
Infotainment, Civic, and Service   218
12.1 Challenges, Actions, and Limitations Faced
by the JRP Project   240

Contributors

Claudia Mellado *is Professor of Journalism in the School of Journalism at the Pontificia Universidad Católica de Valparaíso, Chile. Her research focuses on the study of journalism cultures, journalistic role performance, and comparative studies. She is the principal investigator of the JRP Project (www.journalisticperformance.org). Her work has been extensively published in journals such as* Journal of Communication, International Journal of Press/Politics, Journalism, JMCQ, Journalism Practice, Journalism Studies, *and* Communication Theory. *Her last edited book is* Journalistic Role Performance: Concept, Contexts, and Methods *(Routledge, 2017).*

Adriana Amado *is a researcher at the Universidad Argentina de la Empresa (UADE), Argentina. Her teaching and research focus on social media, journalism, and public communication. She is also a journalist and civic activist in Latin American NGOs. Her last book is* Política pop *(2016).*

Sergey Davydov *is Associate Professor at the National Research University Higher School of Economics in Moscow, Russia. His research interests include the sociology of media, journalism, and public opinion. He is co-editor of the book series* Online Research in Russia *(volumes 2, 3, and 4, in Russian) and editor of the collective monograph* Internet in Russia: A Study of the Runet and Its Impact on Social Life *(in English).*

María Luisa Humanes *is Associate Professor at the Department of Communication Sciences and Sociology, University Rey Juan Carlos in Spain. Her research interests focus on journalistic cultures. She is the head of the project "Models of Journalism in a multi-platform environment," funded by the Spanish Ministry of Science, Innovation, and Universities. She has published about these topics in journals such as* International Journal of Communication, Journalism, *and* International Journal of Press/Politics.

Mireya Márquez-Ramírez *is Associate Professor of Journalism Studies and Media Theory at the Department of Communications, Universidad Iberoamericana, in Mexico City. Her research interests include comparative journalism studies, news production, journalists and violence, and sports journalism. She is Mexico's principal investigator of the* Journalistic Role Performance Project.

Jacques Mick *is Associate Professor of Sociology at the Department of Sociology and Political Science, Federal University of Santa Catarina, Brazil. Since 2011, his research focuses on the work of Brazilian journalists. He has published books and scientific articles on the subject in journals such as* Brazilian Journalism Research *and* Sur Le Journalisme/About Journalism.

Cornelia Mothes *is a postdoctoral researcher at the School of Media and Communication at Technische Universität Dresden, Germany. Her main research interests lie in the field of political communication, political journalism, and media psychology. Her work has been published in journals such as* Communication Theory, Communication Research, *and* Journal of Communication.

Dasniel Olivera *is Associate Professor at the School of Communication of Havana University, Cuba. He wrote his Ph.D. dissertation on change and continuity in the Cuban media, and his research interests are comparative studies of media systems, communication policies, and peace journalism. He received the Award of the Academy of Sciences of Cuba in Social Science Projects Category in 2017.*

Nikos Panagiotou *is Assistant Professor at the School of Journalism and Mass Media Communication, Aristotle University, Greece. He has extensive research work which is currently funded from Google (DNI Initiative fund). He is Greece's principal investigator of the* Journalistic Role Performance Project, *and has published articles in international and Greek journals and in edited volumes. His research interests focus on international journalism, audience studies, and conflict analysis and resolution.*

Svetlana Pasti *is Adjunct Professor at Faculty of Information Technology and Communication Sciences (ITC) at Tampere University, Finland. Her research interests are in journalism studies and comparative research in the BRICS countries. She is author of several books and over 30 peer-reviewed chapters and journals articles such as* Journalism, Journal of Communication, *and* Journalism Studies.

Patric Raemy *is a Ph.D. candidate at the Department of Communication and Media Research, University of Fribourg, and a lecturer in media education at the Zurich University of Teacher Education, Switzerland.*

He researches journalistic roles, journalistic performance, and professional identity.

Sergio Roses *is Associate Professor of Journalism at the School of Communication Science, University of Málaga, Spain. His teaching and research interests include journalists and professionalism, journalistic role performance, and comparative journalism cultures.*

Anna-Maria Schielicke *is a research associate at the Institute of Media and Communication at Technische Universität Dresden, Germany. Her main research interests lie in the field of political communication and media psychology with a focus on populism, stereotyping, and hate-speech.*

Henry Silke *is Lecturer in Journalism at the University of Limerick, Ireland. His research interests include the representation of economics in journalism and working conditions for journalists and digitization. He has published on these topics in journals such as* Digital Journalism, The International Journal of Communication, *and* Critical Discourse Studies.

Agnieszka Stępińska *is Professor at the Faculty of Political Science and Journalism, Adam Mickiewicz University in Poznań, Poland. Her main areas of research are political communication and journalism studies. She leads the Polish team of the* Journalistic Role Performance Project, *as well as a scientific team working on the populist political communication in Poland. Currently, she is an executive editor of the Central European Journal of Communication.*

Gabriella Szabó *is Head of the Department of Political Behavior at the Institute for Political Science of the Centre for Social Sciences, as well as a lecturer at Budapest University of Technology and Economics, Hungary. She has expertise in political communication and media studies, and has extensively published peer-reviewed articles in national and international journals. Her research is funded by the Hungarian National Research, Development and Innovation Office under the grant agreement no. 131990.*

Edson C. Tandoc Jr. *is Associate Professor at the Wee Kim Wee School of Communication and Information at Nanyang Technological University in Singapore. His research focuses on the sociology of message construction in the context of digital journalism and journalistic roles. His work has been extensively published in international peer-reviewed journals.*

Silvio Waisbord *is Professor in the School of Media and Public Affairs at George Washington University. He is the author and editor of*

18 books, including more recently Communication: A Post-Discipline *and* The Communication Manifesto, *both published by Polity Press. He is the former editor-in-chief of the* Journal of Communication *and the* International Journal of Press/Politics. *He has lectured and worked in more than 40 countries in the Americas, Europe, Asia, and Africa. He is a fellow of the International Communication Association.*

Foreword

This book is the culmination of years-long work by a global team of researchers unified by common goals: to better understand how and why journalists perform different roles and to explain the gap between normative visions and actual practices. It takes a decidedly cosmopolitan perspective interested in understanding journalistic norms and practices around the world. It brings together global experts to look at a common set of questions and to produce shared arguments (instead of producing stand-alone chapters). Tapping into a wealth of data, the analysis has a tight focus, brings up nuanced insights, and delivers sharp conclusions. The authors have produced a remarkable book that, like all solid scholarship, tell us something we didn't know and corroborates important arguments.

The book offers rich empirical evidence in support of the argument that journalistic cultures across countries blend various influences and roles.

Recent interest in studying global journalism and "de-westernizing" media and journalism studies has produced a growing English-language literature on journalism from around the world. Certainly, this is a welcome development. It facilitates the inclusion of cases and perspectives and helps to probe conclusions originally produced in a handful of Western countries. However, there is a double risk: to simply add cases from around the world without engaging in common debates and to essentialize journalistic cultures in distinctive geo-political categories. It is important to showcase research from various countries in international journals and book collections, but it does not necessarily foster the kind of conversation necessary for a truly cosmopolitan research community. Also, clustering journalism in geographic-political entities loses sight of constant mixing and borrowing. Similarities, differences, and cross-pollinating dynamics are missed.

To avoid this problem, as this book suggests, we need to be cautious about drawing categorical conclusions about journalistic norms and practices by "nationality" or "region" of the world. What may be analytically expedient, such as understanding press/media systems that overlap with nation-states, may miss important aspects. National (or regional) borders are not perfect containers of porous professional cultures. National groupings are analytically useful as a first approximation to understanding journalism, but it may replicate narrow ways of studying media institutions and journalistic practices.

The book also makes a compelling argument for why we should not take journalists' attitudes and beliefs about their job at face value. Studies about how reporters conceive their work should be mindful of real conditions. Context matters. We cannot (and shouldn't) study journalism in the abstract. Journalistic practice is embedded in organizational and industrial contexts shaped by social factors—economic, political, cultural. This idea is commonsense, but it is still not sufficiently recognized. Personal professional ideals do not easily translate into practice (as anyone who works in any organization knows). What reporters would like to do, and their own professional convictions and ethical principles, are one set of important elements for understanding what happens, but they interact with the rough-and-tumble reality of newsroom work. Virtuous ideals necessitate a considerable degree of personal and collective agency that is not exactly what prevails in hierarchical organizations shaped by multiple forces. Consequently, as this book finds out, there are several gaps between beliefs and practices and abstract principles and concrete decisions that need attention.

Also, conventional journalistic roles are not perfectly separated from each other. Just as in the case of cross-national professional cultures that blend various influences, professional roles are intertwined, too. News stories crystallize the mixing of various ideal roles depending on various factors. This volume clearly identifies this phenomenon as well as the reason why it happens. It tells us that whereas scholars may seek to find typologies that have heuristic value, practices do not necessarily neatly fit in existing categories.

The book also grapples with the problems of past generalizations. It challenges conclusions about the prevalence of certain professional roles in specific countries with plenty of evidence. What makes a "dominant" model dominant? How do we know? At a time of disruptive changes in the news industry and the multiplication of various forms of journalism, old certainties need to be revisited.

By the same token, the book warns us about making universal claims about "journalism" and its relation to core concepts in the literature such as democracy, objectivity, autonomy, investigation, fairness, and so on. The book smartly problematizes the relationship between professional practices and ideals that supposedly govern (or should orient) everyday reporting. Different combinations of roles and ideals unsettle existing grand visions about the linkages between journalism and democratic ideals. Take the multilayered situation of journalism in "new" or "transitional" democracies. Using the latter as an analytical concept is problematic, even though it seems a handy label for classifying journalistic practices and conditions. The reality of journalism, politics, and economics are far more complex that what conventional categories recognize.

In summary, this book makes two major contributions to journalism studies. It calls to interrogate many divides embedded in analytical frameworks and debates. It nudges us to be suspicious of conventional ways of slicing up everything, including journalistic cultures and roles. It reshuffles the way we think about commonalities and differences across divides. It warns us about mindlessly falling back into taxonomies built at a different time. It stimulates our curiosity about how journalism works in different settings.

As a global collective enterprise, the book also invites us to embrace cosmopolitan scholarship to produce analysis grounded in comparative, cross-national data and to overcome existing academic inequalities. It scraps the pyramidal structure of Western-centered global academia. It geographically decenters the analysis by laying out ideas produced by scholars from around the world. At a time when journalism confronts challenges that demand multi-flow conversations, integrated analysis, and action, the book is an admirable example of "thinking together" across multiple borders. The book offers a blueprint for research collaboration that upends conventional ways of thinking about global journalism studies.

Silvio Waisbord

Acknowledgments

This book presents the results of the cross-national *Journalistic Role Performance* (JRP) project (www.journalisticperformance.org).

This study is hosted by the Pontificia Universidad Católica de Valparaíso–Chile (PUCV), and I am deeply grateful for all the institutional support that we have received. My colleagues, enthusiastic students, the campus facilities, and the overall community at PUCV have provided a stimulating environment that has allowed this research project to thrive over the years.

Funding was provided by different sources, such as the national research councils of the participating country teams and/or individual researchers' universities and/or local organizations, to whom we are deeply thankful. We are especially grateful to the Chilean National Fund for Scientific and Technological Development (FONDECYT) for believing in this project from day one, and funding the preliminary phases of the study.

This volume was possible thanks to the efforts and expertise of many scholars and research teams from all over the world. I am indebted to everyone who participated in this endeavor during the various stages of the project's design, planning, management, and data processing.

I am very grateful to the authors of this book for their hard and steady work throughout multiple manuscript drafts. In particular, I would like to thank my colleagues and friends Mireya Márquez-Ramírez, María Luisa Humanes, and Cornelia Mothes for all of their ongoing support and input. Our mutual trust and shared intellectual visions have allowed us produce not only this book, but many publications together.

Thanks to Agnieszka, Gabriella, Sergio, Adriana, Jacques, Henry, Svetlana, Edson, Dasniel, Sergey, Patric, Anna-Maria, and Nikos for your valuable suggestions, commitment, and/or leadership in your respective chapters. The book is much better because of you.

All of my colleagues and co-authors have been a crucial part of everything you will read in the pages that follow. This book is dedicated to them and to the scholars and their research assistants who worked so hard to collect data in their respective countries.

Indeed, the authors of this book also acknowledge the researchers who were part of this project at different stages and conducted content analysis in their respective countries: Kinga Adamczewska, Daniel Beck, Maxi Bongiovanni, Regula Hänggl, Ewa Jurga-Wosik, Lea Hellmueller, Maria Lauber, Olga Logunova, Paschal Preston, Manuel Puppis, Hilda María Saladrigas, Bartlomiej Secler, Eugenia Siapera, Aldo Schmitz, Colin Sparks, Leydi Torres, Moniza Waheed, Andreas Veglis, and Haiyan Wang. We appreciate their effort, commitment, and all of their work. In particular, I feel that it is important to recognize the contributions of our late professor and friend Wolfang Donsbach, who was not only a founding and active member of this project until his passing, but a mentor to all of us.

I would like to thank several top scholars and friends in particular for generously agreeing to read different parts of this book and for providing valuable feedback that contributed a great deal to the quality of the final manuscript: Amaranta Alfaro, Mario Alvarez, Jay Blumler, Sandrine Boudana, Akiba Cohen, Dan Hallin, Dan Jackson, César Jiménez, Henrik Örnebring, Auska Ovando, Clement So, Arjen van Dalen, and Silvio Waisbord. I definitively owe each of you a good bottle of Chilean wine.

Finally, on behalf of my co-authors, I give special thanks to our friends and families, who supported us on this creative and reflective journey.

On a personal note, I dedicate this work to my mother Nora and to my children, Lucas and Julieta, who are the reason why I try to be better every single day.

Claudia Mellado, Santiago, Chile, March 27, 2020.

Part I
Professional Roles and Journalistic Performance

1 Journalistic Role Performance and the News

Claudia Mellado

One of the most frequently discussed subjects in the history of our field is the function that journalism and the media should play in society as interrelated institutions. This discussion centers on the extent to which journalism and the news media should—or should not—serve democracy, citizens, consumers, the market, political elites, the political system at large, or journalists' own intellectual or literary pursuits.

Normative functions are assimilated through a variety of roles that journalists may conceive of and/or perceive as legitimate as part of their job. Some of these journalistic roles are more widely discussed, embraced, and theorized than others.

The roles that journalists claim and/or aim to play and see as important can be performed in the news via specific reporting practices, newsgathering routines, and narrative devices that reflect them. But under what circumstances is the materialization of professional roles actually possible? How is the performance of journalistic roles defined and shaped in the news?

Since focusing on how journalists believe they perform or aspire to perform a certain role only tells part of the story, and given that this only reveals how journalists see their profession and not how their work actually reflects in practice, this book moves beyond early comparative research on journalistic roles. Considering the changes and challenges that journalism as a profession is facing today, this volume provides empirical evidence about the complexity of journalistic cultures. It offers a comprehensive analysis of how news professionals perform different roles across social contexts and news media organizations, how much importance they give to specific professional functions, the way they feel they can perform such roles, how different factors affect the outcome of their work, and the extent to which their performance differs from their ideals of the profession.

This book focuses on the performance of six journalistic roles (the interventionist, watchdog, loyal-facilitator, civic, infotainment, and service), their analytical sub-dimensions, and indicators across different countries, contexts, and topics. It also analyzes the link between norms, perceptions, and practices. We start from the position that regardless of what the expected journalistic norms are, journalistic roles are by no means static, and are instead situational, dynamic, and fluid. We argue that journalistic role performance cannot be fully understood outside of a meaningful context, contesting and challenging pre-established assumptions about a "dominant type" of journalism that prevail in different political, economic, and geographic contexts.

Let us take the following examples as case studies. In 2010, 33 Chilean miners were trapped underground following an accident in the northern part of the country. Cut off from their employers and rescue workers, they feared for their lives for weeks. After 69 days, the world watched as they were rescued one at a time. The record-breaking media coverage of this "real-life miracle" and "happy-ending story" taught all of us about the miners' ordeal and the day-to-day hardships that they endured. Some news outlets and journalists even ran stories about how to survive if you were trapped underground.

The many flags and banners held by cheering crowds as the miners emerged into the sunshine hinted at how important the day was to Chile as a nation. But in the tense lead-up to that dramatic climax, journalists had to follow confusing updates from Chilean officials, covering the increasing number of voices that questioned mining policies and working conditions in that industry, and reporting on the overall tension and uncertainty that prevailed at the rescue site. Some news professionals also relied on infotainment reporting devices to "sell the news" to the audience as the events unfolded. They focused on the miners as "micro celebrities," narrating their life stories and their families' anguish and zooming in on their emotions and private lives.

In late 2019 and early 2020, the world again turned its attention to a unique event: President Donald Trump's impeachment by the U.S. Congress based on allegations that he had tried to illegally coerce Ukrainian officials to investigate his political rival, Joe Biden. The U.S. press already had a tense and antagonistic relation with Trump, who frequently attacked the media for allegedly spreading fake news and attempting to weaken his presidency. Many news organizations had been skeptical, if not openly critical, of his candidacy based on his perceived inability to lead the country. Clearly departing from a tradition of neutrality and objectivity—cherished tenets of the profession in the U.S.—journalists are increasingly commenting on the facticity of Trump's statements, regularly calling out falsehoods. In contrast to similar cases that have been brought before the House, these hearings were the subject of special coverage across media outlets who used all of their resources to scrutinize this historic event for democracy in the U.S. and the world. However, some journalists—and one media outlet in particular—performed quite a different role. Fox News, one of Trump's few allies in the media, did not broadcast live coverage of the impeachment hearings. Instead, the network ran selected sound bites and even video footage with no sound in order to allow its news anchors to interpret events without offering actual live footage.

During the 2020 COVID-19 pandemic, journalism and the media had a valuable opportunity to cover many angles and approaches to the global public health crisis. In several countries, newspapers ran stories that were very critical of governments and national leaders for failing to meet the public's informational needs or for implementing—or failing to implement—the measures that the public or experts deemed suitable.

Stories about containment measures also showcased the loyal-facilitator role. Some highlighted public policies designed to contain the spread of the virus, while others praised foreign governments, local actors, or institutions for putting the public interest and national security first. Meanwhile, the press published endless news stories with tips on how to detect symptoms, what to do, and how to remain safely at home, investigating possible solutions to ordinary problems that might arise as a result of prolonged social isolation. Still other stories focused on entertaining the audience or on the private lives of quarantined individuals, such as the daily occurrences of infected show business celebrities. Sensationalist coverage also contributed to the somewhat apocalyptic, alarmist views that often prevail in times of uncertainty and fear.

At the same time, journalists were quickly gathering citizen testimonies to push for action and sanitary measures, documenting healthcare professionals' concerns about the lack of resources, equipment, hospital staff, and beds. Some news stories even discussed how economic, social, and political systems needed to change to prevent pandemics and their consequences. The media coverage of the Coronavirus pandemic also yielded many examples of the interventionist role. We heard and read multiple personal stories and opinions offered by journalists who sought to signal that there was cause for alarm.

As we can see from these examples, journalistic roles are not mutually exclusive in life or in journalism (Weaver & Willnat, 2012; Mellado, 2015; Lynch, 2007).

In all of these complex episodes, various journalistic roles and their characteristics are performed at once, as multiple missions and news values are accomplished and displayed, sometimes simultaneously, as events unfold (Briggs & Hallin, 2016). Sometimes journalists serve as a watchdog, working to hold the powerful accountable (Bennett & Serrin, 2005). At other times, they play the loyal-facilitator role, giving credence to official claims in supportive, collaborative ways (Christians, Glasser, McQuail, Nordenstreng, & White, 2009). They may also take on the civic role that gives voice to the voiceless and empowers citizens by calling attention to their demands (Curran, 2007), produce news pieces that provide concrete suggestions for everyday life (Eide & Knight, 1999), and thrill the public using infotainment devices (Thussu, 2007). While the use of journalistic voices is more prominent at certain times, as was the case with Trump's impeachment, journalists may also remain more detached in their reporting of other events.

News professionals are not restricted to choosing and performing just one role, as events rarely display the same roles as they unfold. Both the Chilean mine accident and COVID-19 examples show how the interventionist, loyal-facilitator, watchdog, civic, service, and infotainment roles can be presented as suitable angles at different times in the media coverage of an event, and even simultaneously. Both examples also show different types of approaches to the roles. Journalists may move from educating audiences about their rights to advocating for certain causes on their behalf. Other times, it is simply a matter of involvement. The Trump case shows how traditional press scrutiny not only intensified but elicited a more prominent use of the personal voice on the part of the journalist.

But, to what extent did the journalists in charge of covering these events expect to perform all of those roles? As we will see in the various chapters of this book, journalistic practice transcends normative expectations. Journalists must adapt, adjust, and perform multiple roles on a daily basis in response to ever-changing circumstances.

The profession has cherished norms that are often taken as pillars of journalism, such as truth-seeking, monitoring established powers, giving voice to the people, or providing a forum to discuss public affairs (Kovach & Rosenstiel, 2014). However, beyond general agreements on basic assumptions about journalism as a profession (Waisbord, 2013; Örnebring, Karlsson, Fast, & Lindell, 2018), looking at the specific and varied conditions in which journalists work can open our eyes about how professional roles are understood and performed around the world.

The ways of performing these ideals are far from homogenous, and different circumstances may prompt journalists to perform different roles. As Ryfe (2012, p. 21) asserts, "What looks appropriate from one vantage point may seem inappropriate from another." In countries undergoing conflict or crisis, media may prefer to support national unity and harmony in the face of tragedy and crisis (Zelizer & Allan, 2011). For example, the media can set aside their questioning or monitoring of elites or businesses for a time in the aftermath of terrorist attacks or natural disasters. In countries with limited governmental transparency and controlled access to public information, or where elites and economic powers are fully insulated from scrutiny, it would be very hard for journalists to carry out their truth-seeking mission. Furthermore, complete editorial detachment and neutrality would be nearly impossible in countries where the journalists' civic values and levels of independence lead them to openly oppose the government or advocate for social causes. This may also be the case in highly polarized or partisan environments.

Depending on the historical context and sociopolitical moment, then, some journalists portray governments and their policies in a positive light for multiple reasons ranging from national pride to state-development missions to partisan allegiances and collusion, or to reflect political instrumentalization and state intrusion. Others consistently and openly antagonize political elites, for both democratic reasons out of a duty to the profession or for personal political reasons. The giant leap that U.S. media have taken since 2016 regarding their open expression of their opinions about their president is clear evidence of this.

As circumstances change, the idea of journalistic roles as monolithic and taken for granted as good or bad in society seems to oversimplify the complex realities of journalism and the media. For the aforementioned reasons, we believe that the concept of *journalistic role performance* provides a strong theoretical and empirical framework to account for the fluid, dynamic nature of journalistic roles and the ideals-practice links that exist between the evaluative side of journalistic cultures and everyday news practice around the world.

Journalistic Role Performance (JRP): The Project

This book focuses on the circumstances in which journalistic roles are performed in the news, the way in which certain roles interact with each other and present variation across different contexts, and the link between ideals and practice in journalism. In doing so, we present the findings from one of the most wide-ranging collaborative studies in this area of research: the *Journalistic Role Performance* Project *(JRP)*. Ours is an international endeavor that expands the scope of journalism research by including the dimension of news practice in the study of professional cultures.

This effort has two main goals. First, it aims to explain how several professional roles—interventionist, watchdog, loyal-facilitator, service, civic, and infotainment—materialize in print news in various organizational, institutional, and social settings, to account for various contexts and patterns of hybridization. Second, it addresses the link between professional or normative ideals and journalistic practices, explaining the link between the importance that journalists ascribe to different roles, their perceived role enactment, and journalistic role performance.

The analysis of different journalistic roles is based on the relationship between journalism and powerholders, the presence of the journalistic voice in their practices—interventionism vis-à-vis detachment—and the way in which journalism addresses the audience, i.e., as citizens, clients, or spectators. This book also considers the influences that different societal factors, organizational structures, story-level characteristics, and journalists' perceptions exert on the practice of journalism, offering new insights into the nature and complexity of the profession.

Thanks to the collaborative efforts of various scholars, the JRP Project (2013–2018) used a mixed-method design based on content analysis and survey research. National teams first analyzed the performance of professional roles in more than 30,000 news stories from 64 print media outlets from 18 countries. They then surveyed hundreds of journalists working in those outlets to study the link between their perceptions and their professional practice.

For theory-building purposes, in this book we assert that journalists' missions and the performance of journalistic roles can and do take many forms. Our aim is to explore the multiple factors that shape the performance of journalistic roles, ranging from the historical contexts of media systems to the specific country and its type of political regime, the type of news organization where journalists work, and the type of news events at stake.

The world has seen that news professionals have an extraordinary capacity to adapt their missions and their practice to ever-changing circumstances, and to devise and perform duties that evolve in a complex, simultaneous, and often contradictory set of roles. Even though these days of digital revolution and the prevalence of social media prompt many discussions about how journalistic roles are undergoing a process of constant reinvention (Hermida, 2014; Molyneux & Holton, 2015), this is not something totally new. Ever since the "invention" of journalism in the Anglo-Saxon world (Chalaby, 1998), there has been a significant discussion on the different journalistic roles that prevail in less-studied geographical locations (e.g., Mellado, Márquez-Ramírez, Mick, Olivera, & Oller, 2017).

As a sign of the impact that the Western model of journalistic professionalism and its normative theories have had on our understanding of journalistic roles, in many countries the news has often been locked in somewhat rigid journalistic genres that pigeonhole the news in opinion or factual categories. This is why most journalism students around the world are often taught the concept of objectivity very early on. They learn that facts must always be separated from opinions, that hard news are serious while soft news are not—and that they can take some interpretative liberties with these *soft* topics that are not afforded to political news, that journalists must always act as watchdogs but never display loyalty/advocacy towards elites, and that they need to address the audience as citizens regardless the context, the event, or the specific moment in time (Mellado et al., 2013).

While these norms are pedagogical and useful for constructing professional identities and discourses of occupational legitimacy, and to build societal consensus on the accepted functions of the profession, binary expectations rarely work in practice (Waisbord, 2013). Instead, these expectations contribute to ever-growing discrepancies between ideals and practice (Mellado et al., 2020; Tandoc, Hellmueller, & Vos, 2013).

In reality, news events are small and big, extraordinary and ordinary. News coverage often evolves, displaying a variety of angles and actors that require certain types of relationships with powerful actors, audiences, and the use of the journalistic voice. Moreover, having had the opportunity to look at news content from 18 countries and through our efforts to detach ourselves from traditional normative expectations, it has become clear that not all governments—or even politicians—are treated skeptically. In fact, news coverage is sometimes supportive of elites even though the watchdog role of the press has been one of the most discussed and theorized as socially expected, especially in established democracies (Bennett & Serrin, 2005). As most classic ethnographic research on news production concludes, governmental claims or actions tend to go unchecked, and it is actually routine practice to accept official claims as valid (Tuchman, 1978; Fishman, 1980).

By the same token, despite what journalists might aspire to or think, in practice, not all watchdog reporting contributes to political accountability, good governance, or efforts to strengthen democracy (Jacobs & Schillemans, 2016). Roles that focus on democracy-building may clash with those oriented towards consumerism or the market. In fact, despite arguments that infotainment weakens the discussion and visibility of serious public affairs, it is common for journalists to want to engage their audiences with such content. As a result, "hard" news stories may carry traces of infotainment, such as personalization or the appeal to emotions. In other cases, journalists may try to provide a service to the public by offering tips and advice about their everyday needs.

In short, the news and journalism do not work in straightforward ways and their roles are always "open to reimagining" (Baym, 2017, p. 12). In this book, we argue that journalistic roles are situational (Vos, 2017) and dynamic, as opposed to fixed and rigid. Because of this, though the global influence of certain liberal values at the normative level is undeniable (Hanitzsch et al., 2011), at the role performance level—i.e., actual practice—journalistic cultures significantly vary across countries and have a strong context-bound element to them (Mellado, Hellmueller et al., 2017).

Comparative Studies on Journalism and Journalistic Roles

Comparative studies have become a fashionable trend in different research fields, including journalism studies. Over the past few decades, journalism research has focused on explaining how political, economic, cultural, and media-system characteristics have impacted the journalistic profession (Hallin & Mancini, 2004; Esser & Pfetsch, 2004; Esser & Hanitzsch, 2012; Shoemaker & Cohen, 2006). One of the key questions in current comparative research is how similar or different journalistic and media cultures are, and how they are characterized in terms of the information that reaches the public. Moreover, early research also tried to describe the impact of macro political structures and political regimes on the definition of press theories in different parts of the world (e.g., Siebert, Peterson, & Schramm, 1956). These early Manichean approaches have evolved into sophisticated empirical scholarship comparing the impact of political ideologies and partisan allegiances on reporting styles, perceptions, and the performance of journalistic roles across developed democracies (e.g., Donsbach & Patterson, 2004; Van Dalen et al., 2012; Esser & Umbricht, 2013).

Comparative studies need to be specific enough to reflect the characteristics and phenomena occurring in a particular cultural or geographical group or entity, and yet adaptable enough to showcase the differences among individuals and organizations within and across cultures. Scientific research is challenged by this task, as the nature of the journalistic profession might tie many journalistic cultures together at certain levels of analysis or set them apart at others. For example, system-level research (Hallin & Mancini, 2004) in Western democracies has done a fine job in tracking political and media-system similarities across geographically close countries. For their part, survey and content-analysis level research has corroborated the existence of geographical clusters that resemble existing categorizations of media systems (Van Dalen et al., 2012; Esser & Umbricht, 2013).

However, as Mellado Hellmueller and Donsbach (2017, p. 10) have noted, Western models of professionalism have not captured a universal conceptual and empirical understanding of journalism when talking about both "roles as ideals of practice, but also when we talk about the practice of the profession itself." Despite its best efforts to untangle their context-driven nature, comparative research on journalistic cultures is not yet focused enough on the detailed dynamics and nature of roles. We argue that, from the perspective of role performance, roles should not be taken as uniform, whole constructs but, instead, as permeable, hybrid sets of practices and narrative devices. Some aspects of roles can be more prominent depending on the circumstances, or might be casually or systematically triggered by certain factors at the macro, meso, micro, or content level. As a result, in this book we focus on role interaction and the analysis of role sub-dimensions and indicators, which can better illustrate the performance of roles in the news, as well as the factors behind the norms-practice link.

Moreover, most studies have focused on a small set of well-known countries, mainly Western nations (Hallin & Mancini, 2017). Most of these studies reinforce the idea that certain advanced democracies have similar media systems and therefore journalistic cultures, especially in relation to audience approaches and responses to market constraints (Hallin & Mancini, 2004). For example, European media systems—and particularly those of Northern Europe—associated with a Democratic

Corporatist outlook are described as delivering more hard news than their American counterparts, which (at least on television) are more liberal, commercialized, and deliver higher levels of infotainment and soft news (Aalberg & Curran, 2012). Polarized Pluralist media systems are assumed to show more interventionism and partisanship in their news, whereas a Liberal media system is thought to be more detached, factual, and engaged in infotainment, as journalists are said to embrace those roles (Hallin & Mancini, 2004; Donsbach & Patterson, 2004).

Still, this solid body of research tends to cover established democracies only. Despite recent efforts to incorporate a broader range of countries into cross-national studies of journalistic cultures, the call to conduct comparative research outside of the Western world remains and has never been timelier. On the one hand, most important comparative studies of professional roles in the field that engage in the study of both the Western and the non-Western worlds deal with how journalists perceive or conceive their roles (e.g., Hanitzsch et al., 2011; Hanitzsch, Hanusch, Ramaprasad, & De Beer, 2019; Weaver & Willnat, 2012), but not with their actual performance or how these two levels—the evaluative and performative—explain each other. On the other hand, and given the growing predominance of hybrid media systems (Hallin & Mancini, 2012, 2017; Voltmer, 2013), patterns observed in countries that have not been included in existing research—i.e., transitional democracies and non-democracies—are not as straightforward and in many levels of analysis even contradict theoretical assumptions based on established Western democracies. In fact, our results point to different hybridization patterns that tie the press of certain transitional and Western democracies together with respect to the performance of specific roles. We also find that this is not the case for other roles. For example, even if in theory stable democracies provide better structural conditions for journalists' monitoring of elites and their efforts to hold them accountable, the press of some democratic and non-democratic countries can also be grouped together based on their low performance of the watchdog role (see Chapters 4 and 6). This means that not all journalistic cultures fit into fixed categories or meet theoretical expectations with respect to certain factors, i.e., political regime or media system characteristics. Hence, apart from regime type or media system type, the analysis of role sub-dimensions and role interaction can explain several patterns of journalistic role performance. It is therefore crucial to abandon the study of roles as discreet categories and fixed constructs when studying journalistic cultures.

Furthermore, when trying to widen the scope by including a more inclusive and heterogeneous sample of countries in their analyses, scholars are faced with the difficulty of explaining the complexity of journalistic cultures across different political, economic, and social contexts. Two key problems have emerged in this respect that we deem as crucial for our project: first, there is still a worrying lack of comparative research between South-to-South media systems or journalistic cultures that would help to put national research findings and single-country phenomena in perspective. Second, apart from challenging economic indicators, most non-Western countries experience or have experienced similar characteristics that might impact journalistic and media performance, though they may experience them at different levels and ways. Potential similar factors include diverse types of authoritarianism (Geddes, Wright, & Frantz, 2018; Voltmer, 2013), troubled paths towards democratization, a history of colonization (hence resemblance of press and media systems devised by imperialist powers), widespread anti-press and societal violence, weak rule of law, social/racial tensions, elite-oriented presses, limited press freedom and access to information, widespread corruption, collusive press-state relations, or concentrated property of news media, to name a few.

Despite being well-known contextual factors, until now, many of these—except for economic performance, transparency, press freedom, quality of democracy, and few others—have been difficult to measure and compare in quantitative terms, such as clientelism, public advertising budgets, and political parallelism. Few databases include indicators that can account for and measure the different realities, and few indexes provide reliable data for all countries. Also, media-level indicators that include most countries are scarce, making it difficult to calculate the weight of these factors in the overall results of role performance.

Of even greater concern is the fact that many of the studies that do tackle certain countries from the Global South, the developing world, or countries that do not have clear-cut journalistic traditions tend to include them as "the control group." In other words, they are used not to as units of analysis in their own merit, but to refine, reinforce, or disprove particular theories, usually ethnocentric ones (Waisbord, 2019; Willems, 2014; Mellado, Hellmueller et al., 2017).

One of the strongest beliefs and assumptions of our work is that research in our field creates global and significant knowledge about journalism cultures worldwide, precisely in a time when we must question the familiar and the "known," opening the scope to the unexplored. As Waisbord and Mellado (2014, p. 365) emphasize, "De-westernization demands a shift in the analytical mindset. It should make researchers curious about the applicability of concepts, theories, and arguments across settings."

Role Performance as an Emergent Area of Research

Over the past decade, research on journalistic role performance—defined as the study of how particular journalistic norms and ideals are collectively negotiated and result in specific practices—has become very important in our field, providing a more thorough understanding of the processes behind journalistic performance in relation to normative expectations in a fluid media environment.

Understanding how (and why) different journalistic roles are performed around the world is fundamental for this moment in journalism in which the profession, its practices, and its credibility are increasingly being questioned.

As a concept, role performance conceives of journalism as social practice, focusing on the interplay between political economy, agency, and the structure of the media (Voltmer, 2013; Guerrero & Márquez-Ramírez, 2014). This epistemic umbrella allows us to explore journalistic ideals and the way that news is produced in different institutional settings, as well as the constant tension between norms, ideals, and the practices of journalists and news organizations around the world (Weaver & Willnat, 2012).

The study of ideals and practices as crucial elements of journalistic culture creates a valuable outcome: it allows for the analysis of the extent that reporting styles and journalistic decisions are explained by news professionals' role ideals and the extent that journalistic performance can be explained by factors that are not necessarily perceived as relevant on a daily basis.

Our project has developed novel conceptual perspectives, as well as fresh methodological approaches, contributing to and complementing the analysis of journalistic cultures and their integration into the broader field of media and communication. We have developed a standardization of measurements and the operationalization of different professional roles in news content (Mellado, 2015). We also have found more efficient ways to measure professional roles at the evaluative level cross-nationally by asking journalists to rate the importance they ascribe to concrete reporting practices rather than abstract statements on subjective ideals (Mellado et al., 2020).

The project's theoretical and empirical basis has allowed us to produce studies that have analyzed professional role performance in diverse sociopolitical and news production environments (e.g., Márquez-Ramírez et al., 2020; Humanes & Roses, 2018; Mellado, Márquez-Ramírez et al., 2017; Hellmueller & Mellado, 2016; Stępińska, Jurga-Wosik, Adamczewska, Selcer, & Narożna, 2016; Wang, Sparks, & Huang, 2018), supporting the idea that professional roles are fluid, contextual, and shaped by social environments, organizational structures, journalistic routines, and the local context of the news.

In other words, our studies provide empirical support for claims posed by previous revisionist literature (Voltmer, 2013; McCargo, 2012; Frère, 2015; Preston, 2009; Hallin & Mancini, 2017). That is, when looking at a more diverse range of countries that includes not only advanced but also transitional and nondemocratic countries, less clear-cut geographical or political, and media systems emerge. Yes, there are still national journalistic cultures that might appear to support existing theoretical expectations and group together in certain dimensions, but they may be separated by other dimensions or levels of analysis, particularly at the role performance level.

Our previous studies have also helped advance our understanding of the current significance of professional roles in everyday practice. They have shown that while journalistic norms have been established in different systems (Weaver & Willnat, 2012; Hanitzsch et al., 2011; Hanitzsch, Hanusch, Ramaprasad et al., 2019), the way in which journalists see themselves as professionals is not necessarily a mirror reflection of journalistic and media practices (Mellado et al., 2020; Roses & Humanes, 2019). Our previous publications also tried to predict the variation of role performance across several countries. Factors such as the media audience orientation (Humanes & Roses, 2018), macro-variables like press freedom and regime type (Márquez-Ramírez et al., 2020), and media platforms (Hallin & Mellado, 2018) have been identified as relevant for explaining variation in the performance of different roles while also showing that the practice of different roles is embedded in certain topics (Mellado, Márquez-Ramírez et al., 2017).

Despite mounting evidence of the complex news-production conditions that underpin the performance of journalistic roles, it is clear that a careful analysis is still necessary to account for very specific mixtures and nuances of journalistic cultures. Luckily, our research instruments are designed to account for journalistic roles both in general and in disaggregated terms, looking at the specific elements that comprise and give life to professional roles and their performances.

In an effort to continue to develop our contribution to this growing area of research, this book delves into the elements that give life to the performance of different professional roles in societal, organizational, and story-level contexts, explaining the combinations of traits that connect journalists' ideals and practices, how the co-occurrence of different roles generate specific types of hybridizations, and how different journalistic traditions and the historical context can explain variations in journalistic cultures in such a diverse world.

About This Book

This book is based on data spanning a wide range of developed, transitional, and non-democratic contexts and contains the empirical findings of our study. It follows the theoretical volume that was published in January 2017 by Routledge on this topic: *Journalistic Role Performance: Concepts, Contexts and Methods* (Eds. Mellado, Hellmueller & Donsbach). That publication was the first of its kind to theoretically address how journalistic ideals manifest themselves in practice.

This second book applies the framework set out in that previous volume, bringing together scholars from Western and Eastern Europe, Latin America, and Asia. More than an edited volume, this work is a carefully constructed result of hard teamwork. As such, its pages and chapters follow the same thread, though they present their own twists and turns, as authors are in constant dialogue with each other. These scholars have been active contributors to the JRP Project and were the principal investigators in their respective countries. They are leaders in the field in their home nations, and largely work in the research area that this book covers. Of course, they are not just guest authors; they are the soul of the project and have been involved throughout the entire process of the study, engaging in years of collaboration.

Unlike our previous theoretical endeavor, which introduced the concept of journalistic role performance, this book provides an in-depth analysis of how professional role performance behaves cross-nationally. Drawing on the various articles published over the past few years that contain both general explorations and analyses of specific issues of the project, in this book we present both an integrated and fine-grained vision of our results that also expands the scope of the research.

To our knowledge, this is the first book to provide empirical and systematic data that addresses journalistic role performance cross-nationally, studying different roles that tend to be studied separately. Most previous books have reported national or comparative data on journalists' attitudes, values, and norms, mainly focusing on North American and European journalists (Albæk, Van Dalen, Jebril, & de Vreese, 2014), though some do include journalists from around the world (Weaver & Willnat, 2012; Hanitzsch, Hanusch, Ramaprasad et al., 2019; Hanitzsch et al., 2011). While they have made a very important contribution to the field, those studies have approached the analysis of professional roles from just one of its angles, i.e., the conception and or perception of journalists, leaving the performative/practice perspective in the background, or addressing news perception and news content for only a handful of countries (Albæk et al., 2014).

This project is also pioneering in that it includes countries whose journalism models have not been theorized in the same systemic way as those of advanced democracies, and also in analyzing diverse types of news content besides political news. Furthermore, it is important to bear in mind that the entire data set is based on newspapers.

The Chapters of This Book

This book reports findings based on thematic chapters that address how journalistic cultures vary cross-nationally, specifically in relation to different social domains, elements of news production, structural settings, and the challenges that journalists face in performing their journalistic roles. The idea was not to produce chapters that focus on single countries, but to provide a global perspective by writing chapters based on specific topics.

The first part of this book sets the tone for understanding the chapters that follow. It lays out key aspects of the JRP Project that we have been unable to develop in-depth in scholarly journals because of the lack of space to do so. In order to make the work accessible to other colleagues, we describe how the project was organized, the theoretical and methodological framework that grounds it, and the challenges we have faced.

Far from offering a recipe for how to successfully conduct and lead these kinds of transnational, collaborative projects, or even how to master role theory applied to the journalistic field, the first part of this book is an academic effort to share the theoretical and methodological foundations of the project with the scholarly community. It has been a fascinating and fulfilling project, though also laborious, and we hope that it is useful to all of those interested in conducting comparative research on journalism and journalistic roles.

While this chapter outlines the scope of the book, providing an overall understanding of the main areas that underpin the JRP Project and the rationale for the study of journalistic role performance around the globe, in Chapter 2, Mellado offers an in-depth discussion of the theoretical framework of our project. It revisits key theoretical aspects that must be taken into account when studying journalistic roles and also reexamines the concept from different angles and lenses.

Chapter 3, led by Mellado, Mick, and Márquez-Ramírez, focuses on the general design and methodology of our comparative research on journalistic roles and role performance.

The second part of the book explores the manifestation of journalistic roles in actual practice through the analysis of six professional roles in news content across cultures. We pay special attention to the co-occurrences of roles, their interplay, and the hybridization patterns found in different journalistic cultures. Based on the exploration of analytical sub-dimensions and the individual indicators that comprise journalistic roles and research domains, these chapters offer a more detailed look at how journalism is performed in different thematic beats across elite and popular media.

Chapter 4, by Mellado and all of the colleagues who contributed to this book, offers a descriptive overview of the performance of professional roles around the globe. We highlight the overall differences and similarities of journalistic role performance across news content worldwide, setting the stage for the subsequent chapters. These findings refer to the domains we use to analyze journalistic roles, namely journalistic voice, power relations, and audience approaches, as well as six independent roles that emerge from such domains.

Chapter 5 reports findings from the journalistic voice domain of journalistic role performance. Stępińska, Szabó, Amado, and Silke describe how journalists around the world use different types of interventionism when reporting the news, such as journalistic opinion, interpretation, first person, adjectives, and proposal/demand. We also explore how the levels of hybridity in the performance of the interventionist vis-à-vis the disseminator role can be distinguished in different cultures.

Chapter 6 discusses the roles associated with the relationship between journalists and individuals and groups in power, focusing on the materialization of the watchdog and the loyal-facilitator roles in news content. Márquez-Ramírez, Roses, Silke, and Olivera provide examples of how monitoring and loyalism are not as oppositional as they are sometimes made out to be. In fact, our research shows that these roles even work together in some specific contexts. To account for this hybridization, the authors analyze the performance of the watchdog and the loyal-facilitator roles across countries, proposing analytical sub-dimensions for each role: a detached and interventionist orientation to the watchdog role, and the elite-supporting and nation-supporting approaches for the materialization of the loyal-facilitator role.

In Chapter 7, Humanes and Roses examine the different ways in which journalism approaches the audience, analyzing how the civic, service, and infotainment roles manifest themselves in news content, and how they can be distinguished in different cultures. While we find variations in the performance of the different indicators that compose each role across national contexts, media organizations, and news topics, we also show different patterns of role hybridization in the audience approach domain, illustrating how the co-occurrence of these roles is activated in various ways.

The third and final part of the book attempts to explain the performance of different journalistic roles cross-nationally. The chapters included in this section analyze the influences of various factors that can have an effect on different roles, as well as the link between ideals, reporter behaviors, and professional performance.

Recent studies have shown that although journalists may have clear ideas of which professional roles are more important to them, they do not consistently coincide with performance. In Chapter 8, Mellado and Mothes examine the link between the ideals that journalists have of their professional roles around the globe, their perceived role enactment, and their professional performance at two different levels. First, we analyze the disconnect/connection as a gap studying the extent to which journalists can live up to their ideals in news practice. Second, we explore the disconnect/connection as a relationship, looking at whether journalists who adhere to a more specific role are more likely to perform it.

Chapter 9, led by Tandoc, Raemy, Pasti, and Panagiotou, identifies main influences on journalistic role performance at the news-story level, finding that the news topic, news sources, and geographic focus significantly explain particular journalistic role performances.

Considering how journalistic practice has changed fundamentally in today's high-choice digital media environments, especially in newspaper journalism, Chapter 10 focuses on the organizational-level influence on journalistic performance. Mothes, Schielicke, and Raemy argue that the question of how journalism will prevail under such circumstances is intimately linked to how newspaper organizations handle these challenges, and how some of their organizational principles translate into journalistic practices.

Chapter 11 identifies the main influences on journalistic role performance in news content at the societal level, looking at the relationship between different roles and factors that transcend countries. Specifically, Stępińska, Szabo, Silke, and Márquez-Ramírez examine features that are closely related to the media, such as the press, legal, political, and economic environment. They also discuss broader context factors such as the democracy index, indicators of deliberative and participatory democracy, and economic/market freedom in the performance of professional roles.

Finally, Chapter 12 highlights the main findings of our JRP Project, providing conclusions, new insights, limitations, and potential lines of inquiry into the study of role performance cross-nationally.

Together, these chapters provide a more dynamic and overall view of the way in which print journalism conveys a wide range of functions around the world.

Our findings illuminate multiple patterns of hybridization and fluidity of journalistic roles. Although we are able to answer many pending questions, we open many more for future research.

References

Aalberg, T., & Curran, J. (2012). *How media inform democracy. A comparative approach*. Abingdon: Routledge.

Albæk, E., Van Dalen, A., Jebril, N., & de Vreese, C. H. (2014). *Political journalism in comparative perspective*. Cambridge: Cambridge University Press.

Baym, G. (2017). Journalism and the hybrid condition: Long-form television drama at the intersections of news and narrative. *Journalism, 18*(1), 11–26.

Bennett, W. L., & Serrin, W. (2005). The watchdog role. In G. Overholser & K. Hall Jamieson (Eds.), *The press* (pp. 169–188). New York: Oxford University Press.

Briggs, Ch., & Hallin, D. (2016). *Making health public: How news coverage is remaking media, medicine, and contemporary life*. New York: Routledge.

Chalaby, J. (1998). *The invention of journalism*. Basingstoke: MacMillan.

Christians, C. G., Glasser, T. L., McQuail, D., Nordenstreng, K., & White, R. A. (2009). *Normative theories of the media: Journalism in democratic societies*. Urbana, IL: University of Illinois Press.

Curran, J. (2007). Reinterpreting the democratic roles of the media. *Brazilian Journalism Research, 3*(1), 31–54.

Donsbach, W., & Patterson, T. E. (2004). Political news journalists: Partisanship, professionalism, and political roles in five countries. In F. Esser & B. Pfetsch (Eds.), *Comparing political communication: Theories, cases, and challenges* (pp. 251–270). Cambridge: Cambridge University Press.

Eide, M., & Knight, G. (1999). Public—Private service: Service journalism and the problems of everyday life. *European Journal of Communication*, 14(4), 525–547.

Esser, F., & Hanitzsch, T. (Eds.). (2012). *The handbook of comparative communication research*. London: Routledge.

Esser, F., & Pfetsch, B. (Eds.). (2004). *Comparing political communication: Theories, cases, and challenges*. Cambridge: Cambridge University Press.

Esser, F., & Umbricht, A. (2013). Competing models of journalism? Political affairs coverage in U.S., British, German, Swiss, French and Italian newspapers. *Journalism*, 14(8), 989–1007.

Fishman, M. (1980). *Manufacturing the news*. Austin: University of Texas Press.

Frère, M. S. (2015). Francophone Africa: The rise of 'pluralist authoritarian' media systems? *African Journalism Studies*, 36(1), 103–112.

Geddes, B., Wright, J., & Frantz, E. (Eds.). (2018). *How dictatorships work: Power, personalization, and collapse*. Cambridge: Cambridge University Press.

Guerrero, M., & Márquez-Ramírez, M. (2014). *Media systems and communication policies in Latin America*. London: Palgrave.

Hallin, D., & Mancini, P. (2004). *Comparing media systems. Three models of media and politics*. Cambridge: Cambridge University Press.

Hallin, D., & Mancini, P. (2012). *Comparing media systems beyond the Western world*. Cambridge: Cambridge University Press.

Hallin, D., & Mancini, P. (2017). Ten years after. *Comparing media systems*: What have we learned? *Political Communication*, 34(2), 155–171.

Hallin, D., & Mellado, C. (2018). Serving consumers, citizens or elites: Democratic roles of journalism in Chilean newspapers and television news. *The International Journal of Press/Politics*, 23(1), 24–43.

Hanitzsch, T., Hanusch, F., Mellado, C., Anikina, M., Berganza, R., Cangoz, I., . . . Kee Wang Yuen, E. (2011). Mapping journalism cultures across nations: A comparative study of 18 countries. *Journalism Studies*, 12(3), 273–293.

Hanitzsch, T., Hanusch, F., Ramaprasad, J., & De Beer, A. S. (Eds.). (2019). *Worlds of journalism: Journalistic cultures around the globe*. New York: Columbia University Press.

Hellmueller, L., & Mellado, C. (2016). Watchdogs in Chile and the United States: Comparing the networks of sources and journalistic role performances. *International Journal of Communication*, 10, 3261–3280.

Hermida, A. (2014). *Tell everyone: Why we share and why it matters*. Canada: Double Day.

Humanes, M. L., & Roses, S. (2018). Journalistic role performance in the Spanish national press. *International Journal of Communication*, 12, 1032–1053.

Jacobs, S., & Schillemans, T. (2016). Media and public accountability: Typology of an exploration. *Policy and Politics*, 44(1), 23–40.

Kovach, B., & Rosenstiel, T. (2014). *The elements of journalism* (3rd ed.). New York: Crown Publishers.

Lynch, K. (2007). Modeling role enactment: Linking role theory and social cognition. *Journal for the Theory of Social Behaviour*, 37(4), 379–399.

Márquez-Ramírez, M., Mellado, C., Humanes, M. L., Amado, A., Beck, D., Davydov, S., & Wang, H. (2020). Detached or interventionist? Comparing the performance of watchdog journalism in transitional, advanced and non-democratic countries. *International Journal of Press Politics*, 25(1), 53–75.

McCargo, D. (2012). Partisan polyvalence: Characterizing the political role of Asian media. In D. Hallin & P. Mancini (Eds.), *Media systems beyond the western world* (pp. 201–223). New York: Cambridge University Press

Mellado, C. (2015). Professional roles in news content: Six dimensions of journalistic role performance. *Journalism Studies*, 16(4), 596–614.

Mellado, C., Hanusch, F., Humanes, M., Roses, S., Pereira, F., Yez, L., .. Wyss, V. (2013). The pre-socialization of future journalists. *Journalism Studies*, 14(6), 857–874.

Mellado, C., Hellmueller, L., & Donsbach, W. (Eds.). (2017). *Journalistic role performance: Concepts, models and measures*. New York: Routledge.

Mellado, C., Hellmueller, L., Márquez-Ramírez, M., Humanes, M. L., Sparks, C., Stępińska, A., .. Wang, H. (2017). The hybridization of journalistic cultures: A comparative study of journalistic role performance. *Journal of Communication*, 67(6), 944–967.

Mellado, C., Márquez-Ramírez, M., Mick, J., Olivera, D., & Oller, M. (2017). Journalistic performance in Latin America: A comparative study of professional roles in news content. *Journalism*, 18(9), 1087–1116.

Mellado, C., Mothes, C., Hallin, D., Humanes, M. L., Lauber, M., Mick, J., .. Olivera, D. (2020). Investigating the gap between newspaper journalists' role conceptions and role performance in nine European, Asian and Latin American countries. *The International Journal of Press/Politics*. https://doi.org/10.1177/1940161220910106

Molyneux, L., & Holton, A. (2015). Branding (health) journalism: Perceptions, practices, and emerging norms. *Digital Journalism* 3(2), 225–242.

Örnebring, H., Karlsson, M., Fast, K., & Lindell, J (2018). The space of journalistic work: A theoretical model. *Communication Theory*, 28(4), 403–423.

Preston, P. (2009). *Making the news: Journalism and news cultures in Europe*. London, England: Routledge.

Roses, S., & Humanes, M. L. (2019). Conflicts in the professional roles of journalists in Spain: Ideals and practice, *Comunicar*, 27(58), 65–74.

Ryfe, D. (2012). *Can journalism survive? An inside look at American newsrooms*. Cambridge: Polity.

Shoemaker, P., & Cohen, A. (2006). *News around the world: Content, practitioners, and the public*. New York: Routledge.

Siebert, F., Peterson, T., & Schramm, W. (1956). *Four theories of the press*. Urbana, IL: University of Illinois Press.

Stępińska, A., Jurga-Wosik, E., Adamczewska, K., Selcer, B., & Narożna, D. (2016). Journalistic role performance in Poland. *Central European Political Studies*, (2), 37–52.

Tandoc, E., Hellmueller, L., & Vos, T. (2013). Mind the gap: Between role conception and role enactment. *Journalism Practice*, 7(5), 539–554.

Thussu, D. K. (2007). *News as entertainment: The rise of global infotainment*. London: Sage.

Tuchman, G. (1978). *Making news a study in the construction of reality*. New York: Free Press.

van Dalen, A., de Vreese, C., & Albæk, E. (2012). Different roles, different content? A four-country comparison of the role conceptions and reporting style of political journalists. *Journalism, 13*(7), 903–922.

Voltmer, K. (2013). *The media in transitional democracies.* Cambridge, UK: Polity.

Vos, T. (2017). Historical perspectives on journalistic roles. In C. Mellado, L. Hellmueller, & W. Donsbach (Eds.), *Journalistic role performance: Concepts, contexts and methods* (pp. 41–59). New York: Routledge.

Waisbord, S. (2013). *Reinventing professionalism: Journalism and news in global perspective.* Cambridge: Polity

Waisbord, S. (2019). *Communication: A post discipline.* Cambridge: Polity.

Waisbord, S., & Mellado, C. (2014). De-westernizing communication studies: A reassessment. *Communication Theory, 24*(4), 361–372.

Wang, H., Sparks, C., & Huang, Y. (2018). Measuring differences in the Chinese press: A study of People's Daily and Southern Metropolitan Daily. *Global Media and China, 3*(3), 125–140.

Weaver, D., & Willnat, L. (2012). *The global journalist in the 21st century.* Abingdon, UK: Routledge.

Willems, W. (2014). Provincializing hegemonic histories of media and communication studies: Toward a genealogy of epistemic resistance in Africa. *Communication Theory, 24*(4), 415–434.

Zelizer, B., & Allan, S. (2011). *Journalism after September 11* (2nd ed.). London: Routledge.

2 Theorizing Journalistic Roles

Claudia Mellado

Journalism has always been in a perpetual state of change. With each major technological advent or development, the debates about the future of journalism—and particularly the future of newspapers—intensify. Technological transformations are often accompanied by forecasts about the end of "old" technologies and the death of journalism "as we know it" (Curran, 2012; McChesney & Pickard, 2011).

Over the past two decades, scholars have continued to discuss the extent to which digital technologies kill, disrupt, innovate, or present different opportunities for news industries, business models, news production routines, and patterns of audience interaction, consumption, and distribution (McNair, 2009; Anderson, Bell, & Shirky, 2014; Ryfe, 2012; McChesney & Pickard, 2011).

These continuing changes have also presented a good opportunity for journalists and scholars to rethink the profession's ethos and functions (Boczkowski & Anderson, 2017; Peters & Broersma, 2017; Deuze & Witschge, 2020), as well as the potential erosion of journalistic authority (Carlson, 2017). At the core of their concerns is whether conventional societal expectations are reflected in the roles that journalism performs.

Although traditional business models were relatively stable throughout the 20th century, with each incoming "threat" from external actors, pressures, and conditions (Örnebring, 2018; Ryfe, 2012), the profession reestablishes and redraws its boundaries (Waisbord, 2013; Carlson & Lewis, 2015).

While journalists and scholars alike often ascribe great power and independent agency to technology (Örnebring, 2010), digital transformations are not the only important element of journalism's presumed crisis or state of perpetual change (Nielsen, 2016). It is worth remembering that by the last decades of the 20th century, most countries and their media industries were already experiencing the effects of globalization and technological innovation, satellite and cable news, as well as 24/7 news cycles (Cushion & Lewis, 2010). Major changes at the structural level resulted in media industries facing increasing pressures from privatization, market forces, and commercialism (Hallin & Mancini, 2004).

At the same time, in developing countries, major forces apart from market liberalization have impacted news routines and societal expectations about the functions of the profession. Communication reforms, democratization processes, political transitions, and, in some places, the revival of authoritarianism had journalists navigating certain degrees of continuity in their quest for press freedom and autonomy, while some media owners continue to collude with political elites (Hallin & Mancini, 2012; Guerrero & Márquez-Ramírez, 2014; Dobek-Ostrowska & Glowacki, 2015).

Though the news industry and the journalistic profession as a whole have faced challenges, life goes on for journalists around the world who still need to gather information and produce news. Faced with continuing pressures, upheavals, and changes, journalists adapt their work to the various challenges. They are constantly in a state of becoming, exploring and shifting between various roles (Mellado et al., 2017). Thus, journalism scholars should worry less about the supposed death of the profession and its gold standards every time a new type of technology or development comes along, and should instead understand the profession for what it is and what it could be (Zelizer, 2017).

Many aspects of news production, consumption, and distribution might have transformed irreversibly, but news events appear to remain business as usual. Policy implementation processes still need monitoring, marginal groups are still unheard, audiences still need advice on how to handle their ordinary concerns, citizens still need information that allows them to vote, and content still needs to be engaging enough to attract audiences. Hence, it is fair to ask: How can journalism be theoretically analyzed if it is in a constant state of change? Can journalism studies be based on clear-cut models and practices? How can we interpret traditional journalistic norms in this fast-paced environment? How can we better understand the professional roles of journalism in society today?

Acknowledging the ever-changing nature of journalism and its recent transformations, this chapter relies on role theory and role performance research to navigate the fascinating construct of professional roles, reexamining its theoretical grounds and practical applications from different angles and with different lenses.

It is important to clarify that the word *performance* is closely tied to the roles that actors and actresses play at the theater using different "social masks," where sometimes it is more important to "appear good" than to actually "be" good (e.g., Goffman, 1959; Buttler, 1988). From that approach, journalists can be seen as actors that try to show the audience what good professionals they are. While this perspective is very useful, especially for analyzing the "behind-the-scenes" process of news production, this book focuses on the concept of *performance* as the actual practice manifested in the final news product made known to the public.

The first part of the chapter analyzes the optics that have been used to analyze roles in journalism. The remaining pages focus on the concept of professional roles and role performance, its theoretical underpinnings, and the different domains, dimensions, and analytical categories in which it is possible to analyze the intermingled functions of journalism today.

The Roles of Journalism

The term role comes from early Greek and Roman theater, as dramatic text lines were written on "rolls" and then read to the actors by prompters. Since then, the term has been a dramatic one, defined as "the container of all the thoughts and feelings we have about ourselves and others in our social and imaginary worlds" (Landy, 1990, p. 203). It has often been associated with the part played by an actor or actress. Following this logic, Biddle (1986, p. 68) observes that role theory has come to concern itself with "patterned and characteristic social behaviors, parts or identities that are assumed by social participants, and scripts or expectations for behavior that are understood by all and adhered to by performers."

The concept was not exported to psychology, anthropology, and sociology until after the 1930s (Landy, 1993), and was subsequently extended to journalism (e.g., Rosten, 1937; Cohen, 1963; Johnstone, Slawski, & Bowman, 1976), while a huge increase in social science research about "professionalism" and "the professions" is observed overall (Wilensky, 1964).

Of course, because journalism is a "varied cultural practice" and its boundaries are socially constructed and constantly being redefined (Carlson & Lewis, 2015), there are elements of both choice and arbitrariness when defining its roles.

Nevertheless, there is clear evidence that roles, whatever the specific meaning and value assigned to them, can be conceptualized not only as an expected attitude, but also as an expected behavior of individuals who inhabit a particular position in society (Biddle, 1979; Lynch, 2007). In other words, roles serve to analyze cultural and social life in terms of standards (norms), values (ideals), and performance qualities (practices).

Previous studies in journalism have recognized the existence of different dimensions within the construct of professional roles, namely role conception, role perception, role enactment, and role performance (Mellado, Hellmueller, & Donsbach, 2017). These approaches to professional roles basically differentiate between the perceptual level, attitudinal level, and the behavioral level, in accordance with normative demands.

These approaches can also take different forms when they are compared to each other, depending on the level of analysis applied to them. In order to add theoretical context to the different facets journalists can go through, we will now focus on untangling the fusion of the personal and collective sides of professional roles and on the differences between these three broad layers—(given) norms, (take on) ideals, and (played out) performances—in which professional roles are embedded. We will come back to this and discuss it in greater detail in the next section.

Roles as Norms

The field has a rich tradition of theorizing the expected roles and norms of the occupation. The earliest authoritarian, libertarian, Soviet, and social responsibility theories of the press were conceived from the political and normative points of view to teach "what the press should be and do" (and what it should not be and should not do). The legacy work conducted by Siebert, Schramm, and Peterson (1956) outlined categories of models of journalism that either opposed or refined and redefined each other, building connections between socio-political regimes at the macro level and journalistic functions and news content at the micro level. The basic operational assumption of their work was that the regime/political system would determine the type of journalism that exists, with journalism as the dependent variable and political regimes and systems as the independent variables.

This assumption has survived and has influenced media systems theory (Nerone, 1995), paving the way for the comparative media systems research conducted to date. This is especially true of the work that has been done on how national structural and regulatory conditions impact reporting styles and journalists' norms and expectations (Merrill, 2002; Hallin & Mancini, 2004). Differences related to regime type also allowed for bottom-up studies to be conducted on comparative journalism cultures and journalists' norms (see, notably, Benson & Saguy, 2005, for a comparison between the American and French "ideal-types" of journalism).

However, from the perspective of this line of research, it is assumed that certain role expectations and journalistic norms are more desirable than others, such as the watchdog role of the press over the loyalism expressed to elites. Furthermore, the actual materialization of such norms was thought to be unavoidably linked to certain macro-structural conditions, not always considering journalistic agency and news practices (Nerone, 1995).

Still, normative perspectives of the media have been useful to address at least two types of concerns about how the media should be—one dealing with the most suitable regulatory and legal framework for media policies to deliver societal expectations; and the other, addressing how news media "act" or "behave" when performing their chosen or imposed functions and duties (McQuail, 2003). We note that, from this perspective, individual journalistic norms could be subjected to any of those.

From a Weberian perspective, norms can be considered sociological constructs that do not exist in reality but orient practitioners and/or scholars (Benson, 2013). In that sense, norms are closer to ideal types and the notion that the perfect belief can be accomplished in a perfect situation and at a perfect time. While this would be quite rare to find in reality, ideal types are key for organizing our thinking as humans in public and private discourse (Eide, 2017).

For journalists, professional norms are rarely connected to macro structures, and are instead linked to societal expectations. They constitute the core of who they represent, what they should do as professionals, and the missions that the profession asks them to follow (Christians, Glasser, McQuail, Nordenstreng, & White, 2009).

An important element to consider when thinking about journalistic professionalization and how it is embedded in professional roles as norms comes from professional socialization through journalism schools (Schudson, 2001, 2005) and news organizations (Nerone, 2009). News practitioners are exposed to professional and academic discourses about what journalism is and what it should accomplish in society in both of these settings. Consequently, roles can be seen as a key part of the journalistic identity construction process, and as part of the journalistic ideology (Waisbord, 2013; Örnebring, Karlsson, Fast, & Lindell, 2018).

The role metaphor and its use is a good example of how professional roles can be seen as norms. This metaphor links the world and the stage through social masks (Goffman, 1959), and it has been used for decades to explain the relationship between social life and people as taking roles assigned by others (Wilshire, 1991). As Schudson (2001, pp. 149–152) asserts, there are four conditions for the emergence of norms: two related to the self-conscious pursuit of solidarity or group identity, and two that focus on the need to articulate the ideals of social practice across an organization at one point in time or across generations over time.

Reality, of course, is quite more complex than that, as normative expectations can conflict with expectations from reference groups and with journalists' personal ideals.

Although norms are seen as a sort of everlasting core of roles, the expected behavior of the profession and the meaning and function of a role have very deep connections with the individual (the journalist), the organization (the media outlet), and the audience (reference groups). Linking back to Goffman's work (1959), it is possible to argue that journalistic roles are in part also performances for a wider society where it is just as important to be *perceived as* performing a particular role as it is to actually be performing it. For example, in their study of journalists' behavior at the so-called "backstage" of the news production process, and specifically at press conferences, Godler and Reich (2013) found that when journalists repeatedly ask the same "tough" questions, they do not ask the questions because they truly expect politicians to answer them, but so that news professionals will be seen as tenacious. This also links to Carlson's (2017) point about journalists building their own social authority, and the decline of this authority in the face of digital disruption of journalists' boundaries (Hermida, 2014).

At the same time, norms are immersed in complex social contexts in which politics, economy, religion, culture, and several other societal factors converge and diverge. Even normative standards have evolved over time in contexts like the U.S., where, for example, objectivity and disseminative, factual orientations towards storytelling were traditionally cornerstones of the profession (Schudson, 2001). Critical, skeptical, and aggressive questioning practices became more accepted after the Watergate scandal, the civil rights movement, and the failures of the Vietnam War (Feldstein, 2006). Long-standing debates have focused on whether the mission of the press should include functions like encouraging debate (Ettema, 2007) and advocating for public life and social deliberation (Glasser, 1999). This public (or civic) journalism movement (Rosen, 1996) involved reforming journalistic practice by placing respect for the public and their needs at the heart of news (Carey, 2003; Hallin, 1992). Nowadays, ever-changing digital technologies force us to reconsider journalists' mission in light of economic turmoil and the rise of participatory journalism (Peters & Broersma, 2017). We have also been forced to address whether journalistic missions are being redefined by the emergence of international sponsors and foundations that provide funds to conduct journalistic projects (Benson, 2017).

Eide and Knight (1999) have also shown that normative elements of journalism represent the interests of the profession, and while they are always engaged in a tense relationship with the economic and political context, they are not limited to upholding democratic values, or whatever values a political regime defends in a traditional political sense. For example, roles such as service journalism are increasingly part of the profession's engagement with old and new audiences in different societies. As Ryfe (2012) contends, managing to actually reach and engage the audience—given their rising visibility in feedback, clicks, and interaction—is at the core of every newsroom's strategies. In other words, as contexts and news production conditions evolve, norms can also evolve with the profession.

This explains why normatively accepted roles are not the same in all historical contexts, and why they do not necessarily relate to the same performances in all cultures. The chapters of this book show that journalistic roles account for normative ideals in multiple ways that are not always what we might expect them to be.

Roles as Ideals

Traditionally, journalistic roles have been studied from the perspective of ideals (e.g., Hanitzsch et al., 2011; Hanitzsch, Hanusch, Ramaprasad, &

De Beer, 2019; Patterson & Donsbach, 1996; Weaver, Beam, Brownlee, Voakes, & Wilhoit, 2007; Weaver & Willnat, 2012).

While role conception and perception have been used interchangeably in empirical research studies around the world to analyze journalistic ideals (Mellado, Hellmueller, & Donsbach, 2017), these two concepts are different phenomena that every single journalist experiences, whether they are located in the U.S., Germany, China, Argentina, Cuba, or Poland.

Journalists' role conception refers to "the purposes of the profession that journalists conceive as more important at the individual level, where the locus of role evaluation is not necessarily related to social consensus" (Mellado, Hellmueller, & Donsbach, 2017, p. 6; see also Boudana, 2015). The idea of role conception can thus be linked to the idea of self-identification (Ashforth, 2012; Landy, 1993).

Instead, journalists' role perception is more related to perceived role expectations as socially required, and information about their role ideals within the context of the organization and society in which they are embedded. In that sense, it is a "followed script that has been internalized and is located in the larger social structure, but did not necessarily form a mental representation of that role for a particular journalist" (Mellado, Hellmueller, & Donsbach, 2017, p. 6). Note that the word "ideals" in this sense implies a relationship with society, where audiences also—more or less—share the idea that journalists should follow certain values and roles.

Moving from role conception to role perception thus implies changing the level of action of the journalists, and mentally negotiating the discrepancies between their preferences and self-defining values and the values they know need to be embraced and defended in a particular context.

Whether or not we approach professional roles from these two perspectives, perceptions tend to evolve and change more quickly than norms. Various authors have also noted the non-mutually exclusive preferences that journalists may have regarding the roles they would like to play (e.g., Weaver & Willnat, 2012; Hallin, 2017). Hallin (1992, p. 24), for example, asserts that the fragmentation of the audience that took place in the U.S. was not necessarily a negative sign in the 1990s, in that distinctive forms of journalism could emerge for middle-class and working-class audiences and even subgroups of these, reflecting the different tastes and concerns of the audiences while providing each with a serious discussion of the world of politics in the widest sense. Klemm, Hartmann, and Das (2019) analyzed how certain events, such as health crises, cause journalists to shift their role ideals. In their study of German and Finnish journalists, they found that journalists move from a traditional watchdog stance to a more cooperative role with authority. In a different context, El Issawi and Cammaerts (2015) examined how a political upturn also upturned role ideals among journalists. The authors found that the monitorial and facilitative roles prevalent in the early stages of the post-Mubarak era in Egypt were overridden in favor of a radical and collaborative role.

Of course, while journalists can move from their role conceptions or perceptions and enact a role, it does not necessarily mean that their enactment will be transformed into journalistic practice. Role enactment is necessarily a capacity of the specific person in the role (Ashforth, 2012, p. 195), and while the journalist may enact a role, it does not necessarily imply that this will be reflected in the news unless norms and ideals can be transformed into performance.

Within journalism studies, role enactment has been addressed at the evaluative level of analysis—referring to what the journalists think they do, and to the extent to which they believe they can do what is important for them, or for the media outlet where they work—and at the attitudinal level of analysis, referring to the decisions they would make in specific situations in relation to news practices (e.g., Culbertson, 1983; Patterson & Donsbach, 1996; Bro, 2008; Weischenberg, Malik, & Scholl, 2006).

These are two different ways of approaching role enactment. However, they do have something in common, which is that they do not measure actual role performance.

Mellado, Hellmueller, and Donsbach (2017) point out that role enactment as an individual endeavor differs from role performance in that it is very difficult to bring that enactment to the actual news stories. Journalists need to be autonomous enough to accomplish what is individually important to them, but they also need to make a perfect match between what is important for them as professionals, what they believe is important for the media outlet where they work, and what is collectively performed in the process of news production.

Because roles are highly context-specific, the functions that journalists perform in their everyday practice are not necessarily consistent and may even be contradictory.

On the one hand, there can be a lack of individual autonomy that prevents journalists from performing their ideals. On the other hand, elements of external autonomy can influence a specific situation. Indeed, when a role is performed, individuals can transcend their self-interests in favor of the good of their news organizations, of the good of the general public, and according to what should be done in different circumstances (Mothes, 2017). Finally, constraints at the political, economic, or social level can prevent some roles from being performed in the news. As we will discuss in more detail in Chapter 8, journalists' disassociation from or de-identification with specific role performances can also work as a protection device.

Roles as Performance

Although for decades journalism research tended to focus on the evaluative side of professional roles—role conceptions, perceptions, or perceived role enactment—the word "role" has always been linked to its performative side, and with that, to the study of human behavior (Biddle, 1979, p. 11).

While the evaluative level of journalistic cultures deals with the journalist's own formulation of what is important to their work, what is important for their employer, how they think they do their work, and even how the audience perceives the work of journalism in society, the performative level deals with concrete decisions and styles of news reporting, considering different influences that affect journalism and how journalism negotiates those influences.

Let's try to illustrate these differences.

A hypothetical journalist can hold a strong belief that one of her roles as a news professional is to serve the public and preserve a strong and healthy democracy. She works for the most renowned newspaper in her city. Although the political leaning of the paper does not align with her own political sympathies, she has adapted to the job, feels that she has gained status, and has learned how to do the work without burning out. At some point, immersed in that news company and in addition to her initial role conceptions, she may unconsciously feel that she also needs to support her employer's organizational mission, which can be more related to entertaining the public or maintaining the status quo in order to avoid driving away increasingly scarce advertisers.

She is not necessarily giving up her civic mission, and she may perform that role when the opportunity arises, but she is coping with the delicate (and unavoidable) task of concealing ideals and practical constraints. She will have to play various roles at the same time. In some cases, she will have to merge these roles into one. In others, she will have to create a sort of balance to survive to the gap between the two.

As Lynch (2007, p. 379) asserts, assuming that roles are bound by behavior obscures the multiple instances of role overlap or the constant role shuffling and role switching necessary to perform a number of roles in a single context.

If we were to interview our hypothetical journalist about her decisions in specific news event situations, depending on how the questions are formulated, she would claim that she performs particular roles based on either her conceptions or the perceptions she has about the role of her news organization. If we ask her about her perceived enactment in her work, meaning how she evaluates the fulfillment of her ideals, she would probably never be able to match her actual performance. She works with others, and several visible and invisible forces influence her decisions and the way her work is presented to the public.

Now, if we could observe her everyday work routine and then read the pieces that she and her colleagues write, we would realize that they actually show elements of strict civic and infotainment practices and may be mixed with other circumstantial elements of watchdog performance

(Márquez-Ramírez et al., 2020). They may also present a highly personal voice that goes along well with the story, the topic, and the moment in time they are covering. This result would be the role performance. The type of news organization for which journalists work, as well as the social context where that media is located plays, of course, a role in shaping the performance of a role.

A meaningful difference between role performance and the evaluative constituents of journalistic cultures is that while its relevant components are determined in reference to normative criteria, journalistic role performance is, from the outset, not a normative concept (Mellado, 2015).

As outlined at the beginning of this chapter, the analysis of role performance allows for examination of both the news production process, including source search, verification, and negotiations with different groups, and the outcome of newsroom decisions that create the news. In this book, we analyze journalistic role performance as the manifestation of professional roles in the news and as a collective outcome of complex and dynamic decisions that are affected by internal and external factors (Mellado, Hellmueller, & Donsbach, 2017, p. 8).

Paradigm Divide: From the Taken-for-Granted to the Fluid Sense of Professional Roles

Biddle (1986) identifies five perspectives within the role theory field: functional, interactionism, structural, organizational, and cognitive role theory. Though many scholars have weighed in on this subject, the strongest theoretical paradigms in role studies are the structural-functionalist and the symbolic and dynamic interactionism approaches.

It is important to understand how these different perspectives affect journalism studies, and particularly how we study professional roles.

Functional role theory has focused on the "characteristic behaviors of persons who occupy social positions within a stable social system. Roles are conceived as the shared, normative expectations that prescribe and explain these behaviors" (Biddle, 1986, p. 70), whereas symbolic interactionism stresses "the evolution of roles through social interaction, and various cognitive concepts through which individual social actors understand and interpret their own and others' conduct" (p. 72).

Starting from the perspective of symbolic interactionism, dynamic interactionism goes one step further, recognizing the ongoing process by which individuals and contexts impact one another (Hattrup & Jackson, 1996). That is, they recognize that people can shape situations and that situations can also affect people, "such as the unfolding of time produces continuous changes in both persons and the situation" (Ashforth, 2012, p. 20).

In this sense, they expand the scope to include what pragmatic theories in general, and cultural pragmatism in particular, refer to when talking about practices as meaning emerging from the contingencies of individual and collective action.

Drawing on the field of performance studies, cultural pragmatics argue that the materiality of practices should be replaced by the more multidimensional concept of performance, which can be understood beyond the normative world (Alexander, 2004).

According to this theoretical perspective, the concept of performance helps us explain how the integration of groups and collectivities can be achieved through symbolic communications, while continuing to account for cultural complexity and contradiction, institutional differentiation, contending social power, and segmentation.

Another aspect that this approach defends, and that we use to theorize our own models, is the idea that binary distinctions such as good/bad journalism and hard/soft news do not help us understand how journalism and the media work. As Alexander (2004, p. 559) notes, "Normative and empirical theories of power and legitimacy in the contemporary world must come to terms with how the conditions of performativity have changed everywhere." Thus, while rituals are made at one time and place and participants engage in a more instrumental and individualistic type of activity in simpler societies, things are not that straightforward in complex societies, and all actions are symbolic and socially constructed to some degree (p. 566).

Studies on journalistic values, norms, and ideals have tended to position themselves on the functionalist side, emphasizing the normative quality of expectations and the existence of social consensus, assuming that roles are contracted by behavior. For their part, studies on role performance have stood on both the symbolic/dynamic interactionism and cultural pragmatism sides of the road, seeing roles as fluid, non-mutually exclusive, and always negotiable shared understandings in a particular social context.

Our project, and therefore this book, reflects the latter perspective. As we have previously stated, professional roles are socially constructed, situational, and can be combined in various ways that make it impossible to view them as discrete categories (Mellado, 2015; Vos, 2017). Although the journalists may praise specific ideals of the profession and may adhere to specific journalistic norms, it is understandable that their everyday practice is guided by roles that are context-specific and not fixed. For example, and perhaps because of a "looking-glass self" effect (Cooley, 1922; Landy, 1993), each reference group that they encounter may reflect a sense of who they are, shaping how they see their roles in society, and the way that they collectively perform them.

While it is true that formal positions in news organizations tend to become more or less institutionalized as structural-functionalists suggest, professional roles cannot be taken for granted, since the meaning that journalists and different reference groups can give to a role—and the way in which roles are performed in certain contexts and situations—is always a matter of negotiations that occur within different types of structural constraints, as the interactionism and cultural pragmatism approaches stress (Biddle, 1986; Alexander, 2004; Hattrup & Jackson, 1996).

These constraints are not only present in legacy media, where the forces exerted by economic, political, and cultural factors have been widely analyzed (Shoemaker & Reese, 2013). They are also quite present in the actions that occur in social media, where restrictions tend to be located outside of news organizations' boundaries and are mainly related to commercial and economic issues that affect journalists' external autonomy (Mellado & Hermida, 2020).

Ilgen and Hollenbeck (1990) suggest that formal roles and norms are a starting point for negotiation in any type of institution, but they are never an ending point. Of course, this does not mean that roles cannot be more stable or coherent, or that they cannot be tied more closely to some levels than others (Vos, 2017), but they are always in flux, mutating and transforming, allowing different role movements to be made depending on the context.

Addressing professional roles from a socially constructed perspective actually reinforces the sense of journalism as an "interpretative community" (Zelizer, 1993) of norms and practices, which helps maintain journalists' commitment and strengthens their professional position when they interact with reference groups. From this perspective, journalists are not only role takers, but also role players. They can move between their contexts and needs, transforming their understanding of different roles and how the context addresses those roles (Lynch, 2007).

Conceptual Models of Journalistic Roles

To see how all this theoretical discussion works in practice, this section provides a detailed description of the domains, role dimensions, and intermediate models that our study identifies in order to analyze how journalistic roles are performed around the world.

We look at three areas in which the role of journalism can be studied: the "journalistic voice" domain, the "power relations" domain, and the "audience approach" domain, all of which relate to different expectations of journalism in different political, economic, and media contexts.

While previous literature has suggested the use of these three perspectives as dimensions for the analysis of journalistic roles (e.g., Donsbach, 2012; Hanitzsch, 2007), our studies have proposed and then corroborated (e.g., Mellado et al., 2017; Mellado & van Dalen, 2017; Mellado & Vos, 2017) that these are actually three interrelated *domains* from which *independent roles* emerge, which allows us to study professional roles as non-discrete categories.

Domains are, indeed, well-known broader categories in which roles—as independent dimensions—can be analyzed (Landy, 1993, p. 164). It is crucial to establish which domains the various roles belong to because it helps to establish which elements belong to specific roles, which roles belong to a specific domain, and which elements belongs to roles that belong to other domains.

If these three domains were to instead be considered dimensions, it would automatically imply that the roles that belong to those dimensions are the poles of a continuum and thus would be dependent on each other. If we think of two roles as the poles of a continuum, this would mean that if a role is present in one news story, another one cannot be present at the same time; or that if a journalist feels that fulfilling a watchdog role is very important, she or he cannot think that being loyal-facilitator can be equally important at that time. Nevertheless, that is not how professional roles work, as we have explained in previous sections of this chapter. Indeed, a journalist can hold various perspectives on what they must do as a professional when addressing their relationship with those in power or when approaching the audience. A news story can also display different roles at the same time, questioning some officials while praising national policies or defending specific elites. The journalist might be critical of the president but praise the leader of the opposition, for example.

Clearly, these three domains are not the only ones that can be used to investigate professional roles (Mellado, 2015). Indeed, recent studies on journalistic performance analyze new domains of journalistic roles in social media spaces (e.g., Mellado & Hermida, 2020). Nevertheless, the ones analyzed here cover the main traditional professional roles studied in different cultural and social contexts, allowing for cross-national comparative research.

The first is the **journalistic voice**, which deals with the presence of a journalist's voice in his/her reporting. In our project, we address this domain by measuring the presence or absence of the active side of the journalist's voice, namely, **the interventionist role.**

This active stance has traditionally been linked to the participant (Johnstone et al., 1976; Donsbach & Patterson, 2004), advocate (Janowitz, 1975), and missionary roles (Köcher, 1986). The absence of the journalist voice is linked to literature that refers to the neutral or disseminator roles (Cohen, 1963; Weaver & Wilhoit, 1986).

Of the three domains we analyze, this is the only one that presents a unidimensional structure; that is, it is the only one that measures the presence or absence of one role. As such, it is assumed that a higher presence of the journalistic voice renders a higher presence of the interventionist role. Meanwhile, we consider the absence of such a role a sign of a more disseminative stance by the journalist.

The second domain is *power relations*, which is connected to the relationships that journalists have with those in power at different levels. Journalists may see themselves as **watchdogs**, defending the idea of monitoring the powerful and denouncing wrongdoings (Waisbord, 2000; Weaver et al., 2007). In some cases, they even take an antagonistic position with regard to others in order to hold political, economic, and de facto powers accountable (Bennet & Serrin, 2005). At the same time, journalists can see their primary function as acting as **loyal-facilitators**. In other words, as spokespersons of those in power, and through their support for official policies, they can also enhance the sense of belonging to a particular nation. This materializes in two ways: journalism may cooperate with those in power by portraying political elites and their policies in a good light (Christians et al., 2009) or focus on the nation-state by placing emphasis on national triumphs and prestige (Donsbach, 1995; Bishop, 2000).

These two dimensions—the watchdog and the loyal-facilitator roles—are independent from each other, which means that the lower presence of one does not necessarily imply a higher presence of the other. For example, if journalists do not hold those in power accountable or do not feel that is an important function to embrace, they are not necessarily signaling that they will side with those in power. These are different roles that can correlate to each other.

The third and final domain included in our analysis is the *audience approach*, which deals with public service—commercial debate in journalism, including the view of the audience as eager for complex information, giving advice on everyday life, or providing entertainment value (Mellado & van Dalen, 2017). Based on these different understandings of the audience, journalistic roles can be associated with three independent dimensions: the civic, service, and infotainment roles.

The **civic role** appeared first and was linked to the Enlightenment movement, the idea of the public sphere, the struggle for freedom of speech, and the later party press in the 18th and 19th centuries. This role puts democracy first, aiming to empower, educate, and inform citizens (the public) so that they accumulate the knowledge that they need to face and make decisions on complex and controversial topics (Rosen, 1996). The **infotainment role**, which is linked to the emergence of the popular press in the second half of the 19th century—and founded using advertising revenues and directed at mass audiences rather than political subsidy/subscription funding for elite audiences—addresses the public as spectators that need to be entertained and thrilled by stylistic tools, narratives, and/or audiovisual resources (Grabe, Shuhua, & Barnett, 2001). Lastly, the **service role**—which is a more recent role than the previous two, historically speaking—conceives of the audience members mainly as clients, aiming to deliver information and advice about services and products to contribute to their daily lives and provide personal assistance (Eide & Knight, 1999).

These three dimensions are also independent from each other, so the absence of one of them does not necessarily imply the presence of the other two. They can be performed simultaneously, as we note in the introductory chapter in the cases of the Chilean miners and the COVID-19 pandemic, or as we can see in thousands of political stories that add infotainment elements to coverage of citizen movements, or when consumer issues are mixed with democratic messages to empower citizens about how to demand their rights.

Clearly, each role provides a meaningful constellation of related qualities (Landy, 1993, p. 166) that can be measured by specific indicators and statements, depending on whether we are interested in measuring role ideals or role performances. In the case of role performance, each role can be operationalized in terms of its visibility and practical manifestations in news content, with indicators describing specific reporting styles and practices. When leafing through any given newspaper, we can, indeed, consider the following: Is this news article demanding change or calling readers to action, criticizing elites, praising certain policies, providing tips or advice, giving voice to citizens, or engaging in all of this at once?

In relation to ideals, the same indicators can be translated into specific statements that indirectly address how journalists value different roles.

It is important to keep in mind that when a role is conceived, perceived, or performed, the focus tends to be on its specific qualities rather than the whole. That is why it is not very common to find fully performed roles. As you will see in this book, any given news item may display indicators of a role to a greater or lesser extent.

The measures that we use in our models to analyze journalistic roles in the news have been inspired by global studies on role conceptions and journalistic norms. As we explained in this chapter, journalistic ideology is a fundamental tool that journalists can use to differentiate themselves from professionals in other fields, and theirs is a profession that is often exposed to public scrutiny, questioning, and redefinition of its boundaries (Waisbord, 2013; Lewis & Carlson, 2015). Nevertheless, and given that role performance is not a normative construct at the outset, our measurements have been specifically illuminated by multiple media studies (e.g., Benson & Hallin, 2007; Bishop, 2000; Bogaerts, 2011; Eide & Knight, 1999; Grabe et al., 2001; Kurpius, 2002; Ryfe, 2012; Salgado & Strömbäck, 2012; Van Zoonen, 1998; Voakes, 2004; Waisbord, 2000).

Chapter 3 presents the indicators used to measure roles at the evaluative and performative levels (see also the questionnaire and full codebook in Appendix). The composition of each role will be addressed in detail in the following chapters of this book. At the same time, analytical sub-dimensions will be a further division of roles. These are useful for classifying variations in specific qualities of the same roles (see Chapters 5, 6, and 7) and to identify the many nuances that roles take on when they are materialized in certain content, media, and societal contexts.

The following section critically assesses professional roles in all three domains as objects of study, proposing new ways of understanding the interaction between the roles and the constitution of intermediate roles.

Intersection of Roles: Roles as Dimensions and Sub-Dimensions

Journalistic roles are much more complex, nuanced, and rich than the normative literature suggests. As discussed in this chapter, roles are independent, manifold, and not mutually exclusive. On the one hand, roles are typically associated with differentiated social domains because they are oriented to various and specific audiences (Holton, Lewis, & Coddington, 2016). Nevertheless, since these audiences also have multiple roles in society, journalists need to combine them in different ways across news beats, types of media, and political and historical contexts (Hallin & Mancini, 2004; Waisbord, 2013). On the other hand, they tend to be bound by space and time, and therefore take on different levels importance in specific situations.

The interactive, multifaceted, and overlapping nature of professional roles (Lynch, 2007) causes journalists to take on roles shaped by individual and organizational identities. These can be interdependent and even complementary roles (Biddle, 1979). Because of this, roles may change sequentially or simultaneously, and are transformed as an illustration of the multilayered hybridization of journalistic cultures.

Indeed, organizational sociology literature suggests that the co-existence of roles is inherent to any given profession because the professional must respond to ongoing demands, creating a narrative thread that gives coherence to being a professional while performing different roles (Weick, 1996).

All together, we suggest that roles offer multiple possibilities to be materialized in the news through specific indicators and that they can be the most important functions implemented by a journalist in their everyday work. They also have the potential to be performed simultaneously or conceived as relevant, generating intermediate roles (Mellado & Vos, 2017).

In our first model published in 2015, six independent roles emerged from the journalistic voice, power relations, and audiences approach domains: the interventionist, watchdog, loyal-facilitator, service, civic, and infotainment roles (see Figure 2.1).

Based on this framework, several of our previous studies have analyzed journalistic role performance in a variety of socio-political and news-production environments, as well as the gap between ideals and practices.

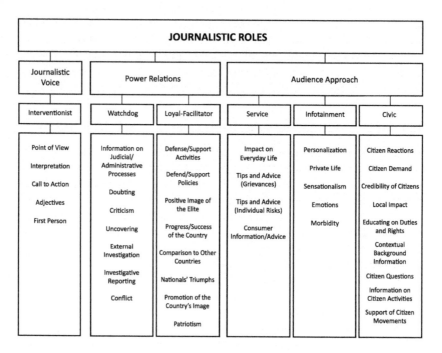

Figure 2.1 Domains, dimensions, and indicators of journalistic roles

Although we have corroborated that these six independent roles relate to each other to some extent, we have not yet provided a guide to how they can be combined and which intermediate roles might emerge.

Following our previous theorization (Mellado, 2015; Mellado & Vos, 2017), in this book we argue that the interventionist role, which is understood as the strong presence of a journalist's individual voice in reporting, is transversal to—and interacts with—other journalistic roles, becoming a sort of meta role that activates journalistic functions generating changes in these same roles (see Chapters 4–7).

For example, if the performance of the watchdog role is coupled with the performance of the interventionist role, it can become more adversarial, as happens when particular journalists may engage in confrontation with political authorities, economic leaders, or any powerful individual or group. The lack of intervention in the performance of the watchdog role instead is closer to a more detached variation of the same role, as it can be seen when journalists expose the wrongdoings of powerful individuals or groups without expressing any opinions, or when they let the sources criticize, question, or uncover wrongdoings. Also, when the loyal-facilitator role positively interacts with the interventionist role, journalism performs a more overtly propagandist role.

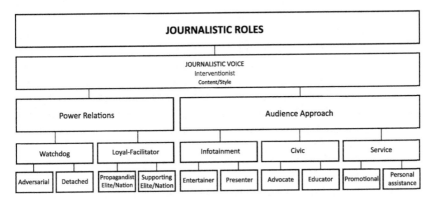

Figure 2.2 Dimensions and sub-dimensions of journalistic roles

Likewise, if the interventionist role is coupled with the performance of the civic role, it can acquire a distinct advocacy tone. This may happen, for example, when journalists claim to be defending citizens from certain evils and take the lead in explicitly supporting social movements. A civic role without a high presence of the journalistic voice is also possible. Actually, this turn of the role is closely related to an educator's stance, in which the journalists provide critical information to the citizens to help them to make political decisions. Meanwhile, the presence of indicators of the service role combined with a strong presence of the journalistic voice in a news story would make the service role closer to a promotional role, as it happens when journalists are particularly emphatic and actively promote certain products or services in the news.

The degree of identification between the infotainment role and the audience is also determined by the production style and specifically by the nature or different types of narrative devices and the use of specific rhetoric styles, such as sensationalism, personalization, elements of private life, emotions, or morbidity. If infotainment elements are combined with a stronger presence of the journalist's voice, this would evolve into expressive-based journalism, which is also found in narrative journalism targeting all kinds of issues. Meanwhile, the lowest presence of the journalist's voice in the infotainment role might seek to exhibit the thrilling qualities of a story, event, scene, or individual on their own merit (see Figure 2.2).

Our study addresses the simultaneous performance of different roles by journalists, news organizations, and national contexts, as well as the potential combination of different roles within one news story. This means that some established democracies and non-democracies, for example, would share the same high or low level of performance of a given role, i.e., civic. Just as role performance is hybrid because the higher presence of one role does not always correlate with the low presence of another, the groups of countries that comprise them are also blended. Some geographically close countries group together for many roles, but they can also group with others. Against this backdrop, this book approaches hybridity as a "sensitizing concept" (Blumer, 1954), which is useful for understanding journalistic cultures around the world to the extent that the different patterns that emerge from the analyses can be conceptualized in specific terms.

The analytical sub-dimensions of roles proposed in this chapter show that professional roles are intermediary translation devices in the dynamic process of practicing the profession. Identifying the practical co-occurrence of each of these combinations allows us to better trace and grasp the specificities of journalistic role performance and will help us to theoretically disentangle the multiple layers of hybridization across and within journalistic cultures. This book gives us the opportunity to look more closely at how this hybridization works and to further develop the theorization set out in these pages.

References

Alexander, J. (2004). Cultural pragmatics: Social performance between ritual and strategy. *Sociological Theory*, 22(4), 527–573.

Anderson, C W., Bell, E., & Shirky, C. (2014). *Post-industrial journalism: Adapting to the present*. Report for the Tow Center for Digital Journalism: New York: Columbia Journalism School.

Ashforth, B. (2012). *Role transitions in organizational life: An identity-based perspective*. NJ: Routledge.

Bennett, W., & Serrin, W. (2005). The watchdog role. In G. Ovelhoser, & K. H Jamieson (Eds.), *The institutions of American democracy: The press* (pp. 169–188). Oxford University Press.

Benson, R. (2013). *Shaping immigration news: A French-American comparison*. Cambridge: Polity.

Benson, R. (2017). Can foundations solve the journalism crisis? *Journalism*, 19(8), 1059–1077.

Benson, R., & Hallin, D. (2007). How states, markets and globalization shape the news: The French and US National Press, 1965–97. *European Journal of Communication*, 22(1), 27–48.

Benson, R., & Saguy, A. (2005). Constructing social problems in an age of globalization: A French–American comparison. *American Sociological Review*, 70(2), 233–259.

Biddle, B. (1979). *Role theory: Expectations, identities and behaviors*. New York: Academic Press.

Biddle, B. (1986). Recent developments in role theory. *Annual Review of Sociology*, 12, 67–92.

Bishop, R. (2000). To protect and serve: The "Guard Dog" function of journalism in coverage of the Japanese-American internment. *Journalism & Communication Monographs, 2*, 64–103.

Blumer, H. (1954). What is wrong with social theory? *American Sociological Review, 19*(1), 3–10.

Boczkowski, P., & Anderson, C. W. (Eds.). (2017). *Remaking the news: Essays on the future of scholarship in the digital age.* Cambridge, MA: MIT Press.

Bogaerts, J. (2011). On the performativity of journalistic identity. *Journalism Practice, 5*(4), 399–413.

Boudana, S. (2015). 'Le spectateur engagé': French war correspondents' conceptions of detachment and commitment. *Journal of European Studies, 45*(2), 137–151.

Bro, P. (2008). Normative navigation in the news media. *Journalism, 9*(3), 309–329.

Buttler, J. (1988). Performative acts and gender constitution: An essay in phenomenology and feminist theory. *Theatre Journal, 40*(4), 519–531.

Carey, J. W. (2003). American journalism on, before, and after September 11. In B. Zelizer, & S. Allan (Eds.), *Journalism after September 11* (pp. 71–89). London and New York: Routledge.

Carlson, M. (2017). *Journalistic authority: Legitimating news in the digital era.* New York: Columbia University Press.

Carlson, M., & Lewis, S. C. (Eds.). (2015). *Boundaries of journalism: Professionalism, practices and participation.* New York: Routledge.

Christians, C., Glasser, T., McQuail, D., Nordenstreng, K., & White, R. (2009). *Normative theories of the media: Journalism in democratic societies.* Urbana, IL: University of Illinois Press.

Cohen, B. (1963). *The press and foreign policy.* Princeton, NJ: Princeton University Press.

Cooley, C. (1922). *Human nature and social order.* New York: Scribner's.

Culbertson, H. (1983). Three perspectives on American journalism. *Journalism Monographs, 83.*

Curran, J. (2012). Technology foretold. In N. Fenton (Ed.), *New media, old news: Journalism and democracy in the digital age* (pp. 19–34). London: Sage.

Cushion, S., & Lewis, J. (Eds.). (2010). *The rise of 24-hour news television: Global perspectives.* New York: Peter Lang.

Deuze, M., & Witschge, T. (2020). *Beyond journalism.* Cambridge: Polity.

Dobek-Ostrowska, B., & Glowacki, M. (2015). *Democracy and media in Central and Eastern Europe 25 years on.* New York: Peter Lang.

Donsbach, W. (1995). Lapdogs, watchdogs and junkyard dogs. *Media Studies Journal, 9*(4), 17–30.

Donsbach, W. (2012). Journalists' role perception. In W. Donsbach (Ed.), *The international encyclopedia of communication* (pp. 1–6). London: Blackwell. First published online 5 June 2008. doi:10.1002/9781405186407.wbiecj010.pub2

Donsbach, W., & Patterson, T. (2004). Political news journalists: Partisanship, professionalism, and political roles in five countries. In F. Esser & B. Pfetsch (Eds.), *Comparing political communication: Theories, cases, and challenges* (pp. 251–270). Cambridge: Cambridge University Press.

Eide, M. (2017). Normative theories and journalistic role performance. In C. Mellado, L. Hellmueller, & W. Donsbach (Eds.), *Journalistic role performance: Concepts, contexts, and methods* (pp. 90–105). New York: Routledge.

Eide, M., & Knight, G. (1999). Public—Private service: Service journalism and the problems of everyday life. *European Journal of Communication, 14*(4), 525–547.

El Issawi, F., & Cammaerts, B. (2015). Shifting journalistic roles in democratic transitions: Lessons from Egypt. *Journalism: Theory, Practice & Criticism, 17*(5), 549–566.

Ettema, J. (2007). Journalism as reason-giving: Deliberative democracy, institutional accountability, and the news media's mission. *Political Communication, 24*(2), 143–160.

Feldstein, M. (2006). A muckraking model: Investigative reporting cycles in American history. *The International Journal of Press/Politics, 11*(2), 105–120.

Glasser, T. (Ed.). (1999). *The idea of public journalism.* New York: The Guilford Press.

Godler, Y., & Reich, Z. (2013). How journalists "Realize" facts epistemology in practice at press conferences. *Journalism Practice, 7*(6), 674–689.

Goffman, E. (1959). *The presentation of self in everyday life.* New York: Doubleday, Anchor.

Grabe, M., Shuhua, Z., & Barnett, B. (2001). Explicating sensationalism in television news: Content and the bells and whistles of form. *Journal of Broadcasting and Electronic Media, 45*(4), 635–655.

Guerrero, M., & Márquez-Ramírez, M. (2014). *Media systems and communication policies in Latin America.* London: Palgrave.

Hallin, D. (1992). Sound bite news: Television coverage of elections, 1968–1988. *Journal of Communication, 42*(2), 5–24.

Hallin, D. (2017). Preface. In C. Mellado, L. Hellmueller, & W. Donsbach (Eds.), *Journalistic role performance: Concepts, contexts, and methods* (pp. 90–105). New York: Routledge.

Hallin, D., & Mancini, P. (2004). *Comparing media systems: Three models of media and politics.* Cambridge: Cambridge University Press.

Hallin, D., & Mancini, P. (2012). *Comparing media systems beyond the Western world.* Cambridge: Cambridge University Press.

Hallin, D., & Mancini, P. (2017). Ten years after comparing media systems: What have we learned? *Political Communication, 34*(2), 155–171.

Hanitzsch, T. (2007). Deconstructing journalism culture: Towards a universal theory. *Communication Theory, 17,* 367–385.

Hanitzsch, T., Hanusch, F., Mellado, C., Anikina, M., Berganza, R., Cangoz, I., . . . Kee Wang Yuen, E. (2011). Mapping journalism cultures across nations: A comparative study of 18 countries. *Journalism Studies, 12*(3), 273–293.

Hanitzsch, T., Hanusch, F., Ramaprasad, J., & de Beer, A. S. (Eds.). (2019). *Worlds of journalism: Journalistic cultures around the globe.* New York: Columbia University Press.

Hattrup, K., & Jackson, S. E. (1996). Learning about individual differences by talking situations seriously. In K. R. Murphy (Ed.), *Individual differences and behavior in organizations* (pp. 507–547). San Francisco: Jossey-Bass.

Hermida, A. (2014). *Tell everyone: Why we share and why it matters.* Canada: Double Day.

Holton, A., Lewis, S., & Coddington, M. (2016). Interacting with audiences. Journalistic role conceptions, reciprocity, and perceptions about participation. *Journalism Studies, 17*(6), 849–859.

Ilgen, D. R., & Hollenbeck, J. R. (1990). The structure of work: Job design and roles. In M. D. Dunnette & L. M. Hough (Eds.), *Handbook of industrial and organizational psychology* (pp. 165–207). Palo Alto, CA: Consulting Psychologists Press.

Janowitz, M. (1975). Professional models in journalism: The gatekeeper and the advocate. *Journalism Quarterly, 52*, 618–626, 662.

Johnstone, J., Slawski, E., & Bowman, W. (1976). *The news people: A sociological portrait of American journalists and their work*. Urbana, IL: University of Illinois Press.

Klemm, C., Hartmann, T., & Das, E. (2019). Fear-mongering or fact-driven? Illuminating the interplay of objective risk and emotion-evoking form in the response to epidemic news. *Health Communication, 34*(1), 74–83.

Köcher, R. (1986). Bloodhounds or missionaries: Role definitions of German and British journalists. *European Journal of Communication, 1*(1), 43–64.

Kurpius, D. (2002). Sources and civic journalism: Changing patterns of reporting? *Journalism & Mass Communication Quarterly, 79*, 853–866.

Landy, R. (1990). The concept of role in drama therapy. *The arts in Psychotherapy, 10*, 175–185.

Landy, R. (1993). *Persona and performance. The meaning of role in drama, therapy, and everyday life*. New York: Guilford.

Lewis, S. C., & Carlson, M. (2015). *Boundaries of journalism: Professionalism, practices, and participation*. New York: Routledge.

Lynch, K. (2007). Modeling role enactment: Linking role theory and social cognition. *Journal for the Theory of Social Behaviour, 37*, 379–399.

Márquez-Ramírez, M., Mellado, C., Humanes, M. L., Amado, A., Beck, D., Davydov, S., Mick, J., Mothes, C., . . . Wang, H. (2020). Detached or interventionist? Comparing the performance of watchdog journalism in transitional, advanced and non-democratic countries. *The International Journal of Press-Politics, 25*(1), 53–75.

McChesney, R., & Pickard, R. (Eds.). (2011). *Will the last reporter please turn out the lights: The collapse of journalism and what can be done to fix it*. New York: The New York Press.

McNair, B. (2009). Journalism in the 21st century—Evolution, not extinction. *Journalism, 10*(3), 347–349.

McQuail, D. (2003). *McQuail's mass communication theory*. London: Sage.

Mellado, C. (2015). Professional roles in news content: Six dimensions of journalistic role performance. *Journalism Studies, 16*(4), 596–614.

Mellado, C., Hellmueller, L., & Donsbach, W. (Eds.). (2017). *Journalistic role performance: Concepts, models and measures*. New York: Routledge.

Mellado, C., Hellmueller, L., Márquez-Ramírez, M., Humanes, M. L., Sparks, C., Stepinska, A., . . Wang, H. (2017). The hybridization of journalistic cultures: A comparative study of journalistic role performance. *Journal of Communication, 67*(6), 944–967.

Mellado, C., & Hermida, A. (2020). The promoter, the celebrity, and the joker: Operationalizing emerging journalistic roles in new media logics. *Presented at the 70th International Communication Association (Virtual) Conference*. Gold Coast, Australia.

Mellado, C., & van Dalen, A. (2017). Challenging the citizen—Consumer journalistic dichotomy: A news content analysis of audience approaches in Chile. *Journalism & Mass Communication Quarterly, 94*(1), 213–237.

Mellado, C., & Vos, T. (2017). Conceptualizing journalistic role performance across platforms. In C. Mellado, L. Hellmueller, & W. Donsbach (Eds.), *Journalistic role performance: Concepts, models and measures* (pp. 106–126). New York: Routledge.

Merrill, J. (2002). The four theories of the press four and a half decades later: A retrospective. *Journalism Studies, 3*(1), 133–136.

Mothes, C. (2017). Biased objectivity: An experiment on information preferences of journalists and citizens. *Journalism & Mass Communication Quarterly, 94*, 1073–1095.

Nerone, J. (1995). *Last rights: Revisiting four theories of the press.* Urbana, IL: University of Illinois Press.

Nerone, J. (2009). To rescue journalism from the media. *Cultural Studies, 23*(2), 243–258.

Nielsen, R. (2016). The many crises of Western journalism: A comparative analysis of economic crises, professional crises, and crises of confidence, in J. Alexander, E. Butler Breese & M. Luengo (Eds.), *The crisis of journalism reconsidered* (pp. 77–97). Cambridge: Cambridge University Press.

Örnebring, H. (2010). Technology and journalism-as-labour: Historical perspectives, *Journalism, 11*(1), 57–74.

Örnebring, H., Karlsson, M., Fast, K., & Lindell, J. (2018). The space of journalistic work: A theoretical model. *Communication Theory, 28*(4), 403–423.

Patterson, T., & Donsbach, W. (1996). News decisions: Journalists as partisan actors. *Political Communication, 13*(4), 455–468.

Peters, C., & Broersma, M. (Eds.). (2017). *Rethinking journalism again: Societal role and public relevance in a digital age.* London: Routledge.

Rosen, J. (1996). *Getting the connections right. Public journalism and the troubles in the press.* New York: Twentieth Century Fund Press.

Rosten, L. C. (1937). President Roosevelt and the Washington correspondents. *Public Opinion Quarterly, 1*(1), 36–52.

Ryfe, D. (2012). *Can journalism survive? An inside look in American newsrooms.* Cambridge: Polity.

Salgado, S., & Strömbäck, J. (2012). Interpretive journalism: A review of concepts, operationalizations and key findings. *Journalism, 13*(2), 144–161.

Schudson, M. (2001). The objectivity norm in American journalism. *Journalism, 2*(2), 149–170.

Schudson, M. (2005). Autonomy of what? In R. Benson & E. Neveu (Eds.), *Bourdieu and the journalistic field* (pp. 214–223). Cambridge: Polity.

Shoemaker, P., & Reese, S. (2013). *Mediating the message in the 21st century: A media sociology perspective.* New York: Routledge.

Siebert, F., Schramm, W., & Peterson, T. (1956). *Four theories of the press.* Urbana, IL: University of Illinois Press.

Van Zoonen, L. (1998). The ethics of making private life public. In K. Brants, J. Hermes, & L. Van Zoonen (Eds.), *The media in question. Popular cultures and public interests* (pp. 113–124). London: Sage.

Voakes, P. (2004). A brief history of public journalism. *National Civic Review, 93*(3), 25–35.

Vos, T. (2017). Historical perspectives on journalistic roles. In C. Mellado, L. Hellmueller, & W. Donsbach (Eds.), *Journalistic role performance: Concepts, contexts and methods* (pp. 41–59). New York: Routledge.

Waisbord, S. (2000). *Watchdog journalism in South America*. New York: Columbia University Press.

Waisbord, S. (2013). *Reinventing professionalism: Journalism and news in global perspective*. Cambridge: Polity.

Weaver, D., Beam, R., Brownlee, B., Voakes, P., & Wilhoit, C. (2007). *The American journalist in the 21st century: U.S. news people at the dawn of a new millennium*. Mahwah, NJ: Erlbaum.

Weaver, D., & Wilhoit, G. C. (1986). *The American journalist: A portrait of U.S. news people and their work*. Bloomington: Indiana University Press.

Weaver, D., & Willnat, L. (2012). *The global journalist in the 21st century*. Abingdon, UK: Routledge.

Weick, K. E. (1996). Enactment and the boundaryless career: Organizing as we work. In M. B. Arthur & D. M. Rousseau (Eds.), *The boundaryless career: A new employment principle for a new organizational era* (pp. 40–57). New York: Oxford University Press.

Weischenberg, S., Malik, M., & Scholl, A. (2006). *Die Souf eure der Mediengesellschaft: Report über die Journalisten in Deutschland*. [The prompters of the media society. Report about journalists in Germany]. Konstanz, Germany: UVK.

Wilensky, H. (1964). The professionalization of everyone? *American Journal of Sociology, 70*(2), 137–158.

Wilshire, B. (1991). *Role playing and identity. The limits of theatre as metaphor*. Bloomington: Indiana University Press.

Zelizer, B. (1993). Journalists as interpretive communities. *Critical Studies in Mass Communication, 10*(3), 219–237.

Zelizer, B. (2017). *What journalism could be*. Cambridge: Polity.

3 Assessing Journalistic Role Performance Cross-Nationally

Comparative Design and Methodology

Claudia Mellado, Jacques Mick, and Mireya Márquez-Ramírez

This book presents the findings of the *Journalistic Role Performance Project (JRP)*. The authors analyze how different journalistic cultures work around the world; the professional roles performed in different social, political, and economic contexts, media outlets, and thematic beats; the factors that explain the performance of specific roles; and the strength or weakness of the link between ideals and practices.

The results discussed in the chapters that give life to this book are based on data gathered from 64 newspapers in 18 countries: Argentina, Brazil, Chile, China, Cuba, Germany, Greece, Hong Kong, Hungary, Ireland, Malaysia, Mexico, the Philippines, Poland, Russia, Spain, Switzerland, and the United States.

We used a three-stage research approach for this project.

Based on standardized operationalization of the watchdog, civic, interventionist, loyal-facilitator, infotainment, and service roles in journalism (see Chapter 2), we first measured journalistic role performance through the presence of each of these roles and their indicators in the news through content analysis. Each role is characterized by different measures of professional practice. While role performance can be studied at earlier stages of the news production process, such as news routines, in this book we focus on the performance of roles as materialized in the final news outcome, i.e., news content.

Second, in order to address the link between ideals and practices, we conducted a survey on role conceptions and perceived role enactment with journalists working at the news outlets included in our sample, further comparing journalists' role ideals with the average performance of their news media organization for each country.

Finally, for each participating country, national teams collected information at the organizational and institutional levels of news media organizations, and at the societal level, e.g., considering staff sizes, audiences, market influences, press freedom, political system factors, and economic factors. Social system and organizational-level variables further provide an explanatory framework for how to explain the ideals-practices gap.

All of the data from the content analysis, survey, and structural context measures were independently collected. This enabled the organization of our work into different levels of analysis: news stories, journalists, news media outlets, and countries. We analyzed the data separately, but also through multi-level techniques in recognition of the nested structure of the data.

This chapter outlines the general design and methodology used by our teams during data collection and analysis processes, and serves as general framework that guides the reading of the empirical chapters.

Sampling of Countries

The study was originally a national project that became international when different colleagues recognized the innovative theoretical framework of this endeavor and committed to collaboratively working on and developing the study, applying the same methodology to different journalistic contexts. The result of this growth was a comparative, cross-national project of considerable size.

Given that our objective was to obtain an intentionally heterogeneous sample, we selected countries to account for a variety of political regimes, geographic regions, and media systems classifications (when available).

Following Hallin and Mancini's Western media systems models, we included countries that represent the Liberal, Democratic Corporatist, and Polarized Pluralist models. We also drew from Democracy Indexes and Freedom of the Press reports to sample transitional democracies and non-democratic countries from different parts of the world.

We made every effort to select countries according to a most-different-systems design. However, although we were able to include nations from Western and Eastern Europe, Latin America, North America, and Asia, it is important to acknowledge that the countries included in the project are far from representative of the vast diversity of media systems that exist around the world.

Content Analysis

Sample Units (Media Outlets)

We conducted a content analysis of the news published in the most important newspapers in the participating countries. Our researchers content-analyzed two to five general interest newspapers per country. The criteria for selecting these newspapers were circulation, media size, reach, audience orientation, ownership, political leaning, and level of influence. The aim was not to match the samples, but to identify the newspapers in each country's media system that were the most representative of their national print contexts (see Table 3.1). For example, some countries have a significant presence of popular or tabloid newspapers. It was therefore crucial to include titles of this type in those particular countries. In others, the media landscape is dominated by newspapers that represent a particular political leaning (e.g., excessive presence of conservative outlets). In others, regional papers have a broader reach.

Table 3.1 Sample Distribution by Country, Newspaper, Audience Orientation, and Total Number of Items

Country	Newspaper	Media Audience Orientation	N
Argentina	Clarín	Popular	1247
	La Nación	Elite	802
	Página/12	Elite	682
Brazil	Folha de S. Paulo	Elite	860
	O Estado de S. Paulo	Elite	745
	O Globo	Elite	834
	Zero Hora	Elite	310
Chile	El Mercurio	Elite	1067
	La Cuarta	Popular	255
	La Tercera	Elite	879
	Las Ultimas Noticias	Popular	381
China	Chengdu Economic Daily	Popular	228
	China Youth Daily	Elite	616
	Peoples Daily	Elite	1301
	Southern Metropolis Daily	Popular	733
	Xinmin Evening	Popular	386
Cuba	Cubadebate	Elite	110
	Cubahora	Elite	99
	Granma	Elite	198
	Juventud Rebelde	Elite	220
Germany	BILD Zeitung	Popular	128
	Frankfurter Allgemeine Zeitung	Elite	526
	Süddeutsche Zeitung	Elite	515
Greece	Eleytheros	Elite	369
	Kathimerini	Elite	532
	NEA	Elite	1131
Hong Kong	Apple Daily	Popular	361
	Ming Pao Daily	Elite	337
	Ta Kung Pao	Elite	825
Hungary	Blikk	Popular	216
	Bors	Popular	231
	Magyar Nemzet	Elite	377
	Nepszabadsag	Elite	263
Ireland	Daily Star	Popular	241
	Irish Independent	Elite	551

Country	Newspaper	Media Audience Orientation	N
Malaysia	Berita hariam	Elite	291
	Harian Metro	Popular	162
	NST	Elite	267
	The Sun	Popular	88
Mexico*	La Jornada	Elite	1192
	La Prensa	Popular	791
	Reforma	Elite	1026
Philippines	Abante	Popular	733
	Philippinde Star	Elite	1488
Poland	Fakt	Popular	303
	Gazeta Wyborcza	Elite	342
	Nasz Dziennik	Elite	230
	Rzeczpospolita	Elite	255
Russia	Moskovskiy Komsomolets	Popular	557
	Rossijskaya Gazeta	Elite	840
Spain	ABC	Elite	521
	El Mundo	Elite	660
	El País	Elite	709
	La Razón	Elite	388
Switzerland	Blick	Popular	501
	La Corriere del Ticino	Elite	594
	Le Matin	Popular	389
	Le Temps	Elite	648
	Neue Zürcher Zeitung	Elite	688
United States	Los Angeles Times	Popular	227
	New York Times	Elite	373
	USA Today	Popular	193
	Wall Street Journal	Elite	264
	Washington Post	Elite	364
			33,640

* We also originally included and coded Mexico's El Universal and El Financiero for this project, but we eventually removed them from the global sample so that the Mexican news (N=4,480) would not be overrepresented.

We decided to focus on print news for a number of reasons despite the fact that we are well aware that newspaper readership is declining around the world. First, newspapers were chosen over other platforms for their potential to set the political agenda and because, in theory, they have the ability to provide more diverse, in-depth, and nuanced coverage of different issues (Skovsgaard & van Dalen, 2013). Second, print newsrooms—even those of regional newspapers—still tend to be larger in terms of staff number and financial, material, and human resources, at least when compared to digital media or radio stations through 2015, the final year of data collection. Third, unlike private or state-run broadcasting networks, the newspaper industry tends to present a lower level of concentration in the participating countries, potentially offering slightly more plurality in terms of newspaper titles. Fourth, there is also a historical argument for focusing on newspapers, since "professional roles" as we understand them grew out of this specific institutional-organizational context. Fifth, the main newspapers of several countries transitioned to online formats during the period in which our sample was taken, and, by doing so, they generally gained more readers (while not necessarily compensating for the loss of financial resources). Finally, we focused on newspaper news because it was more feasible to sample years of media content by analyzing print outlets than analyzing audiovisual media or online news—which are more difficult to track, collect, and save—especially in countries that did not have enough resources to conduct such fieldwork when we started the first wave of this study. It is important to note that each national coordinator funded their own fieldwork due to a global lack of funding.[1]

The timeframe of the overall content analysis comprised two consecutive years between 2012 and 2015. As a result, not all national teams sampled the same years, but they did follow the same procedure and chose the exact same dates of their chosen years. The general guideline for collecting news within this timeframe was for national teams to build a stratified, systematic sample consisting of two constructed news weeks per newspaper per year. This involved ensuring that one newspaper issue from each of the seven days of the week was selected for each semester, and that every month of the year was represented by at least one day, avoiding over-representation of any one period.

Because daily and monthly variations are important factors to consider when conducting a news content analysis, it was crucial to implement a precise system for selecting the data collection dates. We divided each year into two semesters (January 2 to June 30 and July 1 to December 31), and all national teams had to start on a specific date for each period. For example, if the start date of sampling was Thursday, January 12, then, using a 3–4, 3–4 week interval, the next day of data collection would be the following day of the week, three weeks later (i.e., Friday, February 3). After that, the third day of data collection would be Saturday four weeks later (i.e., Saturday, March 3), and so forth. By the end of the first semester, we had covered every day of the week and the first six months of the year. We began this process again in July with a Monday issue. This allowed us to include seven-week days with regular intervals—three and four—between them, avoiding periodicity.

Unit of Analysis

With the full newspaper issues in our hands, we then set the news story as the unit of analysis, hereby understood as the group of continuous verbal and visual elements that refer to the same topic. However, we only included news pieces associated with the national desk. As such, we coded all news published in sections associated with government and legislature, campaigns/elections, police and crime, defense, national security and the military, economy and business, education, environment and climate, transportation, housing and infrastructure, accidents and natural disasters, health, religion and churches, human rights, demonstrations and protests, social problems, and miscellaneous topics for each selected sample unit (newspaper edition). The thematic beats were then recoded into broad topics: politics, economy and business, police and crime, court, social affairs, and general national news.

Stories associated with sports, entertainment, leisure, and so on were left out, as were editorials, opinion columns, and anything not fitting into the unit of analysis concept used, such as items featuring the weather, horoscopes, movie reviews, and puzzles. We also excluded supplements or magazines published by the news outlet as well as front-page teasers, menu bullets, and stand-alone headlines or pictures.

When reading the results of the project as reported in this book, bear in mind that we are only referring to national-desk news. We are aware that this scope might prevent us from comparing how professional roles play out differently around new topics outside of the world of politics and social affairs. Still, we find national desk news to be representative of the full machinery of newsroom dynamics, allowing for a variety of topics, angles, and narratives.

An event, topic, or statement can be covered by a media outlet in more than one story. Therefore, when the same event, statement, or issue was covered in more than one item, these were considered to be individual stories and were coded separately.

With those guidelines in mind, we ended up with a total sample of 33,640 news stories from 64 news outlets.

Measurements

In each country, at least one principal investigator was responsible for collecting data, conducting the study, and liaising with the general project coordinator. He or she received training in sample collection procedures and the application of a common codebook.

Although this codebook was based on previously validated measures of professional roles in news content, the final instrument used for this project was collaboratively adapted, revised, and enriched in order to guarantee intercultural validity.

Then, where appropriate, principal investigators in each participating country recruited and trained two to four independent coders in the application of the codebook translated and back-translated from English to Spanish, Chinese, Portuguese, Russian, Polish, Malay, German, French, Italian, Hungarian, Filipino, and Greek.

We followed a three-step strategy to test for intercoder reliability between and within countries. First, we conducted a pre-test among principal investigators across countries to ensure a common understanding of the codebook. Second, national teams were instructed to run pre-tests on their teams that featured articles not included in the actual sample. The national teams were retrained as many times as necessary to ensure that acceptable intercoder reliability coefficients were achieved. Finally, and once the coding process was finalized, a post-test was conducted to ensure the reliability of the coders in the actual coding process including the 18 countries.[2] Based on Krippendorff's formula (*Ka*), final global intercoder reliability was .75. The variation of intercoder reliability per indicator within each country ranged from .72 to .81 (see global intercoder reliability per role in Table 3.2).

The coding manual included operational definitions of the performance of the six roles analyzed in this first wave of our JRP Project: interventionism, watchdog, loyal-facilitator, service, infotainment, and civic roles (see Appendix).

Five indicators measured the presence of the "interventionist" role, ten indicators measured the "watchdog" role, nine indicators measured the "loyal-facilitator" role, four measured the "service" role, five measured the "infotainment" role, and nine measured the "civic" role.

The six journalistic roles were examined through the explicit presence of specific indicators in news content. Each indicator was measured on a presence—absence (1=yes, 0=No) basis (see individual indicators and global intercoder reliabilities in Table 3.2).

These role dimensions are considered reflective measurement models, where (a) the dimensions exist independent of the measures used, (b) the variation in item measures does not cause a variation in the construct, and (c) adding/dropping an item does not change the conceptual domain of the construct (Wirth & Kolb, 2012). Based on this assumption, confirmatory factor analyses were conducted to test whether the news stories were a reflection of a latent role manifested though concurrent concrete indicators (van Dalen, de Vreese, & Albaek, 2017; Mellado & van Dalen, 2017).

Following CFA results, the individual indicators comprising each role dimension were combined to create a final role score ranging from 0 to 1 (see Appendix). A higher score expresses a higher level of performance in a news story regarding a specific journalistic role and a lower score expresses a lower level of performance of the role. For descriptive purposes, we calculated the raw scores (sum of points divided by the total items in each role). Meanwhile, we used factor scores to run the rest of our analyses. Since each role represents a latent variable, the factor score is technically considered a better measurement of having weighted the indicators that compose it according to how much each item contributes to that latent variable (DiStefano, Zhu, & Mindrila, 2009).

Table 3.2 Survey Items and Coding Indicators for Measuring Role Conception, Perceived Role Enactment, and Role Performance

	Role Conception/Perceived Role Enactment Items (Survey)[*]	Role Performance Indicators (Content Analysis)[**]
Watchdog	• Questioning what powerful individuals or groups say or do • Accusing powerful individuals or groups of holding back important information • Including information on judicial or administrative processes regarding powerful individuals or groups • Providing information on abuses of power or wrongdoing based on extensive inquiry and your own research, rather than simply relying on secondary sources • Quoting sources that question, criticize, or accuse powerful groups or individuals of wrongdoings • To surveil civil society (Cronbach's α = .83/.82)	• Information on judicial/administrative processes • Doubting by the journalist • Doubting by others • Criticism by the journalist • Criticism by others • Uncovering by the journalist • Uncovering by others • Reporting of external investigation • Reporting of conflict • Investigative reporting ($K\alpha$ = .75)
Civic	• Including new voices of the citizen's group or organizations • Informing people on their economic, social, and/or political duties and rights as citizens • Presenting background information and context for citizens regarding specific political events in the news • Mentioning the impact of political decisions beyond the capital and/or the main cities • Including different ideological, political, religious, ethnic, and/or cultural perspectives in a news story (Cronbach's α = .81/.80)	• Citizen perspective • Citizen demand • Credibility on citizens • Education on duties and rights • Local impact • Background information • Citizen questions • Information on citizen activities • Support of citizen movements ($K\alpha$ = .75)

(Continued)

	Role Conception/Perceived Role Enactment Items (Survey)[*]	Role Performance Indicators (Content Analysis)[**]
Interventionist	• Providing your opinion on the facts/issues you are reporting • Formulating your own proposals regarding the development or solution to issues or events • Encouraging the public to behave in a specific way regarding different events or issues • Using evaluative terms about events or persons in your news reporting • To advocate a particular point of view (Cronbach's α = .71/.73)	• Journalist's point of view • Interpretation • Call to action • Adjectives • First person (Kα = .76)
Loyal-Facilitator	• Expressing positive feelings about being from your own country • Presenting official activities and/or national or regional policies in a positive light • Favorably stressing and highlighting the leadership or management skills of institutional powers and leaders • Stressing the political, social, and economic achievements of your own country • Championing the achievement of individuals or groups that belong to your own country or locality • To champion national values (Cronbach's α = .87/.87)	• Defense/support institutional activities • Defense/support national policies • Positive image of the political elite • Positive image of the economic elite • Progress/success of the country • Comparison to other countries • National triumphs • Promotion of the country's image • Patriotism (Kα = .74)
Infotainment	• Featuring one or more individuals and their personal, intellectual, physical, and/or social characteristics • Including explicit references to emotions of people involved in an event • Including details of the private life of people being covered in the news	• Personalization • Private life • Sensationalism • Emotion • Morbidity (Kα = .72)

Role Conception/Perceived Role Enactment Items (Survey)[*]	Role Performance Indicators (Content Analysis)[**]
• Including very concrete details when describing acts of violence, crime, sex scenes, or similar events in the news you are covering (Cronbach's α = .76/.73)	
Service • Indicating how a particular event or action might influence the day-to-day lives of people • Giving tips and practical guidance to the public to deal with practical problems • To provide advice and direction in matters of daily life (Cronbach's α = .61/.67)	• Impact on everyday life • Tips and advice (grievances) • Tips and advice (individual risks) • Information/consumer advice (Kα = .76)

[*] The Cronbach Alpha coefficients were calculated for the full survey dataset of the nine countries.
[**] Krippendorff's alpha coefficients were calculated for the full dataset of news content from the 18 countries.

In spite of all these self-protection measures, there is always a latent possibility of encountering pitfalls in the measuring of journalistic performance, and this project confronted some obstacles related to specific measures that are culturally bound.[3]

For example, coders from different countries may agree that visual morbid curiosity is manifested in the news item if the content captures the reader's attention using explicit images of crime, violence, or sex scenes/scandal in the story. However, what accounts as "explicit" might vary. In generally "safe" countries, a dead body covered by a sheet can be seen as a morbid image of violence and crime, but in a country in which the news is dominated by drug cartel violence, as is the case of Mexico, more graphic images like evidence of a beheading could pass as morbid. Considering that the meaning of the indicator remains the same, we decided that the level of presence of the measure could vary to avoid obscuring the specific traits of the cultures analyzed (see Chapter 12).

Survey of Journalists

Sampling

National teams first assembled a list of all of the journalists who authored news items at the time of data collection in each newspaper. The list had to include their emails and contact details. They then proceeded to survey those journalists to determine whether they were still working for the news organizations represented in the news sample (van Dalen, de Vreese, & Albæk, 2017). Due to a lack of access to potential respondents or lack of sufficient survey responses in many participating countries (journalists often refused to answer the survey), only 11 countries managed to complete data collection at this stage, while acceptable levels of internal consistency were only found for the data from nine countries and 33 news organizations.

The surveys were conducted as web-based questionnaires or face-to-face interviews. The first method proved least successful in some countries, as survey reminders were sent repeatedly but were still dismissed by potential respondents. Given that we used two techniques to obtain the journalists' responses, we later controlled for mode effect.

Journalists were invited to participate in the study through their personal/work emails, telephone, or social media. The surveys were conducted or administered online by trained research assistants from each national team. Journalists were informed of the purpose of the study and were required to sign an informed consent statement prior to completing the survey. All participants gave express consent to participate in our study and were given information about data use, share, and publishing.

In the end, 643 journalists completed the survey, yielding a global response rate of 35%. There were important differences in the response rates of the countries ranging from 10.2% in Germany to 90% in Hong Kong. Indeed, for some countries, the survey sample had a very low response rate. This was another important limitation and was partly due to difficulties encountered in regard to obtaining responses from journalists who belonged to the news organizations analyzed. There are several reasons for this low response rate. Many of the journalists who were contacted no longer worked in those newsrooms when the data were collected. In other countries, some journalists claimed to be suffering from "survey fatigue" and said that they felt overwhelmed by the number of survey requests they receive. Others claimed to have been prohibited from answering surveys of any kind by their bosses.

Measurements

The questionnaire measured journalists' conception of their professional roles as well as their perceived enactment of those roles (see Chapter 8). The survey also measured the journalists' perceived levels of professional autonomy and work and personal characteristics (see full questionnaire in Appendix).

Previous studies expected future research to be able to translate the traditionally abstract statements that are common in survey research on role conceptions (e.g., Hanitzsch, Hanusch, Ramaprasad, & De Beer,

2019; Hanitzsch et al., 2011; Weaver, Beam, Brownlee, Voake, & Wilhoit, 2007; Weaver & Wilhoit, 1996) into specific, recognizable practices for journalists across cultures when rating the importance of professional roles (Mellado et al., 2017; Weischenberg, Malik, & Scholl, 2006). Following that call, and based on the assumption that journalists provide more reliable and valid responses regarding practical issues than abstract normative statements that can have dissimilar meanings across cultures and even within the same newsrooms, the members of this project collaboratively designed 31 statements to measure professional roles at the evaluative level, translating the indicators included in our content analysis into reporting practices that journalists were asked to rate in terms of their individual importance.

Specifically, the survey measures the importance that journalists give to the six professional roles, rating the statements on a five-point scale where 1 was *not important at all* and 5 was *extremely important*.

The survey also asked the journalists to rate the same statements in terms of their perceptions of what they actually do in their work (how common they perceived specific journalistic reporting practices to be in the news stories they published) using a five-point scale where 1 was *not common at all* and 5 was *extremely common*.

We also controlled for 23 normative abstract statements used by previous cross-national surveys of journalists, as you can see in the Appendix of this book (e.g., Hanitzsch et al., 2019, 2011; Weaver et al., 2007; Weaver & Willnat, 2012).

In our instrument, journalists were also asked to indicate their agreement (5-point scale, from *never* to *always*) with three statements associated with their professional autonomy: "When I have a good idea about a topic that I consider important, I always get it covered," "I have freedom to select the news stories I will work on," and "I have freedom to decide which aspects of a news story I should emphasize." These items were averaged to form an index of perceived individual autonomy ($M = 3.60$, $SD = .79$, Cronbach's $\alpha = .81$).

We also measured socio-demographic elements such as age (M= 39.0; SD= 9.8), gender (62.5% male), level of education (90.5% bachelor degree or equivalent), and political leaning from 0 (left) to 10 (right) (M= 4.46; SD= 1.96).

As with the codebook, the master English version of the survey was also translated and back-translated from English into local languages.

With the aim of analyzing the interplay between role conceptions, perceived role enactment, and role performance, our first impulse was to measure the link between individual journalists and the stories they authored in our news sample, as previous studies had done (e.g., Mellado & van Dalen, 2014; Tandoc, Hellmueller, & Vos, 2013; Bergen, 1991).

Nevertheless, we faced an unexpected procedural/logistic level obstacle, as we found that a large percentage of news stories from different outlets across countries failed to include a journalist's name or byline, perhaps reflecting the state of increasing content mimesis in newsrooms around the world (Lee-Wright, Phillips, & Witschge, 2010). In other cases, it was the opposite: news items were signed by several different journalists, reflecting the efforts made by copy editors and editors to collaboratively assemble a story out of several reports. Some countries' internal privacy regulations also made it impossible to obtain the names of journalists or their emails or contact information.

The problem was even more fundamental at the theoretical level.

Given that role performance is a collective outcome of newsroom decisions, linking one piece to just one person could be misleading, as it would assume journalists are fully autonomous and work in a vacuum. Indeed, scholarship on media production and journalistic role performance offers compelling arguments that highlight how role performance focuses on journalism as social practice, where the news is rarely the byproduct of an individual's work, but a hybrid outcome produced by journalists acting within complex institutionalized contexts (Mellado, Hellmueller, & Donsbach, 2017).

Hence, considering that a single news story is the outcome of several decision-making processes involving multiple individuals, our study linked and compared journalists' role conceptions to the average performance of their news organizations.

In this sense, our project moves away from a strict focus on individual-level journalistic links between ideals and practice in favor of a more institutional approach that focuses on the question of how the relationship between journalists and their news organizations affects conception-performance links at different levels (Mellado et al., 2020).

We calculated the average score of each journalist based on his/her answers to the survey questions, representing each role at the conception and perceived enactment level. Considering that the scale range (0–1) used to measure role performance was different from the scale range for measuring role conception and perceived role enactment (1–5), we recoded the average scores for role conception (ranging from 1 to 5) into ranges from 0 to 1, and we transformed both into z-scores.

Each team was expected to undergo an Institutional Review Board (IRB) process or one conducted by a similar entity in their respective universities, with additional reviews being performed at cooperating institutions if necessary (for example, when a member of the research team works at a different institution than the primary investigator). In countries with no IRB, team leaders at minimum used the informed consent template distributed by the project's central coordination team and consulted with them further when needed. For online surveys, informed consent forms had to be presented to respondents during the on-screen survey introduction before the respondent accessed the survey. For face-to-face interviews, local researchers were required to provide a printed and signed version of the informed consent to respondents.

Analytical Strategy

Prior to our main analyses, we conducted separate confirmatory factor analyses (CFAs) for each role analyzed at the performative and evaluative levels for each domain: the journalistic voice, the relationship between journalism and those in power, and audience approaches. CFAs were performed using Mplus 7.0. Within that framework, we empirically tested competing measurement models (see CFA final models fit in Appendix).

At the performance level and evaluative level, the six role dimensions used by this study remain strong, indicating a good fit with the data. The standardized factor loadings for each model were high, and indicator reliabilities (squared multiple correlations) were satisfactory for each individual dimension at the three levels.

Regarding role conception and perceived role enactment, 26 and 27 out of 31 practical statements continued to be part of our scales, respectively, while at the abstract level of measurement, only four out of 23 statements remained, since the others did not have a good fit with the data. These statistical analyses strongly support the idea that more practical statements on reporting practices related to journalistic roles—similar to our indicators for the content analysis—were more effective for measuring role conception and perceived role enactment in a comparative and cross-national way than existing statements on journalistic role conception/perception.

Societal-Level and External Indicators

There is a pressing need for innovative research methodologies that take into account the regional and societal-level specificities of contemporary journalistic production. Studies that include different countries in their samples are especially complex because comparative research involves distinct experiences from the political, economic, cultural, and technological points of view. All of these aspects influence the configuration of journalistic cultures, having varying levels of impact on news production and content depending on specific socio-political contexts and the media platform, medium's political orientation, and reach. Thus, when conducting international comparative research, in addition to observing the data as expressed in news texts, questionnaires, or interviews, the context must be reconstructed by researchers through the selection of aspects that are relevant to that phenomenon.

Research findings, particularly the variation of role performance, can be explained by a number of factors that can be measured, explored, and compared, such as news topic, political leaning, or audience reach. But socio-political variables are not always measurable or comparable.

One of the problems we faced in this regard was the absence of standardized, reliable, and sufficient societal-level variables for comparing all types of countries and political cultures besides the Western world. For example, media systems, market development, government intervention, political parallelism, or journalistic professionalization (Hallin & Mancini, 2004) tend to be theoretical—rather than empirical—constructs and remain open to reinterpretation and scholarly revision in the Western world and beyond. Not all of these dimensions can be easily operationalized and transferred to different countries in a straightforward manner, and the available data might not be as reliable or globally comprehensive as needed even with existing attempts to support media system theory empirically (Brüggemann, Engesser, Büchel, Humprecht, & Castro, 2014).

Moreover, even if taken as theoretical constructs only, many of these media system variables are still useful for comparing and explaining differences in role performance across countries and types of news content, but only in Western democracies. Non-Western media systems are strikingly different, and most are said to be hybrid to some extent, but in ways that are unhelpful for categorizing valid predictive variables.

Ownership patterns and media concentration are also difficult to measure, particularly in comparative terms, as most of the indicators of media concentration or media pluralism have been developed in—and for—very specific geographic contexts. We made every effort to include as many reliable world rankings and contextual variables as possible for our empirical tests (see Chapter 11). While most of them offer illuminating findings related to predicting the performance of certain journalistic roles, researchers in our field have yet to develop a way to standardize measures so that geographic, social, and political contexts can be accounted and controlled for in more precise ways.

Processes for Articulating International Research

In order for any project of this size to be successful, it requires engaged collaborators who can have input into the sampling and data collection processes in their countries, and are able to participate in the writing of research articles, books, and reports that present the results.

The research leaders of our global team represent different countries and worked in similar fields linked to journalism or communication (and in some cases also have connections to other areas, such as politics and various fields of society and culture). This contributed to a certain homogeneity within the group, as did the participants' academic training, with most having focused on communication, journalism, social sciences, or philosophy.

Unfortunately, the absence of a central funding source prevented regular and systematic in situ meetings of the entire international research team. Instead, we encouraged research leaders to meet during various international conferences throughout the years, notably ICA, IAMCR, and AEJMC. Although not all researchers were able to participate, these meetings were important for refining the relationship between overall project coordination and local teams, and for promoting coordination between researchers from different countries—for example, among those working in the same continent or geographic location.

Moreover, during the fieldwork period, the project's general coordination office sent regular guidelines in regard to the standardization of data collection and analysis procedures and other important instructions via email. Discussions about decisions that involved the opinion of all national leaders took place during special meetings and/or were conducted by email. Finally, local team training sessions were conducted by the leaders of each country.

The implementation of the study ran smoothly in some countries but was more complicated in others. In the case of Cuba, for example, researchers had to let government officials read and authorize all materials before they could conduct the study. The Chinese researchers also needed governmental approval. Luckily, we managed to complete both studies on time. This is particularly important in the case of Cuba, as this is the first time that the country's journalism scholars have participated in a research endeavor of this magnitude.

A central factor of international comparative research is control of data quality among teams from different countries. All of the national teams that participated in our project committed to efficiently train both news-content coders and those who conducted interviews with journalists. In order for data to be included in our final dataset, national teams had to submit high-quality—i.e., clean, genuine, and reliable—data for the content analysis and the survey using the template and matrix that they had been given. Initially, many more countries were participating in the project, but national datasets that failed to fit the minimum criteria of quality, consistency, and validity set out in our quality protocols had to be removed from the global dataset(s).

Each dataset was double checked by the country's principal investigator. After that, all national datasets were merged, which generated two final datasets: one for content analysis and one for journalists' surveys. The latter would be merged afterwards with the news content dataset to measure the link between the evaluative and performative levels of journalistic roles. The central coordination team was responsible for conducting the final cleaning of both final datasets.

Our cross-national, collaborative endeavor offers a common theoretical and methodological template which is useful for carrying out comparative research on a local, regional, and large scale, and represents a step towards a more nuanced and in-depth understanding of journalistic cultures worldwide.

While several research pieces have been published individually over the past few years using some of these data, this is the first attempt that our team has made to jointly assess the nuances and differences of journalistic cultures, looking at the nature of professional roles, its sub-dimensions and co-occurrences, the factors that best explain the performance of those roles, and the link between ideals, perceptions, and practices through a global lens. The book aims to provide a better picture of what journalism looks like in the East and West, North and South.

Notes

1 Countries funded their samples in different ways. Several researchers obtained resources from their universities, others applied for national funding, others already had national funding and used some of those funds to cover the project expenses, etc.

2 In order to reduce bias, the body of news was divided randomly among coders in each country for the actual coding.

3 As measurement invariance across groups is "a logical prerequisite to conducting substantive cross-group comparisons" (Vandenberg & Lance, 2000, p. 4), we tested for measurement invariance following the two steps suggested by Muthén and Muthén (2012) for categorical outcomes. Our results point out that all observable variables show the same factor structure with an acceptable fit for both groups, thus supporting the idea that configural invariance exists across countries. Using nested model comparison, our results also show that thresholds and factor loadings were not invariant across countries. Based on residual analysis, we found that the indicators morbid, investigative reporting, patriotism, background information, information/consumer advice, and emotion were not invariant across countries. This suggests that the underlying roles manifest differently in their presses for these items, which might be related to the different cultural-journalistic traditions. The best solution resulted from constraining the thresholds and factor loading for the rest of the indicators so that they were equal in all countries while allowing the loadings of these six indicators to differ across countries. As compared to a model with no constraints, the model assuming equal thresholds and loadings for these observable variables did not negatively affect the fit of the model. This suggests that partial measurement invariance can be supported with our data across countries.

References

Bergen, L. (1991). Journalists' best work. In D. H. Weaver & G. C. Wilhoit (Eds.), *The American journalist: A portrait of U.S. news people and their work* (2nd ed., pp. 194–210). Bloomington, IN: Indiana University Press.

Brüggemann, M., Engesser, S., Büchel, F., Humprecht, E., & Castro, L. (2014). Hallin and Mancini revisited: Our empirical types of Western media systems. *Journal of Communication, 64*(6), 1037–1065.

DiStefano, C., Zhu, M., & Mindrila, D. (2009). Understanding and using factor scores. *Practical Assessment, Research & Evaluation, 14*(20), 1–11.

Hallin, D., & Mancini, P. (2004). *Comparing media systems. Three models of media and politics.* Cambridge: Cambridge University Press.

Hanitzsch, T., Hanusch, F., Mellado, C., Anikina, M., Berganza, R., Cangoz, I., . . . Kee Wang Yuen, E. (2011). Mapping journalism cultures across nations: A comparative study of 18 countries. *Journalism Studies, 12*(3), 273–293.

Hanitzsch, T., Hanusch, F., Ramaprasad, J., & De Beer, A. S. (Eds.). (2019). *Worlds of journalism: Journalistic cultures around the globe.* New York: Columbia University Press.

Lee-Wright, P., Phillips, A., & Witschge, T. (2010). *Changing journalism.* New York: Routledge.

Mellado, C., Hellmueller, L., & Donsbach, W. (Eds.). (2017). *Journalistic role performance: Concepts, models and measures.* New York: Routledge.

Mellado, C., Hellmueller, L., Márquez-Ramírez, M., Humanes, M. L., Sparks, C., Stępińska, A., . . Wang, H. (2017). The hybridization of journalistic cultures: A comparative study of journalistic role performance. *Journal of Communication, 67*(6), 944–967.

Mellado, C., Mothes, C., Hallin, D., Humanes, M. L., Lauber, M., Mick, J., . . Olivera, D. (2020). Investigating the gap between newspaper journalists' role conceptions and role performance in nine European, Asian and Latin American countries. *International Journal of Press/Politics* (accepted for publication).

Mellado, C., & van Dalen, A. (2014). Between rhetoric and practice. *Journalism Studies, 15*(6), 859–878.

Mellado, C., & van Dalen, A. (2017). Challenging the citizen—Consumer journalistic dichotomy: A news content analysis of audience approaches in Chile. *Journalism & Mass Communication Quarterly, 94*(1), 213–237.

Muthén, L. K., & Muthén, B. O. (2012). *Mplus user's guide* (7th ed.). Los Angeles, CA: Author.

Skovsgaard, M., & Van Dalen, A. (2013). The fading public voice: The polarizing effect of commercialization on political and other beats and its democratic consequences. *Journalism Studies, 14*(3), 371–386.

Tandoc, E., Hellmueller, L., & Vos, T. (2013). Mind the gap: Between role conception and role enactment. *Journalism Practice, 7*(5), 539–554.

van Dalen, A., de Vreese, C. H., & Albæk, E. (2017). Mixed quantitative methods approach to journalistic role performance research. In C. Mellado, L. Hellmueller, & W. Donsbach (Eds.), *Journalistic role performance: Concepts, contexts, and methods.* New York: Routledge.

Vandenberg, R., & Lance, C. (2000). A review and synthesis of the measurement invariance literature: Suggestions, practices, and recommendations for organizational research. *Organizational Research Methods, 3*, 4–70.

Weaver, D., Beam, R., Brownle, B., Voake, P., & Wilhoit, C. (2007). *The American journalist in the 21st century: U.S. news people at the dawn of a new millennium.* Mahwah, NJ: Erlbaum.

Weaver, D., & Wilhoit, C. (1996). *The American journalists in the 1990s: U.S. news people at the end of an era.* Mahwah, NJ: Erlbaum.

Weaver, D., & Willnat, L. (2012). *The global journalist in the 21st century.* Abingdon, UK: Routledge.

Weischenberg, S., Malik, M., & Scholl, A. (2006). *Die Souf eure der Mediengesellschaft: Report über die Journalisten in Deutschland.* [The prompters of the media society. Report about journalists in Germany]. Konstanz, Germany: UVK.

Wirth, W., & Kolb, S. (2012). Securing equivalence: Problems and solutions. In F. Esser & T. Hanitzsch (Eds.), *The handbook of comparative communication research* (pp. 469–485). New York: Routledge.

Part II

The Manifestation of Journalistic Role Performance in the News

4 Mapping Professional Roles in News Content Across 18 Countries

A Descriptive Overview

Claudia Mellado, Mireya Márquez-Ramírez, María
Luisa Humanes, Adriana Amado, Cornelia Mothes,
Henry Silke, Agnieszka Stępińska, Gabriella Szabó,
Sergey Davydov, Jacques Mick, Dasniel Olivera,
Nikos S. Panagiotou, Svetlana Pasti, Patric Raemy,
Sergio Roses, Anna-Maria Schielicke, and Edson
Tandoc Jr.

In order to broaden our understanding of journalism as a complex but meaningfully practiced profession, the main goal of this chapter is to map the general differences and similarities in journalistic role performance—specifically in relation to the presence of the interventionist, watchdog, loyal-facilitator, service, infotainment, and civic roles— across and within 18 countries from Asia, Europe, Latin America, and North America. We provide a descriptive overview of the results and trends identified in our project, focusing on the extent to which commonalities of traditional geographies, media system characteristics, and normative frameworks of professional roles hold true in journalistic performance.[1]

Looking at the data as a whole, we found that while the disseminative side of the journalistic voice tends to be stronger than its active side, there is an important performance of the interventionist role in the print press of several countries. In the power relations domain, the watchdog role shows a significantly higher presence than the loyal-facilitator role overall, while print journalists address the audience more often through the performance of the infotainment and civic roles than the service role.

Nevertheless, as expected, the findings show that role performance varies significantly across countries. Specifically, the journalistic roles that explain more country variance are associated to the way that journalists relate to those in power, how they inform and empower the public, and how they use their voices in the news.

Our results offer empirical evidence of the existence of a multilayered hybridization of journalistic cultures across and within countries, with professional cultures displaying types of journalism that do not resemble traditional media system groupings or conventional assumptions about political or regional clusters. In other words, our study shows that the differences and similarities found across countries cannot always be solely attributed to Western and non-Western regions that share the same type of media system, political regime, geographic location, or cultural tradition. While media systems are not static and undergo long-term changes that can be characterized by internal variation (Hallin & Mancini, 2017), the performance of journalistic roles is also subject to shifts produced by historical developments and the fluid context of news-making processes.

It is important to bear in mind that unlike studies that examine the structure of the media, role performance analysis focuses on the practice of journalism, which, as we will see throughout this book, is much more difficult to fit in existing typologies than specific media system categories.

The Hybridization of Journalistic Cultures

Studies on journalistic cultures have systematically analyzed the extent to which journalists from various countries differ in their professional roles (e.g., Hanitzsch et al., 2011; Hanitzsch, Hanusch, Ramaprasad, & de Beer, 2019; Mellado et al., 2017; Weaver & Willnat, 2012). While these studies share the implicit aim of exploring whether countries with similar regional, political, and media system characteristics are also similar in their journalistic cultures, they differ in their approaches (Mellado, 2015, 2019).

Research on comparative role conceptions has tended to assume the perspective that roles are connected to journalistic cultures that, in turn, reflect or result from the configuration of a particular media system (e.g., Christians, Glasser, McQuail, Nordenstreng, & White, 2009; Weaver, 1998). Most survey-based studies have shown that the disseminator and watchdog roles tend to prevail in the liberal model (Hanitzsch et al., 2011; Weaver & Willnat, 2012), whereas more partisan and interventionist types of reporting dominate in Mediterranean countries (Donsbach & Patterson, 2004). Empirical evidence also suggests that loyal-facilitator reporting prevails in developing, transitional, and post-communist settings, whereas journalists from developed economies and competitive media markets are more prone to endorse infotainment/populist tendencies (Hanitzsch et al., 2011; Hanitzsch, Hanusch, Ramaprasad et al., 2019).

By contrast, research on journalistic and media performance (e.g., Esser, 2008; Mellado et al., 2017; Márquez-Ramírez et al., 2020) and revisionist literature on media system studies have highlighted the potential hybridization of journalistic cultures elsewhere (Voltmer, 2013; Guerrero & Márquez-Ramírez, 2014; McCargo, 2012; Frère, 2015;

Preston, 2009; Hallin & Mancini, 2012, 2017). For example, a longitudinal study conducted by Umbricht and Esser (2014; see also Esser & Umbricht, 2013) on print news content in Western European countries and the U.S. found increasing hybridization with more interventionism in U.S. news and more objectivity in European press than what the literature often assumes. The authors argue that the distinction between journalistic styles is less clear-cut than the theoretical models would lead us to expect (Esser & Umbricht, 2013, p. 998).

From an institutional perspective, Hallin and Mancini (2004, 2017) have identified some transitions towards hybrid paths. They suggested, for example, that while media systems of advanced democracies will move towards the liberal, Anglo-Saxon model of objective, fact-based reporting, increased marketization, and commercial pressures, media systems also change over time.

Although previous studies on journalistic professional roles have acknowledged the problem of survey-data perceptions serving as measurements of actual practice (Patterson & Donsbach, 1996; Weaver & Wilhoit, 1996), studies focused on news content in the context of professional roles were rare until the 2010s when this emergent area of research was developed by several authors along with the project that gives life to this book.

As previously illustrated in Chapter 2, we analyze the performance of professional roles based on three main domains from which independent roles emerge: the presence of the journalistic voice (interventionist), the relationships between journalists and de facto power (watchdog and loyal-facilitator), and the way journalism approaches the audience (civic, infotainment, and service).

We argue that if (1) media systems are not monolithic and may even be combined regardless of their geographical and cultural affinity (Hallin & Mancini, 2017; Mancini, 2015); (2) journalistic cultures are not universal; and (3) roles are situational, historical, socially constructed, and affected by different level factors, we should be able to find various elements of hybridization in journalistic cultures as manifested in the performance and intermingling of different roles.

Along with this general main hypothesis, the following research questions will guide this chapter:

RQ1: What are the most important journalistic roles performed in the print news content of the 18 countries analyzed?

RQ2: How do countries differ in terms of the way print journalism performs different journalistic roles?

RQ3: What type of role performance hybridization emerges from the co-occurrence of the interventionist, watchdog, loyal-facilitator, service, civic, and infotainment roles across countries?

Results

Journalistic Voice: The Interventionist Role

Our results suggest that print journalism across the countries under analysis is, in general, more disseminative than interventionist ($M = .21$, $SD = .21$). Nevertheless, significant differences emerge when comparing news across nations in terms of the presence of the interventionist role ($F(17) = 157.078, p < .001; \eta^2 = .08$). The effect size is important, accounting for 8% of overall variance of this role at the national level (Table 4.1 summarizes the presence of all roles by country).

The United States and Argentina show the highest levels of performance of this role. In the case of the U.S., the results tend to contradict normative theories and previous studies on role conception that suggest that the detached journalistic culture of liberal models prevails in Anglo-Saxon journalism (e.g., Weaver & Willnat, 2012; Weaver, Beam, Brownlee, Voakes, & Wilhoit, 2007; Hanitzsch et al., 2011).

Post-communist nations such as Poland, Hungary, and Russia have the next highest levels of performance of the interventionist role along with Greece, Hong Kong, China, and Chile. All of them are transitional democracies with the exception of Greece, an established democracy that experienced major political and economic upheaval during the period analyzed.

In contrast, the country that shows the lowest level of performance of this role is Ireland, followed with some distance by Mexico, Brazil, Malaysia, and the Philippines. While the position of Ireland might be explained by the "informational style of journalism" (Hallin & Mancini, 2004, p. 198) that prevails in liberal media systems, our findings show that Ireland and the U.S. are clearly polar opposites in terms of the interventionist voice, challenging the assumption of similar fact-based, detached journalistic cultures.

At the same time, the absence of the interventionist role in the news published in Malaysia and the Philippines (both countries with scant press freedom) stands in contrast to the results for Cuba, China, and Russia (see Figure 4.1). The latter countries also face serious problems of censorship, but shows significant levels of intervention in their news reporting. This leads us to question the influence of macro structural factors such as press freedom on the extent to which journalists incorporate their voices into the news (see more in Chapter 11). Indeed, these apparently contradictory results go against the belief that a linear relationship exists between having more of a journalistic voice and greater autonomy. As Chapter 5 shows, this is not necessarily the case, because the journalistic voice can be either manifested by explicit content (such as opinion, interpretation, or demand expressed by a journalist) or by a style (the use of adjectives or the use of first person).

The performance of the infotainment role is a trend that seems to be global. The countries with the highest levels of performance of this role are Poland, Germany, Argentina, Chile, and Malaysia followed by the U.S., Russia, and Hungary. China, the Philippines, Ireland, Mexico, and Switzerland all present very low levels of performance of this role. In Spain, which has no popular press, the use of infotainment is rare but still present.

Finally, the results show that in comparative terms, the press from Eastern European countries and the Philippines lead the performance of the service role, followed by Malaysia, Chile, Brazil, and Argentina. Journalism in Cuba, Mexico, Germany, Spain, Switzerland, the U.S., and Ireland performs this role to a lesser extent in the news, although the differences are limited. As separate cases, and in line with the results found for the civic role, the performance of the service role in print news in China and Hong Kong is almost non-existent.

In some cases, the grouping of countries based on the performance of the three audience approach roles does not seem to be very intuitive. For example, the presence of the infotainment role is significantly higher in Germany than in Switzerland, even though their media systems are similar. The same happens with the U.S. and Ireland, and the Philippines and Malaysia, for the service role. Chapter 7 shows that the performance of specific orientations and indicators of each of these roles are indeed context-sensitive, showing different trends of roles hybridization (see Figure 4.3).

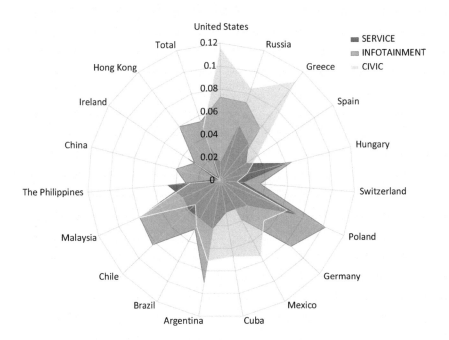

Figure 4.3 Audience approach: Civic, infotainment, and service roles

Performing Multiple Roles: The Co-Occurrence of Journalistic Roles Across Countries

To address our third research question, we first followed the theoretical rationale developed in Chapter 2, measuring the relationship between the interventionist role and the rest of the journalistic roles. We also measured the relationships among the five other roles under the assumption that roles can co-exist and are not mutually exclusive.

As expected, the data reveal the transversal nature of the journalistic voice in the news, showing a significant correlation between the interventionist role and the others. In our analysis, this association was always positive in the overall sample, and was larger between the interventionist and watchdog roles ($r = .221$, $p < .01$), and between the interventionist and infotainment roles ($r = .191$, $p < .01$).

Nevertheless, when we checked the correlations between the interventionist role and the other five roles in each country, we identified interesting trends (see Table 4.2).

First, we found that Spain ($r = .521$, $p < .01$), Greece ($r = .386$, $p < .01$), Poland ($r = .361$, $p < .01$), and to some extent Hungary ($r = .324$, $p < .01$) had the highest correlation between the interventionist and watchdog roles, where journalists use more interventionism while critically

Table 4.2 Correlations Between the Interventionist Role and Other Journalistic Roles by Country

Interventionism/ Country	Watchdog	Loyal	Service	Infotainment	Civic
U.S.	.217**	.042	.072**	.200**	.207**
Russia	.196**	.116**	.046	.287**	.131**
Greece	.386**	.292**	.148**	.059**	.214**
Spain	.521**	.102**	.024	.075**	.067**
Hungary	.324**	.093**	.201**	.079**	.117**
Switzerland	.140**	.211**	.171**	.241**	.087**
Poland	.361**	.054	.107**	−.119**	.180**
Germany	.283**	.217**	−.120**	.443**	.100**
Mexico	.285**	.066**	.127**	.325**	.235**
Cuba	.185**	−.396**	−.063	.090*	.171**
Argentina	.232**	.076**	.066**	.141**	.070**
Brazil	.205**	.151**	.089**	.213**	137**
Chile	−.037	.268**	.232**	.250**	.139**
Malaysia	.154**	−.013	.050	.011	.008
Philippines	−.110**	.116**	.137**	−.022	.032
China	.060**	.332**	.028	.262**	n/a
Ireland	.260**	.086*	.119**	.165**	.018
Hong Kong	.081**	.147**	−.027	.231**	−.012

*$p < .005$, **$p < .001$.

reporting on the elites (and vice versa). This locates them, in general, closer to a more adversarial stance on this role.

The press from Philippines is the only one in which the relationship between these two roles is negative; while in the Chilean press, the data do not show any significant relationship between these roles. For the rest of the countries, the value of the correlation was medium, moderate, or rather low, but significant and positive.

The highest correlation between the interventionist role and the loyal-facilitator role was found in the press from Cuba ($r = -.393$, $p< .01$) and China ($r = .332$, $p< .01$). While the overall relationship between them was positive for the press in China, it was significant but negative in Cuban newspapers, meaning that a higher presence of the interventionist role leads to a lower presence of the loyal-facilitator role. In Cuba, journalists seem to avoid using the interventionist role when portraying the country in a positive light. In the press from the U.S., Poland, and Malaysia, the data do not show any significant co-occurrence of these two journalistic roles, while the relationship was positive and significant to varying degrees in the rest of the countries.

In relation to the audience approach domain, we found a strong tendency to blend the performance of the interventionist role with the info-tainment role in the print media of most of the countries. This relationship is particularly strong in Germany ($r = .442$, $p< .01$), followed by Mexico ($r = .325$, $p< .01$). Only two countries —Malaysia and the Philippines— did not show a significant correlation for this combination, while the Polish press showed a low but significant negative overall association ($r = -.119$, $p< .01$). Given that these are roles that express the subjectivity of the journalist or audience, this suggests that the relationship between the two roles can be strongly tied to the narrative transformations of contemporary media—including newspapers—based on emerging digital styles (Beckett & Deuze, 2016).

The highest significant and positive correlation values between the interventionist role and the service role were found in the press from Chile ($r = .232$, $p< .01$) and Hungary ($r = .201$, $p< .01$). This association was not statistically significant in the case of Russia, Spain, Cuba, Malaysia, Hong Kong, and China. For the rest of the countries—with the exception of Germany—the values of the correlations were rather low, even though the association was always positive. Given that we analyze sections that form part of the National Desk, it is possible that journalists resist the temptation to offer more personal advice on political issues and rely on the voices of expert sources when they do so.

Finally, we found the highest values of positive correlation between the interventionist and civic roles in Mexico, Greece, and the U.S., showing that these journalistic cultures are closer to an advocate orientation. In these three cases, there were many protests and citizen actions during the years analyzed. This may suggest that journalists who work in environments with at least some individual freedoms combine the two roles when the situation merits such action in order to report on the news in a more active way. Meanwhile, the correlation of these two roles was not statistically significant in the Asian press or in Ireland.

Besides the transversal relationship between the interventionist and other journalistic roles, we also found a significantly higher co-occurrence of the performance of the two public service oriented roles—the watchdog and the civic roles—at the global level ($r = .239, p< .01$).

When we broke the results down by country, the most popular association is indeed the co-occurrence of the watchdog and civic roles. This correlation is particularly high in the case of the Cuban ($r = .404, p< .01$), Mexican ($r = .384, p< .01$), and, to a lesser extent, Greek ($r = .223, p< .01$), and U.S. ($r = .241, p< .01$) presses. In the print press from the U.S., we also found the strongest association between the infotainment and civic roles ($r = .365, p< .01$).

Meanwhile, the civic and loyal-facilitator roles correlate most strongly in Cuba ($r = -.446, p< .01$) and Malaysia ($r = .212, p< .01$), but in opposite directions, showing traits unique to the local cultures and how "loyalism" can materialize in certain contexts (see Chapters 6 and 11).

We identified an even stronger combination in Malaysia—namely that of the civic and service roles ($r = .313, p< .01$). The same trend is present in Spain ($r = .200, p< .01$) and Mexico ($r = .229, p< .01$) to a lesser extent. Finally, the U.S. ($r = .181, p< .01$) and Germany ($r = .173, p< .01$) share a tendency to spectacularize political wrongdoings, though this correlation is not as strong as those found for other role combinations. Our results show a significant connection between the infotainment and watchdog roles in their print media. The dramatization of political scandals has been a traditional style of covering corruption and political operations. While Umbricht and Esser (2014) found, for example, an increase in scandalization, emotionalization, and private life over time in the U.S. and U.K. presses, Hallin and Papathanassopoulos (2002, p. 176) note that clientelist relationships exist to some degree in all modern societies, and that this has been the case in Germany where the media dramatize political scandals.

Conclusion

The aim of this chapter was to test the thesis of hybridization in journalistic cultures, examining how countries differ and can be grouped together with respect to the performance of multiple professional roles in the news.

Specifically, our study finds compelling evidence of the multilayered hybridization of journalistic cultures at the performative level. These results reflect the presence of fluid and dynamic journalistic roles in the news, which display theoretically contrasting traits to a greater extent than media system and role conception research has shown. Journalistic cultures are not universal and role performance hybridity differs across media systems, political regimes, and regional boundaries. While previous studies identified certain levels of consistency across countries for key characteristics of the roles adopted by media professionals, we show that a combination of traits seems to be the norm rather than the exception. Specifically, our research shows that professional roles increasingly intermingle at the performative level, especially when a broader sample of countries is used along with types of news that go beyond the front page or the coverage of political events alone.

For example, standard assumptions made in the literature on media system research suggest that media outlets from advanced democracies with more solid media markets and higher levels of journalistic professionalization would tend to engage in the watchdog role more prominently. By contrast, it is expected that media from transitional or non-democratic countries would display the loyal-facilitator role more, while journalists working in consolidated market economies are thought to engage in the performance of the infotainment and service roles to appeal to audiences. Earlier research on role conceptions also suggests that journalists in transitional and developing countries are more likely to play the interventionist role (Hanitzsch et al., 2011; Weaver, 1998; Weaver & Willnat, 2012).

However, our results do not provide strong support for these expectations. Moreover, our data show that within theorized countries such as those in Western Europe and the U.S., and within transitional democracies and non-democratic countries, journalists perform different roles in the news, displaying different combinations and intermediate outcomes.

The only perspective that shows some global homogeneity is the idea that the disseminative stance of journalists dominates compared to the interventionist stance. These results align with earlier assumptions based on the media system (Hallin & Mancini, 2004) and especially on role conception studies (Hanitzsch et al., 2011; Hanitzsch, Hanusch, Ramaprasad et al., 2019; Weaver & Willnat, 2012). Regardless of region or political status, journalists use a more fact-based, opinion-free template, although results vary significantly in their adoption of a more active stance, as Chapter 5 shows.

By contrast, we must view roles that involve the adoption of a certain stance on powerful institutions or audiences from a different angle (see Chapters 6 and 7). Globally, the watchdog, infotainment, and civic roles followed suit in order of importance, whereas the loyal-facilitator role was the least visible across countries, except in Cuba. This is one of the few countries in our sample that meets theoretical expectations regarding high levels of interventionism and loyalism and low infotainment, and where the characteristics of its political system strongly shape the news.

80   *Claudia Mellado et al.*

It is also important to note that role performance differences do not fully support previous media system typologies for advanced democracies, as studies that empirically tested different variables against these systems suggest (Brüggemann, Engesser, Büchel, Humprecht, & Castro, 2014). The only cases in which advanced democracies classified on the basis of specific media system models share clear commonalities were Spain and Greece, which are grouped together in the power relations domain, and Germany and Switzerland, which are close in relation to the journalistic voice domain. We note, however, that the latter two countries often have little in common with each other in relation to the infotainment role.

Our data also show strong support for the manifold hybridization of journalistic cultures in transitional democracies and non-democratic countries. Transitional democracies do not form a unified cluster in any role. Instead, they are distributed across groups with advanced democracies and non-democratic regimes when analyzed by domain and globally. Furthermore, the evidence does not suggest that journalists in transitional democracies are more likely to be interventionist (Hanitzsch et al., 2011; Weaver & Willnat, 2012).

Regarding potential regional grouping, the data reveal that some countries tend to align with common expectations for some domains, albeit only partially. For example, although they always appear closer to countries that are very different from them in terms of political regimes and geographic location, China and Hong Kong present similar results for all of the domains analyzed. We found the same to be true with Russia, Hungary, and Poland for the journalistic voice domain, and with Russia and Poland in the case of the audience approach domain. This supports existing claims in the literature that examines similar trends in post-communist countries (Gross & Jakubowicz, 2013).

At the national level, the print press from countries like Ireland supports the expectations of a liberal media system tending towards a disseminative type of reporting. Print journalistic cultures such as that of the U.S. rank higher in contrasting traits such as interventionism (Esser & Umbricht, 2013), with an intermediate position regarding, for example, the watchdog role. Indeed, Greece and Spain, which comprise the Polarized Pluralist theorized media system model—and that experienced political and economic turmoil in the years of the sample—exhibit a higher performance of the watchdog role than the United States.

In short, our results reflect a normative-practice gap and question the notion of a clear-cut divide between and within Western and non-Western journalistic cultures. Although hybridity seems to be a global phenomenon, it manifests in different ways in the performance of multiple and non-mutually exclusive professional roles across a diverse group of countries.

Supporting our theoretical expectations, we found strong evidence of a significant co-occurrence of professional roles used simultaneously by journalists around the world, and specifically in some countries, to inform the public and report the news. While the literature has often referred to Western models as the standard and considers non-Western models to be a deviation, our results suggest that there is no single dominant journalistic model in specific regions or political systems, and that journalistic cultures are based on a combination of role performances. For example, the diversity found in the performance of professional roles across and within countries shows that similar structural conditions could end up producing different performances, while different structural conditions could result in similar ones. Our findings revealed that, for example, this is the case in China and Switzerland and in Argentina and Germany for several roles.

While the values of correlation between the interventionist role and the watchdog role were highest in several advanced and transitional democracies, we did not find a clear pattern of connection between performing the watchdog role or the loyal-facilitator role and interventionism in non-democratic countries. In China, for example, there is a significant positive correlation between the loyal-facilitator role and interventionism, while in Cuba has a significant but negative correlation of the same combination of roles.

This may be due to the fact that, unlike normative values, which are more easily transferred through journalism education and global discourses of professionalism (Deuze, 2005; Zelizer, 2017), journalistic roles manifest in ways that are more difficult to fit into existing ideal media system typologies and political or regional clusters when analyzed comparatively and cross-nationally (Mellado et al., 2017). Although we can make some intuitive assumptions about the systematic performance of some roles in different systems, the call for journalists might vary depending on the context. In this sense, role performance can be influenced by the nature of professional roles and their specific logic of negotiations (Ashforth, 2012), the events unfolding (Shoemaker & Cohen, 2006; Benson & Hallin, 2007), the period of the occurrence or the historical moment (Ryfe, 2016), and the nature of the news (Waisbord, 2013).

This chapter sets the stage for the next chapters of this book. Chapters 5, 6, and 7 break down these general findings, offering analyses of the analytical sub-dimensions of each role as well as their indicators, which will be a useful way of classifying variations in specific qualities of the roles.

Note

1 This chapter is based on the article "The Hybridization of Journalistic Cultures," which appeared in the *Journal of Communication.*

82   *Claudia Mellado et al.*

References

Ashforth, B. (2012). *Role transitions in organizational life: An identity-based perspective*. NJ: Routledge.

Beckett, C., & Deuze, M. (2016). The role of emotion in the future of journalism. *Social Media + Society*. doi:10.1177/2056305116662395

Benson, R., & Hallin, D. (2007). How states, markets and globalization shape the news: The French and US national press, 1965–97. *European Journal of Communication, 22*(1), 27–48.

Brüggemann, M., Engesser, S., Büchel, F., Humprecht, E., & Castro, L. (2014). Hallin and Mancini revisited: Four empirical types of western media systems. *Journal of Communication, 64*(6), 1037–1065.

Christians, C. G., Glasser, T. L., McQuail, D., Nordenstreng, K., & White, R. A. (2009). *Normative theories of the media: Journalism in democratic societies*. Urbana, IL: University of Illinois Press.

Deuze, M. (2005). What is journalism? Professional identity and ideology of journalists reconsidered. *Journalism, 6*(4), 442–464.

Donsbach, W., & Patterson, T. (2004). Political news journalists: Partisanship, professionalism, and political roles in five countries. In F. Esser and B. Pfesch (Eds.), *Comparing political communication: Theories, cases, and challenges* (pp. 251–270). Cambridge: Cambridge University Press.

Esser, F. (2008). Dimensions of political news cultures: Sound bite and image bite news in France, Germany, Great Britain, and the United States. *The International Journal of Press/ Politics, 13*(4), 401–428.

Esser, F., & Umbricht, A. (2013). Competing models of journalism? Political affairs coverage in US, British, German, Swiss, French, and Italian newspapers. *Journalism, 14*(8), 989–1007.

Frère, M. S. (2015). Francophone Africa: The rise of 'pluralist authoritarian' media systems? *African Journalism Studies, 36*(1), 103–112.

Gross, P., & Jakubowicz, K. (2013). *Media transformations in the post-communist world: Eastern Europe's tortured path to change*. Lanham, MD: Lexington.

Guerrero, M., & Márquez-Ramírez, M. (2014). *Media systems and communication policies in Latin America*. London: Palgrave.

Hallin, D., & Mancini, P. (2004). *Comparing media systems: Three models of media and politics*. Cambridge: Cambridge University Press.

Hallin, D., & Mancini, P. (Eds.). (2012). *Comparing media systems beyond the Western world*. Cambridge: Cambridge University Press.

Hallin, D., & Mancini, P. (2017). Ten years after comparing media systems: What have we learned? *Political Communication, 34*(2), 155–171.

Hallin, D., & Papathanassopoulos, S. (2002). Political clientelism and the media: Southern Europe and Latin America in comparative perspective. *Media, Culture & Society, 24*(2), 175–195.

Hanitzsch, T., Hanusch, F., Mellado, C., Anikina, M., Berganza, R., Cangoz, I., . . . Kee Wang Yuen, E. (2011). Mapping journalism cultures across nations: A comparative study of 18 countries. *Journalism Studies, 12*(3), 273–293.

Hanitzsch, T., Hanusch, F., Ramaprasad, J., & de Beer, A. S. (Eds.). (2019). *Worlds of journalism: Journalistic cultures around the globe*. New York: Columbia University Press.

Mancini, P. (2015). The news media between volatility and hybridization. In J. Zielonka (Ed.), *Media and politics in new democracies: Europe in a comparative perspective* (pp. 28–34). Oxford: Oxford University Press.

Márquez-Ramírez, M. Beck, D., Roses, S., Mothes, C., Panagiotou, N., Silke, H., . . . Mellado, C. (2020). Detached or interventionist? Comparing the performance of watchdog journalism in transitional, advanced and non-democratic countries. *The International Journal of Press-Politics, 25*(1), 53–75.

Mazzoleni, G. (2012). *La comunicazione politica*. Bologna: Il Mulino.

McCargo, D. (2012). Partisan polyvalence: Characterizing the political role of Asian media. In D. Hallin & P. Mancini (Eds.), *Media systems beyond the western world* (pp. 201–223). New York: Cambridge University Press.

McMenamin, I., Flynn, R., O'Malley, E., & Rafter, K. (2013). Commercialism and election framing: A content analysis of twelve newspapers in the 2011 Irish general election. *The International Journal of Press/Politics, 18*(2), 167–187.

Mellado, C. (2015). Professional roles in news content: Six dimensions of journalistic role performance. *Journalism Studies, 16*(4), 596–614.

Mellado, C. (2019). Journalists' professional roles and role performance. In Jon F. Nussbaum (Ed.), *Oxford research encyclopedia of communication*. Oxford: Oxford University Press. Published Online February 2019, pp. 1–23. doi:10.1093/acre-fore/9780190228613.013.832

Mellado, C., Hellmueller, L., Márquez-Ramírez, M., Humanes, M. L., Sparks, C., Stepinska, A., . . . Wang, H. (2017). The hybridization of journalistic cultures: A comparative study of journalistic role performance. *Journal of Communication, 67*(6), 944–967.

Olivera, D., & Torres, L. (2020). El rol profesional leal-facilitador en el periodismo cubano. Un análisis a partir del contenido de las noticias de cuatro medios nacionales entre los años 2012 y 2013 (The performance of a loyal-facilitator role in Cuban journalism. An analysis based on the news from four national newspaper between 2012 and 2013). In O. Martínez (Ed.), *Miradas heterogéneas a las ciencias sociales desde los métodos econométricos* (pp. 81–111). Ciudad de México: Universidad Iberoamericana.

Patterson, T. E., & Donsbach, W. (1996). News decisions: Journalists as partisan actors. *Political Communication, 13*(4), 455–468.

Preston, P. (2009). *Making the news: Journalism and news cultures in Europe*. London, England: Routledge.

Ryfe, D. (2016). The importance of time in media production research. In C. Paterson., D. Lee., Saha, A., & Zoellner, A (Eds.), *Advancing media production research* (pp. 38–50). Hampshire, UK: Palgrave Macmillan.

Shoemaker, P., & Cohen, A. (2006). *News around the world: Content, practitioners, and the public*. New York: Routledge.

Umbricht, A., & Esser, F. (2014). The evolution of objective and interpretative journalism in the Western press: Comparing six news systems since the 1960s. *Journalism and Mass Communication Quarterly, 91*(2), 229–249.

Voltmer, K. (2013). *The media in transitional democracies*. Cambridge: Polity.

Waisbord, S. (2013). *Reinventing professionalism: Journalism and news in global perspective*. Cambridge: Polity.

Weaver, D. (1998). Journalists around the world: Commonalities and differences. In D. H. Weaver (Ed.), *The global journalist: News people around the world* (pp. 455–480). Cresskill, NJ: Hampton.

Weaver, D., Beam, R. A., Brownlee, B. J., Voakes, P. S., & Wilhoit, G. C. (2007). *The American journalist in the 21st century: U.S. news people at the dawn of a new millennium*. Mahwah, NJ: Lawrence Erlbaum.

Weaver, D., & Wilhoit, C. (1996). *The American journalists in the 1990s: U.S. news people at the end of an era*. Mahwah, NJ: Erlbaum.

Weaver, D., & Willnat, L. (Eds.). (2012). *The global journalist in the 21st century*. New York: Routledge.

Zelizer, B. (2017). *What journalism could be*. Cambridge: Polity.

5 Journalistic Voice

The Performance of the Interventionist Role

Agnieszka Stępińska, Gabriella Szabó, Adriana Amado, and Henry Silke

One lasting "big question" in our field is how much of the journalistic voice should be heard in the media. Should journalists just report on what they see or learn from their sources and let the audience members interpret the events on their own? Or should journalists perhaps explain and comment on the story they are covering?

The answer to that question leads to normative considerations of expectations of journalists determined by cultural, social, and political conditions. Not surprisingly then, most previous studies on the disseminative or interventionist stance of journalism as a profession have been conducted from such a normative perspective (for a review of concepts and literature, see, for example, Benson, 2008; Eide, 2017; Christians, Glasser, McQuail, Nordenstreng, & White, 2009), journalistic role conceptions studies (Hanitzsch et al., 2011; Hanitzsch, Hanusch, Ramaprasad, & de Beer, 2019) or media research (Patterson, 1993; Barnhurst & Mutz, 1997; Strömbäck & Dimitrova, 2011; Strömbäck & Shehata, 2007; Djerf-Pierre & Weibull, 2008; Strömbäck & Esser, 2009; Esser & Umbricht, 2014).

The analyses that draw on these perspectives provide interesting distinctions and definitions of two types of journalistic voice in news stories: disseminator (or descriptive) and interventionist. While descriptive, fact-oriented, and source-driven journalism is more focused on providing answers to questions of who, when, where, and what, interventionist journalism is more focused on why (Salgado & Strömbäck, 2012). The former, also called a "reporter voice" by Thomson and White (2008, p. 228), manifests by refraining from any judgement and keeping to a detached description of the facts. The latter, called the "commentator voice" (Thomson & White, 2008), is based on journalists' contribution as participants in the news, including interpretation, overt commentary, or speculation about the future consequences of current affairs.

Such a distinction aligns with Benson and Hallin's (2007) definition of interpretive and opinion-based journalism. According to the authors, "interpretation is a kind of empirical discourse, but goes beyond current facts, setting or historical context to speculate on such things as significance, outcomes and motives," while giving opinions refers to the "exercise of judgement, either normative (what is good or bad) or empirical (what is true or false)" (p. 32). Djerf-Pierre and Weibull add a critical component to the presence of the journalistic voice and characterize it as "four entwined features: critical expertise, speculation, advocacy, and meta-journalism" (2008, p. 209). In practice, journalists act as experts or commentators, interpreting political reality for their audience: "Taking the role of ombudsmen of the public, journalists advocate the presumed interests and needs of the public/audience" (Djerf-Pierre & Weibull, 2008, p. 209). On the other hand, Hanitzsch (2007, p. 373) notices that journalism cultures that follow an interventionist approach may either "act on behalf of the socially disadvantaged or as mouthpiece of a political party or other groups whose interests are at stake."

That leads us to professional role conceptions among journalists. These have been systematically studied for more than six decades based on the distinction between two main categories: "neutral" and "participant" journalism (e.g., Cohen, 1963; Johnstone, Slawski, & Bowman, 1976; Donsbach & Klett, 1993; Patterson & Donsbach, 1996; Donsbach & Patterson, 2004; Bro, 2008; Hanitzsch et al., 2011, 2019; Weaver & Wilhoit, 1986, 1996; Weaver et al., 2007; Weaver & Willnat, 2012).

For example, Donsbach and Patterson (2004) recognize two dimensions when analyzing the presence of the journalistic voice in news stories: passive-active and advocate-neutral. The first refers to the degree to which journalists act independently from those who are interested in what will be published (autonomy and accountability), while the second reflects the extent to which journalists take sides on certain issues (opinions, interpretations, suggestions, or speculations). However, as will be discussed in our findings, autonomy of journalists does not necessarily point to more interventionism, while lack of autonomy does not necessarily prevent interventionist journalism, as the journalistic voice may be used in support of a political or business interest.

Bro (2008) also suggests a two-dimensional model. While an active-passive dimension is linked to the purpose of news reporting, a representative-deliberative dimension reflects news reporters' perspective. In particular, the passive journalist will mostly be focused on simply disseminating news stories, while the active journalist will be concerned with the effect of the news. Likewise, while the representative stance is focused on a fact-oriented description of events, the deliberative stance is devoted to actively helping people participate in the public sphere (Bro, 2008, p. 319).

The interventionist role has mostly been studied from the perspective of a non-Western ideal of development journalism (Hanitzsch, Hanusch, & Lauerer, 2016) with an inherent normative component. However, the performance of the interventionist role is not a new phenomenon in the Polarized Pluralist model developed in the Mediterranean media systems of southern Europe, where newspapers have close ties to political parties and journalists represent a literary style of writing that favors commentary and interpretations over fact-based reporting (Donsbach & Klett, 1993; Hallin & Mancini, 2004; Esser & Umbricht, 2014). This is not a new development in advanced democracies and is reflected in changes in the Anglo-American tradition in the performance of the press during the last decades (Esser & Umbricht, 2014).

Indeed, some scholars claim that the increase in interventionist coverage on the part of journalists represents a significant change in political news content that has developed over the last few decades (Patterson, 1993; Barnhurst & Mutz, 1997; Strömbäck & Dimitrova, 2011; Strömbäck & Shehata, 2007; Djerf-Pierre & Weibull, 2008). For example, Esser and Umbricht (2014, p. 240) show that indicators of the interventionist role became more important over time in media systems that had been previously perceived as mostly focused on descriptions of the facts. Salgado, Strömbäck, Aalberg, and Esser (2017) draw on the observations contained in their study, tracing a greater presence of interventionist elements in the U.S. and French journalistic cultures than in Portugal and Spain.

Against this backdrop, our project analyzes the "journalistic voice" domain as dealing with the presence-absence of the interventionist stance of journalists in their reporting, following Mellado's (2015) operationalization. The presence of the interventionist side is journalist-centered, where news professionals have a voice in the story (Wang, Sparks, Lü, & Huang, 2016) and sometimes act as advocates for different groups in society. The absence of the intervention by journalists would then lead to a latitude in the disseminator voice, which gives importance to the distance between the journalists and the facts they are reporting (Mellado, 2015).

Given that this chapter primarily focuses on role performance, we claim that the level of interventionism is lower when journalists report the facts in a detached and neutral way without any indication of evaluation, interpretation, judgment, or statements about which side (s)he is on or her/his position, while it is higher when more of those elements are present in the news.

These two ways of reporting conform to a unidimensional structure, whereby a greater level of participation by the journalist implies higher levels of interventionism, and vice versa (see Chapter 2).

According to several scholars, the increase in interventionist journalism can be explained by the rise of critical professionalism, skepticism towards official sources, and journalism's striving for independence from outside influences (Patterson, 1993, pp. 66–67, 80–81). Zaller (2001) and Benson and Hallin (2007) link its presence to the degree of journalistic interdependence and the closeness of the relationship between the press and politics: the more political actors try to control the news, the more journalists will try to report something else instead. McNair (2000, p. 7), on the other hand, claims that the emergence and increasing use of both political public relations and news management and the commercialization of journalism (the need to construct more compelling news products) support tendencies towards interpretive journalism.

Journalistic Interventionism and Its Indicators

Since the journalistic voice domain is always present in one form or another (more or less interventionist), assessing its various forms requires both conceptualization and operationalization.

For the purposes of this study, we examine the performance of the interventionist role through the presence of five specific indicators in the news: the journalist's opinion, interpretation, call for action, use of evaluative adjectives, and use of first person (Mellado, 2015), where the higher their presence, the higher the level of performance of the interventionist role.

The approach used in the comparative study reveals similarities and differences between journalists across countries regarding the extent to which news professionals go beyond a detached description of the facts in the stories they produce, as Chapter 4 outlines.

We also provide an in-depth discussion of the specific indicators and split them into two main analytical sub-dimensions: (1) those related to the content of a news item (the message delivered by a journalist, including arguments, explanations, and instructions) and (2) those related to the style (how a journalist presents the message).

Consequently, we may distinguish between two types of interventionism: a content-determined interventionism and a style-determined interventionism. The former is based on two elements. The first is the extent to which journalists provide an *interpretation*; this can be traced by the extent that the news item includes a journalistic explanation of the causes or meanings and/or suggestions of possible consequences of certain facts/actions. Secondly, they express their *point of view*—a reference to the author or authors' explicit personal perspective and/or presentation of *a call for action* to propose changes or demand action. For example, a journalist can offer some interpretation of the outcome of the general election by emphasizing his/her predictions on what will happen if the opposition were to win alongside a clear point of view on that outcome. The latter is rooted in journalists' tendency to *use qualifying adjectives* and/or *use the first person* in news stories by being a witness to a story, appropriating an action, or giving an opinion. For example, while reporting on the funeral of three children who were tragic victims of infanticide, the journalist's voice can be reflected in the use of words such as "anguish," "despair," and "darken."

Each of these indicators can appear separately or be accompanied by other indicators related to the same role, and by indicators belonging to other journalistic roles.

Such a distinction allows us to recognize different types of interventionism in the news across countries depending on the predominance of any of these sub-categories in the news. Furthermore, different combinations of interventionist indicators (both of content and style) may lead to either an explanatory form of interventionist role performance manifested by the presence of interpretations, opinions, and the use of adjectives; or an instructive form, expressed by calls for action formulated by journalists and emphasized by the use of the first person. As a result, splitting the indicators reveals more nuances of the hybridization of journalistic cultures and, specifically, of the performance of professional roles in the news.

The prevalence of specific role performances depends on a set of story-level, organizational, and societal-level factors that will be discussed in detail in Chapters 9–11. In this chapter, we follow previous studies on the presence of journalistic voice in news stories that emphasize the importance of political regime, media commercialism, and a type of news story in order to provide insight into the performance of the interventionist role across the presses of the countries under study.

In view of this goal, the following research questions will guide this chapter:

> *RQ1: What type of interventionist role is performed in print journalism around the globe?*
> *RQ2: What internal variations can be found in the performance of the interventionist role in print journalism across and within countries?*

We ran Anova tests to measure the significance and effect sizes of differences in the presence of both types of interventionism (content-based and style-driven) across countries and in relation to the political regime (advanced democracy, transitional democracy, and non-democratic), audience orientation (popular/elite), and type of news story (journalistic genre). We also ran Pearson correlations between the particular indicators of the interventionist role and between the interventionist role and other roles overall and for each country.

Results

Distribution of Indicators Measuring the Performance of the Interventionist Role

As indicated in Chapter 4, the countries that show the highest global means for the interventionist role are the U.S., followed by transitional democracies, non-democratic countries, and Polarized Pluralist countries from Europe. These include Argentina, Poland, Hungary, Hong Kong, Greece, China, Chile, and Russia. By contrast, the country that showed the lowest global mean was Ireland.

Based on that general result, and following the distinction between two sub-dimensions of the interventionist role, we traced which types of indicators constitute the interventionist role in a particular country.

Anova tests showed significant differences in the presence of both types of interventionism (content-based and style-driven) across countries ($F_{content}$ (17,3362)=164.127; p<.001; F_{style} (17,3362)=255.802; p<. 001). The effect size was relevant for the content-based interventionist approach ($\eta2=$ .08) and particularly important for the style-driven type of interventionism ($\eta2=$ .12).

Figure 5.1 shows that the countries with the highest presence of the content-based side of the interventionist role were Poland (M= .30, SD= .31), the United States (M= .28, SD=27), Germany (M= .27, SD=.20), Greece (M=26, SD=.29), and Argentina (M=.25, SD=.26). Meanwhile, the countries with the highest presence of the style-driven side of the interventionist role were Argentina (M= .38, SD= .23), the US (M= .37, SD= .23), Chile (M=.35, SD=.25), the Philippines (M=.34, SD=.25), Hungary (M=.34, SD=.37), Russia (M=.32, SD=.34), and China (M=.32, SD=.29).

Only two of the countries in our sample show the highest average score for both of these groups: the U.S. and Argentina. This implies that both types of interventionism are very well-established in their journalistic cultures, while other countries display quite different types of interventionism. For example, Germany has a comparatively strong content part

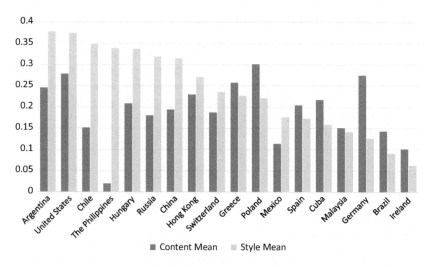

Figure 5.1 Content- and style-related indicators of the interventionist role (means)

(see previous paragraph) and a weak style part (M= .13, SD= .22). The press from the Philippines and Chile, on the other hand, present the largest gap between the use the content-related indicators ($M_{Philippines}$= .02, SD= .09; M_{Chile}=.15, SD=.22) and the use of the style-related indicators ($M_{Philippines}$=.40 SD= .23; M_{Chile}= .34, SD= .25), presenting the largest difference between both means. Other countries rank medium in both (in Switzerland $M_{content}$= .19, SD= .24 and M_{style}=.24, SD=.28; in Spain $M_{content}$=.21, SD=26, M_{style}=.17, SD=25; in Cuba $M_{content}$=.22, SD=.27, M_{style}=.16, SD=29) or relatively low in both (in Malaysia $M_{content}$=15, SD=.26 and M_{style}=.14, SD=28). Unsurprisingly, the country that scored very low in both sub-dimensions of the interventionist role was Ireland ($M_{content}$= .10, SD= .23, M_{style}= .06, SD=.17).

After calculating the average score of each country in the two sub-dimensions of the interventionist role (content- and style-related), we conducted an in-depth analysis of the presence of the specific indicators that comprise those two analytical approaches.

First, in regard to the content-driven mode of interventionism, we found that interpretation (36.2%) and opinion (15.6%) are two of the most frequent indicators of intervention present in the overall sample, while calls for action provided by journalists are less frequently present (3.7%). For the style-oriented approach to interventionism, our data show that as many as 44.3% of news stories include the use of evaluative adjectives, while only 4.8% exhibit the use of the first person.

The examination of specific content-related indicators in the news in particular countries shows that journalists share their opinions quite often in Greece, Poland, the U.S., Hungary, and Argentina (over 20% of news items), while hardly any news items include a journalist's opinion in Asian countries such as the Philippines, China, and Hong Kong (around 2%). In spite of this, interpretations were present in more than 50% of news stories in two of these countries—China and Hong Kong—and in Germany, the U.S., and Poland. At the same time, more than 30% of the news included interpretations in Cuba, Argentina, Hungary, Russia, Switzerland, Spain, and Brazil, all countries with different political backgrounds. In the Philippines, by contrast, the performance of interpretation was present in less than 4% of the news analyzed. The third content-exposed indicator, call to action, was less frequently present in the news overall, as previously described. In fact, this indicator was only present in more than 5% of the news in Greece, Poland, Malaysia, Chile, and Russia (see Figure 5.2).

As far as a style is concerned, the findings reveal that journalists quite often use evaluative adjectives when reporting on events (see Figure 5.3). In the U.S., Argentina, the Philippines, Chile, China, and Hong Kong, more than 50% of the news includes its presence, while in Switzerland, Spain, Hungary, Greece, and Mexico, between 30 and 40% of news pieces include evaluative terms. On the other hand, the use of the first person is less frequent across countries, with a presence in no more than 20% of the items, except in Hungary (28.9 percent).

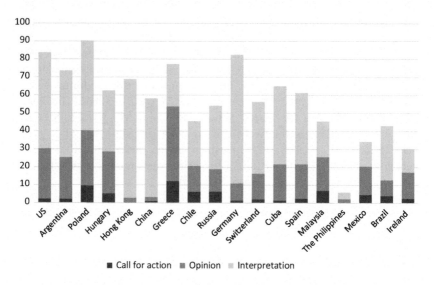

Figure 5.2 Presence of content-related indicators of the interventionist role (percentage)

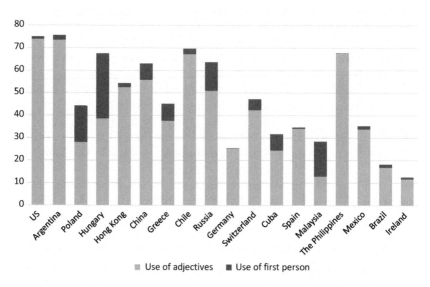

Figure 5.3 Presence of style-related indicators of the interventionist role (percentage)

Furthermore, we found significant associations between the presence of the following indicators in the whole sample: calls for action and journalist's point of view (r=.239, p<.01), and call for action and the use of the first person (r=.127, p<.01). Although weak, we also found a significant correlation between the presence of journalists' call for action and interpretation (r=.093, p<.01), and between call for action and the use of adjectives (r=.083, p<.01). It seems that a call for action made by a journalist is often accompanied by his/her opinion, first-person narration, and by an interpretation of the events that includes suggestions and qualifying adjectives. The other possible relationships between the indicators of the interventionist role (opinion with interpretation, opinion and the use of adjectives, opinion and first person, interpretation and first person, and interpretation and the use of adjectives) did not significantly correlate with each other in our overall sample.

Presence of the Interventionist Role in Different Types of Political Regimes

Based on the first descriptive results, we were interested in determining whether the political regime of a country plays a significant role.

Indeed, Anova tests show that the type of regime has a significant effect on the performance of the interventionist role (F(2, 34511)=56.186; p<.001). However, our study shows that a high level of interventionism was present in both advanced democracies and non-democratic regimes. In fact, the mean value of a presence of interventionist indicators was the highest among the non-democratic countries (M= .23, SD= .20), followed by the advanced democracies (M= .22, SD= .22).

Specifically, our findings show that there were more news items including journalists' interpretation (63%), evaluative adjectives (51%), and the first person (7%) in the non-democratic regimes than in the advanced democracies and transitional democracies (see Table 5.1). On the other hand, opinions were more frequently included in news items in the advanced democracies (22%) than in transitional democracies (14%) and non-democratic regimes (5%). Based on that observation, we argue that journalists are more eager to express their view on the events or issues they are covering (journalists say what *they* think) in countries with a stable democratic regime, while there is a tendency towards providing

Table 5.1 Presence of Indicators of the Interventionist Role by Regime Type (Percentage)

	Advanced democracies	Transitional democracies	Non-democratic regimes
CONTENT			
Interpretation	39.9	31.0	53.1
Opinion	22.0	14.2	5.1
Call for action	4.1	4.0	1.2
STYLE			
Use of adjectives	39.7	45.4	50.7
Use of first person	3.1	5.1	7.3

explanation and interpretation (journalist say what *the audience members* should think) in non-democratic regimes.

Presence of the Interventionist Role in Different Types of Media

For the purposes of our project, we collected news from newspapers with different audience orientations: popular and elite. When we examined the differences in the presence of the interventionist role in both groups, we found a significantly higher performance of the interventionist role ($t(33,638)=9.66$; $p<.001$) in the popular press ($M=0.23$, $SD=0.21$) as compared to the elite press ($M=0.20$, $SD=0.22$).

Specifically, chi-square tests showed that a significant relationship exists between the media audience orientation of the newspaper (popular or elite) and the use of the first person by journalists (χ^2 (1, $N=33,640)=90.74$; $p<.001$), as well as the use of adjectives ($\chi 2$ (1, $N=33,640)=305.38$; $p<.001$). Journalists who write for popular newspapers more frequently use style-related indicators of interventionism in their reporting than journalists in the elite press (see Table 5.2). However, there were no significant differences between the popular and elite press in the overall sample in regard to the presence of opinion, interpretation, and calls for action.

Specifically, we noticed that the presence of adjectives was highest in the popular press in Chile (88%) and Argentina (74%), while the use of the first person is found most frequently in the popular press in Hungary (38%) and Spain (34%) (see Table 5.3).

Some countries have characteristics that contradict the dominant pattern of higher presence of interventionism in the popular press, namely where: (1) the use of first person was similarly low (around 1–2%) in both types of the news media (U.S., Mexico, Argentina, Ireland, Hong Kong, and the Philippines), (2) the use of first person was similarly relatively high (around 14–16% in Poland), or (3) the use of adjectives was higher in the elite press than in popular press (the U.S., China, Germany, Poland, and Mexico).

Table 5.2 Presence of Indicators of the Interventionist Role in the Popular and Elite Press (Percentage)

	Indicators of the model		*CONTENT (%)*			*STYLE (%)*	
	M	SD	*Opinion*	*Interpretation*	*Call for action*	*Use of adjectives*	*Use of first person*
Popular	0.23	0.21	14.5	36.6	4.0	53.5	6.8
Elite	0.20	0.22	16.0	35.9	3.7	42.6	4.2

Table 5.3 Presence of Style-Related Indicators of the Interventionist Role in the Popular and Elite Press Across Countries (Percentage)

	USE OF FIRST PERSON (%)		USE OF ADJECTIVES	
	Popular press	Elite press	Popular press	Elite press
U.S.	1.0	1.1	44.8	86.1
Argentina	2.8	1.4	74.5	72.7
Poland	14.2	16.8	18.2	31.8
Hungary	37.7	24.8	61.1	23.0
Hong Kong	0.3	2.2	67.0	48.0
China	4.9	8.9	49.7	60.0
Greece	–	7.6	–	37.6
Chile	3.9	1.9	87.6	60.6
Russia	23.5	5.6	58.3	46.2
Germany	1.6	0.0	21.1	25.7
Switzerland	7.1	3.7	53.3	42.4
Cuba	–	7.3	–	24.4
Spain	34.1	0.6	–	34.1
Malaysia	14.0	16.1	11.2	13.6
The Philippines	0.0	0.2	61.3	70.8
Mexico	0.9	1.5	29.7	35.4
Brazil	–	1.3	–	16.9
Ireland	0.0	1.1	8.3	13.2
TOTAL	6.8	4.8	53.5	42.6

The Performance of the Interventionist Role in Different Types of News Stories

Not surprisingly, the presence of the interventionist role was significantly higher $(t(33,637)=-39.8; p<.001)$ in features and reportage news stories $(M=0.33, SD=0.25)$ than in briefs and news reports $(M=0.19, SD=0.20)$.

However, the performance of the interventionist role is not restricted to features and reportages. For example, more than 40% of the briefs and articles in the global sample included evaluative adjectives, while one third of these story types included interpretations provided by journalists.

Specifically, interpretation was present in more than 50% of items published in briefs or articles in Germany, Hong Kong, and China; in more than 40% of items in the U.S. and Argentina; and in more than one third of briefs and articles in Poland, Switzerland, and Spain. More than 20% of briefs and articles in Greece, the U.S., Poland, and Argentina included an opinion.

By contrast, the use of the first person or calls for action made by journalists is almost absent in briefs and articles in the global sample (3.8% and 2.9%, respectively). Figure 5.4 shows a distribution (in percentages) of both content-related and style-related indicators of the interventionist

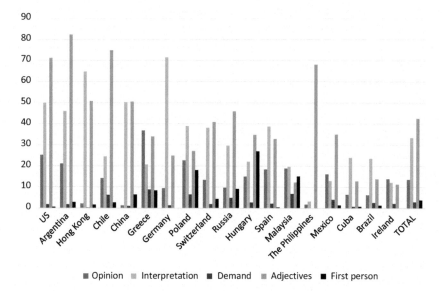

Figure 5.4 Indicators of the interventionist role in briefs and articles (combined) across countries

role in two types of news stories (briefs and articles combined) across countries.

Presence of the Interventionist Role Across Different News Topics

The findings presented in Table 5.4 show that a significantly higher level of interventionism is found in pieces that cover certain news topics (F $(17,34469)=21.275$; $p<.001$). Opinions expressed by journalists were the most present in news topics such as housing, infrastructure, public works, and health and social problems. Journalists were similarly eager to share their opinions on political events such as elections and protests/demonstrations.

Interpretation, meanwhile, can be found most frequently in news items covering defense, military, and domestic security, as well as highly relevant public issues such as housing, education, transportation, and economy. The call for action made by the journalists was more frequently found in news items on social problems, housing, transportation, and police, as well as energy and environment. While evaluative adjectives were found transversally in news items across all thematic beats, the use of the first person was traced most frequently in items on education, social problems, housing, defense, energy and environment, and religion.

Table 5.4 Presence of the Indicators of the Interventionist Role in the News (Percentage, Means, and Standard Deviations)

	Overall role		Content indicators (%)			Style indicators (%)	
	M	SD	Opinion	Interpre-tation	Call for action	Adjectives	First person
Government, legislature	0.21	0.22	15.6	39.8	3.6	40.0	4.7
Elections, campaign	0.20	0.22	21.1	37.3	3.4	44.7	4.3
Police, crime	0.18	0.20	12.1	27.1	9.6	42.7	4.2
Court	0.17	0.21	14.2	29.9	2.3	36.4	3.5
Defense, military	0.21	0.19	9.2	41.9	2.6	46.7	6.2
Economy, business	0.21	0.21	14.4	39.6	3.5	44.3	3.5
Education	0.23	0.21	14.1	41.8	4.5	46.4	6.2
Energy, environment	0.24	0.22	16.6	40.3	6.2	49.9	6.5
Transportation	0.24	0.21	14.9	42.3	6.6	52.6	4.6
Housing, infrastructure	0.25	0.23	22.4	40.7	5.0	51.6	6.3
Accidents, disasters	0.18	0.20	9.5	26.6	3.0	45.9	2.9
Health	0.21	0.21	20.3	32.7	4.9	42.9	6.0

In summary, according to our results, the performance of the interventionist role tends to be higher in news items covering (1) topics that are relevant to ordinary citizens, such as housing, social problems, education, and transportation; (2) strategic issues that citizens might be less familiar with such as defense, military, and domestic security; (3) political events such as elections and protests; and (4) complex issues such as economy or energy, environment, and climate change.

Conclusion

The performance of the interventionist role of journalism is important for understanding how journalism informs in a given society. While some studies on role conceptions have shown general patterns of this regard (Hanitzsch et al., 2016), we found an absence of clear-cut patterns based on political regime characteristics or regions. The performance of the interventionist role is not limited to partisan media cultures, nondemocratic countries, or autonomous media systems (Strömbäck & Dimitrova, 2011; Esser, 2008).

Nevertheless, the distinction between the content-related and style-related indicators of the interventionist role introduced in this chapter allow us to recognize nuances in journalistic cultures around the world and shed more light on the presence of different forms of the journalistic voice in the news. Firstly, our findings question the supremacy of the Anglo-American press model that is said to be based on factual and neutral reporting, thus limiting the journalistic voice while linking it to interpretation instead of the practices of sharing opinions or demanding specific actions (Donsbach & Klett, 1993; Hallin & Mancini, 2004; Hanitzsch et al., 2011). Moreover, the U.S. print press shows the highest levels of both types of interventionism: content-related and style-driven. These findings align with previous research (Benson & Hallin, 2007; Esser & Umbricht, 2014) that shows higher levels of interpretation and opinion than expected.

Interestingly, the U.S. interventionist style (a combination of the content- and style-related indicators) is far different from Ireland, which provides a clear example of the disseminator role and classic model of the fact-oriented, informational style of journalism that exists in the liberal model described by Hallin and Mancini (2004, p. 198; see also Nechushtai, 2018).

Meanwhile, our data partly support generalizations made on the Western European tradition of a bigger presence of the journalistic voice in the news media (Donsbach & Klett, 1993; Hallin & Mancini, 2004). Indeed, we can find relatively high levels of content-related indicators of the interventionist role in Germany (interpretation) and Greece (interpretation, opinion, and proposal), and a moderate level in Spain (interpretation and opinion). All of these European countries have lower means of the style-related indicators than the North and South American and Asian countries in our sample. In other words, we argue that Western European journalism is oriented towards explicitly expressed explanations, evaluations, and expectations. Furthermore, looking at Germany, Greece, and Spain, we can see differences in the performance of the interventionist role between the Democratic Corporatist model and the Polarized Pluralist model, following the Hallin and Mancini models of media systems (2004). While in the former (Germany) journalists focus mostly on interpretations of covered facts, in the latter (Greece and Spain) they frequently present their own opinions and call for actions.

Our study also shows that autonomy does not always explain the presence of interventionism. In fact, the global mean value of the presence of interventionist indicators was the highest among non-democratic countries, followed by advanced democracies and transition democracies. Nevertheless, we cannot easily follow the research on interventionism as a non-Western ideal of development journalism (Hanitzsch et al., 2016) either for several reasons.

First, as we mentioned previously, the two countries with the highest global means of both types of indicators of the interventionist role (content- and style-related)—the U.S. and Argentina—represent two different groups in terms of democracy development (advanced democracy and transitional democracy, respectively). Second, the distinction between countries in relation to the presence of content-oriented and style-oriented types of interventionism cuts across regime types.

We argue that journalists can be more interventionist in advanced and transitional democracies because they are more autonomous, because they are defending specific causes, or because of a high level of political parallelism (partisanship press). This is the case in Argentina (Amado & Waisbord, 2015) and Poland (Stępińska, Jurga-Wosik, Adamczewska, Secler, & Narożna, 2016), where the interventionist role is a moderate way to express political support through interpretation, opinion, and adjectives.

On the other hand, the performance of the interventionist role in non-democratic regimes cannot be interpreted as an indicator of greater autonomy of journalists and the media, but rather as a form of influence of political elites (political party in power). In other words, in more authoritarian regimes, dimensions such as active-passive (Donsbach & Patterson, 2004) do not serve as an alternative to understanding this role outside of the Western context. In countries like China or Cuba, journalists can be interventionist because they need to defend the state or they can be afraid of saying something against them, embracing self-censorship.

A predominant presence of adjectives across news media in most of the countries under study (with the U.S., Argentina, Chile, and the Philippines as leaders) can be explained by functions they can play in different circumstances (for Latin America—see Waisbord, 2013 and Ramírez Gelbes et al., 2018). Adjectives are tools for giving a colorful style to the article without necessarily providing an explicit opinion. In democratic countries, they can be used to attract the audience's attention (popular press) or strengthen the opinion and interpretation provided by a journalist (elite press). In the case of countries with barriers to free expression, evaluative adjectives can be used to express subjectivity in a more discreet fashion.

The significant presence of adjectives in both advanced democracies and transitional democracies may be related to a strong influence of "literary journalism" (Wolfe & Johnson, 1973) or "narrative journalism" (Tulloch, 2014), which prefers multiple points of view for enriching sociological interpretation of the events and proposes another way to achieve accuracy that is based not on fact but on exhaustive descriptions of the circumstances (Harbers & Broersma, 2014). Narrative journalists "organize and represent social reality through the filters of personal experience and moral judgment, and the individual reporter's prior knowledge, experiences, values and convictions provide the frame of reference" (Habrers & Broersma, 2014, p. 644). Instead of reporting "bare" facts, they aim to convey their experience of an event or situation (see also Ettema, 2009).

A second major finding of this chapter is that there was no significant difference between the popular and elite press when it came to content-related indicators, that is, the presence of opinion, interpretation, and calls to action within this role. By contrast, these two types of newspapers differ significantly in terms of the presence of style-related indicators, that is, the use of the first person by the journalists in the news as well as the use of adjectives.

Although newspapers are part of legacy media, they are not outside of the personal style that is currently the rule in digital environments. Since they need to compete with other types of media, they can also adapt their style. Beckett and Deuze (2016. p. 4) note that,

> for journalism to sustain its social, political, and economic added value distinct from the general flow of information and comment, it must reassert the value of critical, independent, constructive journalism with a reconceptualized idea of human interest at its center.

The fact that elements of the interventionist role can be found in countries that differ in terms of political regime is of interest, and this leads us to encourage further comparative studies on journalistic role performance that will explore both similarities and differences across countries in different media platforms.

References

Amado, A., & Waisbord, S. (2015). Divided we stand: Blurred boundaries in Argentine journalism. In M. Carlson & S. Lewis (Eds.), *Boundaries of journalism: Professionalism, practices, and participation* (pp. 51–66). New York: Routledge.

Barnhurst, K. G., & Mutz, D. (1997). American journalism and the decline in event-centred reporting. *Journal of Communication, 47*(4), 27–53.

Beckett, C., & Deuze, M. (2016). On the role of emotion in the future of journalism. *Social Media + Society, 2*(3). Retrieved from https://journals.sagepub.com/doi/full/10.1177/2056305116662395

Benson, R. (2008). Normative theories of journalism. In W. Donsbach (Ed.), *The international encyclopedia of communication* (pp. 2561–2597). Oxford: Wiley-Blackwell.

Benson, R., & Hallin, D. (2007). How states, markets and globalization shape the news. The French and US National Press, 1965–97. *European Journal of Communication, 22*(1), 27–48.

Bro, P. (2008). Normative investigation in the news media. *Journalism, 9*(3), 309–329.

Christians, C. G., Glasser, T. L., McQuail, D., Nordenstreng, K., & White, R. A. (2009). *Normative theories of the media: Journalism in democratic societies.* Urbana, IL: University of Illinois Press.

Cohen, B. (1963). *The press and foreign policy*. Princeton, NJ: Princeton University Press.

Djerf-Pierre, M., & Weibull, L. (2008). From public educator to interpreting ombudsman: Regimes in political journalism in Swedish public service broadcasting 1925–2005. In J. Strömbäck, M. Ørsten, & T. Aalberg (Eds.), *Communicating politics: Political communication in Nordic countries* (pp. 195–214). Gothenburg: Nordicom.

Donsbach, W., & Klett, B. (1993). Subjective objectivity. How journalists in four countries define a key term of their profession. *International Communication Gazette, 51*(1), 53-83.

Donsbach, W., & Patterson, T. (2004). Political news journalists: Partisanship, professionalism, and political roles in five countries. In F. Esser & B. Pfetsch (Eds.), *Comparing political communication: Theories, cases, and challenges* (pp. 251–270). Cambridge, UK: Cambridge University Press.

Eide, M. (2017). Normative theories and journalistic role performance. In C. Mellado, L. Hellmueller, & W. Donsbach (Eds.), *Journalistic role performance. Concepts, context, and methods* (pp. 90–105). New York: Routledge.

Esser, F. (2008). Dimensions of political news cultures: Sound bite and image bite news in France, Germany, Great Britain, and the United States. *International Journal of Press/ Politics, 13*(4), 401–428.

Esser, F., & Umbricht, A. (2014). The evolution of objective and interpretative journalism in the Western press: Comparing six news systems since the 1960s. *Journalism and Mass Communication Quarterly, 91*(2), 229–249.

Ettema, J. S. (2009). The moment of truthiness: The right time to consider the meaning of truth-fulness. In B. Zelizer (Ed.), *Changing faces of journalism. Tabloidization, technology and truthiness* (pp. 114–126). London and New York: Routledge.

Hallin, D., & Mancini, P. (2004). *Comparing media systems: Three models of media and politics*. Cambridge, UK: Cambridge University Press.

Hanitzsch, T. (2007). Deconstructing journalism culture: Toward a universal theory. *Communication Theory, 17*(4), 367–385.

Hanitzsch, T., Hanusch, F., Mellado, C., Anikina, M., Berganza, R., Cangoz, I., Coman, M., Hamada, B., Hernández, M.E., Karadjov, C.D., Moreira, S.V., Mwesige, P.G., Plaisance, P.L., Reich, Z., Seethaler, J., Skewes, E.A., Noor, D.V., & Yuen, K.W. (2011). Mapping journalism cultures across nations. *Journalism Studies, 12*(3), 273–293.

Hanitzsch, T., Hanusch, F., & Lauerer, C. (2016). Setting the agenda, influencing public opinion, and advocating for social change: Determinants of journalistic interventionism in 21 countries. *Journalism Studies, 17*(1), 1–20.

Hanitzsch, T., Hanusch, F., Ramaprasad, J., & de Beer, A. (Eds.). (2019). *Worlds of journalism. Journalistic cultures around the globe*. New York: Columbia University Press.

Harbers, F., & Broersma, M. (2014). Between engagement and ironic ambiguity: Mediating subjectivity in narrative journalism. *Journalism, 15*(5), 639–654.

Johnstone, J. W. C., Slawski, E. J., & Bowman, W. W. (1976). *The news people: A portrait of American journalists and their work*. Urbana, IL: University of Illinois Press.

McNair, B. (2000). *Journalism and democracy: An evaluation of the political public sphere*. London: Routledge.

Mellado, C. (2015). Professional roles in news content: Six dimensions of journalistic role performance. *Journalism Studies*, 16, 596–614.

Nechushtai, E. (2018). From liberal to polarized liberal? Contemporary US news in Hallin and Mancini's typology of news systems. *The International Journal of Press/Politics*, 23(2), 183–201.

Patterson, T. E. (1993). *Out of order*. New York: Vintage.

Patterson, T. E., & Donsbach, W. (1996). News decisions: Journalists as partisan actors. *Political Communication*, 13, 455–468.

Ramírez Gelbes, S., Dillon, P., Gil Buetto, R., Panza, M., Bombau, T., di Virgilio, B., . . . Siano, V. (2018, enero–junio). Adjetivos e información: la intervención de la subjetividad en la prensa escrita digital de América Latina. *Contratexto*, 29, 47–63.

Salgado, S., & Strömbäck, J. (2012). Interpretive journalism: A review of concepts, operationalizations and key findings. *Journalism*, 13(2), 144–161.

Salgado, S., Strömbäck, J., Aalberg, T., & Esser, F. (2017). Interpretive journalism. In C. de Vreese, F. Esser, & D. N. Hopmann (Eds.), *Comparing political journalism* (pp. 50–70). London and New York: Routledge.

Stępińska, A., Jurga-Wosik, E., Adamczewska, K., Secler, B., & Narożna, D. (2016). Journalistic role performance in Poland. *Central European Political Studies*, 2, 37–52.

Strömbäck, J., & Dimitrova, D. V. (2011). Mediatization and media interventionism: A comparative analysis of Sweden and the United States. *The International Journal of Press/Politics*, 16(1), 30–49.

Strömbäck, J., & Esser, F. (2009). Shaping politics: Mediatization and media interventionism. In K. Lundby (Ed.), *Mediatization: Concept, changes, consequences* (pp. 205–223). New York: Peter Lang.

Strömbäck, J., & Shehata, A. (2007). Structural biases in British and Swedish elections news coverage. *Journalism Studies*, 8(5), 798–812.

Thomson, E., & White, P. R. R. (Eds.). (2008). *Communicating conflict: Multilingual case studies of the news media*. London: Continuum.

Tulloch, J. (2014). Ethics, trust and the first person in the narration of long-form journalism. *Journalism*, 15(5), 629-638.

Waisbord, S. (2013). Democracy, journalism, and Latin American populism. *Journalism*, 14(4), 504–521.

Wang, H., Sparks, C., Lü, N., & Huang, Y. (2016). Differences within the mainland Chinese press: A quantitative analysis. *Asian Journal of Communication*, 27(2), 1–18.

Weaver, D. H., & Wilhoit, G. C. (1986). The American journalist: A portrait of US news people and their work. Bloomington.

Weaver, D. H., & Wilhoit, G. C. (1996). *The American journalist in the 1990s: U.S. news people at the end of an era*. Mahwah, NJ: Lawrence Erlbaum Associates.

Weaver, D. H., & Willnat, L. (Eds.). (2012). *The global journalist in the 21st century: News people around the world*. New York: Routledge.

Wolfe, T., & Johnson, E. W. (Eds.). (1973). *The new journalism*. New York: Harper and Row.

Zaller, J. R. (2001). The rule of product substitution in presidential campaign news. In E. Katz & Y. Warshel (Eds.), *Elections studies: What's their use?* (pp. 247–270). Boulder, CO: Westview.

6 Power Relations

The Performance of the Watchdog and Loyal-Facilitator Roles

Mireya Márquez-Ramírez, Sergio Roses, Henry Silke, and Dasniel Olivera

Imagine that we meet for coffee in any given country in the hypothetical company of a local journalist. Striking up a conversation about the general mission of journalism in their particular context would likely lead to a discussion of the type of relationship that should be forged between journalists, media, and powerholders. Some coffee companions would be inclined to support the view that regardless of the circumstances and events, journalists must always act as critical *watchdogs* of established powers. Expected to "call attention to the breakdown of social systems and the disorder within public institutions that cause injury and injustice" (Ettema & Glasser, 1998, p. 3), watchdog reporting should find hidden evidence of social ills, official deception, and institutional corruption (Bennett & Serrin, 2005, p. 170). Journalists should then routinely ask tough and probing questions to hold the powerful accountable while keeping "at reasonable distance from the targets of investigation" (Waisbord, 2000, p. 6). In scrutinizing powerholders, journalists could also become their antagonists, actively criticizing their behaviors (Clayman, Heritage, Elliott, & McDonald, 2007) and explicitly declaring themselves as their opponents.

Plenty of journalists would also believe that, in certain circumstances, they must play a *loyal-facilitating* role. For example, some would defend the idea that supporting political institutions, elites, and policies could be necessary for preserving peace and security, boosting national pride and morale, helping to build national institutions or preserving the societal values of consensus or harmony over conflict. In countries with a "development journalism" approach, the press plays a central role in disseminating governmental or national policies (Wong, 2004, p. 26). In democracies, journalism that "advocates" for certain causes or actors, "according to its instrumentality for the social groups they support" (Donsbach, 2012) is also common. In sum, regardless of the place, journalists routinely collaborate with local, regional, national, or even transnational governments "passively or unwittingly, reluctantly or wholeheartedly" (Christians, Glasser, McQuail, Nordenstreng, & White,

2009, p. 197), acting as government partners and as nation builders (Mellado, 2015; Romano, 2005). In authoritarian or post-authoritarian societies, this can be the default expected function of the press, as leaders often use this loyal-facilitating approach as to justify government control of mass media, to instrumentalize journalists, and to promote state policies (Shah, 2008).

For these reasons, regardless of journalists' expectations, normative professional roles can be quickly transcended by the ordinary realities of news-making dynamics and local sociopolitical environments. Health crisis, world-stage sporting events, war, conflict and violence, natural disasters, political and economic crisis, social polarization, trials and judiciary processes, corruption, or simple routine meetings of world leaders and their entrenched coverage procedures can either shift between actors and institutions, and activate or deactivate different types of reporting with relation to established powers, from monitoring vigilance to supporting loyalty.

Even in the same newspaper issue, certain events sometimes elicit more critical coverage, i.e., a corruption case, while other stories display a more promotional approach towards elites, i.e., a decrease in a city's crime figures. In this chapter, we show that the watchdog and loyal-facilitator roles are neither as straightforwardly antagonistic nor monolithic as they are sometimes portrayed to be, and are instead dynamic, hybrid, situational, and fluid (Mellado, Hellmueller, & Donsbach, 2017; Mellado, Hellmueller et al., 2017).

Also, because journalistic roles are mutating and often contingent upon the circumstances, the relationship between journalists and established powers can—and often does—change, going back and forth between being supportive and critical depending on actors and circumstances. For example, if we were drinking our coffee in Athens during the Greek economic crisis, we would read a more nationalistic and defensive view of the country rather than being exposed to the Greek-blaming narrative that prevailed in most European newspapers (Papathanassopoulos, 2015). The questioning, criticism, and uncovering in nationalistic Greek newspapers would perhaps more frequently target EU bodies and Germany because of the austerity measures imposed by the European Union and the International Monetary Fund in exchange for a bailout.

Across the Atlantic Ocean, a journalist from Brazil's slightly more progressive *Folha de São Paulo* would probably hold different views than one from the conservative *O'Globo*. The former title was more critical of the mass protests against left-leaning Dilma Rousseff's government in the lead-up to the World Cup and Rio Olympic Games, whereas the latter was surprisingly more supportive of street protestors (Shahin, Zheng, Sturm, & Fadnis, 2016), but perhaps only conveniently, resulting of the paper's antagonism towards a perceived political foe.

Other potential tablemates might voice support for any given national leader, policy, or action that in their view was needed to preserve national prestige, order, or security against a perceived rival or enemy, or in a hostile, conflictive environment. Patriotic narratives during the U.S.-led war on Iraq—and later on Syria—were abundant in the U.S. press, offering an "us versus them" narrative (Zelizer & Allan, 2011). Journalists would justify the need to support the government and help protect American interests in the battle against what they termed as terrorism.

Across different types of political regimes, there would be plenty of examples of journalists covering the voices and utterances of political and economic elites uncritically, supportively, and sometimes even enthusiastically (Christians et al., 2009; Starkman, 2014). The U.S. is not the only place where nationalistic tropes are common in times of war. The "war on terrorism" functions as a framework to promote nationalism and self-censorship in Russia, too (Simons & Strovsky, 2006). In the Irish news media, the coverage of the financial crisis defended and legitimated the status quo by privileging "narrow economic frames over societal considerations" (Preston & Silke, 2014, p. 22).

In countries with state-party rule, like Cuba, the loyal-facilitator and interventionist roles would tend to reflect the media's adherence to the Communist Party and its guidelines and strict control. However, journalists in Havana would probably justify the continuing support for the Revolution's national policies and elites on defense grounds following the U.S.-imposed economic embargo.

In some situations, journalists can be expected to function as mouthpieces of established powers and resort to self-censorship not on the grounds of political partisanship or nationalism alone, but as a conduit of safety and protection for journalists covering sensitive issues (Hughes & Márquez-Ramírez, 2017).

Hence, considering the multiple factors and conditions involved in news production, this chapter analyzes the ways in which the watchdog and the loyal-facilitator roles materialize in news content worldwide. We have identified two sub-dimensions of watchdog and loyal-facilitator roles. We observe *detached* and *interventionist* approaches to the monitoring function (Márquez-Ramírez et al., 2020) and *elite-supporting* and *nation-supporting* orientations to the loyal-facilitator role (Mellado, 2015). The following sections explain their theoretical foundations.

Detachment and Interventionism When Monitoring Elites

The process of monitoring powerful actors does not entail a fixed set of practices, as not all watchdog reporting is equal. Journalists try their best to use whatever resources they have at their disposal to question those with power. However, most critical stories or ordinary denunciations rarely lead to Watergate-like consequences. As Coronel (2010, pp. 112–113) acknowledges, watchdog journalism can cover "a range of exposure journalism, regardless of where it is published or aired, and regardless of the quality, target, and initiator of the investigation."

For monitoring purposes, journalists can choose "between actively seeking to influence the political process and trying to function as impartial conduits for political reporting" (Donsbach, 2012, p. 2; Trenz, Conrad, & Rosén, 2009). The concept of "media interventionism" is useful for understanding the logic behind this distinction (Esser, 2008). Given that the journalistic voice domain is transversal to the performance of more specific roles (Mellado, 2015; see also Chapter 2), detachment and interventionism are journalistic styles that can deeply impact the practice of monitoring through journalists' own voices or those of third parties or sources.

The detached orientation to watchdog reporting means that in keeping a distanced, neutral, dispassionate tone, the questioning, criticizing, or uncovering of wrongdoing constituent of the watchdog role can be achieved through the words of sources and third parties, while the journalist may remain neutral in the narrative. By contrast, in the interventionist orientation, it is the journalist him/herself who speaks, posing questions or making allegations using the first person, arguing, or giving opinions in a more adversarial tone (Entman, 2003; Clayman et al., 2007).

With respect to newsgathering, in the detached orientation, scandals and exposés often arise from third parties, such as external investigations, reports, trials, and monitoring agencies (Ettema & Glasser, 1998). In fact, this is the most common route to fostering accountability, as the media primarily serve an indirect rather than direct role in this process (Jacobs & Schillemans, 2016). In its more interventionist variation, journalists draw on their own research and in-depth investigations. They are heavily involved in the processes of questioning, criticizing and denunciation of wrongdoing through their own voice rather than their sources. For these reasons, journalists and media houses are sometimes seen as adversaries and engage in open conflict and antagonism with political elites, a particular actor or institutions (Mellado, 2015).

Supporting Elites and the Nation

Despite being "too pervasive ant too historically important [a role] to be swept aside" (Christians et al., 2009, p. 196), the loyal-facilitator role—sometimes called collaborative—has been largely neglected and scarcely theorized in academic literature, particularly in Western democracies. As Christians and colleagues acknowledge, the very idea of collaboration (with established powers) implies a relationship with the state or other centers of power "that clashes with the libertarian idea of a free and autonomous press" (2009, p. 196). However, as a theoretically rich and widely present role, its spirit and performance is deeply ingrained in the everyday processes of news production, story narrative, and reporting in different parts of the world (Mellado, 2015).

The view that the loyal-facilitator role is somehow straightforwardly opposed to the watchdog role (Hanitzsch, 2007) is not only dichotomous but also erratic. The polarity embedded in many of the normative and theoretical perspectives of the classic authoritarian or Soviet theories of the press—by which the media merely serve as agitators, vehicles, propagandists, and mouthpieces for their respective regime (Siebert, Peterson, & Schramm, 1956)—contradict the mounting evidence that the performance of the watchdog role does not automatically translate into the exclusion of the loyal-facilitator role (Mellado, Hellmueller et al., 2017).

The loyal-facilitator role also possesses very specific traits that are often rooted in elite-centered news production routines and narratives. Mellado (2015) proposes two analytical orientations by which the loyal-facilitator role takes shape. The first relates to the support of elites. In this orientation, journalists serve as loyal spokespersons for those in power, conveying a positive image of political or economic elites or supporting official policies. Journalists cooperate with powerholders and accept the information they provide as legitimate and credible (Bagdikian, 1992; Manning, 2001).

This dimension entails an explicit defense and promotion of certain actions carried out by governments, institutions, and actors either by overtly supporting institutional activities conducted by the political or economic elite, or by promoting national and regional policies (Bishop, 2000; Donohue, Tichenor, & Olien, 1995). A more intensive version of this approach entails the positive portrayal of the political and economic elites (Donohue et al., 1995; Hertsgard, 1989). The news can stress or highlight leadership, management skills, or personal characteristics through the use of positive adjectives to refer to certain actors in power.

Following Mellado's (2015) categorization, a second approach to the loyal-facilitator role moves the focus from powerful individuals to the nation as a unit. This "nation-supporting" analytical sub-dimension manifests when promoting patriotism and portraying a positive image of one's country, encouraging the sense of belonging, and strengthening national prestige (Verma, 1988; Bishop, 2000). Another element of the *nation-supporting* sub-dimension is the presence of patriotic elements within the news story. Following Ward (2010, p. 216), Mellado (2015) distinguishes a communal patriotism—which represents loyalty to one's land, language, and customs—and political patriotism associated with love for one's political values, structure, and ideals.

Considering the aforementioned sub-dimensions of the watchdog and loyal-facilitator roles, we pose the following research questions to guide this chapter:

RQ1: *In what ways do the watchdog and loyal-facilitator roles and their specific sub-dimensions materialize in news content across 18 countries?*

RQ2: *How do these roles materialize in comparisons across topics and political leanings?*

RQ3: *What patterns of hybridization can be observed when correlating different role sub-dimensions, news topics, and countries?*

We ran Anova tests for each sub-dimension of the watchdog and loyal-facilitator roles to measure the significance and effect sizes in relation to country variation, political leaning—left, center, and right—and news topic. We also ran Pearson correlations between the watchdog and loyal-facilitator roles and their sub-dimensions with respect to news topics.

Results

Two Approaches of Watchdog Role Performance in the News

In the global news sample, both orientations to watchdog reporting show an unequal presence. Specifically, the interventionist approach has a much lower level ($M = .03$, $SD = .09$) and the detached orientation is three times higher ($M = .09$, $SD = .16$). Around the world, scrutiny does not tend to emanate from journalists' own voice, but from sources and external investigations. Tables 6.1 and 6.2 show the performance of these two analytical sub-dimensions of watchdog journalism.

Likewise, lukewarm forms of scrutiny prevail in both orientations. In the detached watchdog approach (see Table 6.1), the highest indicators were criticism by sources (14.4%) and sources' doubting (9.6%). By contrast, uncovering denunciations by third parties and the publication of external investigations scored significantly lower globally (6.6% and 6.5%, respectively).

As Table 6.2 shows, in the interventionist approach, journalists' doubting (5.9% of the sample) and journalists' criticism (5.2%) are the most important indicators, nearly doubling the rate of journalists' own uncovering of wrongdoing (2.1%). The reporting of conflict between news media and those in power was considerably low and nearly anecdotal (1.0%).

Despite these general trends, we found statistically significant differences across countries in both approaches ($F_{\text{detached}}(17)= 190{,}419$; $p< .001$; $F_{\text{interventionist}}(17)= 194{,}048$; $p< .001$).

Table 6.1 The Detached Orientation of the Watchdog Role Across Countries

	Global	Hong Kong	Ireland	China	Philippines	Malaysia	Chile	Brazil	Argentina	Cuba	Mexico	Germany	Poland	Switzerland	Hungary	Spain	Greece	Russia	United States
Detached sub-dimension (Mean)	.09	.01	.08	.02	.08	.06	.03	.13	.13	.02	.14	.15	.16	.04	.12	.15	.12	.09	.16
SD	.16	.06	.18	.07	.17	.14	.08	.22	.19	.07	.21	.23	.22	.10	.21	.2	.18	.14	.19
Indicators (%)																			
Coverage of judiciary processes $X^2=1297.179$, $p < .001$	9.0	1.1	10.5	1.2	9.3	8.8	2.4	15.9	14.7	.0	10.4	16.7	8.9	3.9	16.7	15.8	8.0	6.2	15.3
Doubting by sources $X^2=1426.033$, $p < .001$	9.3	1.6	7.8	2.8	9.1	13.7	3.0	12.7	11.7	2.4	15.2	12.1	26.5	1.3	13.0	8.10	14.2	16.2	6.10
Criticism by sources $X^2=2270.980$; .001	14.4	3.0	14.1	2.1	6.3	5.3	5.3	15.2	20.5	2.6	18.5	27.8	28.1	8.8	21.8	24.6	25.9	12.5	31.
Uncovering by sources $X^2=1682.548$, $p < .001$	6.6	.70	1.30	.50	5.1	1.2	1.2	10.4	12.4	2.4	15.9	7.50	5.0	2.2	8.2	16.9	9.6	2.0	4.40
External investigation $X^2=1383.161$, $p < .001$	6.5	.30	4.40	1.2	8.9	3.0	1.0	12.7	4.80	.30	9.2	9.5	12.7	6.0	2.4	7.7	4.6	7.3	22.3

Table 6.2 The Interventionist Orientation of the Watchdog Role Across Countries

	Global	Hong Kong	Ireland	China	Philippines	Malaysia	Chile	Brazil	Argentina	Cuba	Mexico	Germany	Poland	Switzerland	Hungary	Spain	Greece	Russia	United States
Interventionist sub-dimension (Mean)	.03	.00	.02	.00	.00	.03	.00	.04	.04	.01	.04	.02	.09	.01	.06	.09	.11	.04	.02
SD	.09	.02	.08	.03	.02	.09	.03	.12	.11	.06	.11	.08	.18	.04	.14	.17	.18	.11	.09
Indicators (%)																			
Doubting by the journalist X^2= 2438.441, $p < .001$	5.9	.20	3.3	.90	.20	2.0	1.1	7.3	7.0	2.4	3.6	4.2	18.5	.90	10.6	21.9	13.3	9.7	1.9
Criticism by the journalist X^2= 3065.333, $p < .001$	5.2	.30	4.7	.70	.30	.90	.30	3.0	7.30	1.6	3.1	3.8	14.7	1.00	8.7	14.4	26.1	5.9	2.5
Uncovering by the journalist X^2= 706.445, $p < .001$	2.1	.10	.40	.10	.10	.20	.20	3.7	2.90	.30	3.3	.90	6.4	.30	4.8	4.8	6.3	2.6	1.5
Reporting of conflict X^2= 940.963, $p < .001$	1.0	.50	.00	.20	.00	8.9	.10	2.0	.90	.00	.00	.10	.70	.10	.20	1.7	3.7	.30	.20

As observed in Figure 6.1, the countries with the highest presence of the interventionist orientation are Greece, Spain, and Poland. A second group consisting of Hungary, Brazil, Russia, Argentina, and Mexico shows a medium level of the interventionist watchdog. Malaysia, the United States, Ireland, and Germany, for their part, display a moderate presence, whereas the interventionist sub-dimension is nearly absent in Cuba, Switzerland, China, Chile, Hong Kong, and the Philippines.

The results are different for the detached sub-dimension of watchdog reporting. The United States and Poland are on the forefront of detached watchdog reporting. A second group showing an intermediate level consists of Germany, Hungary, Argentina, Mexico, Spain, Greece, and Brazil. For their part, the Philippines, Ireland, Russia, and Malaysia have a moderate presence of this sub-dimension, while the news in Switzerland, Chile, Cuba, China, and Hong Kong display a very marginal level. Still, in most countries, the detached orientation tends to hold a stronger presence than the interventionist version.

Some countries present asymmetrical performance of both sub-dimensions of the watchdog role. For example, the U.S. and Germany appear to have more stable journalistic cultures, presenting a higher level of detached watchdog reporting across their news and a much lower presence of the interventionist orientation. Other countries present nearly null levels of both types, like Cuba, China, Hong Kong, and Chile, or moderate levels of both, as is true of Switzerland, Malaysia, Ireland, and the Philippines. By contrast, high or at least medium levels of both sub-dimensions characterize Greece, Poland, and Spain.

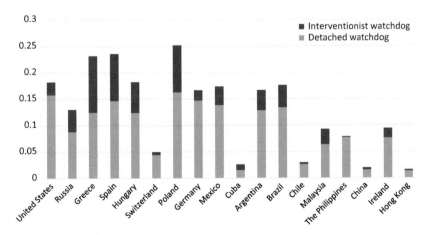

Figure 6.1 The interventionist and detached orientations of the watchdog role across countries (mean)

Beyond differences across countries, the presence of the detached and interventionist types of news vary greatly across topics ($F_{\text{Interventionist}}$ (17) = 22.968, p < .001; F_{Detached} (17) = 147.576, p < .001).

As Figure 6.2 shows, the detached watchdog performance varies greatly depending on the topic, meaning that when journalists quote sources who question, are critical of, or uncover those in power, it is mainly about news related to court issues, human rights, protests and demonstrations, and the police and crime. By contrast, news about accidents and natural disasters, economy and business, housing and infrastructure, or transportation are not strongly associated with this type of reporting.

The watchdog interventionist performance is more stable across some news topics. Journalists are more likely to challenge official powers using their own voice when reporting on subjects such as politics—where officials are more likely to disclose or leak public information—or with topics that involve abuses of power or social problems at the core of society. However, topics such as accidents and natural disasters, transportation, education, and the economy tend to receive less scrutiny, as journalists are less likely to openly confront established powers when reporting news on these topics.

Some topics present greater asymmetry across the two sub-dimensions. For example, news about courts and human rights display high levels of detached watchdog and a medium to medium-low level of interventionist watchdog, perhaps because journalists tend to provide coverage of the legal processes carried out by prosecuting bodies, and to activists and NGOS releasing their own reports and investigations on human rights abuses.

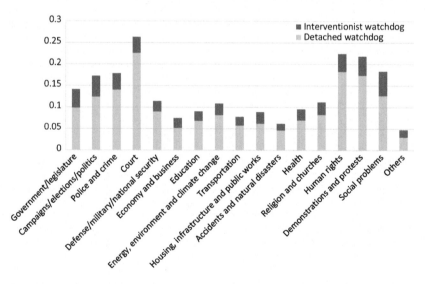

Figure 6.2 The interventionist and detached variations of the watchdog role across news topics (mean)

On the other hand, protests and demonstrations is the only topic with a high presence of both types of watchdog reporting, followed by social problems, campaigns, and news about police and crime. These are topics that strike at the core of society and in which third parties role have a great interest in disclosing and publicizing information. However, there is plenty of information to be dug out by journalists on their own in these areas. By contrast, journalists do not normally scrutinize breaking news events like accidents and natural disasters or topics like transportation, education, and (not-surprisingly) the economy and business.

Another variable that is closely linked to watchdog journalism is political leaning ($F(2) = 84.710$, $p < .001$). There are important differences across different types of political orientations, as newspapers situated in the center-right of the spectrum are slightly more likely to play the watchdog role in general ($M = .07$, $SD = .12$) than those in the left ($M = .06$, $SD = .11$) or center ($M = .05$, $SD = .10$).

These differences are smaller—and indeed lower—in the case of the detached watchdog ($F(2) = 40.19$, $p < .001$). We find a lower presence of this sub-dimension in newspapers close to the center ($M = .08$, $SD = .16$) compared to left-leaning ($M = .09$, $SD = .18$) or right-leaning newspapers ($M = .10$, $SD = .18$).

We found greater differences in the case of the interventionist watchdog ($F(2) = 10.400$, $p < .001$). Newspapers leaning to the right displayed twice as much interventionist watchdog activity ($M = .04$; $SD = .12$) as those on the left or center ($M = .02$; $SD = .09$), perhaps because many conservative tabloid or broadsheet newspapers that openly oppose left-leaning governments are more likely to use their own voice to be critical when reporting on exposés.

Two Approaches to the Loyal-Facilitator Role in the News

Both orientations to the performance of the loyal-facilitator role are practically null in most countries. We have, however, found some exceptions in Cuba, the country with the highest levels of both sub-dimensions ($M_{\text{Elitessupporting}} = .41$, $SD = .32$; $M_{\text{Nation supporting}} = .28$, $SD = .28$).

The comparison across countries of both sub-dimensions show statistically significant differences accordingly ($F_{\text{Elites supporter}}(17) = 501.728$, $p < .001$; $F_{\text{Nationsupporter}}(17) = 343.764$, $p < .001$).

Globally, as shown in Table 6.3, in the elite-supporting orientation, the order of importance with respect to its indicators was as follows: defense/support of activities (7.1% of the news) and positive image of the political elite (7.4%) recorded the highest levels in global news, closely followed by the defense or support of policies (5.9%) and much farther by the positive image of the economic elite (2.7%).

With respect to the nation-supporting orientation, Table 6.4 shows that the indicators with the highest presence in the sample for this orientation

Table 6.3 The Elite-Supporting Orientation of the Loyal-Facilitator Role Across Countries

Elite-Supporting sub-dimension	United States	Russia	Greece	Spain	Hungary	Switzerland	Poland	Germany	Mexico	Cuba	Argentina	Brazil	Chile	Malaysia	Philippines	China	Ireland	Hong Kong	Global
(Mean)	.01	.06	.08	.04	.02	.01	.01	.01	.05	.41	.04	.03	.01	.19	.00	.05	.03	.01	**.06**
SD	.05	.15	.18	.12	.08	.05	.08	.05	.16	.32	.12	.10	.06	.21	.04	.12	.13	.05	**.12**
Indicators (%)																			
Defense or support of activities X²= 3853.409, p <.001	.40	9.70	9.60	2.80	3.70	.60	2.30	.80	5.30	51.20	4.80	3.70	1.90	20.20	.40	8.00	1.90	.90	**7.1**
Defense or support of policies X²= 3871.302, p <.001	.30	5.90	10.50	4.90	1.50	.40	1.40	.90	4.80	48.00	3.70	2.20	.90	12.10	.20	5.10	2.40	.70	**5.9**
Positive image of the political elite X²= 4238.968, p <.001	1.80	6.10	11.60	4.30	.80	1.30	.80	.70	8.50	41.60	3.10	1.20	1.60	37.40	.80	4.80	3.80	2.30	**7.4**
Positive image of economic elite X²= 1757.395, p <.001	.70	.90	.50	2.20	.50	.70	.90	1.30	2.20	22.60	3.00	2.90	.50	5.30	.20	1.10	2.90	.10	**2.7**

Table 6.4 The Nation-Supporting Orientation to the Loyal-Facilitator Role Across Countries

	United States	Russia	Greece	Spain	Hungary	Switzerland	Poland	Germany	Mexico	Cuba	Argentina	Brazil	Chile	Malaysia	Philippines	China	Ireland	Hong Kong	Global
Nation-Supporting sub-dimension (Mean)	.01	.05	.03	.02	.01	.01	.02	.01	.03	.28	.02	.04	.01	.05	.02	.02	.01	.00	.04
SD	.06	.12	.10	.07	.06	.04	.09	.05	.10	.28	.09	.13	.06	.12	.06	.06	.07	.03	.09
Indicators (%)																			
Progress/success X^2= 2205.316, p < .001	1.5	9.7	4.20	4.2	.70	.50	2.7	4.5	5.4	37.6	2.4	6.2	1.8	11.5	1.8	5.2	3.9	.9	5.82
Comparison to other countries X^2= 483.448, p < .001	1.8	3.0	4.90	.80	.70	1.00	1.9	1.00	1.8	8.1	3.00	5.4	1.7	2.8	.50	.80	1.4	.40	2.28
National triumphs X^2= 3495.536, p < .001	.80	3.9	2.10	.80	1.60	.70	4.4	.10	1.7	37.6	2.0	4.0	1.2	3.3	5.8	.20	1.0	.00	3.96
Promotion of the country's image X^2= 3203.823, p < .001	1.1	4.4	1.00	1.20	1.70	.20	1.4	.10	2.6	32.4	1.2	3.4	.90	6.7	.70	.60	.50	.30	3.36
Patriotism X^2= 2750.416, p < .001	.90	3.6	1.60	1.30	1.10	.10	.70	.00	1.5	25.5	1.0	.80	.90	2.6	.20	.80	.50	.10	2.40

were progress and success (5.8% of the news) followed by national triumphs (3.9%) and promotion of the country's image (3.36%). The rest of the indicators scored only half as much as the most important indicator.

As observed in Figure 6.3, Cuba stands alone at the top of the list with nearly four out of ten news items displaying support for elites and nearly three out of ten items showing nationalism. Second-place Malaysia recorded half as much such activity reflecting the elite-supporting orientation.

Nearly at the bottom of the list, Greece and Russia display a very moderate level of both or at least one sub-dimension, whereas for the nation-supporting orientation, Mexico, China, and especially Brazil are fourth in the slightly higher visibility of support towards the nation. We find another group with a minimal presence of both dimensions consisting of Argentina, Spain, Ireland, and Poland. Finally, nearly a null presence of the role and both sub-dimensions is recorded in Hungary, Chile, Hong Kong, Germany, the U.S., Switzerland, and the Philippines. While this is a surprising result for nations with important state interventions in their media, it does not mean that those countries do not actually have a loyal press.

Our results also show some predominance of a specific analytical sub-dimension. For example, the biggest asymmetries are found in Malaysia, Cuba, and Greece, where the elite-supporting approach is significantly more important than the nation-supporting approach. The same pattern, although at a very moderate level, can be found in China and Mexico. The contrary occurs in Brazil and the Philippines, where the nation-supporting dimension slightly prevails over the other. This is also true, though to a much lower degree, in Poland and the United States.

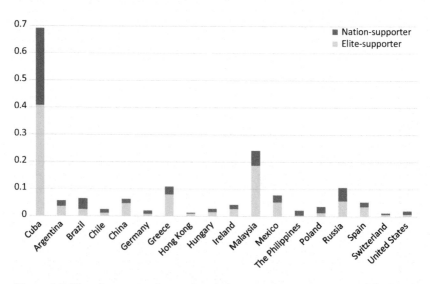

Figure 6.3 The elite-supporting and nation-supporting orientations of the loyal-facilitator role across countries (means)

The loyal-facilitator role ($F(17) = 40.586, p < .001$) and both of its sub-dimensions ($F_{Elitessupporter}(17) = 41.083, p < .001; F_{Nationsupporter}(17) = 39.275, p < .001$) also vary across news topics and are statistically significant.

According to Figure 6.4, the topics more closely associated with the elite-supporting orientation are housing and infrastructure, government and legislature, education, and defense. Likewise, the topics more closely related to the nation supporter sub-dimension are defense, housing, education, the economy and business, and health.

There are topics in which the elite-supporting orientation prevails, as in government news, housing and infrastructure, and campaigns and politics. There are no topics in which the opposite occurs, but there are indeed cases in which the presence of both sub-dimensions is very similar, such as news on religion, health, or human rights. Likewise, we find topics for which both sub-dimensions of the loyal-facilitator role have a higher or middle-higher presence, such as defense, and economy and business. By contrast, news about accidents and natural disasters, court, and police and crime show a minimal presence of both sub-dimensions.

Finally, significant differences also were found with respect to the political orientation of newspapers. Differences slightly increase when observing the elite-supporting orientation ($F_{Elites\ supporting} (2) = 220.343, p < .001$). Left-leaning papers ($M = .06, SD = .17$) reflected twice as much support for elites as centrist papers ($M = .03, SD = .12$) or those on the right ($M = .02, SD = .10$), perhaps reflecting the predominance of the role

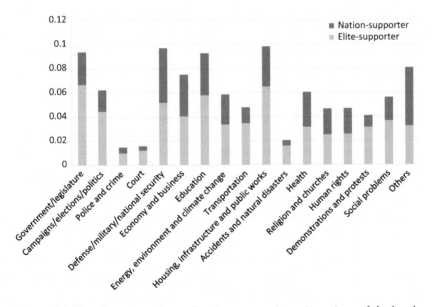

Figure 6.4 The elite-supporting and nation-supporting orientations of the loyal-facilitator role across news topics (means)

in the Cuban sample. In the case of the nation-supporting sub-dimension $(F_{Nationsupporter} (2) = 76.330, p <.001)$, the differences were smaller, with left-leaning newspapers again showing a slightly higher presence ($M = .03$, $SD = .12$) than those in the center right ($M= .02$, $SD= .09$) and center ($M = .02$, $SD = .08$).

News and Power: The Hybridization of Journalistic Roles

In previous sections, Chapter 4 illustrated the type of role performance hybridization that emerges from the co-occurrence of the interventionist, watchdog, loyal, service, civic, and infotainment roles across countries. Looking at the sub-dimensions of the watchdog and the loyal-facilitator roles, a similar trend of hybridization can be observed. For example, in countries with a great degree of state control and political instrumentalization, such as Cuba, the lowest presence of elite support in the news positively correlates with a higher level of detached watchdog ($r = -.216$, $p < .01$), whereas in Russia, news that displays support for the nation tends to hinder the detached watchdog orientation ($r = -.183, p < .01$).

Although we could expect similar results in countries with acute political and economic crises like Greece—given its high political instrumentalization and parallelism—in this country, we observe a great degree of hybridization, as the detached watchdog orientation is positively correlated to the elite-supporting orientation ($r = .170, p < .01$), meaning that Greek newspapers use third parties to doubt, criticize, or uncover wrongdoing by some actors while being supportive of other political elites.

In an authoritarian liberal system like Hong Kong, transitional democracies like Chile, and liberal democracies like the United States, Switzerland, and Germany, meanwhile, no significant correlations were found among the orientations of the watchdog and the loyal-facilitator roles, meaning that the sub-dimensions of these roles behave decisively independent from one another, at least at the national media system level.

Our results found that the hybridization of the watchdog and loyal-facilitator role performances is indeed contextual to news topics. For example, news about demonstrations and protests present a positive correlation between the interventionist watchdog and the elite-supporting dimensions ($r = .238, p < .01$), meaning that when news media cover social protests, they tend to openly criticize and support certain elites, though not necessarily the same elites. Topics such as transportation and court news also show significant correlations between the interventionist watchdog and the elite-supporting orientations ($r = .120, p < .01$). Moreover, stories about military and national security show a positive correlation between the interventionist watchdog and the nation-supporting orientation ($r = .167, p < .01$), with news scrutinizing military affairs also showing traces of nation support and patriotism.

We also analyzed correlations between the analytical sub-dimensions of both the watchdog and the loyal-facilitator roles and news topics to discern even more specific patterns of hybridization that yielded significant values in specific countries and topics. Furthermore, we observed five types of hybridization between the watchdog and the loyal-facilitator roles and their sub-dimensions in different countries.

a) *The watchdog and loyal-facilitator roles as allies for certain topics.* In Greece, the watchdog role is positively correlated with the loyal-facilitator role in news about military affairs ($r = .637, p < .01$), protests and demonstrations ($r = .362, p < .01$), court news ($r = .286, p = .01$), and economic news ($r = .216, p < .01$). The positive correlation pattern over protests is also displayed in Argentina ($r = .270, p = .01$) and Brazil, ($r = .383, p < .01$) where the press both question and support certain elites in regard to these topics. Moreover, Malaysia also presented this pattern in news about police and crime ($r = .351, p < .01$).

In Russia ($r = -.260, p < .01$), Argentina ($r = -.161, p < .01$), and Malaysia ($r = -.337, p < .01$), there is a negative correlation between both roles and governmental news, meaning that when newspapers are acting vigilant towards the government or the congress, they are not also supporting political elites. The same pattern is found in Russia ($r = -.345, p < .01$) and Cuba ($r = -.222, p < .05$) in news about economy and business, and in Brazil in news about police and crime ($r = -.148, p < .01$).

b) *Interventionist scrutiny that supports the nation.* We found a positive correlation in the United States between news about politics and elections ($r = .335, p < .01$), courts ($r = .293, p < .01$), the economy ($r = .224, p < .05$), and government ($r = .164, p < .05$). Russia displays this pattern as well in news about courts ($r = .426, p < .01$) and Greece in news about military affairs ($r = .745, p < .01$).

c) *Interventionist scrutiny that supports elites.* We found this positive correlation in the United States about election news ($r = .185, p < .01$). Only Russia ($r = .471, p < .01$) and Greece ($r = .416, p < .01$) presented this pattern in news about courts. Greece also shows this pattern in military and defense news ($r = .423, p < .01$), and news about social protests ($r = .389, p < .01$). We also found this pattern in Malaysia in news about police and crime ($r = .367, p < .01$). This type of hybridization was especially present in news on social protest in Brazil ($r = .708, p < .01$). By contrast, we observed a negative correlation in Malaysia in news about government ($r = -.318, p < .01$), and politics and elections ($r = -.271, p < .01$). Paradoxically, in Cuba, both sub-dimensions are negatively correlated in economic news ($r = -.209, p < .05$).

d) *Detached scrutiny that supports elites.* This pattern was present in Germany about governmental news ($r = .164$, $p < .05$), although a stronger relationship is found in Malaysia on police and crime news ($r = .361$, $p < .01$), and in Greece on economic news ($r = .295$, $p < .01$) or protests ($r = .249$, $p = .05$). Argentina ($r = .322$, $p < .01$) and Brazil ($r = .259$, $p < .05$) also display this type of hybridization in news about protests. In Russia ($r = -.244$, $p < .01$) and Malaysia ($r = -.301$, $p < .01$), the correlation is negative in news about government and legislature. Also in Malaysia, the same pattern is repeated in news about politics and elections ($r = -.205$, $p < .05$).

e) *Detached scrutiny that supports the nation.* We find this pattern in the United States on economic news ($r = .200$, $p = .01$). In Greece, this pattern is found in news about politics and elections ($r = .153$, $p = .01$). In Brazil, the correlation is negative in news about police and crime ($r = -.185$, $p < .01$).

Conclusion

This chapter takes a step forward in the research of journalistic roles by looking "within" the watchdog and loyal-facilitator roles to unveil specific patterns of hybridization in their performances. A trip around the world shows the multiple ways in which journalism and the news media position themselves around institutional powers and engage in scrutiny or defense of actors, policies, and institutions. In this sense, this chapter provides evidence of the diverse facets and nuances of watchdog journalism and the many ways that journalists also perpetuate the status quo and defend national interests in their reporting.

We specifically looked at two analytical role sub-dimensions that show a new layer of research findings about the fluidity of journalistic roles in certain environments and their dependence on specific topics and situations in others. Like all journalistic roles, professional functions related to the relationship between journalism and those in power are contextual and situational, and manifest themselves in different ways across different countries, newspapers' political leanings, and news topics.

With respect to the watchdog role, we found that the interventionist approach to monitoring is more dependent on country characteristics, as authoritarian regimes tend to restrict the practice of watchdog journalism overall. Journalists need conditions of security, access of information, freedom, and autonomy to use their voice and confront established powers. In transitional democracies with a highly commercialized and concentrated media environments, watchdog journalism is arguably relegated. Moreover, we corroborated that media systems in established democracies like the U.S. and Germany have stable (mostly detached) journalistic cultures, whereas countries with political conflicts elicit more versatility in the monitoring of powers.

A new variable not sufficiently explored in our previous work is media political leaning. This variable is more closely related to the interventionist orientation to watchdog reporting. As media-system literature (Hallin & Mancini, 2004) asserts, partisanship and interventionism seem to go hand in hand even when scrutinizing powers, but only when there are at least minimal conditions of freedom and democracy. Greece turned out to be a flagship example of this trend. By contrast, the topic of the news is a variable that is more closely associated with the detached version of the watchdog role, suggesting that some types of beats have naturalized news production routines and rituals of objectivity and detachment. In other words, the ordinary practices of covering certain topics may discourage journalists from prominently using their voice.

Meanwhile, national-level differences significantly shape the loyal-facilitator role and both of its dimensions. The elite-supporting approach varied considerably across countries, suggesting that, in fact, reporting favorably about the government in Malaysia and Cuba differs vastly from such practice in more stable democracies like the United States and Switzerland. The nation-supporting orientation is also strongly associated with the type of political regime, although this sub-dimension is more scattered across different types of countries, suggesting that its elements of nationalism and patriotism are, in fact, context-driven rather than regime-driven. Also, expectedly, the political leaning of the medium considerably impacts the elite-supporting dimension, corroborating the partisan nature of news coverage in certain newspapers. However, in global terms, neither political leaning nor the news topic have significant impact on the performance of the nation-supporting role.

In general terms, while the detached approach is more globally found in the news than the interventionist orientation, its contextual nature forces us to observe different patterns across countries and across news topics and newspaper's political leanings. This is also valid for the two loyal-facilitator approaches. The elite-supporting dimension is more common than the nation-supporting one in most of the cases, but the gap between the two analytical dimensions of the loyal-facilitator role is smaller than within the watchdog role.

Although we found evidence of role and sub-role hybridization, the global performance of the loyal role was lower than expected across countries. In order to better understand its contextual performance, we have to delve deeper into the data to find patterns of hybridization in the news media of smaller group of countries. Interaction between watchdog and loyal roles would be activated when journalists report on specific news topics such as courts, military affairs, protests and demonstrations, police and crime, elections or the economy. The patterns of co-occurrence of interventionist scrutiny and support for the elites, as well as detached scrutiny and support for the elites, were present in several countries, though they were concentrated in a reduced number of topics, meaning journalists support some elites while at the same time are critical of other elites, suggesting possible partisan motivations behind some watchdog reporting in certain newsbeats. The co-occurrence of interventionist scrutiny that at the same time supports the nation spans fewer countries but affects almost all news topics, especially in the U.S., as reporting can get openly critical if journalists perceive that the country is departing from national values or standards. Hence, a key finding is that while the U.S. has one of the most detached approaches to the watchdog role in this study, this detachment is often accompanied by a support to the nation, whereas more openly interventionist scrutiny often also supports elites. These results should open new avenues for future research that delves into the nature of journalism and power relations. Theoretically, scrutiny and loyalism might appear as two opposites of a pole, but a trip to the world of journalistic practices might actually show how deeply intertwined both roles are.

References

Bagdikian, B. (1992). *The media monopoly*. Boston, CA: Beacon Press.

Bennett, W. L., & Serrin, W. (2005). The watchdog role. In G. Overholser & K. Hall Jamieson (Eds.), *The press: The institutions of American democracy* (pp. 169–188). New York: Oxford University Press.

Bishop, R. (2000). To protect and serve: The 'Guard Dog' function of journalism in coverage of the Japanese-American internment. *Journalism & Communication Monographs*, 2(2), 64–103.

Christians, C. G., Glasser, T. L., McQuail, D., Nordenstreng, K., & White, R. A. (2009). *Normative theories of the media: Journalism in democratic societies*. Urbana, IL: University of Illinois Press.

Clayman, S., Heritage, J., Elliott, M., & McDonald, L. (2007). When does the watchdog bark? Conditions of aggressive questioning in presidential news conferences. *American Sociological Review*, 72(1), 23–41.

Coronel, S. (2010). Corruption and the watchdog role of news media. In P. Norris (Ed.), *Public sentinel: News media and governance reform* (pp. 111–136). Washington, DC: The World Bank.

Donohue, G. A., Tichenor, P. J., & Olien, C. N. (1995). A guard dog perspective on the role of media. *Journal of Communication*, 45(2), 115–132.

Donsbach, W. (2012). Journalists' role perception. In W. Donsbach (Ed.), *The international encyclopedia of communication* (pp. 1–6). London: Blackwell. doi:10.1002/9781405186407.wbiecj010.pub2

Entman, R. (2003). *Projections of power: Framing news, public opinion, and U.S. foreign policy*. Chicago: University of Chicago Press.

Esser, F. (2008). Dimensions of political news cultures: Sound bite and image bite news in France, Germany, Great Britain, and the United States. *The International Journal of Press/ Politics*, 13(4), 401–428.

Ettema, J., & Glasser, T. (1998). *Custodians of conscience*. New York: Guilford Press.

Hallin, D., & Mancini, P. (2004). *Comparing media systems: Three models of media and politics*. Cambridge: Cambridge University Press.

Hanitzsch, T. (2007). Deconstructing journalism culture: Towards a universal theory. *Communication Theory, 17*, 367–385.

Hertsgard, M. (1989). *On bended knee: The press and the Reagan presidency*. New York: Schocken.

Hughes, S., & Márquez-Ramírez, M. (2017). Examining the practices that Mexican journalists employ to reduce risk in a context of violence. *International Journal of Communication, 11*(23), 499–521.

Jacobs, S., & Schillemans, T. (2016). Media and public accountability: Typology of an exploration. *Policy and Politics, 44*(1), 23–40.

Manning, P. (2001). *News and news sources: A critical introduction*. London: Sage.

Márquez-Ramírez, M., Mellado, C., Humanes, M. L., et al. (2020). Detached or interventionist? comparing the performance of watchdog journalism in transitional, advanced and non-democratic countries. *International Journal of Press Politicis, 25*(1), 53–75.

Mellado, C. (2015). Professional roles in news content: Six dimensions of journalistic role performance. *Journalism Studies, 16*(4), 596–614.

Mellado, C., Hellmueller, L., & Donsbach, W. (Eds.). (2017). *Journalistic role performance: Concepts, contexts and methods*. New York: Routledge.

Mellado, C., Hellmueller, L., Márquez-Ramírez, M., et al. (2017). The hybridization of journalistic cultures: A comparative study of journalistic role performance. *Journal of Communication, 67*(6), 944–967.

Mellado, C., Márquez-Ramírez, M., Mick, J., et al. (2017). Journalistic performance in Latin America: A comparative study of professional roles in news content. *Journalism, 18*(9), 1087–1116.

Papathanassopoulos, S. (2015). European media views of the Greek crisis. In S. Staffers (Ed.). *The media and financial crisis: Comparative and historical perspectives* (pp. 103–118). London: Routledge.

Preston, P., & Silke, H. (2014). Ireland—From neoliberal champion to "The Eye of the Storm". *Javnost- The Public, 21*(4), 5–23.

Romano, A. (2005). Asian journalism: News, development and the tides of liberation and technology. In A. Romano & M. Bromley (Eds.), *Journalism and democracy in Asia* (pp. 1–14). London: Routledge.

Shah, H. (2008). Development journalism. In W. Donsbach (Ed.), *The international encyclopedia of communication* (pp. 1–6). London: Blackwell. Retrieved from https://doi.org/10.1002/9781405186407.wbiecd031

Shahin, S., Zheng, P., Sturm, H. A., & Fadnis, D. (2016). Protesting the paradigm: A comparative study of news coverage of protest in Brazil, China and India. *The International Journal of Press/Politics, 21*(2), 143–164.

Siebert, F., Peterson, T., & Schramm, W. (1956). *Four theories of the press*. Urbana, IL: University of Illinois Press.

Simons, G., & Strovsky, D. (2006). Censorship in contemporary Russian journalism in the age of the war against terrorism. A historical perspective. *European Journal of Communication, 21*(2), 189–211.

Starkman, D. (2014). *The watchdog that didn't bark. The financial crisis and the disappearance of investigative journalism*. New York: Columbia University Press.

Trenz, H., Conrad, M., & Rosen, G. (2009). Impartial mediator or critical watchdog? The role of political journalism in EU constitution-making. *Comparative European Politics, 7*(3), 342–363.

Verma, Y. (1988). *The press in Nepal: An appraisal.* Kathmandu: Pratibha.
Waisbord, S. (2000). *Watchdog Journalism in South America.* New York: Columbia University Press.
Ward, S. (2010). *Global journalism ethics.* Montreal: McGill—Queen's University Press.
Wong, K. (2004). Asian-based development journalism and political elections: Press coverage of the 1999 general elections in Malaysia. *International Communication Gazette, 66*(1), 25–40.
Zelizer, B., & Allan, S. (2011). *Journalism after September 11* (2nd ed.). London: Routledge.

7 Audience Approach

The Performance of the Civic, Infotainment, and Service Roles

María Luisa Humanes and Sergio Roses

In their daily practices, journalists make certain assumptions about their target audience. Far from viewing the audience as mere receivers of news (Anderson, 2011, p. 537), such professionals form a mental picture of the public and try to meet their needs. These may be individual needs associated with everyday issues, collective needs linked to social affairs, or the need to be informed in an entertaining way (Mellado, 2015).

However, figuring out who the audience is and what it wants from journalism is no easy task. For example, Gans (2004) draws attention to the disconnect between journalists and readers due to the former's inability to imagine an audience consisting of millions of people and their lack of trust in the audience's ability to know what news is.

Audience needs vary over time, and they may also depend on the geographic, political, and social context. Despite advances in technology and the possibilities it offers for knowing who the audience is, journalists may remain disconnected from part of their audience if they do not address contextual and cultural factors in the societies where they work. In this sense, the media and journalists must constantly redefine their roles to conform to audience expectations about their mission in society (Costera Meijer, 2003; Atkinson, 2011; Mellado, López-Rabadán, & Elortegui, 2017).

Based on the definitions of the audience (DeWerth-Pallmeyer, 1997), journalists take practice-related decisions that affect news content, adapting it to what they believe their audience requires.

Audience approaches are associated with the professional culture of journalism (Mellado & van Dalen, 2017) and with ideas about what the function of the media should be in a particular society and for the individuals who form part of it.

The literature has traditionally highlighted two ways of conceptualizing the audience, either as citizens or as consumers (Skovsgaard & Bro, 2017). The former is influenced by normative theories of the press in democratic Western societies (see Christians, Glasser, McQuail, Nordenstreng, & White, 2009). For example, public interest theory, theory of the Fourth Estate, Habermas' public sphere theory, and social responsibility theory all suggest that individuals seek to be well informed by the news in order to take action and make decisions in the most rational way possible. This vision urges journalists to fulfill the social purpose of defending the public good. The second classical conceptualization of the audience focuses on what they demand as consumers. The link between that vision and tabloidization is deemed a threat or failure of the system, with the commercialization of the media blamed for the degradation of the critical and rational debate on matters of public interest that Habermas proposed (Johansson, 2007). According to Atkinson (2011, p. 106), "The myth of 'consumer sovereignty' rests on the crude utilitarian notion that people know what they want, rather than being cumulatively conditioned by what is made available."

This opposing vision of two "classes" of audience and, ultimately, of two journalistic roles as opposite and as symbols of "good" and "bad" journalism (e.g., Franklin, 2005) has been superseded by new approaches (Eide & Knight, 1999; Costera Meijer, 2003; Brants & De Haan, 2010; Atkinson, 2011) that have opened up audience conceptualizations to new types.

Specifically, Mellado and van Dalen (2017) found that audiences can be approached from at least three different angles: the infotainment, service, and civic models. Their study shows that approaching the audience as consumer or citizen are not two poles of one continuum, and that a consumer orientation consists of two different dimensional structures: service and entertainment. They also establish that these different approaches do not lead to mutually exclusive journalistic roles or to good or bad forms of journalism, as our results will show. For example, in the U.S. press we found a significant co-occurrence between the infotainment and the civic roles.

Based on the assumption that professional roles continuously evolve, and focusing on journalistic role performance in relation to the way journalism approaches the audience, this chapter analyzes the performance of the civic, infotainment, and service roles in the news across countries. We also examine the presence of analytical sub-dimensions and the indicators that compose each role in different types of news, as well as the hybridization of these roles in the news and the inter-country variation thereof.

Journalistic Roles and Audience Approaches

The Civic Role

This role is linked to the tradition of public (or civic) journalism (Rosen & Merrit, 1994) and is therefore about empowering and motivating the audience to get involved in social life, fostering civic awareness of the public sphere.

During and after the Vietnam War and the Watergate scandal, a tendency towards aggressive journalism contributed to a loss of credibility of the U.S. media (Hallin, 1992; Patterson, 1993). While journalists believed that good journalism was based on acting as watchdogs over those in power and contributing to a well-informed society (Croteau & Hoynes, 2001; Weaver, Beam, Brownlee, Voakes, & Wilhoit, 2007), the public emphasized a civic focus (Holton, Coddington, & Gil de Zúñiga, 2013). To win back the audience, the journalistic profession chose to engage in the civic journalism movement (Nerone, 2018), endeavoring to reform journalistic practice by placing respect for the public and its needs at the heart of the news (Carey, 2002).

As outlined in Chapter 2, the performance of the civic role is characterized by news coverage of citizens' demands. On the one hand, the advocate orientation promotes citizen activities, shows the demands of the audience, and lends support to social movements. Journalists who follow this approach prioritize civic engagement and taking action in the public sphere. This sub-dimension includes six indicators of the civic role: citizen reactions, citizen demand, credibility of citizens, support of citizen movements, citizen questions, and information on citizen activities. The educator sub-dimension reflects the journalist's function as a guide who provides content that allows citizens to make decisions. This orientation includes three indicators: local impact, educating on duties and rights, and contextual background information.

The Infotainment Role

The infotainment role addresses news content in a way that evokes emotions, personalization, morbid curiosity, and sensational elements in an effort to relax and entertain the audience, who are viewed as spectators (Mellado, 2015). This role could materialize in two ways, as developed in Chapter 2. In the first (Entertainer), the journalist embraces the elements of infotainment themselves, which would link this role to a more interventionist stance. For example, a journalist could show his own feelings of sadness in a news story that reports on immigrant children detained by the border police. On the other hand, a less active infotainment role can be found when this is not linked to an interventionist stance on the part of the journalist. For example, when a news story includes photos of migrant children crying.

Though the popular press has provided information and entertainment since the early 19th century, the infotainment role is not limited to a single type of media outlet (such as the popular press) or to specific content (such as "soft" news). Rather, it has become a cross-cutting journalistic style. Media managers pursue revenue by making news content more attractive to the audience. This is how "consumer-driven journalism"

(Skovsgaard & Bro, 2017) or "market-driven journalism" (McManus, 1994) came about.

In the 1980s, managers displaced journalists (Underwood, 1993) and commercialization spread from North America to the rest of the world driven by neoliberalism (McChesney, 2001). Media systems shifted away from politics and towards commerce through liberalization in Europe (Hallin & Mancini, 2004) and in non-Western contexts such as Latin America (Guerrero & Márquez-Ramírez, 2014). In China, the process has been driven by the state itself (Zhao, 2012, p. 158).

The commercialization of the news has resulted in tabloidization (Esser, 1999; Sparks & Tulloch, 2000), raising a number of concerns about the public interest. This includes the lack of classic values of journalism (Altschull, 1995), a prevalence of economic criteria in the newsroom (Picard, 2004), the McDonaldization of the news (Franklin, 2005), and effects of political cynicism (Jebril, Albæk, & de Vreese, 2013). Normative visions aside, current journalistic practice shows that the spread of the infotainment function cuts across media outlets, thematic beats, and journalistic genres (Esser, 1999; Sparks & Tulloch, 2000). In that sense, one contemporary challenge is to better understand the ways in which infotainment and public service-oriented roles are combined.

The Service Role

The service role is linked to the global idea of the audience as clients who are to be given advice and guidance about their individual needs (Eide & Knight, 1999, p. 525). This approach responds to the complexity of "late modernity," in which individuals do not just act as citizens in the traditional political sphere or via organized civil society, and do not just seek entertainment. In fact, they are both consumers and clients, "breaking" the traditional dichotomy (Mellado & van Dalen, 2017). Specifically, it has been asserted that service journalism is aimed at "a hybrid social subject" (Eide & Knight, 1999, p. 527).

This role is performed when the news addresses the impact of events on the audience's everyday lives, provides tips and advice on both complaints and individual risks, offers consumer information and advice, and provides personal assistance. Specifically, four indicators were measured in the performance of the service role in the news: impact on everyday life, tips and advice (grievances), tips and advice (individual risks), and consumer advice (for more information, see Chapters 3 and 4). While the first three indicators are more related to personal guidance, the last is more oriented towards helping the audience as consumers.

This type of journalism has been likened to news content that is detached from the classic newsbeat structure (politics, economy, courts, police and crime). Indeed, Underwood refers to this type of content as "news-you-can-use," i.e., news on medicine, personal finance, diets, self-help, and, in general, any type of content that is not too complex and is detached from public issues and government activities (2001, p. 101).

Eide has noted that service journalism not only attends to individual needs, but also "lends itself to collective, political action as it shares common ground—the problematization of the everyday life-world—with the social movements, advocacy and activism groups that are the driving force in sub-politics" (2017, p. 198). That argument has led us to assert that service journalism is not necessarily limited to certain news topics, such as health and lifestyle. Rather, it can be a new way of informing on public affairs as well.

The Situational and Contextual Influence on Role Performance

Journalistic role performance is sensitive to the context and situations in which journalism is practiced (Mellado, Hellmueller, & Donsbach, 2017). For example, political systems implement and promote different degrees of citizen participation in politics, which could give rise to differences in the manifestation of the civic role. Similarly, although the commercialization of the media appears to be a global tendency, we should not forget that its development is closely linked to the spread of neoliberal capitalism.

Furthermore, journalists could activate the civic role to mobilize citizens at critical political moments, such as during a transition to democracy or a pre-war period. In this respect, roles might change as a result of the historical context.

Bearing in mind that professional roles are not mutually exclusive and that they overlap in practice (Mellado, 2015), we identify potential hybridizations of roles within the audience approach domain. A first combination is the co-occurrence of the civic and the infotainment roles. As an example of this hybridization we could think about a story involving same-sex marriage legalization in a country, where elements of personalization are included through an image of the intertwined hands of two women (one of which has a name tattooed on it), while the photo caption alludes to their recent marriage. The content may focus on the citizen's right to same-sex marriage, illustrated by a graph listing the other countries in which it is previously allowed.

A second potential hybridization is that of the civic and service roles. A news story can include elements of each role. For example, a story can include the civic role by covering a project developed by two activists to offer electoral information in a city before general elections. In addition to providing information and giving voice to citizens, the story can also offer tips on how to exercise their right to vote, materializing the service role.

Another story can describe how hundreds of people try to leave an area devastated by a hurricane, including complaints from citizens and their claim that their government is not reacting to the crisis. Meanwhile, the service role can be included through a discussion of the hurricane's specific consequences for the everyday lives of residents of that area.

A third hybridization may occur between the service and infotainment roles. In these cases, journalists provide tips on how to manage everyday life, consumer information, and advice and elements of personalization, sensationalism, private life, emotions, or morbidity. For example, a news story can give information about how an old woman annoyed her neighbors with her parrot's singing and how this affected their daily routine. In addition, the news may add a psychological characterization of the elderly protagonist of the story.

Finally, another type of hybridization can be found when a co-occurrence of elements of the three roles takes place. For example, a story on telework to avoid infection from COVID-19 that includes elements of the civic role by informing the public of their labor rights, offers advice on what to do if a worker suffers an accident at home (service role), and includes elements of personalization by providing information on the experiences of two people who telework.

Based on this framework, the following research questions guide the next sections of this chapter:

RQ1: How do the civic, infotainment, and service roles and their indicators materialize in news content across 18 countries?
RQ2: How do these roles and their indicators materialize when comparing across political regime, media audience orientation, and thematic beats?
RQ3: What patterns of co-occurrence can be observed in the performance of the civic, infotainment, and service roles across countries?

We ran Anova and chi-square tests to analyze the presence of each role, their analytical sub-dimensions, and specific indicators across countries, news topics, and types of papers. We also ran Pearson correlations to test the co-occurrence of the three roles within the domain audience approach cross-nationally.

Performing the Civic, Infotainment, and Service Roles in News

Two Approaches to the Civic Role in News

The performance of the civic role was measured by the presence-absence of nine content indicators (see Chapter 3) used to identify two analytical sub-dimensions according to the focus given to the story: the civic-advocate and civic-educator orientations.

In our overall sample of news stories across countries, the presence of the advocate orientation of the civic role was slightly higher than the civic-educator sub-dimension ($M_{civic-advocate}$ = .08, SD = .19; $M_{civic-educator}$ = .06, SD = .14; $t(17118)$ = 3.585, $p < .001$).

Theoretically, the advocate orientation of the civic role is associated with a greater presence of the interventionist role. In fact, we found a significant correlation between our advocate sub-dimension and the interventionist role in the sample, although it was lower compared to correlations between interventionist and other roles (see Chapter 4).[1] Furthermore, our data show that the correlation between the educational orientation and the interventionist role is weaker than its correlation to the advocate sub-dimension.

Overall, the most prevalent indicators of the advocate orientation were the inclusion of citizen statements or reactions to political decisions that affect them (8.3%). News showing citizen demands (4.9%) and support for citizen activities and information on activities organized by citizens came second in order of importance (4.4%), whereas the presence of support for social movements was the lowest (1.5%). In the educator approach of this role, the presence of contextual background information is the most frequent indicator (9.9%), followed by the inclusion of local impact of political decisions (5.9%) (see Table 7.1).

Nevertheless, statistically significant differences were found in both sub-dimensions of the civic role across countries ($F_{civic-advocate}(17,16764)$ = 187.441, $p < .001$; $F_{civic-educator}(17, 33622)$ = 641.305, $p < .001$).

As shown in Figure 7.1, the presence of the advocate sub-dimension was highest in Argentina (M = .50, SD = .17), Mexico (M = .45, SD = .26) and Ireland (M = .42, SD = .27), and lowest in Greece (M = .11, SD = .24), the U.S., (M = .10, SD = .18), Russia (M = .09, SD = .16), Malaysia (M = .06, SD = .16), the Philippines (M = .06, SD = .15), Cuba (M = .06, SD = .18), Spain (M = .04, SD = .13), and Brazil (M = .03, SD = .12). It has a moderate presence in the rest of the countries and was absent from China and Hong Kong.

The presence of the civic-educator orientation was significantly higher in the news of most of the countries that ranked the lowest in the advocate analytical sub-dimension, such as Greece (M = .14, SD = .19), the U.S., (M = .14, SD = .17), Malaysia (M = .11, SD = .19), and Russia (M = .11, SD = .17). By contrast, the civic-educator approach was almost negligible in Hungary (M = .02, SD = .08), Switzerland (M = .02, SD = .07), and Ireland (M = .01, SD = .07).

We examined whether the newspapers of countries with advanced democratic systems tend to perform the civic role and its two analytical sub-dimensions more than the rest of the countries in our study. Although we found statistically significant differences in both cases

Table 7.1 Analytical Sub-Dimensions and Indicators of the Civic Role (Means and Percentages)

	United States	Greece	Russia	Malaysia	Cuba	Argentina	Poland	Mexico	Spain	Ireland	Hungary	Switzerland	Germany	Brazil	Chile	Philippines	China	Hong Kong	Total
Advocate sub-dimension (Mean)	.10	.11	.09	.06	.06	.50	.36	.45	.04	.42	.36	.27	.35	.03	.37	.06	.00	.00	.08
SD	.18	.24	.16	.16	.18	.17	.21	.26	.13	.27	.21	.14	.16	.12	.17	.15	.00	.02	.18
Indicators (%)																			
Citizen reaction	27.2	12.4	2.9	9.5	1.4	13.6	17.4	11.1	8.1	6.6	6.0	2.8	8.9	4.7	5.2	3.5	.0	.2	8.3
χ^2 (17, N=33640) = 1951.095, p < .001																			
Citizen demand	4.6	9.0	5.8	6.6	7.2	11.1	8.1	8.8	6.5	3.3	3.8	2.2	6.3	4.3	1.3	2.5	.0	.2	4.9
χ^2 (17, N=33640) = 844.765, p < .001																			
Credibility of citizens	15.1	1.2	4.2	7.1	9.4	14.0	9.6	6.0	1.0	6.6	2.2	.7	1.8	1.8	.6	1.1	.0	.0	4.4
χ^2 (17, N=16782) = 26052.417, p < .001																			
Support of citizen movements	.8	7.1	1.1	5.1	.3	2.4	1.9	2.9	2.0	1.8	1.6	.1	.1	1.0	.3	.2	.0	.0	1.5
χ^2 (17, N=33640) = 76.450, p < .001																			
Citizen questions	2.2	5.0	2.1	2.2	2.9	1.4	.5	2.4	.8	.4	.6	.0	.7	2.3	.2	.1	.0	.0	1.2
χ^2 (17, N=33640) = 484.709, p < .001																			
Information on citizen activities	5.3	15.2	4.2	1.5	.8	7.5	7.2	6.1	6.0	2.9	4.4	1.8	1.8	2.8	2.6	3.0	.0	.0	4.4
χ^2 (17, N=33640) = 1098.823, p < .001																			
Educator sub-dimension (Mean)	.14	.14	.11	.11	.08	.05	.05	.09	.04	.01	.02	.02	.07	.07	.05	.04	.00	.00	.06
SD	.17	.19	.17	.19	.18	.15	.13	.17	.14	.07	.08	.07	.15	.15	.12	.12	.00	.00	.14
Indicators (%)																			
Local impact	9.0	11.0	9.4	6.8	15.6	6.5	5.6	1.1	4.9	1.9	1.8	1.3	12.1	7.4	4.0	7.9	.0	.0	5.9
χ^2 (17, N=33640) = 945.011, p < .001																			
Educating on duties and rights	1.1	7.7	7.0	3.2	2.7	1.7	3.8	3.5	.5	.3	.6	.1	5.6	3.0	2.0	5.9	.0	.0	2.6
χ^2 (17, N=33640) = 777.472, p < .001																			
Contextual background information	39.1	21.3	21.9	22.3	11.5	5.9	4.3	16.8	5.8	.8	.9	4.0	9.5	13.6	11.7	.8	.0	.0	9.9
χ^2 (17, N=33640) = 3387.096, p < .001																			

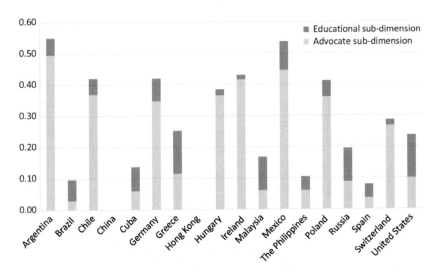

Figure 7.1 The advocate and educational sub-dimensions of the civic role across countries (means)

$(F_{\text{civic-advocate}}(2, 17116) = 375.369, p < .001; F_{\text{civic-educator}}(2, 34311) = 245.780,$ $p < .001)$, the results show important nuances.

While advanced democracies tend to score higher for the civic-educator approach ($M_{\text{advanceddemocracies}} = .07$, $SD = .15$; $M_{\text{transitionaldemocracies}} = .06$, $SD = .14$, $M_{\text{nondemocracies}} = .01$, $SD = .08$), the presence of the civic-advocate orientation is significantly higher in the press of transitional democracies ($M_{\text{advanceddemocracies}} = .09$, $SD = .19$; $M_{\text{transitionaldemocracies}} = .11$, $SD = .21$, $M_{\text{nondemocracies}} = .01$, $SD = .08$) with the exception of two advanced democracies, Greece ($M = .14$, $SD = .19$) and the United States ($M = .14$, $SD = .17$), where the educator-oriented sub-dimension is also high.

Significant differences were also found in the performance of the civic role and its two sub-dimensions ($F_{\text{civic}}(16, 34496) = 292.123, p < .001$; $F_{\text{civic-educator}}(16, 34496) = 168.472, p < .001$; $F_{\text{civic-advocate}}(16, 17101) = 181.368, p < .001$) in regards to news topic.

Considering the civic role overall, four news topics rank the highest: demonstrations and protests ($M = .27$, $SD = .24$), social problems ($M = .17$, $SD = .23$), human rights issues ($M = .13$, $SD = .19$), and housing, infrastructure, and public works ($M = .10$, $SD = .16$). Specifically, three topics are associated with the presence of both sub-dimensions of the civic role: demonstrations and protests ($M_{\text{civic-educator}} = .25$, $SD = .17$; $M_{\text{civic-advocate}} = .37$, $SD = .30$), social problems ($M_{\text{civic-educator}} = .17$, $SD = .23$; $M_{\text{civic-advocate}} = .30$, $SD = .31$), and human rights issues ($M_{\text{civic-educator}} = .12$, $SD = .20$; $M_{\text{civic-advocate}} = .23$, $SD = .26$).

We note that political and economic news hardly displayed any of the characteristics of the civic role, as shown in Figure 7.2.

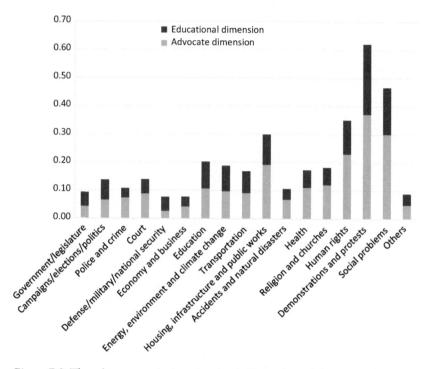

Figure 7.2 The advocate and educational sub-dimension of the civic role across news topics (means)

The Performance of the Infotainment Role

As indicated in Chapter 4, the performance of the infotainment role was slightly higher than the civic role, higher than the service role, and showed statistically significant differences across countries.

Overall, the most frequent indicator of the infotainment role in news is personalization, which appeared in 10% of the stories analyzed. It was followed by emotions and sensationalism (7.1% and 5.1%, respectively), the presence of elements of individuals' private lives (3.9%), and morbidity, both visual (2.1%) and verbal (.7%) (see Table 7.2).

However, we found significant differences in their presence across countries (see Table 7.2). While personalization was more frequent in Greece (22%), Russia (19.8%), and the United States (17.7%), the inclusion of private life was higher in Malaysia (11.1%), Argentina (9.9%), and the United States (9.2%). Meanwhile, sensationalism was most common in Chile (15.1%), Germany (12.3%), and Argentina (11.2%), and emotions were found mainly in news content from Argentina (14.1%), Chile (15.1%), Germany (14.5%), and Poland (12.1%). Lastly, morbidity was more frequent in Poland (7.9%), Malaysia (7.2%), and Argentina (6.1%).

Table 7.2 Indicators of the Infotainment Role (Percentages)

Indicators (%)	Total	Hong Kong	China	Philippines	Chile	Brazil	Germany	Switzerland	Hungary	Ireland	Spain	Mexico	Poland	Argentina	Cuba	Malaysia	Russia	Greece	United States
Personalization $\chi^2(17, N=33640) = 117.397$, $p < .001$	17.7	16.3	1.3	8.1	12.5	15.6	13.4	5.7	8.2	5.9	4.4	1.9	15.2	9.9	.2	7.1	19.8	22.0	1.7
Private life $\chi^2(17, N=33640) = 78.010$, $p < .001$	9.2	3.9	1.8	.8	4.2	4.6	3.0	2.6	6.6	3.2	1.3	1.7	5.8	9.9	.0	11.1	4.0	1.3	3.9
Sensationalism $\chi^2(17, N=33640) = 1467.994$, $p < .001$	2.5	3.0	1.5	.5	15.1	.8	12.3	3.9	8.1	1.5	1.2	6.9	9.2	11.2	.0	7.2	3.1	2.4	5.1
Emotions $\chi^2(17, N=33640) = 819,901$, $p < .001$	8.0	10.2	10.8	4.7	15.1	4.5	14.5	6.9	11.1	5.3	1.7	6.2	12.1	14.1	.2	12	11.2	2.7	8.4
Morbidity $\chi^2(17, N=33640) = 659.274$, $p < .001$	.9	1.5	.2	1.7	1.7	1.2	3.0	.9	4.4	.3	.4	3.5	7.9	6.1	0	7.2	2.2	4.6	2.4

While the infotainment role was present in both the elite ($M = .04$, $SD = .10$) and popular press ($M = .08$, $SD = .16$), its performance was significantly higher in the latter ($t(1) = 26.430$, $p < .001$) across all its indicators.

The performance of the infotainment role also varied across news topics ($F(16, 34496) = 113.386$, $p < .001$), and was higher in news on police and crime ($M = .10$, $SD = .18$), accidents and natural disasters ($M = .09$, $SD = .17$), and religion ($M = .09$, $SD = .15$). Chapter 9 shows how these variations manifest in practice when controlling the organizational and country-level variables.

When the infotainment role is combined with the interventionist role, we find a form of more expressive journalism aimed at all issues. Our data support this argument for all topics, though we found variations. The hybridization of both roles is stronger in news about accidents and natural disasters ($r = .302$, $p < .001$), and also significant—although lower—in news on politics ($r = .179$, $p < .001$).

All indicators of this role have an above average presence in news on police and crime: personalization (16.2%), elements of private life (7.7%), sensationalism (10.2%), emotions (14.1%), and morbidity (12.6%).

Meanwhile, news on human rights is more closely associated with the presence of personalization (15.8%) and private life (9%), while news on religion combined mostly elements of private life (8.5%) with personalization (12.9%) and sensationalism (12.2%). News on accidents and natural disasters shows the highest levels for emotions (18.5%) and personalization (12.2%). Finally, personalization is the most frequent indicator in news on politics (15%) (see Figure 7.3).

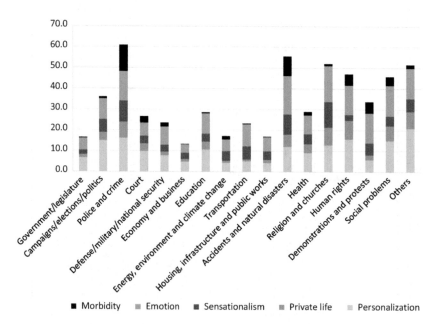

Figure 7.3 Elements of infotainment role performance across news topics (mean and percentage)

The Performance of the Service Role

In the overall sample, significant differences were found when comparing the presence of this role across countries (see Chapter 4). The more salient side of this role in news is related to its personal assistance subdimension. Indeed, impacts on everyday life—that is, when the journalists refer to the consequences or meanings that certain facts or events have for everyday life—were most present. The presence of this indicator was highest in Eastern and Western European countries such as Poland (15.2%), Russia (13.1%), Greece (11.3%), Germany (10.8%), and Hungary (10.2%), and lower in Switzerland (4.4%), the United States (2.9%), China (0.6%), and Hong Kong (0.4%) (see Table 7.3).

The second most important indicator of the service role was the presence of advice related to products or services. This characteristic was most present in transitional democracies such as the Philippines (10%) and Chile (6%)—two countries with a neoliberal economy— followed by Brazil (4.6%), Argentina (4.5%), and Hungary (4%).

The two remaining indicators of service journalism refer to tips and advice that journalists offer. In general, these indicators were less present in the news, and were only found to have a greater presence in the three Eastern European countries included in our study—Russia (3.4% and 2.6%), Hungary (6.3% and 3.5%), and Poland (6.2% and 5.2%).

The elite and popular press present significant differences in regard to the service role (t (1) = 2.248, p < .02), with the elite press showing a higher performance of this role (M = .035, SD = .11 vs. M = .031, SD = .11)—a trend that repeats for all indicators. Nevertheless, Chapter 10 will show that the effect of audience orientation on the performance of service role disappears when controlling by country, as well as by several organizational-level factors.

The presence of the service role was also highly dependent on the topic ($F(16, 34496)$ = 114.309, p < .001). Stories on health had the highest presence (M = .12, SD = .21), followed by news on transportation (M = .09, SD = .17) and housing, infrastructure, and public works (M = .09, SD = .17). Its lowest presence was found in news on politics (M = .01, SD = .06), defense (M = .01, SD = .07), and police and crime (M = .01, SD = .07).

When considering the presence of each indicator, impact on everyday life was the most frequent across all news topics (see Figure 7.4). On other hand, data showed an above-average presence in all indicators of the service role in news on health (21.4% for everyday life impact, 5.7% and 12.1% for advice on facing grievances or risks in daily life, and 9.4% for consumer advice) and transportation (20.6% for everyday life impact, 4% and 4.6% for advice on facing grievances or risks in daily life, and 6.2% for consumer advice). News on housing, infrastructure, and public works also had a higher presence of impact on everyday life elements (21.7%), and consumer advice (6.9%). Among traditional "hard" news topics, only economy and business has a greater presence of the consumer advice indicator (8.7%).

Table 7.3 Indicators of the Service Role (Percentages)

	Total	Hong Kong	China	Philippines	Chile	Brazil	Germany	Switzerland	Hungary	Ireland	Spain	Mexico	Poland	Argentina	Cuba	Malaysia	Russia	Greece	United States
Impact on everyday life	6.5	.4	.6	5.2	5.1	6.9	1.8	4.4	1.2	6.8	6.5	6.8	15.2	8.2	6.7	8.5	13.1	11.3	2.9
Tips (grievances)	1.5	.1	.1	.6	1.4	1.6	.6	.5	6.3	2.3	.7	1.6	6.2	2.1	3.3	.4	3.4	1.0	.8
Tips (individual risks)	1.9	.5	.5	3.1	2.7	1.9	.3	.8	3.5	2.0	2.5	1.2	5.2	2.2	1.0	3.0	2.6	1.9	.8
Consumer advice	2.9	.1	.1	1.0	6.0	4.6	.9	2.2	4.0	2.7	1.2	1.6	2.7	4.5	.3	2.7	1.1	1.9	1.7

Impact on everyday life: $\chi^2 (17, N=33640) = 746.786$, $p < .001$

Tips (grievances): $\chi^2 (17, N=33640) = 526.424$, $p < .001$

Tips (individual risks): $\chi^2 (17, N=33640) = 232.424$, $p < .001$

Consumer advice: $\chi^2 (17, N=33640) = 788.349$, $p < .001$

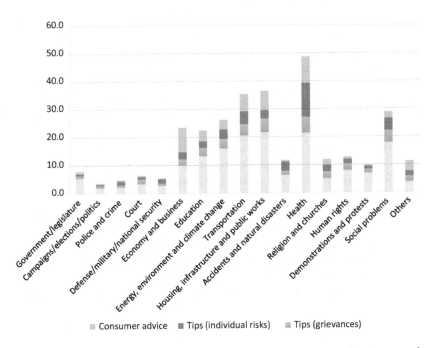

Figure 7.4 Elements of service role performance across news topics (mean and percentage)

The Hybridization of Roles Within the Audience Approach Domain

Following the potential hybridizations outlined in the "Situational and Contextual Influence on Role Performance" section of this chapter, we looked at the news stories to see which co-occurrences were more present.

In relation to the civic-infotainment hybridization, we identified a significant but weak link between the roles ($r = .092$, $p < .01$) in the overall sample, although the co-occurrence of the infotainment role with the civic-advocate sub-dimension was stronger ($r = .160$, $p < .01$).

However, this pattern changes significantly when analyzing national differences. The highest correlations between the civic and infotainment roles were indeed found in the U.S., ($r = .365$, $p < .01$) and, to a lesser extent, in Argentina ($r = .128$, $p < .01$).

The second potential hybridization was the co-occurrence of the service and civic roles. In our overall data, this hybridization was stronger ($r = .149$, $p < .01$) than the civic-infotainment combination, and slightly stronger than the advocate sub-dimension ($r = .187$, $p < .01$). Again, our results significantly vary when analyzing national differences. The highest correlations between the civic and service roles were found in Malaysia ($r = .313$, $p < .01$), Mexico ($r = .229$, $p < .01$), and Spain ($r = .199$, $p < .01$).

The third potential hybridization was the co-occurrence of the info-tainment and service roles. In our overall data, these two roles did not significantly correlate ($r = -.001, p = .915$). Nevertheless, when looking at each national case, we found a significant link between the roles in Spain ($r = .142, p < .01$) and Mexico ($r = .173, p < .01$).

While we only found significant correlations between the three roles in these two countries, service and civic ($r_{Spain} = .199, p < .01; r_{Mexico} = .229, p < .01$), infotainment and civic ($r_{Spain} = .122, p < .01; r_{Mexico} = .168, p < .01$), and infotainment and service ($r_{Spain} = .142, p < .01; r_{Mexico} = .173, p < .01$), this is more indicative of a trend than a rule. Indeed, as you can see in the illustrative examples provided in the first section of this chapter, specific stories from any country can potentially combine elements of these three roles.

These role hybridizations vary across media with different audience orientations. For example, while elite newspapers show a significant co-occurrence of the civic and service roles ($r = .170, p < .01$) and between the civic and infotainment roles ($r = .122, p < .01$), such associations are almost non-existent in popular newspapers.

Lastly, we found that role hybridization varied across news topics. The co-occurrence of the civic and infotainment roles was mostly found in news on social problems, demonstrations, human rights, health, acci-dents and natural disasters, housing, infrastructure and public works, transportation, and courts and politics. Meanwhile, the association between the civic and service roles was found in almost all news topics. Finally, the combination of the service and infotainment roles mostly appears in news on social problems.

Conclusion

This chapter analyzes the performance of the service, civic, and infotain-ment roles as well as their sub-dimensions and indicators, the relation-ships between these roles, and their co-occurrences across the print press from 18 countries. It also addresses the connections between key varia-bles such as political regime, news topic, and media audience orientation.

Focusing separately on each of the roles, we found that the civic role was performed in two ways—advocate and educator—and that the pres-ence of both was similar in the overall sample. The first type of civic journalism is based mainly on the presence of citizen statements about political decisions that affect them. In this respect, the citizen voice was more often a response or reaction to the political actions of third par-ties than a reflection of citizens' own initiatives or political discourses. In other words, the role manifested more clearly as a window through which citizens could express opinions about the political agenda set by authorities and less as a loudspeaker for citizens to set their own. In fact, the presence of explicit citizen credibility and support for social movements was comparatively low. The presence of the civic-educator orientation of the civic role seemed to manifest to a greater extent as the provision of information that citizens could use to make more informed decisions, and was less a reflection of a genuinely educational function through which active citizenship could be practiced. Contextual background information was provided almost twice as much as data on the local impact of political decisions, and almost four times as much as information on citizens' rights and duties.

In regard to inter-country variation, some countries present an important gap between the performance of the civic-advocate and civic-educator sub-dimensions of the role, where the first dominated over the second. Specifically, the print press of advanced or transitional democratic systems overall showed more presence of the civic-educator than non-democratic countries. This was not the case for the print press in the U.S. and Greece, possibly due to the fact that the performance of the civic role was more present than the average compared to the rest of the countries. An important finding was that the presence of the citizens' loudspeaker and support functions was higher in the print press from transitional democracies. Moreover, we found that the civic-advocate orientation was most common in the print press of Central and Eastern European countries and from most Latin American countries.

The advocate and educator orientations of the civic role also manifest differently according to news topic. They were more closely associated with stories on demonstrations and protests, social problems, and human rights. However, it is worth noting the almost negligible presence of the citizen role in news on government actions and the economy. Those topics still seem to be a closed off from the citizen reaction.

When the media and journalists try to entertain and relax the audience, they mostly use personalization, emotions, and sensationalism—a pattern that is common across countries. Thus, the results generally show that characteristics based on morbid fascination and people's private lives are not a dominant trait of the performance of this role in the national desk sections of print journalism.

The characteristics of this role were more present in news on crimes and accidents and natural disasters, where the keys to competing for the audience's attention were sensationalism, personalization, and details of the protagonists' private lives. This was also the case for news on religion and churches. For example, news on sexual abuse by members of the clergy was often covered as a scandal, underscoring emotions and personalization of victims or perpetrators. In news on human rights, rather than referring to legislative or political debates, there was a tendency to resort to personalization.

Lastly, the service role basically manifests through its personal assistance orientation, with the exceptions of the print press from the Philippines and Chile, where a consumer advice approach seems to be more prevalent in accordance with their neoliberal economic system. Furthermore, when comparing the presence of the indicators of the service role across news topics, "impact on everyday life" was also the most frequent in all news topics. In this respect, the results support the argument put forward by Eide and Knight (1999, p. 545) about "the problematization of the everyday life-world" as the common ground shared by service journalism. This was reinforced by some of our data. In topics where the presence of the civic role was above average (human rights, demonstrations, public works, and social problems), the personal assistance side of the service role was more salient. Thus, in news on protests, e.g., a strike by the taxi sector over competition from private car-hire companies, we might find both the advocate sub-dimension of the civic role and information about how this impacts individuals' everyday lives.

We also found that the presence of the infotainment role and its indicators was twice as high in the popular press, although its presence in elite titles was also relevant. In the service role, the type of media outlet only made a difference when looking at its personal assistance orientation, which was more frequent in the elite press. That could be understood as a strategy adopted by more serious newspapers to attract or expand their audience.

Regarding potential role hybridization within the audience approach domain, we found an important link between the infotainment and civics roles in the U.S., between the infotainment and service roles in Argentina, and between the civic and service roles in Malaysia and Mexico. Moreover, all potential combinations were present in two countries—Spain and Mexico.

The findings set out in this chapter also show that the hybridization of roles tends to be transversal to all news topics, and that elite-oriented newspapers engage more in the hybridization of roles and specifically the combination of the civic role with elements of infotainment and service journalism. Instead, the three roles tend to be performed independently in the popular press.

The lower performance of the service role may be due to the characteristics of our sample, which only includes content from national desk sections. The presence of this role might increase if the analysis is extended to other beats.

Note

1 An exception appears in the case of the Irish press, where a negative correlation is found ($r = -.287$, $p < .001$) according to the detached journalistic culture of the press in that country.

References

Altschull, J. H. (1995). *Agents of power: The media and public policy.* New York: Longman.

Anderson, C. W. (2011). Deliberative, agonistic, and algorithmic audiences: Journalism's vision of its public in an age of audience transparency. *International Journal of Communication, 5,* 19.

Atkinson, J. (2011). Performance journalism: A three-template model of television news. *The International Journal of Press/Politics*, 16(1), 102–129.

Brants, K., & De Haan, Y. (2010). Taking the public seriously: Three models of responsiveness in media and journalism. *Media, Culture and Society*, 32(3), 411–428.

Carey, J. (2002). American journalism on, before, and after September 11. In B. Zelizer & S. Allan (Eds.), *Journalism after September 11* (pp. 89–108). London: Routledge.

Christians, C. G., Glasser, T., McQuail, D., Nordenstreng, K., & White, R. A. (2009). *Normative theories of the media: Journalism in democratic societies.* Chicago: University of Illinois Press.

Costera Meijer, I. (2003). What is quality television news? A plea for extending the professional repertoire of newsmakers. *Journalism Studies*, 4(1), 15–29.

Croteau, D., & Hoynes, W. (2001). Media, markets and the public sphere. Retrieved September 6, 2015, from https://370bojangeorgievski,dejanandon ovandzanetatrajkoskahofstramass112.files.wordpress.com/2009/02/media-markets-the-public-sphere-croteauhoynes.pdf.

DeWerth-Pallmeyer, D. (1997). *The Audience in the News.* Mahwah, NJ: Erlbaum.

Eide, M. (2017). The culture of service journalism. In N. N. Kristensen, & K. Riegert (Eds.), *Cultural journalism in the Nordic countries* (pp. 195–204). Göteborg: Nordicom.

Eide, M., & Knight, G. (1999). Public/private service: Service journalism and the problems of everyday life. *European Journal of Communication*, 14(4), 525–547.

Esser, F. (1999). Tabloidization of news: A comparative analysis of Anglo-American and German press journalism. *European journal of communication*, 14(3), 291–324.

Franklin, B. (2005). The local press and the McDonaldization thesis. In A. Stuart (Ed.), *Journalism: Critical issues* (pp. 137–150). New York: Open University Press.

Gans, H. J. (2004). *Deciding what's news: A study of CBS evening news, NBC nightly news, Newsweek, and Time.* Evanston, IL: Northwestern University Press.

Guerrero, M., & Márquez-Ramírez, M. (Eds.). (2014). *Media systems and communication policies in Latin America.* Nueva York: Palgrave.

Hallin, D. C. (1992). Sound bite news: Television coverage of elections, 1968–1988. *Journal of Communication*, 42(2), 5–24.

Hallin, D. C., & Mancini, P. (2004). *Comparing media systems: Three models of media and politics.* Cambridge: Cambridge university press.

Holton, A. E., Coddington, M., & Gil de Zúñiga, H. (2013). Whose news? Whose values? Citizen journalism and journalistic values through the lens of content creators and consumers. *Journalism Practice*, 7(6), 720–737.

Jebril, N., Albæk, E., & de Vreese, C. H. (2013). Infotainment, cynicism and democracy: The effects of privatization vs personalization in the news. *European Journal of Communication*, 28(2), 105–121.

Johansson, S. (2007). 'They Just Make Sense': Tabloid newspapers as an alternative public sphere. In R. Butsch (Ed.), *Media and public spheres* (pp. 83–95). London: Macmillan.

McChesney, R. W. (2001). Global media, neoliberalism, and imperialism. *Monthly Review-New York, 52*(10), 1–19.

McManus, J. H. (1994). *Market-driven journalism: Let the citizen beware?* Thousand Oaks, CA: Sage Publications.

Mellado, C. (2015). Professional roles in news content: Six dimensions of journalistic role performance. *Journalism Studies, 16*(4), 596–614.

Mellado, C., López-Rabadán, P., & Elortegui, C. (2017). (For) Citizens or spectators? Chilean political journalism and its professional models for approaching the audience. *Palabra Clave, 20*(1), 14–46.

Mellado, C., & van Dalen, A. (2017). Challenging the citizen—Consumer journalistic dichotomy: A news content analysis of audience approaches in Chile. *Journalism and Mass Communication Quarterly, 94*(1), 213–237.

Nerone, J. (2018). Lessons from American history. In N. J. Woodhull & R. Snyder (Eds.), *Journalists in Peril* (pp. 125–132). New York: Routledge.

Patterson, T. E. (1993). *Out of order.* New York: Vintage.

Picard, R. G. (2004). Commercialism and newspaper quality. *Newspaper Research Journal, 25*(1), 54–65.

Rosen, J., & Merritt Jr., D. (1994). Public journalism: First principles. In *Public journalism: Theory and practice.* Dayton: Kettering Foundation.

Skovsgaard, M., & Bro, P. (2017). Journalistic roles in the mediated public sphere. In C. Mellado, L. Hellmueller, & W. Donsbach (Eds.), *Journalistic role performance. Concepts, contexts, and methods* (pp. 78–92). New York: Routledge.

Sparks, C., & Tulloch, J. (Eds.). (2000). *Tabloid tales: Global debates over media standards.* London: Rowman and Littlefield.

Underwood, D. (1993). *When MBA's rule the newsroom.* New York: Columbia University Press.

Underwood, D. (2001). Reporting and the push for market-oriented journalism: Media organizations as businesses. In W. L. Bennett & R. M. Entman (Eds.), *Mediated politics: Communication in the future of democracy* (pp. 99–116). Cambridge: Cambridge University Press.

Weaver, D., Beam, R., Brownlee, B., Voakes, P., & Wilhoit, G. C. (2007). *The American journalist in the 21st century. U.S. news people at the dawn of a new millennium.* Mahwah, NJ: Erlbaum.

Zhao, Y. (2012). Understanding China's media system in a world historical context. In D. Hallin & P. Mancini (Eds.), *Comparing media systems beyond the Western world* (pp. 143–176). Cambridge: Cambridge University Press.

Part III

Explaining Journalistic Role Performance

8 Measuring the Link Between Professional Role Conceptions, Perceived Role Enactment, and Journalistic Role Performance Across Countries

Claudia Mellado and Cornelia Mothes

Drawing on pioneering research based on experiments or quasi-experiments that examine the relationship between ideas and action, several studies conducted before the 21st century suggested that journalists' perceptions and attitudes could be reflected in their professional practices (e.g., Starck & Soloski, 1977; Culbertson, 1983; Patterson & Donsbach, 1996; Drew, 1975).[1] One of the reasons for this is the fact that most of those studies used perceptions and/or attitudes as a proxy measure for actual role performance.

Over the past decade, revisionist literature on journalistic roles has documented the inevitable discrepancies between rhetoric and practices in journalism (Bro, 2008; Tandoc, Hellmueller, & Vos, 2013; van Dalen, de Vreese, & Albaek, 2012; Mellado & van Dalen, 2014; Weischenberg, Malik, & Scholl, 2006), where the ways journalists see themselves as professionals do not necessarily mirror role performance (Mellado et al., 2020).

The risks associated with relying solely on journalists' self-reports to study journalistic cultures have been the focus of significant inquiry in journalism research (Ryfe, 2020; Weischenberg et al., 2006). Given the various factors that influence journalistic practice, it has become more and more important to assess the link between ideals and performance. This is especially critical in a context in which the credibility and social responsibility of the profession are being questioned and the public's skepticism towards, and dissatisfaction with, the performance of the media are increasing (Brants, 2013; Waisbord, 2013).

Some studies of professional ideals and practices have focused on the relationship between role conception and role performance, exploring whether journalists who identify with certain roles end up performing them (Starck & Soloski, 1977; Culbertson, 1983; van Dalen et al., 2012; Tandoc et al., 2013). Another line of inquiry centers on the link between ideals and practice as a gap, analyzing factors that create discrepancies between journalistic ideals and performance (Mellado & van Dalen, 2014; Humanes & Roses, 2018).

In addition to substantially contributing to our understanding of the significance of journalistic ideals in everyday practice, most of this research also poses a series of theoretical and methodological challenges. These mostly deal with the level of analysis used to compare ideals and performance, treating news as an individual outcome rather than a collective one (for an overview, Mellado et al., 2020).

In this chapter, we analyze the interplay between journalistic ideals and professional practice based on an understanding of role performance as a collective and socially constructed outcome. We examine both the gap and the relationship between individual role conceptions, perceived role enactment, and average role performance in journalists' work in newspapers from nine countries in Europe, Asia, and Latin America. We believe that exploring the ideal/performance link from both perspectives is a compelling way to provide evidence to nurture debates around contemporary journalism.

More than a decade ago, Weischenberg et al. (2006) argued that the study of role conception alone was not of relevance, as it does not impact the news, particularly in the case of political journalism. The data analyzed in this chapter show that the disconnect between journalistic ideals and practices of professional roles impacts journalism overall.

As this chapter demonstrates, while role performance and normative journalistic standards vary strongly from country to country when measured separately, journalistic cultures generate similar gaps between journalists' ideals and media organizations' performance across all countries. This is especially true for the civic and watchdog roles, which are directly linked to the democratic functions of the profession. Our results also reveal that the extent to which journalists' role conceptions match their perceived role enactment, and the extent to which both match actual role performance differ significantly across countries, especially in public influence-oriented roles, such as the interventionist and the loyal-facilitator role.

We have also identified a significant association between normative conceptions and perceived role enactment with actual role performance for four professional roles. However, we found no significant relationship between what journalists deem important or perceive as reality for the watchdog and civic oriented roles and how their organizations perform these roles.

Studying the Link Between Rhetoric and Practices

The ideal/practice link has been studied from two main perspectives.

Some research focuses on the link as a relationship, exploring whether journalists who adhere more to a specific role are more likely to perform it. Bergen (1991) offers content data from 131 journalists in her study of role conceptions. She questioned U.S. journalists, asking them to submit what they considered to be their "best work." The analysis showed that news professionals' role conceptions correlated weakly to their performance. Also in the U.S., Tandoc et al. (2013) compared the role conceptions of the disseminator, mobilizer, adversarial, and investigator roles of 56 journalists with their individual performance, and found that only the mobilizer role conception predicted its corresponding performance. Similarly, the study led by Scholl and Weischenberg (1998) in Germany showed that while journalists stated that they performed the roles important to them to a large degree, the performance of these roles was not highly present.

Other studies have addressed the link between ideal and performance by focusing on the gap or distance between the two. For example, Mellado and van Dalen (2014) compared the role conception of 102 Chilean journalists with the news stories they produced at the individual level, finding that organizational influences and belonging to a news beat significantly increased the gap. Roses and Humanes (2019) analyzed the disconnect between journalists' role conceptions and their perceived role enactment in the Spanish press, finding a significant role conflict, especially in the watchdog, civic, and disseminator roles. Earlier studies from our project focused on institutional influences on conception/performance gaps and showed that the differences between ideals and performance are transversally greater across countries in terms of roles that are generally more closely related to democratic functions of journalism, such as keeping the powerful accountable and educating citizens to make better political decisions (Mellado et al., 2020).

While studies examining the link as a gap and as a relationship tend to share a similar theoretical interest and empirical approach, they lead to somewhat different conclusions. For example, Scholl and Weischenberg (1998) found that despite the existence of a significant gap between the conception and performance of journalists on "explaining complex issues," ideals and practices were significantly correlated. In an effort to provide a comprehensive picture of the ideal/performance link across diverse journalistic cultures, we will therefore examine both the gap and the relationship between role conceptions and role performance. We will further extend these perspectives by looking at journalists' perceived role enactment as a potential intersection between ideals and practice, and the inherently imperfect match among them.

The Inherently Imperfect Match Between Role Conception, Perceived Enactment, and Performance

As Chapter 2 illustrates, there are meaningful differences between role conception, perceived role enactment, and role performance as objects of study. Although perceived role enactment more directly addresses behavioral outcomes than role conceptions do, and thus epistemically lies between normative ideals and actual performance, both role conception and perceived role enactment can be located at the evaluative level—dealing with how journalists conceive of their roles or perceive the implementation of their roles, respectively. For its part, role performance as a concept is located at the performative level, which is where the actual practice of journalism comes into play. Role conceptions and perceived enactment are mostly measured through self-reports (surveys, in-depth interviews) and, in the case of perceived enactment, also through experiments. Role performance is addressed through content analysis, newsroom observation, and the like.

Hence, when aiming to extend this research by studying the link between role conception, perceived enactment, and role performance simultaneously, a mixed-methods approach is required (as developed in Chapter 3) to gain substantial insights into the nature of the link between ideals/perceptions and practices (van Dalen, de Vreese, & Albæk, 2017). For instance, a strong link can occur either through a strong performance of a highly relevant/perceived role or through a low importance/ perceived enactment of a role that is rarely performed. Also, negative association can be observed when role performance is more pronounced than conceptions/perceptions. In any of these cases, the link would be strong, but can only be substantiated if data from diverse methodological approaches are combined.

Although a great deal of academic discussion has been developed over the past few decades about the (in)existence of a link between ideals and practice, media studies and role performance research have systematically suggested several reasons for a disconnect between the evaluative side of journalistic cultures and role performance.

One important aspect to consider when conducting comparative research on professional roles is that the suppositions made in classical studies on role conceptions about the level of professionalism and internal freedom of journalists do not necessarily apply equally to different societies. As Hallin (2017, p. xv) notes,

> [t]he long-standing practice of studying journalism around the world by doing surveys of journalists' role conceptions, for example, rests implicitly on a model of the media derived from Western systems with high levels of journalistic professionalism: it makes the most sense if we assume that journalists are the key actors in the production of news, that they have enough autonomy that their individual role conceptions matter, and that the system is egalitarian enough that it makes sense to count each individual equally. In many systems, all of those assumptions may be quite far from reality, and it will be particularly important in analyzing these systems to think

systematically about what forces might disrupt or modify the linkage between role conception and role performance.

Similarly, while most studies on roles measure journalistic performance at the individual level, news content is not necessarily produced by only one journalist. Rather, it is created with other colleagues within highly complex institutions and political contexts, and is therefore a collective outcome (Boczkowski, 2011; Mellado, 2015; Mellado et al., 2020; Ryfe, 2020; Schudson, 2011).

Even if a journalist is highly committed to advocating for the public and providing individuals with the information they need to make political decisions, he or she would not be able to produce a civic-oriented piece if the story focused on events totally unrelated to civic life, or if the journalist is working for a media outlet that focuses on entertaining, or in a country where the political context prevents him or her from going against the status quo.

Moreover, journalists write for different platforms and topics, so they frequently perform multiple roles while working on a single piece. The work can also change dramatically from one day to the next, and journalists must occasionally put aside their gold standards to address situations that require specific role performances. Indeed, the outcome of their work is decided by many people, and a single news piece can be the product of many different reporters, while editors and other newsroom leaders make final decisions. As Laurent (1978, p. 221) puts it, "the same people perceive . . . very differently the same event depending upon which hierarchical glasses they are invited to wear."

On top of all this, journalists tend to write for many different audiences at the same time, especially in the digital ecosystem in which we are immersed. This means that a single news story must meet different requirements that can be associated with the merging of diverse roles.

In view of all of this, we argue that the absolute value of the "gap" or of the "relationship" between ideals/perceptions and practices has no substantive meaning unless we focus on the source of that variation and on what the link is the expression of. It is important to keep in mind that when a role is performed alongside or with other roles, the focus tends to be on the specific qualities of the role rather than its totality (Landy, 1993). As such, it is not very common to find fully performed roles despite what some role ideals might suggest.

As the link is context-dependent, specific social settings or organization configurations may result in different associations between ideals and performance. For example, repressive political regimes have censored the media, harassing, persecuting, and even killing journalists to prevent them from informing the public in a timely manner or from going against those who wield political power. Economic factors such as state advertising and the way the elites decide to carve up the media turf within a country may also influence the link between norms, ideals, and practices. Cultural values shared by the members of a given society could also affect how journalists negotiate their roles. For instance, in certain journalistic cultures that have developed under the banner of societal models marked by collective well-being and harmony, such beliefs can moderate the relationship between ideals/perceptions and practices within the profession in a manner that differs from what is found in countries where cultural values are not so transversally shared.

Likewise, organizations have historically used different forms of internal management. Specifically, organizational behavior literature focuses on the relationship between meaning and control. This includes the existence of normative control, which can be carried out by facilitating sense-making, inducing journalists to internalize specific roles, and giving them a sense of belonging (Ashfort, 2012). For example, Greil and Rudy (1984), showed how certain rites that occur when people join a specific organization can shape their identity within the organization.

Brunsson (1993, p. 489) refers to the body/soul dichotomy of individuals, defining the soul as the locus of thought and ideas, and the body as the instrument of action. While ideas and actions are considered separate phenomena, they can be related in normative and descriptive terms in that individuals' ideas may reflect their actions, and vice versa. As such, although an organizational process of socialization and internal control must be monitored in order to turn ideas into specific actions, this process will also involve "a certain degree of subordination" on the part of the members of the organization (p. 490).

The problem here is that human beings are expected to have a plurality of preferences. In the case of journalists, working at a media outlet entails being in contact with coworkers, sources, and other reference groups, all of which can impact the effectiveness of the normative control that news organizations exert. At the same time, what can be done in a specific context cannot always be said, but the fact that we cannot say certain things does not mean that we cannot do them, or believe that they ought to be done. Finally, while actions can be socially constructed each time a particular action occurs, ideas may change faster than behaviors, since actions require organized coordination between many people (Ashfort, 2012).

Indeed, the process of socialization within news organizations does not necessarily imply that journalists accurately perceive the work of those news organizations, which are formed by different people from different cultures at different levels.

Studies have found that journalists can also experience internal discrepancies and conflicts between roles at the individual level (Klemm, Das, & Hartmann, 2019; Hooker, King, & Leask, 2012). When journalists cannot be coherent with their ideals, they can address those discrepancies by "bringing (oneself) into line with the environmental forces" (Rothbaum, Weisz, & Snyder, 1982, p. 5). For example, Klemm et al.

(2019) find changes in the way German and Finnish journalists covering public health crises see their roles, shifting from watchdog to being co-operative and supporting the public interest.

As Wyss (2008) and Brunsson (1993) suggest, lack of coherence may also be approached by rationalizing non-compliant actions as a strategy for managing the news. According to these authors, lowering the journalist's efforts and expectations may shield them from the disappointment of role inconsistencies. Similarly, Mothes (2014) finds that journalists may dis-identify with behaviors that are not aligned with their role conceptions in order to reduce their emotional dissonance, thereby reinforcing the strength of their ideals without actually performing them.

Various studies on perceived journalistic autonomy have additionally shown that although institutionalized controls exist, journalists might not be able to see the impact of economic, political, and structural pressures on the practice of their work (e.g., Hanitzsch & Mellado, 2011). These studies also suggest that normalization (also called naturalization or de-identification) shapes the meaning that journalists give to different structural media factors (Mellado & Humanes, 2012, p. 999), transforming what is extraordinary or unexpected into more or less ordinary things (Ashforth & Kreiner, 2002; Rosenthal, 1990).

At the same time, journalists can activate an internal compensatory process (Heckhausen & Schulz, 1995; Mothes, 2014). Many studies on cognitive dissonance show that it is difficult to remain detached from common practices for too long because behavior must appear rational and make sense to each individual (Festinger, 1957).

Whether it is exerted by the societal context, the organization, or internally by the journalist, higher levels of control thus seem to create less space to deviate from/or to pursue a role in the contextual space in which journalists develop their work. Against this backdrop, this chapter will be guided by the following research questions:

> *RQ1a: Does the size of the gap between journalists' role conception, their perceived role enactment, and the average performance of their news media organizations vary across the interventionist, watchdog, civic, loyal, service, and infotainment roles?*
> *RQ1b: Are these variations stable across countries?*
> *RQ2b: To what extent do journalists' role conception and perceived role enactment relate to the average performance of their news media organizations?*
> *RQ2b: Which roles show the strongest relationship between conceptions/perceptions and performance?*

In order to analyze the link between journalists' role conception, perceived role enactment, and role performance, we compared each journalist's role conception/perception to the average role performance of their respective organization. We first calculated the average score of each journalist based on their answers to the survey questions representing each role. Then, we calculated the average score of role performance for each media outlet with regard to each role, considering all of the news stories from each outlet (see Chapter 3 and Appendix). We recoded the average scores for role conception/perception (ranging from 1 to 5) into scores of 0 to 1, because the scales used to measure role performance were different from the scales measuring role ideals.

To measure the link between conception, perception, and performance as a gap, we calculated the absolute differences between each two. We subtracted the average role performance score of each media outlet from the average role conception/perception score of each journalist from that outlet, and subtracted the average perception score from the average conception score. Note that the absolute values of the "gap" scores have no substantive interpretation because we have no way of knowing what level of presence of a particular role in news content would correspond to the journalist's assignment of levels of importance, as we argued in the previous section of this chapter. The focus of our analysis is the relative sizes and directions of these gaps, with positive values in the case of conception-performance gaps. This suggests that roles are more important to journalists, or perceived to be accomplished more by the journalists' news organizations, compared to actual role performance measured via content analysis.

We used all measures separately to assess the link between conception/perception and performance as a relationship and correlated them using different statistical procedures.

Results

The Link as a Gap

Three gaps were analyzed to address *RQ1a/b*. The first was the difference between journalists' role conceptions and the average performance of their news media organization. The second set of analyses addressed the level of discrepancy between journalists' perceived role enactment and role performance. Finally, we calculated the distance between journalistic ideals and reported behaviors. Our analyses suggest that the trends are similar across countries in terms of which role generates the largest/smallest gap. Although most gaps significantly deviate from zero in all three types of gaps, they are larger between journalists' conceptions/perceptions and their media performance than between their ideals and perceived enactment.

Role Conception—Role Performance Gaps

The six roles analyzed in our project differed significantly in the size of their conception-performance gaps across countries, $F(5,$

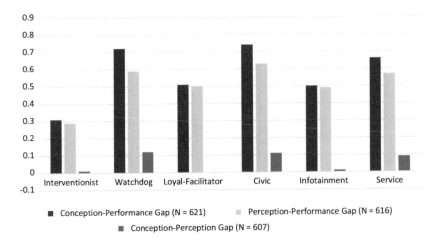

Figure 8.1 Average conception-performance, perception-performance, and conception-perception gaps for six journalistic roles across countries

3100) = 718.884, $p < .001$, $\eta^2 = .54$ (see first bars, Figure 8.1). The largest gaps occurred with regard to the civic role ($M = 0.74$, $SD = 0.16$) and the watchdog role ($M = 0.72$, $SD = 0.17$). This finding indicates that the discrepancies between ideals and performance are largest in public service-oriented roles across all countries, and hence in roles that are traditionally at the heart of the democratic functions of journalism as a profession.

Interestingly, while the overall smallest conception-performance gap occurred for the interventionist role in the global sample ($M = 0.31$, $SD = 0.17$), the very same role revealed the largest country differences, $F(8, 627) = 27.67$, $p < .001$, $\eta^2 = .26$ (see Figure 8.2), along with the loyal-facilitator role, $F(8, 624) = 26.68$, $p < .001$, $\eta^2 = .26$ (see Figure 8.4). In other words, the agreement between what journalists would like to do and the average performance of their news media organization varies significantly more between countries for these roles than for any other roles. In the case of the interventionist role, for example, China, Ireland, and Brazil showed substantially greater gaps than Spain, Argentina, Germany, and Chile.

Meanwhile, the smallest country differences in conception-performance gaps occurred with regard to the service role, $F(8, 627) = 7.06$, $p < .001$, $\eta^2 = .08$ (see Figure 8.7), followed by the infotainment role, $F(8, 628) = 8.61$, $p < .001$, $\eta^2 = .10$ (see Figure 8.6). Hence, the smallest country differences in conception-performance gaps occurred for roles that are most clearly related to more consumer-oriented roles, rather than roles that primarily address journalists' relationship to the political sphere, including civil society.

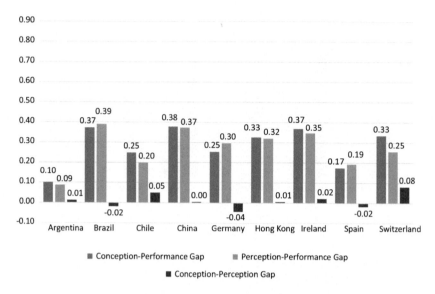

Figure 8.2 Country differences in conception-performance gap, perception-performance gap, and conception-perception gap for the interventionist role

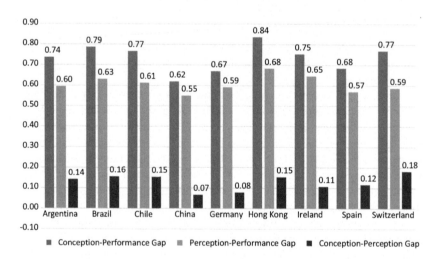

Figure 8.3 Country differences in conception-performance gap, perception-performance gap, and conception-perception gap for the watchdog role

Perceived Role Enactment—Role Performance Gaps

The six roles also differed significantly in the size of the gaps between perceived enactment and performance across countries. Although these perception-performance gaps varied significantly between roles,

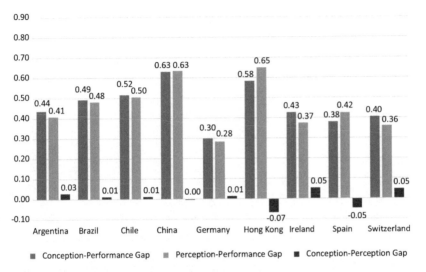

Figure 8.4 Country differences in conception-performance gap, perception-performance gap, and conception-perception gap for the loyal-facilitator role

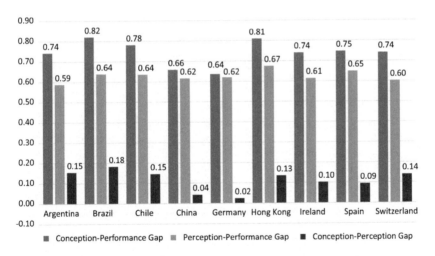

Figure 8.5 Country differences in conception-performance gap, perception-performance gap, and conception-perception gap for the civic role

differences were comparatively less pronounced than in conception-performance gaps, $F(5, 3075) = 399.673$, $p < .001$, $\eta^2 = .39$ (see second bars, Figure 8.1). The largest perception-performance gaps again occurred with regard to the civic role ($M = 0.63$, $SD = 0.14$) and the watchdog role ($M = 0.59$, $SD = 0.16$), while the smallest gaps occurred for the

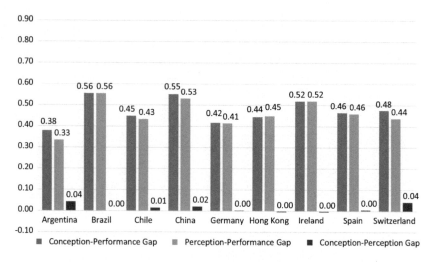

Figure 8.6 Country differences in conception-performance gap, perception-performance gap, and conception-perception gap for the infotainment role

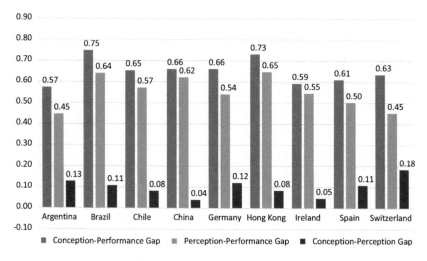

Figure 8.7 Country differences in conception-performance gap, perception-performance gap, and conception-perception gap for the service role

interventionist role ($M = 0.29$, $SD = 0.17$). Hence, discrepancies between ideals and performance, and between perceived enactment and actual performance, are largest in public service-oriented roles across countries.

Regarding country differences, we found the same pattern as for the conception-performance gap. While the overall smallest gap pertained to the interventionist role, this role showed the largest country differences, $F(8, 623) = 32.68$, $p < .001$, $\eta^2 = .30$ (see Figure 8.2), again followed by the loyal-facilitator role, $F(8, 620) = 27.47$, $p < .001$, $\eta^2 = .26$ (see Figure 8.4). The smallest country differences in perception-performance gaps were linked to the two roles that showed the largest overall gaps across countries; that is, the civic role, $F(8, 619) = 1.54$, $p = .139$ (see Figure 8.5) and the watchdog role, $F(8, 623) = 4.17$, $p < .001$, $\eta^2 = .05$ (see Figure 8.3).

Taken together, these findings suggest that journalists in all countries show similarly large gaps between how they perceive their performance in terms of public service-oriented roles (i.e., civic and watchdog) and what their news organizations actually do in this respect.

Role Conception—Perceived Role Enactment Gaps

Lastly, the six roles also differed significantly in the size of conception-perception gaps, that is, in the size of discrepancies between what journalists deem important from a normative-ideal point of view, and what they perceive as being actually performed in their media organizations' news coverage. Although roles differed in this respect, these differences were much less substantial than their conception-performance gaps and perception-performance gaps, $F(5, 3030) = 107.29$, $p < .001$, $\eta^2 = .15$ (see third bars, Figure 8.1). As we saw in the previous two types of gaps, the biggest conception-perception gaps occurred with the watchdog role ($M = 0.12$, $SD = 0.18$) and the civic role ($M = 0.11$, $SD = 0.15$). The overall smallest gaps occurred for the interventionist role ($M = 0.01$, $SD = 0.12$), loyal-facilitator role ($M = 0.002$, $SD = 0.15$), and infotainment role ($M = 0.01$, $SD = 0.12$).

The biggest country differences in conception-perception gaps occurred—although at a much smaller scale than the former types of gaps—with the civic role, $F(8, 615) = 11.35$, $p < .001$, $\eta^2 = .13$ (see Figure 8.5). Hence, the differences in the gap between journalists' civic duty and the perceived enactment of that duty are comparatively larger between countries than the differences in the gaps for the other roles.

All of the other roles showed very small differences among countries, and the infotainment role shows non-significant differences $F(8, 625) = 1.16$, $p = .325$ (see Figure 8.6), which could be associated with economic pressures and changes in audience needs that are transversal in contemporary society.

The Link as a Relationship

In order to address *RQ2a/b*, we analyzed the link between role conception and perceived role enactment with role performance as a relationship instead of as a gap.

Overall, the analyses revealed that roles showing the greatest gaps in the previous section also showed the smallest correlations between individual conceptions and perceptions on the one hand, and actual role performance on the other. In other words, gap analyses and relationship analyses in our data indicate similar patterns of a disconnect between ideals and practices across countries, although the fine-grained information they provide is different.

Specifically, multilevel analyses controlling for variance between countries reveal that only four out of six roles show discernible connections between normative conceptions and perceived role enactment with actual role performance—that is, the interventionist, loyal-facilitator, infotainment, and service roles (see Table 8.1).

These four roles are basically the ones that, by definition, accept that particular interests affect news coverage, either from the political sphere (i.e., interventionist and loyal-facilitator) or the economic sphere (i.e., infotainment and service).

In other words, journalists who give more importance to these roles (i.e., role conception) or think they are capable of performing them (i.e., perceived role enactment) are more likely to perform these roles within their news organization. With the exception of the loyal-facilitator role, the relationship is stronger between perceived role enactment and role performance than between role conception and role performance. This again reflects the larger gaps between conceptions and practice compared to the gap between perceptions of practice and actual practice.

Instead, the two roles most strongly related to the ideal of professional journalism and its public service function (i.e., watchdog and civic) did not show any significant relationship between what journalists deem important (i.e., role conception) or perceive as reality (i.e., perceived role enactment) and how their organizations perform these roles. Hence, the biggest gaps found in our analyses (see Figure 8.1) translated into nonsignificant relationships when investigating the link between conception, perception, and performance as a relationship, showing that journalists' evaluations of news performance tend to exist relatively independent of real media performance for these two journalistic roles.

Conclusion

This chapter contributes to our understanding of the significance of journalistic ideals in daily news practice by assessing the link between journalistic role conception, individually perceived role enactment, and media role performance both as a gap and as a relationship.

Not surprisingly, we found the largest gaps between evaluative and performative measures of journalistic roles, and especially between journalists' role conceptions and the performance of these roles by newspapers. Accordingly, the smallest gaps emerged between the two evaluative

Table 8.1 Strength of the Relationship Between Role Conceptions vs. Perceived Role Enactment and Role Performance (Unstandardized Regression Coefficients; Standard Errors in Parentheses)

	Interventionist			Watchdog			Loyal-facilitator		
	Model 1	Model 2	Model 3	Model 1	Model 2	Model 3	Model 1	Model 2	Model 3
Fixed Effects									
Intercept	.21*** (.02)	.19*** (.02)	.18*** (.02)	.06** (.01)	.05** (.01)	.05** (.01)	.02*** (.003)	.01** (.004)	.02** (.004)
Role Conception	–	.03** (.01) (ß = .08)	–	–	.01 (.01)	–	–	.01*** (.003) (ß = .15)	–
Perceived Role Enactment	–	–	.05*** (.01) (ß = .13)	–	–	.01 (.01)	–	–	.01** (.003) (ß = .13)
Covariance Parameters (ID)									
Residual	.002*** (.000)	.002*** (.000)	.002*** (.000)	.001*** (.000)	.001*** (.000)	.001*** (.000)	.0002*** (.000)	.0002*** (.000)	.0002*** (.000)
Intercept Country	.003* (.002)	.004* (.002)	.004* (.002)	.001* (.001)	.001* (.001)	.001* (.001)	.0001* (.000)	.0001* (.000)	.0001* (.000)
−2LL	−2213.28	−2193.49	−2188.92	−3022.86	−2974.11	−2964.38	−3659.42	−3615.97	−3586.20
AIC	−2207.28	−2185.49	−2180.92	−3016.86	−2966.11	−2956.38	−3653.42	−3607.97	−3578.20

	Civic			Infotainment			Service		
	Model 1	Model 2	Model 3	Model 1	Model 2	Model 3	Model 1	Model 2	Model 3
Fixed Effects									
Intercept	.03** (.01)	.03** (.01)	.03** (.01)	.05*** (.01)	.03** (.01)	.03* (.01)	.03*** (.01)	.02** (.01)	.02** (.01)
Role Conception	–	.002 (.002)	–	–	.04*** (.01) (ß = .18)	–	–	.01** (.003) (ß = .09)	–
Perceived Role Enactment	–	–	.002 (.003)	–	–	.06*** (.01) (ß = .26)	–	–	.01*** (.003) (ß = .12)
Covariance Parameters (ID)									
Residual	.0001*** (.000)	.0001*** (.000)	.0001*** (.000)	.001*** (.000)	.001*** (.000)	.001*** (.000)	.0002*** (.000)	.0002*** (.000)	.0002*** (.000)
Intercept Country	.001* (.000)	.001* (.000)	.001* (.000)	.001* (.000)	.001* (.000)	.001* (.000)	.0002* (.000)	.0002* (.000)	.0002* (.000)
−2LL	−4257.12	−4175.80	−4143.54	−2445.11	−2453.84	−2475.22	−3627.10	−3592.52	−3598.26
AIC	−4251.12	−4167.80	−4135.54	−2439.11	−2445.84	−2467.22	−3621.10	−3584.52	−3590.26

Note. *** $p < .001$; ** $p < .01$; * $p < .05$

dimensions of role ideals measured via self-reports; that is, role conception and perceived role enactment.

When looking at the specific roles affected, our results indicate that in terms of all three types of gaps, but most clearly in terms of the two gaps comparing evaluative and performative indicators of role ideals (i.e., conception-performance gaps and perception-performance gaps), discrepancies are the largest for public service-oriented roles such as the watchdog and civic roles (see Chapters 4, 6 and 7). As is described in earlier research, our analyses imply that particular roles relating to journalism as a profession that serve the public good appear to be the most difficult to perform in actual news. With public service-oriented roles revealing the largest gaps in terms of conception-performance and conception-perception discrepancies, these findings indicate that journalists are indeed aware of the discrepancies between their ideals and what their media organizations actually do, and that they may use some internal strategies to deal with such discrepancies, as discussed in the theoretical framework of this chapter.

As even conception-perception gaps approximately reproduce the relative magnitude of conception-performance and perception-performance gaps—showing the most pronounced discrepancies in the watchdog and civic roles—journalists appear to be aware that roles are not always as well implemented as they would like them to be. Journalists seem to adequately perceive gaps between ideals and institutional behavior. However, conception-perception gaps were generally much less pronounced, which might indicate that journalists deal with conception-performance discrepancies by reconciling them at the perceptional, evaluative level. That is, journalists may—intentionally or unintentionally—adapt their views of reality (i.e., of how their media organizations perform specific roles) to their normative ideals (i.e., how they would personally like to perform specific roles) in order to solve the dissonance between both, which was shown to be most likely in the case of public service-oriented ideals. Although the reverse path would also be possible, that is, the adaptation of ideals to reality, this seems less likely due to the pronounced gaps between individual role conceptions and actual role performance.

The smallest discrepancies across all three types of gaps occurred in regard to roles that allow journalists' individual viewpoints (e.g., interventionist), political (e.g., loyal-facilitator), and economic influences (e.g., infotainment) to affect the news to some extent.

Taken together, these findings suggest that journalists are generally better able to adequately recognize and even implement roles that aim to influence the audience than public service-oriented roles, which tend to be strongly affected by structural and social-level factors (see Chapters 10 and 11).

Our analyses of the link as a relationship between ideals and news practices also revealed that the performance of roles that more readily accept that particular interests affect news coverage (i.e., interventionist, loyal-facilitator, infotainment, service) was closely associated with the journalists' role conception and perceived role enactment, with correlations of between ß = .08 and ß = .26. By contrast, the two public service-oriented roles showed no relationship between role conception, perceived role enactment, and actual performance.

Indeed, our findings reveal that ideals and perceptions of the civic and the watchdog roles were not negatively related to the performance of these two roles, which might well have been an outcome of the relationship analysis given the pronounced gaps found for the two roles. Instead, they do not relate to role performance at all. This is a key result of our analyses, and might be seen as another indication of the limitations that journalists face in regard to adequately reflecting on and implementing their role ideals. It may also be taken as another sign of journalists rationalizing or dis-identifying with discrepancies between perceptions and behaviors. Previous research has found that this is especially likely to occur when these discrepancies relate to roles that touch on the core democratic functions of professional journalism, which undoubtedly include watchdog and civic orientations.

Surprisingly, while journalistic cultures differ substantially in terms of role conception and role performance, the countries in our sample showed similarly evident gaps between journalists' conceptions/perceptions and their newspaper organizations' performance. With regard to perception-performance gaps, these similarities between countries are most pronounced for the civic and watchdog roles. In other words, journalists across countries showed similarly large gaps between how they evaluate the performance of these roles and how their newspapers actually engage in them. By contrast, largest differences between countries emerged with regards to the interventionist and the loyal-facilitator role. This was true for both perception-performance gaps and conception-performance gaps, while country differences were smallest for consumer-oriented roles such as service and infotainment. These results could, on the one hand, indicate how specific journalistic traditions affect journalists' ability to put their ideals into practice, as we see in the case of the interventionist role (see Chapter 5). On the other hand, they could be an effect of the different contexts in which journalists operate across the countries analyzed.

Our study broadens the scope of inquiry for future scholarship. Specifically, more work is needed to investigate which individual, organizational, or societal control-level actions render specific gaps and relationships between journalistic ideals and journalistic performance across and within countries. At the same time, future studies must address the extent to which the patterns we identified hold true when analyzing the performance of journalistic roles in other traditional media platforms and social media spaces.

Note

1 Kerrick, Anderson, and Swales (1964) and Greenberg and Tannenbaum (1962) also used experimental designs, although their evidence suggests that reporters' attitudes have little impact on their performance.

References

Ashforth, B. (2012). *Role transitions in organizational life: An identity-based perspective.* NJ: Routledge.
Ashforth, B., & Kreiner, G. (2002). Normalizing emotion in organizations: Making the extraordinary seem ordinary. *Human Resource Management Review, 12*(2), 215–235.
Bergen, L. (1991). Journalists' best work. In D. H. Weaver & G. C. Wilhoit (Eds.), *The American journalist: A portrait of U.S. news people and their work* (2nd ed., pp. 194–210). Bloomington, IN: Indiana University Press.
Boczkowski, P. (2011). *News at work: Imitation in an age of information abundance.* Chicago: University of Chicago Press.
Brants, K. (2013). Trust, cynicism, and responsiveness: The uneasy situation of journalism in democracy. In C. Peters & M. Broersma (Eds.), *Rethinking journalism: Trust and participation in a transformed news landscape* (pp. 15–27). New York: Routledge.
Bro, P. (2008). Normative navigation in the news media. *Journalism, 9*(3), 309–329.
Brunsson, N. (1993). Ideas and actions: Justification and hypocrisy as alternatives to control. *Accounting, Organizations and Society, 18*(6), 489–506.
Culbertson, H. (1983). Three perspectives on American journalism. *Journalism Monographs, 83.*
Drew, D. (1975). Reporters' attitudes, expected meetings with source and journalistic objectivity. *Journalism Quarterly, 52*(2), 219–271.
Festinger, L. (1957). *A theory of cognitive dissonance.* Evanston, IL: Row, Peterson.
Greenberg, B. S., & Tannenbaum, P. H. (1962). Communicator performance under cognitive stress. *Journalism Quarterly, 39*(2), 169–178.
Greil, A., & Rudy, D. (1984). Social cocoons: Encapsulation and identity transformation organizations. *Sociological Inquiry, 54,* 260–278.
Hallin, D. (2017). Preface. In C. Mellado, L. Hellmueller, & W. Donsbach (Eds.), *Journalistic role performance: Concepts, models and measures* (pp. xi–xvi). New York: Routledge.
Hanitzsch, T., & Mellado, C. (2011). What shapes the news around the world? How journalists in eighteen countries perceive influences on their work. *International Journal of Press/Politics, 16,* 404–426.
Heckhausen, J., & Schulz, R. (1995). A life-span theory of control. *Psychological Review, 102,* 284–304.
Hooker, C., King, C., & Leask, J. (2012). Journalists' views about reporting avian influenza and a potential pandemic: A qualitative study. *Influenza and Other Respiratory Viruses, 6*(3), 224–229.
Humanes, M. L., & Roses, S. (2018). Journalistic role performance in the Spanish national press. *International Journal of Communication, 12*(22), 1032–1053.

Kerrick, J. S., Anderson, T. E., & Swales, L. B. (1964). Balance and the writer's attitude in news stories and editorials. *Journalism Quarterly*, *41*(2), 207–215.

Klemm, C., Das, E., & Hartmann, T. (2019). Changed priorities ahead: Journalists' shifting role perceptions when covering public health crises. *Journalism*, *20*(9), 1223–1241.

Landy, R. (1993). *Persona and performance. The meaning of role in drama, therapy, and everyday life*. New York: Guilford.

Laurent, A. (1978). Managerial subordinancy: A neglected aspect of organizational hierarchies. *Academy of Management Review*, *20*, 311–342.

Mellado, C. (2015). Professional roles in news content: Six dimensions of journalistic role performance. *Journalism Studies*, *16*(4), 596–614.

Mellado, C., & Humanes, M. L. (2012). Modeling perceived professional autonomy in Chilean journalism. *Journalism*, *13*(8), 985–1003.

Mellado, C., Mothes, C., Hallin, D., Humanes, M. L., Lauber, M., Mick, J., . . Olivera, D. (2020). Investigating the gap between newspaper journalists' role conceptions and role performance in nine European, Asian and Latin American countries. *International Journal of Press/Politics* https://doi.org/10.1177/1940161220910106

Mellado, C., & van Dalen, A. (2014). Between rhetoric and practice. *Journalism Studies*, *15*(6), 859–878.

Mothes, C. (2014). *Objectivity as a professional cornerstone in journalism: A dissonance-theoretical comparison of journalists and non-journalists*. Baden-Baden: Nomos.

Patterson, T., & Donsbach, W. (1996). News decisions: Journalists as partisan actors. *Political Communication*, *13*(4), 455–468.

Rosenthal, D. (1990). *At the heart of the bomb: The dangerous allure of weapons work*. Reading, MA: Addison-Wesley.

Roses, S., & Humanes, M. L. (2019). Conflicts in the professional roles of journalists in Spain: Ideals and practice. *Comunicar*, *58*(XXVII), 65–74.

Rothbaum, F., Weisz, J. R., & Snyder, S. S. (1982). Changing the world and changing the self: A two-process model of perceived control. *Journal of Personality and Social Psychology*, *42*(1), 5–37.

Ryfe, D. M. (2020). The role of self-reports in the study of news production. *Journalism*, *21*(3), 349–364.

Scholl, A., & Weischenberg, S. (1998). *Journalismus in der Gesellschaft. Theorie, Methodologie und Empirie [Journalism in society: Theory, methodology, and empirical results]*. Opladen, Wiesbaden: Westdeutscher Verlag.

Schudson, M. (2011). *The sociology of news* (2nd ed.). New York: W.W. Norton & Co.

Starck, K., & Soloski, J. (1977). Effect of reporter predisposition in covering controversial story. *Journalism Quarterly*, *54*(1), 120–125.

Tandoc, E., Hellmueller, L., & Vos, T. (2013). Mind the gap: Between role conception and role enactment. *Journalism Practice*, *7*(5), 539–554.

van Dalen, A., De Vreese, C., & Albæk, E. (2012). Different roles, different content? A four-country comparison of the role conceptions and reporting styles of political journalists. *Journalism*, *13*, 903–922.

van Dalen, A., De Vreese, C., & Albæk, E. (2017). Mixed quantitative methods approach to journalistic role performance research. In C. Mellado, L.

Hellmueller, & W. Donsbach (Eds.), *Journalistic role performance: Comcepts, contexts, and methods* (pp. 189–205). New York: Routledge.

Waisbord, S. (2013). *Reinventing professionalism: Journalism and news in global perspective.* Cambridge: Polity.

Weischenberg, S., Malik, M., & Scholl, A. (2006). *Die Souf eure der Mediengesellschaft: Report über die Journalisten in Deutschland.* [The prompters of the media society. Report about journalists in Germany]. Konstanz, Germany: UVK.

Wyss, V. (2008). Das Doppelgesicht des redaktionellen Managements: 'Heuchelei' in der Qua- litätssicherung [The two-faced nature of editorial management: 'Hypocrisy' in quality management]. In B. Pörksen, W. Loosen, & A. Scholl (Eds.), *Paradoxien des Journalismus. Theorie—Empirie—Praxis* [*Paradoxes in journalism: Theory, empirical findings, and media practice*] (pp. 123–143). Wiesbaden: VS Verlag für Sozialwissenschaften.

9 Journalistic Role Performance
A News-Story-Level Approach

Edson Tandoc Jr., Patric Raemy, Svetlana Pasti, and Nikos Panagiotou

This chapter focuses on the impact of news story elements on journalistic role performance.

While early literature presumed that journalists' role conceptions would manifest in their output (e.g., Culbertson, 1983), a growing body of studies has examined the link between journalistic role conception and performance, addressing both news outputs (Mellado et al., 2020; Mellado & Van Dalen, 2013; Tandoc, Hellmueller, & Vos, 2013) and the ways in which journalists perform their roles outside of traditional and organizational outlets, such as on their social media accounts (Tandoc, Cabañes, & Cayabyab, 2019; Mellado & Ovando, 2020).

While this body of work is illuminating, journalistic performance is also influenced by different factors at multiple levels. One area that has been overlooked by previous studies is the impact of elements and characteristics in news stories on the presence of different professional roles in the news. Most of the time, individual journalists affiliated with news organizations do not have exclusive control over the final content of their news outputs. Some factors that dictate journalistic content, and hence journalistic performance, are beyond journalists' control. This includes the focus of news events or issues, their location, and the sources involved in these events, all of which shape how these events are represented in the news. These news-level-story factors can also affect the type and extent of journalistic role performances that manifest in the news.

Such factors are related to, if not shaped by, news routines. Numerous studies have examined the ways in which news routines shape news selection (e.g., Atton & Wickenden, 2005; Gans, 1979; Shoemaker, Eichholz, Kim, & Wrigley, 2001). Therefore, news routines might also be able to account for the extent to which journalists are able to perform particular roles as manifested in the news content they produce. News routines ingrained in journalists through a process of socialization—which are therefore usually beyond the control of individual reporters and editors—can also explain the link between journalistic role conception and performance (see Chapter 8).

Few studies have explored routinized journalistic performance focusing on the manifestations of routines at the news-story-level. In this chapter, we explore (1) elements that rely more on routinized actions and might be coupled with journalistic roles and (2) how these elements affect journalistic role performance in news content. We also discuss why news should not only be seen as the result of journalists' individual decisions, but also as the output of routinized organizational processes (Mellado, Hellmueller, & Donsbach, 2017), while exploring which elements could be connected to routinized actions and role performance. Finally, the influence of these elements on role performance is empirically tested and discussed. Since news stories are nested within news organizations, which are in turn nested within countries, we controlled for the effects of organization and country differences.

The Coupling of News-Story-Level Factors and Role Performance

Many scholars critically discuss the link between journalists' role ideals and their manifestations in news content. Studies focusing on the link between role conception and performance often stumble over the neglect of routinized and hence less reflected news work. News routines refer to the "patterned, repeated practices and forms media workers use to do their jobs" (Shoemaker & Reese, 1996, p. 105). In a profession marked by unexpected events, news routines help journalists make their daily work more predictable and reduce uncertainty by standardizing day-to-day procedures (Tandoc & Duffy, 2019). This is useful given how journalists are confronted by "finite organizational resources and an infinite supply of potential raw material" (Shoemaker & Reese, 2013, p. 168). News routines also facilitate a news organization's control over its journalists (Berkowitz, 1997), as well as journalists' control over their profession (Karlsson, 2010). For example, journalists tend to classify events they encounter as hard news, soft news, spot news, developing news, or continuing news. Each type comes with particular expectations and work demands, providing some form of control in an otherwise uncontrollable and unexpected situation (Tuchman, 1978). Following this, it can be assumed that journalists not only classify events as certain story types, but also write them in a certain routinized style.

News routines stem from three domains: the demands of the audience, the goals of the organization, and the impact of suppliers of content (Shoemaker & Reese, 2013). For example, news values—a set of criteria used or invoked to evaluate events as newsworthy—represent judgments of what would interest and meet the expectations of audiences, ensuring the sustainability of news production. The routines of fact-checking and objectivity also ensure that organizations are protected from libel suits or allegations of bias (Shoemaker & Reese, 2013; Tuchman, 1972). These domains affect the kinds of routinized practices used in newsrooms and the extent to which they are deployed. They can also explain similarities across different organizations and media cultures. Thus, news routines link individual journalists to their respective news organizations and to the journalism profession as a whole. By standardizing news production, news routines also tend to homogenize news outputs. However, they also operate within larger organizational and socio-cultural contexts. To understand the effects of news routines on news outputs, we also need to account for variations in journalistic cultures.

In this chapter, we focus on the impact of news-story-level factors, which we define as manifestations of news routines, on the performance of roles in the news. In the following sections we discuss three potential influences of news routines in role performance: news topic, which manifests the beat system; news sources, which shape sourcing patterns; and geographic focus, which impacts both the scope of the story and the news value of proximity.

News Topics

News organizations depend on information, and journalists must therefore know where and how to find stories. The beat system has become a basic routine across news organizations. Journalists are assigned to particular thematic or geographic beats, and wait for or find newsworthy events or information to report about (Reich, 2014). Journalists working the same beat can be expected to have shared perspectives (Schudson, 2003; Donsbach, 2004). The focus of an article can affect how it is reported and may shape role performance. Studies have found that role performance varies depending on thematic beats as measured in terms of news topic (Mellado & Lagos, 2014) and that certain news topics predict the performance of civic and watchdog roles (Hellmueller, Mellado, Blumell, & Huemmer, 2016).

Hellmueller and Mellado (2016) have shown that news stories citing political sources much more often refer to the watchdog role in the United States than in Chile, where journalists using political sources perform the interventionist, infotainment, or civic journalistic roles instead. Focusing on the watchdog model, Hellmueller et al. (2016) also found that in newspaper coverage about politics in the United States, the watchdog model is frequently performed in stories dealing with the government, police and crime, while the civic role is more strongly present in stories covering issues such as human rights, demonstrations, and religion. Humanes and Roses (2018) report a strong performance of the watchdog role in news items about police and crime in Spanish newspapers, while this role is less represented in economic news. The service role is typically performed in pieces about health, accidents and natural disasters, social problems, education, transportation, and energy and environment, while the infotainment role has the strongest presence in news items covering police and crime, accidents and natural disasters, health, social problems, and human rights (Humanes & Roses, 2018). In their study of Latin American journalistic cultures, Mellado et al. (2017) found a high presence of the interventionist role in news stories on social issues. For their part, Chinese journalists often perform this role when they write about energy, environment, economy and business, and education (Wang, Sparks, Lü, & Huang, 2017). However, these studies were conducted within specific country or regional contexts. Given that this chapter draws on data across multiple countries, we propose the following research question:

RQ1: Controlling for the effects of organization and country, which news topics are associated with which types of role performance?

News Sources

In addition to obtaining news from their beats, journalists rely on news sources for their supply of stories. But sourcing patterns are heavily dependent on the availability and ease of access to particular news sources. As a result, news selection becomes highly susceptible to the influence of elite sources, often at the expense of minority voices (e.g., Franklin & Murphy, 1991; Schlesinger, 1978; Tandoc & Skoric, 2010). Therefore, news sources also structure how journalists do their jobs and shape how news gets produced. For example, scholars have noted how public relations practitioners have influenced the news as journalists turn to them for information (Cottle, 2000; Lewis, Williams, & Franklin, 2008), giving rise to what some refer to as information subsidies. These subsidies make journalists dependent on a steady supply of information that is heavily reliant on public relations (Turk, 1985). Indeed, a consistent criticism of the impact of news routines is that they drive reporters to individuals and groups that are already in a position to provide them with news stories, such as government officials and politicians. Such sourcing patterns can affect the content of the news that is produced (Shoemaker & Reese, 2013).

Information sources include individuals, documents, press releases, and other media reports (Soley, 2008). News topic usually affects the choice of source. For unplanned events, "reporters locate individuals who were involved in, or who observed, the event" (Soley, 2008, p. 1). For beat news stories, reporters use routine sources who tend to be of higher status, male, and have more influence than the average citizen (Soley, 2008, p. 1). Gans (1979, p. 125) argues that journalists "find it easier to make contact with sources similar to them in class position, as well as race, age, and other characteristics." For example, Zeldes and Fico (2005) found that female journalists in the U.S. were more likely to use female sources than male journalists; in other countries, such as China and India, news organizations send female journalists "to charm" male political officials (Gudipaty et al., 2018, p. 117).

The digitization of journalism has generated new sourcing patterns for journalists and the public. The relationship between journalists and their news sources is changing. Social media has provided news sources with a platform to directly broadcast their opinions or announcements without going through journalists. Ordinary audience members have become news sources, too. Individuals can use their mobile phones and social media accounts to report on newsworthy events they witness first-hand. Still, studies find that sourcing patterns in newspapers remain unchanged, privileging elite sources even in the age of social media (Paulussen & Harder, 2014; Tandoc, 2018).

Economic factors such as the reduction of resources in newsrooms can cause journalists to rely on external sources such as PR services, news agencies, and pre-packaged information material. In authoritarian political systems like China and Russia, state media journalists are assigned the roles of *propagandist* and *social organizer*. Their main sources of information are the government and state agencies. These sourcing patterns, which are skewed towards the elite, can pose threats to the quality of news because they may lead to a reduction in the diversity of sources and their verification (Davis, 2002, 2008; Johnston & Forde, 2009). Sourcing patterns also have implications for role performance. For example, while journalists identify with a particular role, the extent to which they can perform that role is affected by the quality and range of information they can access from available sources. Thus, guided by this work on the impact of sources of news content, we also explore how sourcing patterns shape journalistic performance. Therefore, we ask:

RQ2: *Controlling for the effects of organization and country, which types of sources are associated with which role performances?*

Geographic Focus

Finally, the scope of a news story can also shape it. Scope refers to the "contextual spin that journalists put on an event" (Shoemaker & Reese, 2013, p. 176). Scope is related to but broader than proximity, which refers to "the closeness of the media organization to an event" (Shoemaker & Reese, 2013, p. 176). An event's proximity—both geographic and psychological—to the news organization can affect how it is eventually presented to the audience in terms of scope. For example, a farmer's reduced yield in a small town far from the metropolis might be geographically distant from the news organization, but it can be presented as emblematic of decreasing state support and protection of agriculture in the country. Thus, a story's geographic focus can affect both the extent to which an event gets covered and how it is reported.

Proximity is often considered a news value that makes an event or issue newsworthy. If an event or an issue is geographically or psychologically close or relevant to a news organization, that news organization will be more likely to report on it. Studies have explored the link between geographic focus and news outputs, mainly focusing on local journalists. For example, Harnischmacher (2015) found that local journalists view local relevance, proximity, and immediacy as important factors, and see more sensationalistic factors such as negativity and unexpectedness (and also personalization) as rather unimportant. Arnold and Wagner (2018) compared the reporting style of metropolitan and local newspapers in Germany and found that local newspapers were more likely to report more service-oriented news, but did so less critically and with less controversial articles and background information. By contrast, metropolitan newspapers' content seems to be more relevant, critical, and diverse. Statham (2008) found greater differences between transnational and sub-national European newspapers than between cross-national variations. Transnational journalists make more efforts to influence European Union actors than their national colleagues. Boukes and Vliegenthart (2017) found that regional newspapers tend to focus on the so-called tabloid news factors: personification and negativity. Regional news also tends to include more ordinary people as sources in their articles (Reich, 2012).

Unlike most media in large urban centers, local journalists often follow the core aim of promoting the common good of the community by fostering social networks and community dialogue (Richards, 2013). Local journalists seem to see themselves as strong advocates for their communities and their development. As such, they serve as a check on local governments to ensure that such development takes place (Hanusch, 2015). These articles make it clear that the geographic focus of the journalists or the events matter and are closely linked. Local journalists will logically be closer to local events and issues. Since studies found that journalists seem to care about issues pertaining to their own communities, the performance of particular roles might also be affected by the geographic scope of the story. Therefore, we also explore the link between the geographic focus of the news story and the role performance manifested in that story. Thus, we ask:

> RQ3: *Controlling for the effects of organization and country, how is the geographic focus of the story related to the presence of different professional roles in the news?*

Analytical Strategy

We first explored the link between a story's central theme and the role performance manifested in it. As expected, government/legislature accounts for the highest number of articles (25.3%), followed by economy (18.5%), and police (13.4%). The dominance of government/legislature as a news topic holds true in most countries except for Switzerland, Germany, Brazil, Chile, Philippines, and Ecuador, where the most reported news topic is economy/business; Ireland, where the most-reported topic is police/crime; and Malaysia, where the most-reported topic is campaigns/elections (see Table 9.1).

To understand the impact of sourcing patterns, we first account for the impact of the number of sources mentioned in the story. This refers to the total number of sources quoted. Next, we examined the effect of using document and human sources. A document source is a publication or other record or document that provides information and may be used in other publications as well. Examples of document sources include official records, press releases, and publications, or when the news item quotes another news media report. Some 33.2% of all articles use document sources, while 63.5% use human sources. Finally, we coded for the presence of each of the following types of sources: anonymous, media, expert, civic society, ordinary people, business, and state/political party.

The geographic focus of the story refers to the geographic area where the news item takes place. If there is a mix of geographic foci, the coders coded for the geographic area that was emphasized based on frequency or space. A news story was coded as 1) local, if the story focused on the metropolitan area within which the media outlet is published; 2) non-local/national, if the story focused on a region outside of the media source's metropolitan area or the nation as a whole; and 3) international, if the story took place in a different nation.

Given that this chapter is focused on the impact of news-story-level characteristics, the analysis also controlled for variation in role performance due to organizational characteristics or country-level factors. Therefore, in our three-level model, we predicted each of the role performances based on story-level factors while controlling for variation at the level of organization and country.

Results

To examine the link between news-story-level factors (i.e., topics, sourcing patterns, and geographic focus) and journalistic role performance, we ran a series of multilevel models. We accounted for news-story-level factors—news topics, sourcing patterns, and geographic focus—to predict each of the six role performances mapped out in Chapter 4 and discussed in detail by Chapters 5, 6, and 7: interventionist, watchdog, loyal-facilitator, service, infotainment, and civic roles. Since organizational and country-level influences might also affect role performance (see Chapters 10 and 11), we controlled for these variations by including

Table 9.1 Topics, Sources, and Geographic Focus

Domain	Items	Overall	Russia	Greece	Spain	Hungary	Switzerland	Poland	Germany	Mexico	Cuba
Topic	Government/legislature	25.3	42.1	24.8	22.2	29.7	25.6	19.2	16.0	34.2	36.4
	Campaigns/elections/politics	11.8	5.4	24.7	10.2	9.7	10.3	14.6	22.2	13.5	6.8
	Police and crime	13.4	15.0	4.6	19.1	23.7	13.6	15.0	11.4	16.7	.4
	Courts	4.2	4.3	4.0	4.6	3.6	1.6	8.4	2.0	1.9	1.2
	Defense/military/national security	2.4	2.7	2.2	1.9	1.1	.6	1.7	3.9	.8	20.4
	Economy and business	18.5	5.0	17.1	23.4	6.9	29.7	10.6	24.8	6.3	8.2
	Education	3.5	2.9	1.7	2.4	5.0	1.4	3.9	4.0	2.4	4.6
	Energy, environment, and climate change	2.4	2.6	2.9	1.9	1.7	2.2	1.1	3.7	1.9	.6
	Transportation	1.9	2.8	1.1	.9	1.7	1.1	.9	1.8	.9	4.0
	Housing, infrastructure, and public works	1.8	5.0	.2	.4	1.3	1.9	3.1	1.7	.9	2.4
	Accidents and natural disasters	4.2	3.5	1.3	1.9	3.8	5.9	3.8	1.2	2.9	9.2
	Health	3.8	2.9	3.7	2.9	6.4	2.3	5.0	2.8	3.1	.6
	Religion and churches	1.0	.4	.1	2.3	1.1	.6	3.7	1.3	1.7	5.2
	Human rights	1.2	.5	1.7	1.5	.4	.7	1.1	.4	3.4	36.4
	Demonstrations and protests	2.6	2.0	5.8	3.4	2.6	1.2	3.9	1.1	4.9	6.8
	Social problems	2.0	2.9	4.0	.9	1.5	1.2	4.2	1.5	4.7	.4

(Continued)

Table 9.1 (Continued)

Domain	Items	Overall	Russia	Greece	Spain	Hungary	Switzerland	Poland	Germany	Mexico	Cuba
Sources	Number of sources (Mean)	2.31	2.02	1.79	1.85	2.64	1.74	3.37	2.79	1.74	1.67
	Document source	33.2	21.7	47.0	34.3	38.5	52.4	34.0	47.3	28.8	17.4
	Human source	72.0	79.2	48.9	73.0	81.4	46.7	86.7	79.7	62.1	77.7
	State/political party source	56.8	58.4	51.5	64.3	52.8	42.1	63.8	64.4	66.8	29.5
	Business source	16.2	4.7	21.7	12.8	10.6	24.9	16.9	25.3	6.6	15.5
	Civic society source	11.9	6.7	16.0	9.4	11.8	10.7	18.5	13.9	15.0	25.2
	Ordinary people source	13.9	9.9	5.5	6.8	19.9	8.8	19.1	7.5	9.6	18.0
	Media source	11.7	2.7	25.4	5.9	21.6	15.1	15.2	16.7	4.6	6.9
	Expert source	14.3	14.6	7.2	15.2	25.9	7.6	31.2	19.8	7.4	30.3
	Anonymous source	12.3	7.5	10.2	4.3	12.2	1.8	12.7	1.8	3.0	0.0
Geographic Focus	Local	28.2	29.0	22.9	50.2	38.9	6.8	23.8	11.1	37.7	27.8
	National	61.2	62.5	54.6	33.9	51.8	86.0	67.7	80.2	53.9	55.7
	International	10.6	8.5	22.5	15.9	9.3	7.2	8.5	8.6	8.5	16.6

(Continued)

Table 9.1 (Continued)

Domain	Items	Argentina	Brazil	Chile	Malaysia	Philippines	China	Ireland	Ecuador	Hong Kong	United States
Topic	Government/legislature	26.1	23.5	11.9	17.3	11.7	45.5	9.5	11.2	33.4	17.8
	Campaigns/elections/politics	11.3	13.1	17.6	22.2	8.2	.4	8.0	17.3	.9	16.7
	Police and crime	16.2	10.6	12.6	12.4	19.8	6.9	18.7	5.2	10.4	14.5
	Courts	5.4	2.8	6.6	3.1	4.7	1.5	16.8	14.6	.6	7.1
	Defense/military/national security	1.0	1.1	1.7	3.1	4.1	4.6	.4	3.8	9.0	3.5
	Economy and business	15.0	31.5	22.5	7.0	31.7	16.2	17.1	15.7	16.1	9.0
	Education	2.1	3.0	4.3	8.7	2.1	7.6	3.9	5.0	2.7	3.8
	Energy, environment, and climate change	1.5	2.5	2.4	1.5	3.1	3.2	.5	3.7	2.2	3.8
	Transportation	3.0	.4	3.7	1.7	1.6	3.0	1.3	3.5	3.8	1.5
	Housing, infrastructure, and public works	1.9	1.7	3.3	4.7	1.7	1.3	1.7	3.5	1.0	.8
	Accidents and natural disasters	3.3	1.1	5.1	7.4	5.5	5.6	7.5	5.2	10.5	7.3
	Health	3.4	3.0	3.9	3.5	2.7	3.6	9.2	3.4	3.9	7.3
	Religion and churches	.6	.4	.8	3.1	.8	.0	.8	.7	.1	1.3
	Human rights	2.3	1.0	.1	.6	.4	.2	.1	3.8	2.3	.9
	Demonstrations and protests	5.1	3.4	2.3	1.9	.8	.2	2.4	1.1	2.7	.7
	Social problems	1.8	1.1	1.4	1.9	1.2	.3	1.9	2.3	.7	3.9
Sources	Number of sources (Mean)	1.93	2.65	2.05	1.26	1.70	3.13	2.26	1.91	2.78	5.18
	Document source	37.1	37.8	25.0	4.1	20.6	31.3	23.9	23.8	27.9	41.2
	Human source	63.5	87.2	77.7	97.3	80.3	67.7	88.5	61.9	74.4	93.7
	State/political party source	43.8	53.7	53.4	58.7	56.8	69.8	52.0	46.3	57.2	76.0
	Business source	10.5	23.6	19.2	7.7	18.5	12.7	20.1	5.5	12.7	34.3
	Civic society source	16.0	13.8	9.9	14.7	12.2	3.3	14.1	4.6	4.1	20.2
	Ordinary people source	14.4	9.3	16.2	14.4	4.7	23.3	28.2	9.3	29.7	29.8
	Media source	13.1	13.0	3.8	2.7	4.6	9.5	5.6	4.3	39.5	14.8
	Expert source	10.2	21.0	9.2	10.8	4.6	15.6	8.1	10.1	21.1	33.8
	Anonymous source	16.3	9.6	12.7	1.2	4.1	41.2	9.7	2.1	43.7	9.9
Geographic Focus	Local	52.8	9.1	58.6	41.3	62.0	1.7	1.8	33.8	0.1	9.9
	National	34.0	82.5	31.7	56.9	22.6	89.1	94.6	49.3	88.2	88.9
	International	13.1	8.4	9.7	1.7	15.4	9.2	3.7	17.0	11.7	1.3

the random intercepts for these two higher levels in the models, while the story-level factors were included as fixed effects (see Table 9.2).

RQ1 asked about which news topics are related to which journalistic role performances. When it comes to predicting the interventionist role, all news topics except housing and social problems were negatively related. We observed the strongest negative relationships between the interventionist role and stories about courts (b = -.07, p < .05, β = -.06), accidents (b = -.07, p < .05, β = -.09), and the police (b = -.06, p < .05, β = -.09). When it comes to the watchdog role performance, all topics except economy and religion were positive predictors. The topics with the strongest relationship to the watchdog role performance include courts (b = .08, p < .05, β = .14), police (b = .05, p < .05, β = .14), government (b = .03, p < .05, β = .11), and campaigns (b = .04, p < .05, β = .11). This makes sense, as the watchdog function is often aimed at keeping the state in check.

When it comes to loyal-facilitator role performance, all topics except government, housing, the economy, and education were significant predictors, but only defense was a positive predictor. The strongest negative effects were exerted by police (b = -.02, p < .05, β = -.06) and court (b = -.02, p < .05, β = -.04) topics. It seems that writing about crime and justice stories ran counter to the performance of the loyal-facilitator role, which is marked by cooperating with the establishment. In terms of service role performance, all topics except defense, religion, human rights, and protests were significant predictors, with campaigns, police, and courts as negative predictors. The strongest effects were seen from health (b = .09, p < .05, β = .13), economy (b = .03, p < .05, β = .10), and transportation (b = .07, p < .05, β = .08) topics. Indeed, these topics tend to involve people's day-to-day lives.

In terms of infotainment role performance, all topics except accidents and human rights were significant predictors, but only police and religion were positive predictors. Understandably, the strongest negative predictors are government (b = -.03, p < .05, β = -.10) and economy (b = -.04, p < .05, β = -.12). Finally, when it comes to the civic role, all topics except police, courts, and religion were significant positive predictors, with the strongest effects from protests (b = .19, p < .05, β = .24), social problems (b = .10, p < .05, β = .11), and housing (b = .06, p < .05, β = .06). Indeed, these are news topics that concern social issues.

RQ2 asked about the impact of sourcing patterns on journalistic role performance. The analysis found that number of sources had significant and positive effects on interventionist (b= .013, p < .05, β = .13), watchdog (b = .007, p < .05, β = .14), loyal (b= .011, p < .05, β = .24), service (b = .001, p < .05, β = .02), infotainment (b = .003, p < .05, β = .05), and civic (b = .002, p < .05, β = .04) role performances. When it comes to using document and human sources, the analysis found that the use of document sources had very small positive effects on the performance of the interventionist (b = .01, p < .05, β = .02), watchdog (b = .01, p < .05, β = .04), and service (b = .004, p < .05, β = .02) roles. It had a small negative effect on the loyal-facilitator (b = -.002, p < .05, β = -.001) role, and no significant relationship with the performance of the infotainment and civic roles. By contrast, the use of human sources had small positive relationships with the performance of the interventionist (b = .02, p < .05, β = .04) and infotainment (b = .02, p < .05, β = .001) roles. It had a marginal and negative effect on service (b = -.005, p < .05, β = -.02) and civic (b = -.003, p < .05, β = -.01) roles, but no significant relationship with the performance of either the loyal-facilitator or watchdog roles.

We now focus on specific sources. When it comes to the interventionist role, all types of sources except civil society and media sources are positive predictors, and the strongest predictor is the use of ordinary people (b = .03, p < .05, β = .05). In terms of the watchdog role, all types of sources except expert and anonymous sources are significant positive predictors, and civil society sources are the strongest predictor (b = .02, p < .05, β = .06), underscoring the important role of civil society in keeping governments in check. When it comes to the loyal-facilitator role, all types of sources except civil society and ordinary people are positive predictors, with the use of state and political party sources as the strongest predictor (b = .008, p < .05, β = .04). In terms of the service role, all types of sources except state and political party sources are significant predictors, but media and anonymous sources are negative predictors. As expected, the expert source was the strongest predictor among all sources (b = .02, p < .05, β = .06) for the performance of the service role. All types of sources except anonymous sources are significant predictors for the infotainment role, but only ordinary people and media sources are positive predictors, with ordinary people as the strongest predictor (b = .08, p < .05, β = .22). In terms of the civic role, all types of sources except business and media are significant predictors, but media, expert, and anonymous sources are all negative predictors. The strongest predictors are ordinary people (b = .07, p < .05, β = .20) and civil society (b = .06, p < .05, β = .16) sources.

Finally, RQ3 asked about the link between the story's geographic focus and the performance of different roles. While there were significant and negative relationships between geographic focus (measured from local to international) and the performance of loyal-facilitator, service, infotainment, and civic roles, these were marginal in terms of magnitude. A small but significant positive relationship between geographic focus and the performance of the loyal-facilitator role was found (b = .01, p < .05, β = .06). This suggests that the more stories tend to focus on local events or issues, the more likely it is that the stories will exhibit the loyal-facilitator role (see Table 9.2). Negative relationships were found with service (b = -.002, p < .05, β = -.01), infotainment (b = -.003, p < .05, β = -.01), and civic (b = -.004, p < .05, β = -.02) roles.

Table 9.2 Story-Level Effects on Journalistic Role Performance

	Interventionist			Watchdog			Loyal-facilitator			Service			Infotainment			Civic		
	b (SE_b)	Lower	Upper	b (SE_b)	Lower	Upper	b (SE_b)	Lower	Upper	b (SE_b)	Lower	Upper	b (SE_b)	Lower	Upper	b (SE_b)	Lower	Upper
		95% CI			95% CI			95% CI			95% CI			95% CI			95% CI	
Fixed Effects																		
Intercept	.188 (.012)	.161	.215				.038 (.012)	.002	.074	.022 (.007)	.008	.036	.058 (.007)	.043	.072			
News Topic																		
Government/Legislature	-.030 (.004)	-.039	-.022	.034 (.002)	.030	.038				.008 (.002)	.003	.012	-.034 (.002)	-.039	-.029	.015 (.002)	.011	.020
Campaigns	-.015 (.005)	-.024	-.005	.037 (.002)	.032	.042	-.010 (.002)	-.014	-.006	-.014 (.003)	-.019	-.008	-.011 (.003)	-.016	-.005	.016 (.003)	.011	.021
Police	-.059 (.005)	-.068	-.050	.051 (.002)	.047	.056	-.021 (.002)	-.024	-.017	-.009 (.003)	-.014	-.004	.022 (.003)	.017	.027			
Courts	-.072 (.007)	-.085	-.059	.086 (.003)	.080	.093	-.024 (.002)	-.030	-.019	-.011 (.004)	-.018	-.004	-.019 (.004)	-.026	-.011			
Defense	-.036 (.008)	-.052	-.020	.026 (.004)	.018	.034	.012 (.003)	.005	.019				-.025 (.005)	-.034	-.016	.017 (.004)	.009	.025
Economy	-.027 (.005)	-.036	-.019							.033 (.002)	.028	.038	-.044 (.003)	-.049	-.039	.009 (.002)	.004	.013
Education	-.034 (.007)	-.047	-.020	.011 (.003)	.004	.018				.033 (.004)	.026	.041	-.035 (.004)	-.043	-.027	.038 (.004)	.031	.045
Energy	-.019 (.008)	-.035	-.003	.014 (.004)	.006	.022	-.009 (.003)	-.015	-.002	.038 (.004)	.030	.047	-.043 (.005)	-.052	-.034	.034 (.004)	.026	.043
Transportation	-.021 (.008)	-.039	-.004	.014 (.004)	.005	.022	-.008 (.004)	-.016	-.001	.066 (.005)	.056	.075	-.044 (.005)	-.054	-.034	.036 (.005)	.027	.045
Housing				.014 (.005)	.005	.023				.057 (.005)	.047	.067	-.052 (.005)	-.062	-.041	.061 (.005)	.052	.071
Accidents	-.069 (.006)	-.081	-.056	.013 (.003)	.007	.020	-.020 (.003)	-.026	-.015	.012 (.004)	.005	.019				.010 (.003)	.004	.017

(Continued)

Table 9.2 (Continued)

	Interventionist			Watchdog			Loyal-facilitator			Service			Infotainment			Civic		
		95% CI			95% CI			95% CI			95% CI			95% CI			95% CI	
	$b\ (SE_b)$	Lower	Upper	$b\ (SE_b)$	Lower	Upper	$b\ (SE_b)$	Lower	Upper	$b\ (SE_b)$	Lower	Upper	$b\ (SE_b)$	Lower	Upper	$b\ (SE_b)$	Lower	Upper
Fixed Effects																		
Health	-.054 (.007)	-.068	-.041	.011 (.003)	.004	.018	-.013 (.003)	-.019	-.008	.086 (.004)	.078	.093	-.030 (.004)	-.038	-.022	.025 (.004)	.018	.032
Religion	-.033 (.012)	-.057	-.009				-.018 (.005)	-.028	-.007				.015 (.007)	.002	.029			
Human Rights	-.026 (.011)	-.048	-.004	.045 (.006)	.034	.056	-.019 (.005)	-.028	-.009							.060 (.006)	.049	.071
Protests	-.040 (.008)	-.055	-.024	.045 (.004)	.037	.052	-.013 (.003)	-.020	-.007				-.034 (.004)	-.043	-.026	.193 (.004)	.185	.201
Social Problems				.031 (.004)	.023	.040	-.018 (.004)	-.025	-.010	.041 (.005)	.031	.050	-.010 (.005)	-.020	-.001	.101 (.005)	.092	.110
Sources																		
Number of sources	.013 (.001)	.012	.015	.007 (.000)	.006	.007				.001 (.000)	.000	.002	.003 (.000)	.002	.004	.003 (.000)	.002	.004
Document Sources	.009 (.003)	.004	.014	.014 (.001)	.011	.016	-.002 (.001)	-.005	.000	.004 (.000)	.002	.007						
Human Sources	.017 (.003)	.011	.024							-.005 (.002)	-.008	-.001	.020 (.002)	.016	.023	-.003 (.002)	-.006	.000
State/Political Sources	-.009 (.003)	-.015	-.003	.013 (.001)	.011	.016	.008 (.001)	.005	.010				-.012 (.002)	-.015	-.009	.003 (.001)	.001	.006
Business Sources	.009 (.003)	.002	.016	.008 (.002)	.005	.011	.007 (.005)	.004	.010				-.004 (.002)	-.008	.000			
Civic Society Sources				.023 (.002)	.019	.027							-.015 (.002)	-.019	-.011	.063 (.002)	.060	.067
Ordinary People Sources	.028 (.004)	.021	.035	.004 (.002)	.000	.007				.010 (.002)	.006	.013	.077 (.002)	.073	.081	.074 (.002)	.070	.077

(Continued)

Table 9.2 (Continued)

	Interventionist b (SE_b)	95% CI Lower	95% CI Upper	Watchdog b (SE_b)	95% CI Lower	95% CI Upper	Loyal-facilitator b (SE_b)	95% CI Lower	95% CI Upper	Service b (SE_b)	95% CI Lower	95% CI Upper	Infotainment b (SE_b)	95% CI Lower	95% CI Upper	Civic b (SE_b)	95% CI Lower	95% CI Upper
Fixed Effects																		
Media Sources				.014 (.002)	.011	.018	−.003 (.002)	−.006	.000				.004 (.002)	.000	.009			
Expert Sources	.018 (.003)	.011	.024				.003 (.001)	.000	.006	.022 (.002)	.018	.026	−.009 (.002)	−.013	−.005			
Anonymous Sources	.020 (.004)	.013	.027				−.006 (.002)	−.009	−.002	−.010 (.002)	−.014	−.006				−.012 (.002)	−.015	−.008
Geographic Focus							.011 (.001)	.009	.013	−.002 (.002)	−.004	.000	−.003 (.001)	−.005	−.001	−.005 (.001)	−.007	−.003
Covariance Parameters (ID)																		
Residual	.039 (.000)	.038	.039	.010 (.000)	.009	.010	.007 (.000)	.007	.007	.012 (.000)	.011	.012	.012 (.000)	.012	.013	.010 (.000)	.010	.010
Random Intercepts																		
Intercept Organization	.004 (.001)	.002	.006	.001 (.000)	.000	.001	.000 (.000)	.000	.000	.001 (.000)	.000	.001	.002 (.000)	.001	.002	.001 (.000)	.000	.001
Intercept Country	.002 (.001)	.000	.005	.001 (.000)	.000	.002	.005 (.002)	.003	.010	.001 (.000)	.000	.001	.001 (.000)	.000	.002	.001 (.000)	.000	.002
AIC (df)	−13783.8 (31)			−60108.6 (31)			−70771.0 (31)			−54386.8 (31)			−51845.0 (31)			−59050.1 (31)		
BIC (df)	−13460.6 (31)			−59785.4 (31)			−70447.8 (31)			−54063.6 (31)			−51521.8 (31)			−58726.9 (31)		

Note. Only results with $p < .05$ were retained.

Conclusion

The study of journalistic roles has expanded from focusing on what journalists conceive of as their roles to examining and measuring the manifestations of roles in journalistic performance. While examining role conceptions is important, different studies have established that journalists' personal traits and beliefs account for a small part of what shapes journalistic content (Mellado et al., 2020; Mellado et al., 2017; Mellado & Van Dalen, 2013; Tandoc et al., 2019; Tandoc & Takahashi, 2014). For example, traditional news outputs are usually susceptible to the demands, expectations, and limitations of the organizations that journalists find themselves in across different cultures.

As studies in journalistic roles expanded to examine news outputs, an increasing number of projects have found discrepancies between role conception and role performance. One explanation that has been proposed is the role of the organizational context surrounding news outputs. But one area of news production that has not been sufficiently explored when it comes to accounting for journalistic role performance is the characteristics of the news story themselves. This chapter started off with the assumption that news-story-level factors, which we argue are related to, if not shaped by, news routines, can help account for journalistic role performance. In coupling news-story-level factors with journalistic role performance, this chapter focused on three main components: news topic, sourcing patterns, and geographic focus of the story. While this is a novel approach to understanding journalistic performance, it is consistent with the idea that influences on news content go beyond the control of individual journalists. For example, specific topics are associated with certain types of sources and occur within a particular geographic focus that journalists themselves have to respond to but cannot control.

This study finds that news topic, news source, and geographic focus influence journalistic role performances. For example, state-related topics such as government issues, campaigns, and police and court stories positively relate to the performance of the watchdog role, while economy, transportation, and health topics were positively related to service role performance. Similarly, the use of civil society and ordinary people as sources was also related to the performance of the civic role. This provides support for the assumption that roles are context driven (Mellado, 2019), which means that certain topics tend to be associated to particular roles. In terms of geographic focus, the more local a story is, the more likely it is to exhibit the loyal-facilitator role; as the story becomes decoupled from a local perspective, the more likely it is to exhibit service, infotainment, and civic roles. Overall, these findings provide empirical support for the assumption that factors outside the control of individual journalists—such as the nature of the issues or events they cover and report on—also affect the extent to which particular roles can be performed. Moving forward, it is important to continue to theorize and examine the link between news-story-level factors and journalistic role performance, as the field continuously refines its explanation of journalistic role performance.

This chapter found that story-level characteristics are related to manifestations of journalistic roles in news content. However, it is also plausible that the relationship is more correlational than causal. That is, story-level factors might also be manifestations of particular role performances. This is something that future projects can help unpack. It is true that the story-level factors tested in this chapter refer to those that tend to be beyond the control of journalists, but this is not always the case. For example, while a news story about a government issue obviously entails the use of government sources, a journalist seeking to perform a civic role might also seek out the perspectives of ordinary people who will be affected by the issue. While reporters around the world are assigned to a specific geographic or thematic beat, in some media markets, shrinking newsroom sizes have led to the increase in the number of general assignment reporters or those who are assigned to any issue or event on a per-need basis. Thus, selection of news topics to pursue can also be a reflection of a journalist's individual judgment, such as the goal of performing a particular role. The extent to which the journalist can perform this role also partly depends on the nature of the story, including the topic, sources, and geographic considerations. Accounting for news story factors is therefore crucial to understanding journalistic role performance.

References

Arnold, K., & Wagner, A. (2018). Die Leistungen des Lokaljournalismus. Eine empirische Studie zur Qualität der Lokalberichterstattung in Zeitungen und Online-Angeboten. *Publizistik*, 2, 177–206.

Atton, C., & Wickenden, E. (2005). Sourcing routines and representation in alternative journalism: A case study approach. *Journalism Studies*, 6(3), 347–359. doi:10.1080/14616700500013200810

Berkowitz, D. (1997). *Social meanings of news: A text-reader*. Thousand Oaks, CA: Sage.

Boukes, M., & Vliegenthart, R. (2017/2020). A general pattern in the construction of economic newsworthiness? Analyzing news factors in popular, quality, regional, and financial newspapers. *Journalism*, 21(2), 279–300.

Cottle, S. (2000). New(s) times: Towards a 'second wave' of news ethnography *Communications*, 25, (1), 19–41.

Culbertson, H. (1983). Three perspectives on American journalism. *Journalism Monographs*, 83, 1–33.

Davis, A. (2002). *Public relations democracy: Public relations, politics and the mass media in Britain*. Manchester and New York: Manchester University Press.

Davis, A. (2008). Public relations in the news. In B. Franklin (Ed.), *Pulling newspapers apart: Analysing print journalism* (pp. 256–264). London: Routledge.

Donsbach, W. (2004). Psychology of news decisions: Factors behind journalists' professional behavior. *Journalism*, 5(2), 131–157.

Franklin, B., & Murphy, D. (1991). *Making the local news: Local journalism in context*. London: Routledge.

Gans, H. (1979). *Deciding what's news* (1st ed.). New York: Pantheon.

Gudipaty, N., Ramaprasad, J., Pasti, S., Lago, C., Li, X., & Rodny-Gumede, Y. (2018). Gender: Towards equality? In S. Pasti & J. Ramaprasad (Eds.), *Contemporary BRICS journalism: Non-Western media in transition* (pp. 104–129). London and New York: Routledge.

Hanusch, F. (2015). Transformative times: Australian journalists' perceptions of changes in their work. *Media International Australia, 155*(1), 38–53. doi.org/10.1177%2F1329878X1515500106

Harnischmacher, M. (2015). Journalism after all: Professionalism, content and performance -A comparison between alternative news websites of traditional newspapers in German local media markets. *Journalism, 16*(8), 1062–1084.

Hellmueller, L., & Mellado, C. (2016). Watchdogs in Chile and the United States: Comparing the networks of sources and journalistic role performance. *International Journal of Communication,10*, 3261–3280.

Hellmueller, L., Mellado, C., Blumell, L., & Huemmer, J. (2016). The contextualization of the watchdog and civic journalistic roles: Reevaluating journalistic role performance in U.S. newspapers. *Palabra Clave, 19*(4), 1072–1100.

Humanes, M., & Roses, S. (2018). Journalistic role performance in the Spanish national press. *International Journal of Communication, 12*, 1032–1053.

Johnston, J., & Forde, S. (2009). Not wrong for long': The role and penetration of news wire agencies in the 24/7 News Land-scape. *Global Media Journal: Australian Edition, 3*(2), 1–16.

Karlsson, M. (2010). Rituals of transparency. *Journalism Studies, 11*(4), 535–545. doi:10.1080/14616701003638400

Lewis, J., Williams, A., & Franklin, B. (2008). A compromised fourth estate? UK news journalism, public relations and news sources. *Journalism Studies, 9*(1), 1–20. doi:10.1080/14616700701767974

Mellado, C. (2019). Journalists' professional roles and role performance. In *Oxford research encyclopedia of communication*. Oxford: Oxford University. doi:10.1093/acrefore/9780190228613.013.832

Mellado, C., Hellmueller, L., & Donsbach, W. (Eds.). (2017). *Journalistic role performance: Concepts, contexts, methods.* London and New York: Routledge.

Mellado, C., Hellmueller, L., Márquez-Ramírez, M., Humanes, M. L., Sparks, C., Stepinska, A., . . Wang, H. (2017). The hybridization of journalistic cultures: A comparative study of journalistic role performance. *Journal of Communication, 67*(6), 944–967. doi:10.1111/jcom.12339

Mellado, C., & Lagos, C. (2014). Professional roles in news content: Analyzing journalistic performance in the Chilean national press. *International Journal of Communication, 8*, 2090–2112.

Mellado, C., Mothes, C., Hallin, D., Humanes, M. L., Lauber, M., Mick, J., . . Olivera, D. (2020). Investigating the gap between newspaper journalists' role conceptions and role performance in nine European, Asian and Latin American countries. *The International Journal of Press/Politics* (accepted for publication).

Mellado, C., & Ovando, A. (2020). How Chilean journalists use social media: Digital transformation and new forms of visibility and identity creation. *Palabra Clave* (accepted for publication).

Mellado, C., & Van Dalen, A. (2013). Between rhetoric and practice. *Journalism Studies, 15*(6), 859–878. doi:10.1080/1461670x.2013.838046

Paulussen, S., & Harder, R. A. (2014). Social media references in newspapers. *Journalism Practice, 8*(5), 542–551. doi:10.1080/17512786.2014.894327

Reich, Z. (2012). Journalism as bipolar interactional expertise. *Communication Theory, 22*(4), 339–358.

Reich, Z. (2014). 'Stubbornly Unchanged': A longitudinal study of news practices in the Israel press. *European Journal Communication, 29*, 351–370.

Richards, I. (2013). ERA 2012: Prelude to the aftermath? *Australian Journal Review, 35*(1), 11–13.

Schlesinger, P. (1978). *Putting 'reality' together*. Beverly Hills, CA: Sage.

Schudson, M. (2003). *The sociology of news*. New York: W. W. Norton and Co.

Shoemaker, P. J., Eichholz, M., Kim, E., & Wrigley, B. (2001). Individual and routine forces in gatekeeping. *Journalism and Mass Communication Quarterly, 78*(2), 233–246.

Shoemaker, P. J., & Reese, S. D. (1996). *Mediating the message: Theories of influences on mass media content* (2nd ed.). White Plains, NY: Longman.

Shoemaker, P. J., & Reese, S. D. (2013). *Mediating the message in the 21st century: A media sociology perspective*. New York: Routledge.

Soley, L. (2008). News sources. In W. Donsbach (Ed.), *The international encyclopedia of communication* (pp. 1–5). John Wiley & Sons, Ltd. doi:10.1002/9781405186407.wbiecn029

Statham, P. (2008). Making Europe news: How journalists view their role and media performance. *Journalism, 9*(4), 398–422.

Tandoc, E. (2018). Five ways Buzzfeed is preserving (or transforming) the journalistic field. *Journalism, 19*(2), 200–216. doi:10.1177/1464884917691785

Tandoc, E., Cabañes, J. A., & Cayabyab, Y. M. (2019). Bridging the gap: Journalists' role orientation and role performance on Twitter. *Journalism Studies, 20*(6), 857–871. doi:10.1080/1461670X.2018.1463168

Tandoc, E., & Duffy, A. (2019). Routines in journalism. In *Oxford research encyclopedia of communication*. Oxford: Oxford University Press.

Tandoc, E., Hellmueller, L., & Vos, T. P. (2013). Mind the gap: Between role conception and role enactment. *Journalism Practice, 7*(5), 539–554. doi:10.10 80/17512786.2012.726503

Tandoc, E., & Skoric, M. (2010). The pseudo-events paradox: How pseudo-events flood the Philippine press and why journalists don't recognize it. *Asian Journal of Communication, 20*(1), 33–50. doi:10.1080/01292980903440830

Tandoc, E., & Takahashi, B. (2014). Playing a crusader role or just playing by the rules? Role conceptions and role inconsistencies among environmental journalists. *Journalism, 15*(7), 889–907. doi:10.1177/1464884913501836

Tuchman, G. (1972). Objectivity as strategic ritual: An examination of newsmen's notions of objectivity. *American Journal of Sociology, 77*(4), 660–679. doi:10.2307/2776752

Tuchman, G. (1978). *Making news: A study in the construction of reality*. New York: Free Press.

Turk, J. V. (1985). Information subsidies and influence. *Public Relations Review, 11*(3), 10–25. doi:10.1016/S0363-8111(85)80078-3

Wang, H., Sparks, C., Lü, N., & Huang, Y. (2017). Differences within the mainland Chinese press: A quantitative analysis. *Asian Journal of Communication, 27*(2), 154–171.

Zeldes, G. A., & Fico, F. (2005). Race and gender: An analysis of sources and reporters in the networks' coverage of the 2000 presidential campaign. *Mass Communication and Society, 8*(4), 373–385. doi:10.1207/s15327825mcs0804_5

10 Journalistic Role Performance
An Organizational-Level Approach

Cornelia Mothes, Anna-Maria Schielicke, and Patric Raemy

In the past decades, journalistic media have undergone dramatic changes spurred by the proliferation of the Internet, with newspapers being particularly affected by these changes (e.g., Thurman & Fletcher, 2019). New competitors on the information market, digital access to free content, declining circulation, and decreasing advertising revenue have intensified economic pressures on newspapers to such an extent that the focus of newspapers today has increasingly shifted from how to inform their readership to how to prevent a further loss of readers. In addition, intensified political polarization in the digital era has exacerbated public distrust of journalistic media (Arceneaux, Johnson, & Murphy, 2012; Jackob et al., 2019), which further accelerates economic pressures on media companies.

To keep newspapers competitive in high-choice, polarized media environments, newspapers have gradually adopted business strategies that substantially affect the work of journalists. Since newspaper organizations have transitioned into more profit-oriented industries, journalism has become more market-driven, with journalistic principles increasingly competing with business principles (Reese & Shoemaker, 2016; Underwood & Stamm, 1992). At the same time, economic pressures, along with technological developments, have triggered increased media convergence as a result of resource cuts and the growing need of newspaper companies to produce contents for various platforms (García-Avilés, Kaltenbrunner, & Meier, 2014; Menke et al., 2016). As a consequence, today's newspapers fulfill their public service function in a tense context of competing priorities arising from journalistic principles, business principles, and technological principles—an interplay of conflicting interests that makes the nature of news organizations and journalism more complicated (Reese & Shoemaker, 2016).

The present chapter examines how these organizational factors affect the way journalistic values are selectively performed in daily newspaper coverage. We will specifically look at effects of journalistic, business, and technological principles on journalistic role performance with regards to the six roles conceptualized and validated in earlier research (e.g., Mellado, 2015; Mellado & van Dalen, 2014), that is, the interventionist role; the two politics-oriented journalistic roles (i.e., watchdog, loyal-facilitator), addressing journalists' involvement in political processes and their relationship to political actors; and the three audience-oriented journalistic roles (i.e., infotainment, civic, service), addressing journalists' relationship to their readers as members of civil society and/or as clients and spectators. Based on this conceptualization, our analyses revealed a relative "balance of power" between journalistic and business principles in newspaper organizations in terms of their effects on journalistic role performance, corroborating the existence of a professional paradox in journalism, with organizational factors simultaneously helping promote and curtail journalistic independence.

Journalistic Principles: Independence as a Cornerstone

Although journalism lacks some of the essential prerequisites of a profession, journalists of the same cultural background tend to share a common idea of what journalism should achieve for society. This idea is most strongly related to an "overarching commitment to public service" (Singer, 2007, p. 81), according to which journalists' first and foremost loyalty should be to the citizenry (Kovach & Rosenstiel, 2007). This commitment is most clearly reflected in their main professional standard of journalistic independence, which is not only a central part of ethical codes and legal regulations across journalistic cultures, but is also conceived of as the basis for journalistic reliability and professional autonomy (e.g., Kovach & Rosenstiel, 2007; Singer, 2007).

On an organizational level, journalistic independence is most clearly reflected in the ethical codes that newsrooms establish to guide proper journalistic behavior. These codes usually specify legitimate as well as illegitimate practices in order to clarify more general ethical guidelines established within the journalistic profession. Although such guidelines were shown to have no direct impact on journalists' perceptions of their professional autonomy (Reich & Hanitzsch, 2013), they are likely to affect journalistic behavior more indirectly by leading journalists to internalize the expectations imposed by their superiors and to adapt their behavior accordingly (Breed, 1955; Wyss, 2003). How this conformity translates into journalistic role performance is still an open question, although roles more clearly addressing independence—probably most of all by an absence of the "loyal-facilitator" ideal—may more likely be affected by ethical codes. Due to the lack of empirical evidence to back up this assumption, however, we will investigate the following research question:

> RQ1: How do editorial codes of ethics affect newspapers' role performance with regards to interventionism, politics-oriented roles (i.e., watchdog, loyal-facilitator), and audience-oriented roles (i.e., infotainment, civic, service)?

A second indicator of journalistic independence on an organizational level refers to the media's responsibility of not letting their political orientation, as often laid down in editorial policies, affect news coverage. The question as to how this responsibility is met in practice has mainly been measured by the extent of partisan bias in media coverage, derived by comparing the general political leaning of news outlets with their coverage of political issues, agendas, and candidates (for an overview, see D'Alessio & Allen, 2000; Eberl, Boomgarden, & Wagner, 2015). When partisan media bias is present in media coverage, this is usually taken as a sign of journalism being affected by political influences, but also by economic interests. By biasing news coverage towards a particular point of view, media companies cater towards likeminded users to attract and retain audiences in highly contested news markets (Agirdas, 2015; Gentzkow & Shapiro, 2010).

Although demand-driven media coverage and placing commercial needs before professional ones may proliferate in high-choice digital media environments—which is especially likely in newspaper markets that have been most significantly affected by the fundamental changes in the digital era—empirical evidence on the impact of media's political leaning on partisan media bias remains inconsistent (e.g., Eberl et al., 2015; Eisinger, Veentra, & Koehn, 2007; Haselmeyer, Wagner, & Meyer, 2017). Moreover, although there is some evidence on how slant affects the overall quality of news coverage, such as the focus on substance or the inclusion of sources (e.g., Dunaway, Davis, Padgett, & Scholl, 2015), there is little empirical insight into how political leaning generally affects journalistic quality beyond media bias. For instance, do media outlets with a clear editorial commitment to a certain political orientation generally report in a more interventionist way than centrist media? Or do they even differ in terms of politics-oriented roles such as the "watchdog" or the "loyal-facilitator" role? On the other hand, could political orientation—by addressing consumer needs—potentially lead to more audience-oriented news coverage?

These questions have likely received less attention in research so far, as such influences can vary greatly depending on the political context in which media organizations operate, both in terms of the political system in general and the specific political situation (e.g., Agirdas, 2015). Left-leaning media outlets in democratic societies with right-wing governments, for instance, may present very different characteristics than outlets in democracies with left-wing governments—not to mention non-democratic countries. However, in times of increasing political polarization and contested media credibility, the question arises whether political leaning is generally related to different ways of news reporting compared to newspapers without a clear political stance. We will therefore investigate the following research question:

> *RQ2: How does political leaning affect newspapers' role performance with regards to interventionism, politics-oriented roles (i.e., watchdog, loyal-facilitator), and audience-oriented roles (i.e., infotainment, civic, service)?*

Business Principles: Growing Economic—and Political—Imperatives

While journalistic principles mainly address how newspaper organizations implement professional standards of journalistic independence in their daily news routines, business principles are generally related to the opposite question—that is, how media industries restrict this independence through economic imperatives. Bucher and Schumacher (2008) refer to this conflicting situation as one of the most fundamental "paradoxes" in journalism that is closely linked to the question of professional autonomy (see, e.g., Benson, Powers, & Neff, 2017; Waisbord, 2013). Although an investment in high-quality journalism can help secure economic success (e.g., Meyer, 2004; Rosenstiel & Mitchell, 2004), it is becoming increasingly difficult for the newspaper industry to guarantee journalistic quality in times of declining market demand. As a consequence, Fenton (2010) points out that "as news is a business, the business of news is increasingly not the business of journalists" (p. 565).

The available research mainly refers to this development as an increasing soft news orientation of journalistic media, resulting in more entertaining, dramatized, and sensationalistic news content to appeal to an oversaturated audience (for an overview, see Reinemann, Stanyer, Scherr, & Legnante, 2011). This strategy appears to succeed, at least in the short term and for some audience segments (Bas & Grabe, 2015; Mothes, Knobloch-Westerwick, & Pearson, 2019). However, comparative content analyses suggest that this trend in news coverage strongly depends on the audience orientation of news outlets, with commercial television channels and tabloid newspapers showing a significantly higher increase over time and higher overall share of soft news than public-service television channels and elite newspapers (e.g., Curran, Salovaara-Moring, Cohen, & Iyengar, 2010; McLachlan & Golding, 2000). Different editorial profiles thus translate into differences in news styles. We therefore expect that audience orientation will have a significant impact on journalistic role performance particularly with regards to the "infotainment" role:

H1: "Infotainment" role performance will be more pronounced in popular newspapers than elite newspapers.

Although it is likely that infotainment is related to other audience-oriented roles, mostly the primarily consumer-oriented "service" role, and may come at the expense of politics-oriented role performance, particularly with regards to the critical-analytical "watchdog" role, it is an open question as to how audience orientation specifically affects the performance of these roles, which leads to the following research question:

RQ3: How does newspaper audience orientation affect role performance with regards to other audience-oriented roles (i.e., civic, service), interventionism, and politics-oriented roles (i.e., watchdog, loyal-facilitator)?

A second indicator often used to examine the impact of business principles on news coverage is media ownership (Hamilton, 2004; Shoemaker & Reese, 2013). In this case, the question of journalistic independence refers less to editorial policies aiming to address particular needs of the audience than to specific interests of newspaper owners. These interests can vary greatly from social welfare to commercial interests to government support (Elejalde, Ferres, & Herder, 2018). Although ownership types differ across countries and media types, a widely accepted approach is to distinguish newspaper companies that are privately held, owned by large corporations, or state-run (Benson, Neff, & Hessérus, 2018; Picard & van Weezel, 2008).

As state-owned media exert more political control over editorial decisions than other ownership types, journalists working for newspapers owned by the state feel that they have significantly less professional autonomy (Reich & Hanitzsch, 2013) and are subject to more external political influence (Hanitzsch & Mellado, 2011). According to Hanitzsch and Berganza (2012), political control exercised by the state is closely related to the aim of "banning information from being published or forcing journalists to focus on the 'official' version of public events" (p. 807). Hence, in order to stay in power, governments that own media companies tend to use their economic influence to manipulate news coverage in a way that supports the incumbent government and prevents voters from making informed decisions (Djankov, McLiesh, Nenova, & Shleifer, 2003). Accordingly, the political imperatives that the government issues should most strongly relate to politics-oriented journalistic roles that directly address journalists' relationship to the government, that is, the government-critical "watchdog" role and the government-friendly "loyal-facilitator" role. We will therefore test the following hypothesis:

> *H2:* State-owned newspapers will perform lower on the "watchdog" role (*H2a*) and higher on the "loyal-facilitator" (*H2b*) than other ownership types.

Whether journalistic role performance is affected by state ownership beyond government-related roles is less clear. We will therefore additionally examine the following research question:

> *RQ4: How does state ownership affect newspapers' role performance with regards to the "interventionist" role and audience-oriented roles (i.e., infotainment, civic, service)?*

While newspapers owned by the state are primarily influenced by political imperatives, newspapers under corporate ownership—especially chain-owned newspapers traded on the stock market—are mainly dominated by the commercial interests of the management, which not only leads to less perceived autonomy among journalists working for highly market-oriented companies (Ferrucci, 2018), but can also involve substantial quality cutbacks: While privately owned newspapers, which are often influenced less by economic pressures, were shown to provide more substantive, issue-focused news, newspapers under corporate ownership aim to achieve profit maximization primarily by featuring more emotionalized, less informative, and less civic-oriented soft news stories (Benson et al., 2018; Dunaway, 2008; Ferrucci, 2015; Underwood & Stamm, 1992). However, differences between corporate and private ownership vary greatly across individual organizations—mainly depending on the size of organizations (Dunaway & Lawrence, 2015)—and lead to inconclusive findings regarding how exactly ownership type affects journalistic role performance with regards to corporate and private ownership (e.g., Benson et al., 2018; Hanitzsch & Berganza, 2012; Henkel, Thurman, & Deffner, 2019; Reich & Hanitzsch, 2013). We therefore investigate the following research question:

> *RQ5: Do newspapers under corporate ownership differ from newspapers under private ownership with regards to interventionism, politics-oriented roles (i.e., watchdog, loyal-facilitator), and audience-oriented role performance (i.e., infotainment, civic, service)?*

Technological Principles: Changing Newsroom Practices

While business principles are becoming more and more dominant in highly competitive news markets, they are accompanied by significant technological changes within newsrooms. The technological trend that probably has had the greatest impact on the editorial work of journalists at the organizational level of newspapers in recent years is often referred to as "newsroom convergence"—that is, the increasing convergence of individual editorial departments into newsrooms producing content for different media outlets within the same company (Boczkowski, 2010; García-Avilés et al., 2014; Menke et al., 2016). The restructuring of individual newsrooms into cross-media productions or even fully converged news desks controlled by a central management can be understood as a response to the growing demands on newspaper organizations to cover different channels with as little additional expenditure of time and personnel resources as possible.

These "bundling strategies" (Bonin, 2016) are seen as necessary for the print market to survive in the digital world (Dimitrov, 2014). In fact, newsroom convergence provides many opportunities for media organizations to share content, sources, and facilities between different editorial departments and to support digital collaboration between newsrooms in many respects, including greater audience involvement (García-Avilés et al., 2014). Hence, convergence is also related to a substantial transformation of newsroom practices. This usually goes hand in hand with a centralization of operations, an increase in efficiency, and a reduction of resources available for news gathering and reporting (García Avilés, Meier, Kaltenbrunner, Carvajal, & Kraus, 2009). However, it is not clear whether these technological changes also lead to changes in role performance. Studies focused on the impact of newsroom convergence in different media types and systems suggest that journalistic routines and practices have been surprisingly unaffected by technological change (see, Bonin, 2016; Domingo & Paterson, 2011; Menke et al., 2016; Usher, 2014). Against this empirical background, we investigate the following research question:

> RQ6: *Does newsroom convergence affect the journalistic role performance of newspapers in terms of interventionism, politics-oriented roles (i.e., watchdog, loyal-facilitator), and audience-oriented roles (i.e., infotainment, civic, service)?*

Measures of Journalistic, Business, and Technological Principles

To measure organizational impacts via dominant indicators of business, journalistic, and technological principles in newsrooms, information on the key characteristics of the newspapers in our sample was obtained by the research collaborators in each respective country based on literature reviews of available national research, document analyses, and personal inquiry.

Regarding journalistic principles, we first measured whether a given newspaper had established *editorial codes of ethics* to define and guide proper journalistic behavior. Following Reich and Hanitzsch (2013), the presence of such ethical guidelines was measured by a dichotomous variable indicating whether or not the given newsrooms have implemented editorial codes of conduct specifying legitimate behavior to guide journalistic practice (0 = *no*, 1 = *yes*). In general, editorial policies with regards to journalistic ethics existed in 67% of the newspapers examined in the present study.

To further address journalistic principles by examining the impact of *political leaning*, the political orientation of the newspapers in our sample was measured on a five-point scale (*left, center-left, center, center-right, right*). For the statistical analyses, this variable was recoded into a categorical variable that indicates whether a given newspaper is known to follow a liberal, left-leaning editorial policy (*left, center-left*); a conservative, right-leaning editorial policy (*center-right, right*); or a centrist, ideologically neutral policy (*center*). Across all countries, 27% of the newspapers analyzed represented a more leftist ideology, 38% a more conservative ideology, and 35% a centrist orientation.

Regarding business principles, two predictors were included: The newspapers' *audience orientation* indicated whether a given newspaper mainly addresses a politically interested niche audience (*elite press*) or a broader, rather diverse readership (*popular press*; for a similar approach, see Mellado, Humanes, & Márquez-Ramírez, 2018). In total, 75% of the newspapers analyzed were classified as elite newspapers, while 25% were identified as popular newspapers.

The second indicator of business principles pertained to *media ownership*, capturing whether the newspapers in our sample were owned and primarily controlled by private groups, single owners, or families (*private ownership*); by publicly traded corporations (*corporate ownership*); or by the government (*state ownership*). This media ownership typology is based on previous research (e.g., Benson et al., 2018; Dunaway & Lawrence, 2015; Reich & Hanitzsch, 2013) and was adapted for the newspaper market. Of the newspapers in our sample, 17% were owned by the state and 17% were owned by large corporations without major private shareholders, while the majority (66%) were owned by private entities.

Regarding technological principles that shape newsroom cultures, a cross-nationally developed, ideal-type measure of *newsroom convergence* was used to identify which of the following three categories the newspapers in our sample tended to fall into: full integration, cross-media, or isolated platform (e.g., García Avilés et al., 2009). If newspapers belonged to organizations that have combined the news production infrastructure for multiple platforms in one newsroom controlled by a centralized management, the strongest manifestation of newsroom convergence was coded (*full integration*). If the newspaper presented a work environment with specific newsrooms for different platforms that were linked through multimedia-administrators or synchronized multimedia-routines coordinated by a central management, a moderate degree of newsroom convergence was coded (*cross-media*). If a newspaper has an autonomous newsroom without any systematic cooperation across platforms in terms of news gathering, news production, and news distribution, the lowest level of newsroom convergence was coded (*isolated platform*). A moderate level of newsroom convergence was most pronounced in our sample, with 50% of the newspapers published in cross-media environments, followed by 39% produced by news organizations that have transitioned to full integration, and 12% produced by entirely autonomous newsrooms.

Results

To investigate the effects of organizational impacts on journalistic role performance with regards to interventionism, the two politics-oriented roles (i.e., watchdog, loyal-facilitator), and the three audience-oriented roles (i.e., infotainment, civic, service), multilevel models were conducted, one for each journalistic role. Each model contained three levels, with news articles nested in media organizations and countries. As the aim of this chapter is not to examine predictors at the societal level (for societal effects, see Chapter 11) but on the organizational level, the country level is included only to determine whether the estimated organizational effects can be expected to be stable across countries. Additionally, the individual level is included to determine the extent to which news articles vary in their performance of the six roles and how much of this variance can be attributed to their belonging to higher grouping factors, such as newspapers and/or countries. This procedure allowed us to compare the variance between articles with the variation between newspapers and countries. To account for these article-, organizational-, and societal-level differences in role performance, the random intercepts of the two higher levels (i.e., newspaper, country) were included in all models, while organizational predictors were included as fixed effects.

Across all six role performance indicators, the analyses based on these random intercept models revealed that role performance most clearly varied on the individual article level (see Tables 10.1 and 10.2, *covariance parameters: residual*) and on the newspaper level (see Table 10.1 and 10.2, *covariance parameters: intercept newspaper*). The analyses thus indicate significant impacts of factors related to the individual news-story-level (see Chapter 9) and the organizational level of newspaper outlets. In two out of six roles, additional country differences were identified (see Tables 10.1 and 10.2, *covariance parameters: intercept country*). The performance of the "loyal-facilitator" and "civic" roles showed significant variations between countries. Hence, countries differed most with regards to roles that most clearly reflect differences in the political context of media systems—by representing two "extreme" points of political role performance as either serving the government (i.e., loyal-facilitator) or operating on behalf of the citizenry (i.e., civic). By contrast, more traditional democratic role ideals such as the "watchdog" and the "detached observer" (indicated by an absence of interventionism), and economically driven roles such as the "infotainment" and "service" roles were not affected by country differences and, thus, to a certain extent, appear to have undergone global standardization processes. For further discussion of country differences and commonalities, see Chapter 11.

In order to shed further light on the specificities of the significant differences in role performance that occurred between newspaper organizations, the authors included organizational factors as fixed effects. This led to an increased model fit in three out of six roles as compared to the intercept-only models (see Tables 10.1 and 10.2, χ^2_{Change} in $-2LL$). Accounting for differences between articles, newspapers, and countries, the organizational factors examined here can be considered critical in explaining variance in role performance with regards to the "watchdog" role, the "loyal-facilitator" role, and the "infotainment" role. It is therefore not surprising that these three roles show the strongest effects of organizational predictors on role performance, although the effect sizes are relatively small.

Most pronounced in this context are effects related to business principles as represented by audience orientation and ownership type. "Infotainment"—as the only audience-oriented role that showed a significant improvement in model fit after the inclusion of organizational predictors—was mainly influenced by media audience orientation (*H1*). Specifically, elite newspapers were found to be significantly less likely than popular newspapers to utilize infotainment in their news coverage ($b = -.047, p = .011, \beta = -.16$). Apart from infotainment, audience orientation did not exhibit any further effects on journalistic role performance (*RQ3*).

Ownership type, in contrast, primarily affected the two politics-oriented roles that showed a significant increase in the goodness-of-fit after the inclusion of organizational predictors (i.e., watchdog, loyal-facilitator). In line with *H2a and H2b*, the analyses revealed that newspapers owned by the state exhibited a significantly lower performance of the "watchdog" role ($b = -.047, p = .011, \beta = -.16$) and a significantly higher performance of the "loyal-facilitator" role ($b = .046, p = .009, \beta = .18$). Subsequent post-hoc variance analyses with Bonferroni correction also showed that state-owned newspapers differed in this regard from both newspapers owned by corporations—which served as the reference point in our multi-level models—and privately owned newspapers. While state-owned newspapers showed the lowest performance of the "watchdog" role ($M = .02, SD = .06$), corporate newspapers ($M = .06, SD = .11$) and private newspapers ($M = .07, SD = .12$) performed this role to a

Table 10.1 Organizational Effects on the Performance of the Interventionist and Politics-Oriented Journalistic Roles

	Interventionist			Watchdog			Loyal-Facilitator		
	b (SE_b)	p	95%CI	b (SE_b)	p	95%CI	b (SE_b)	p	95%CI
Fixed Effects									
Intercept	.194 (.041)	< .001	.113; .276	.024 (.019)	.193	−.013; .062	.054 (.021)	.014	.011; .096
Editorial Code of Ethics (0 = No, 1 = Yes)	.017 (.027)	.513	−.036; .070	−.003 (.012)	.821	−.027; .021	−.026 (.011) ß = −.12	.018	−.047; −.005
Political Leaning (0 = Center)									
Left Leaning	.064 (.028) ß = .13	.025	.008; .120	.032 (.012) ß = .13	.012	.007; .057	.005 (.010)	.635	−.015; .024
Right Leaning	.007 (.022)	.763	−.038; .051	.005 (.010)	.641	−.015; .025	.002 (.008)	.814	−.014; .018
Audience Orientation (0 = Popular, 1 = Elite)	−.009 (.019)	.652	−.046; .029	.010 (.008)	.226	−.007; .027	.009 (.006)	.155	−.004; .022
Media Ownership (0 = Corporate Ownership)									
Private Ownership	.013 (.024)	.597	−.035; .060	.011 (.011)	.309	−.010; .032	−.004 (.008)	.658	−.020; .013
State Ownership	−.025 (.040)	.534	−.105; .055	−.047 (.018) ß = −.16	.011	−.084; −.011	.046 (.017) ß = .18	.009	.012; .079
Newsroom Convergence (0 = Isolated Platform)									
Cross-Media	−.029 (.035)	.413	−.099; .041	.024 (.016)	.139	−.008; .055	−.009 (.012)	.475	−.033; .016
Full Integration	−.001 (.039)	.990	−.079; .078	.029 (.018)	.009	−.006; .065	.006 (.014)	.653	−.022; .035
Covariance Parameters (ID)									
Residual	.041 (.000)	< .001	.040; .041	.011 (.000)	< .001	.011; .011	.007 (.000)	< .001	.007; .007
Intercept Newspaper	.003 (.001)	< .001	.002; .005	.001 (.000)	< .001	.000; .001	.000 (.000)	< .001	.000; .001
Intercept Country	.003 (.002)	.064	.001; .008	.001 (.000)	.058	.000; .002	.005 (.002)	.003	.002; .009
χ^2_{Change} in −2LL	8.836			19.754*			24.434**		
AIC (df)	−12324.816 (12)			−57908.325 (12)			−71734.098 (12)		
BIC (df)	−12223.426 (12)			−57806.936 (12)			−71632.709 (12)		

Table 10.2 Organizational Effects on the Performance of Audience-Oriented Journalistic Roles

	Infotainment			Civic			Service		
	$b\ (SE_b)$	p	95%CI	$b\ (SE_b)$	p	95%CI	$b\ (SE_b)$	p	95%CI
Fixed Effects									
Intercept	.130 (.024)	<.001	.082; .177	.033 (.020)	.107	-.007; .073	.058 (.019)	.004	.019; .096
Editorial Code of Ethics (0 = No, 1 = Yes)	-.022 (.014)	.130	-.051; .007	-.008 (.013)	.547	-.034; .018	-.029 (.012) ß = -.12	.022	-.053; -.005
Political Leaning (0 = Center)									
Left Leaning	.006 (.017)	.718	-.029; .041	.027 (.013) ß = .10	.044	.001; .054	.007 (.014)	.630	-.021; .034
Right Leaning	.001 (.013)	.914	-.025; .028	.003 (.011)	.759	-.018; .025	.007 (.011)	.516	-.015; .029
Audience Orientation (0 = Popular, 1 = Elite)	-.042 (.012) ß = -.15	.001	-.067; -.018	.006 (.009)	.497	-.012; .024	.001 (.010)	.907	-.018; .020
Media Ownership (0 = Corporate Ownership)									
Private Ownership	-.005 (.015)	.728	-.035; .025	.000 (.011)	.969	-.023; .022	-.019 (.012)	.125	-.042; .005
State Ownership	-.030 (.021)	.173	-.073; .014	-.025 (.020)	.212	-.064; .015	-.008 (.018)	.681	-.044; .029
Newsroom Convergence (0 = Isolated Platform)									
Cross–Media	-.024 (.021)	.252	-.066; .018	.018 (.017)	.284	-.016; .052	.015 (.017)	.395	-.020; .049
Full Integration	-.019 (.023)	.416	-.065; .027	.021 (.019)	.274	-.017; .059	.003 (.019)	.859	-.034; .041
Covariance Parameters (ID)									
Residual	.014 (.000)	<.001	.014; .014	.013 (.000)	<.001	.013; .013	.013 (.000)	<.001	.012; .013
Intercept Newspaper	.002 (.001)	<.001	.001; .003	.001 (.000)	<.001	.001; .001	.001 (.000)	<.001	.001; .002
Intercept Country	.000 (.000)	.965	.000; .000	.001 (.000)	.019	.000; .002	.000 (.000)	.439	.000; .003
χ^2_{Change} in -2LL	21.298**			8.539			8.605		
AIC (df)	-49192.905 (12)			-52587.990 (12)			-52928.358 (12)		
BIC (df)	-49091.515 (12)			-52486.601 (12)			-52826.968 (12)		

significantly higher degree; $F(2, 34511) = 581.37$, $p < .001$, $\eta^2 = .033$). Similarly, state-owned newspapers differed significantly from private and corporate newspapers with regards to the "loyal-facilitator" role, showing substantially higher performance of this role ($M = .07$, $SD = .15$) than both corporate ($M = .02$, $SD = .07$) and private newspapers ($M = .03$, $SD = .08$); $F(2, 34511) = 521.56$, $p < .001$, $\eta^2 = .029$. Beyond these two roles, state ownership did not show any additional effects on role performance ($RQ4$). This was true of other types of media ownership as well ($RQ5$).

Besides business principles which, to a certain extent, also encompass political imperatives, especially in terms of state ownership, the "loyal-facilitator" and "watchdog" roles were additionally—although to a smaller extent—affected by journalistic principles. Regarding $RQ1$, our analyses revealed that the "loyal-facilitator" role was performed less in news organizations that have established editorial codes of conduct to guide proper journalistic behavior ($b = -.026$, $p = .018$, $\beta = -.12$). Newsrooms with clear editorial policies were thus less inclined to report the news in a government-favorable way than newsrooms without a clear editorial commitment to ethical standards. Editorial codes of ethics also affected news coverage with regards to the "service" role, as the second role model besides the "loyal-facilitator" role that primarily serves external needs, in this case by addressing the consumer interests of the audience rather than state interests. With regards to the "service" role, ethical codes again reduced the newspapers' performance of this role ($b = -.029$, $p = .022$, $\beta = -.12$), implying that service-orientation is less pronounced in news organizations that clearly commit themselves to ethical standards via editorial guidelines.

In contrast to the "loyal-facilitator" and "service" roles, the critical-analytical "watchdog" and "civic" roles remained unaffected by editorial codes of ethics, but were instead influenced by newspapers' political leaning ($RQ2$) as the second indicator of journalistic principles examined in the present study. Our analyses revealed that left-leaning, more liberal newspapers showed a greater tendency than centrist newspapers to perform both the "watchdog" role ($b = .032$, $p = .012$, $\beta = .13$) and the "civic" role ($b = .027$, $p = .044$, $\beta = .10$). The same pattern was not evident in right-wing, more conservative newspapers.

Additionally, newspapers' political leaning also affected the performance of the "interventionist" role, with left-leaning, more liberal newspapers again performing higher on interventionism than centrist newspapers ($b = .064$, $p = .025$, $\beta = .13$), while no differences were found between centrist and right-wing, more conservative newspapers.

While both business and journalistic principles implemented at the organizational level of news organizations affected journalistic role performance to some extent, depending on the specific role considered, the technological context in which news is produced—measured by the degree of newsroom convergence—did not show any substantial impact on role performance (*RQ6*).

Conclusion

Journalistic practice has fundamentally changed in today's highly competitive digital media environments. This is particularly true of newspaper journalism, which is facing declining circulation and advertising revenue. The question of how journalism will prevail under these circumstances is thus closely intertwined with the question of how newspaper organizations handle the challenges that the newspaper industry faces. Although changes in news organizations are evident, the present analysis aimed to clarify whether and how these organizational principles translate into journalistic performance.

Based on the interventionist role, two politics-oriented roles (i.e., watchdog, loyal-facilitator) and three audience-oriented roles (i.e., infotainment, civic, service), our analyses suggest that organizational factors primarily affect journalistic role performance through business principles applied in newsrooms. With regards to audience orientation, our findings corroborate earlier research (e.g., Curran et al., 2010; McLachlan & Golding, 2000) by showing that—across countries—newspapers addressing politically interested niche audiences (i.e., elite press) provided less infotainment than newspapers targeting a wider, more diverse audience (i.e., popular press), supporting *H1*. However, the performance of other audience-oriented roles, as well as politics-oriented roles and the interventionist role, remained unaffected by audience orientation (*RQ3*), suggesting that commercial pressures induced by increasing competition in digital information environments do not automatically result in an overall transformation of journalistic practices.

In regard to the second business principle explored in the present chapter—ownership type—our analyses showed significant effects on role performance. Reflecting the ambivalent findings in previous research (e.g., Benson et al., 2018; Henkel et al., 2019), no substantial differences were found between private and corporate ownership (*RQ5*). However, future research should investigate these impacts on a more nuanced level by differentiating more clearly between different company sizes, as the size of media organizations may be more critical to role performance than ownership type alone (Dunaway & Lawrence, 2015). In contrast to economic imperatives, political imperatives related to ownership type were found to be more influential. In line with *H2a/b* and consistent with existing research (e.g., Djankov et al., 2003; Hanitzsch & Berganza, 2012), state-owned newspapers performed significantly higher on the government-supporting "loyal-facilitator" role and significantly lower on the government-critical "watchdog" role. Hence, government-owned newspapers appear to effectively focus their attention on the two journalistic roles that most clearly present either the potential for or threat of governments staying in power, while roles that are less promising or threating to governments remained untouched (*RQ4*).

Strengthening journalistic principles in newsrooms could potentially counteract the external forces imposed by economic and political imperatives. In fact, our findings suggest that implementing ethical codes in newsrooms can serve as an effective means to confine external influences on professional journalism to the benefit of journalistic independence, as they come into play specifically in relation to journalistic roles that refer to the economic and political demands that most clearly exceed the core public service function of professional journalism: the commercially driven "service" role and the politically driven "loyal-facilitator" role (*RQ1*). Hence, newsrooms with established ethical standards were less inclined to report on public issues in a government-favorable way, and less likely to focus on audiences as clients than newspapers without a clear editorial commitment to journalistic ethics.

While the performance of journalistic roles that primarily accommodate external (rather than professional) demands may thus be restrained by reinforcing journalistic ethics in news organizations, an additional strengthening of core professional roles—especially those related to critical-analytical journalism—mainly operates via political leaning (*RQ2*). As our findings show, liberal newspapers were likely to perform both the "watchdog" and the "civic" role to a greater extent. This finding may indicate a higher tendency among left-wing newspapers to engage in the analytical and investigative monitoring of the political status quo, and the guidance of citizens in critical-reflexive thinking and action, potentially because of a generally more active approach to political change. Since the "watchdog" and "civic" roles are to a certain extent both associated with a more active involvement of journalists—either as representatives of the media as a "fourth estate" or as civic advocates helping citizens acquire political competence and knowledge about their opportunities for political participation—it is not surprising that liberal newspapers were also found to perform higher on the "interventionist" role.

Although both the "watchdog" and the "civic" roles may be performed in a more detached manner (see Chapters 6 and 7), the repetition of the impact pattern of political leaning on the performance of more politically active journalistic roles suggests that liberal newspapers generally pursue a more critical-reflective, progressive, and interventionist approach to news reporting, even across countries with different political systems and government orientations. Future research is needed, however, to examine whether this more active journalistic involvement is linked to a higher likelihood of partisan media bias. To avoid false conclusions, analyses should consider the moderating impact of the specific political context in which newspapers of different political leanings operate and how this impact may change over time with changes in government or the political system in general.

In contrast to business and journalistic principles, technological principles did not show any significant effects on role performance in our analyses ($RQ6$). On the one hand, this result aligns with earlier findings suggesting that although newsroom structures have fundamentally changed in digital news environments, journalistic principles and routines have remained relatively stable over time (e.g., Bonin, 2016; Usher, 2014). However, our measure of newsroom convergence may also have been too insensitive to what Hanusch (2017) describes as the next stage of converged news environments by pointing to the "potential advent of more specialized news work for specific platforms . . . with stories commissioned for a particular platform only" (p. 1582). Future research should take these finer-grained developments in converged news environments into account to better understand if and how journalistic routines and standards are adapted to the requirements of specific platforms. These include both traditional ones like print, television, and radio, and digital platforms such as online news sites, Twitter accounts, or Facebook pages.

Overall, our analyses of the six journalistic roles have shown that although organizational factors influence journalistic role performance, the extent of these effects is moderate when controlling for article-level and country-level differences. This finding reflects the immense complexity of today's news production and speaks to the various interdependencies and often conflicting demands to which journalists and the media are exposed every day. We have taken this complexity into account to show the impact of organizational factors on the work of journalists. Such factors both facilitate external influence, thereby curtailing journalistic independence, and strengthen journalistic independence through counter-measures against external influence. It will be crucial for the future of newspaper journalism to keep an eye on how this "balance of power" will be decided, and to identify the factors that cause potential shifts in these power relations—factors that most likely lie beyond the organizational level in the broader societal context, as it has a decisive impact on the structural foundations of organizational cultures and professional autonomy.

References

Agirdas, C. (2015). What drives media bias? New evidence from recent newspaper closures. *Journal of Media Economics*, 28, 123–141.

Arceneaux, K., Johnson, M., & Murphy, C. (2012). Polarized political communication, oppositional media hostility, and selective exposure. *The Journal of Politics*, 74, 174–186.

Bas, O., & Grabe, M. E. (2015). Emotion-provoking personalization of news: Informing citizens and closing the knowledge gap? *Communication Research, 42,* 159–185.

Benson, R., Neff, T., & Hessérus, M. (2018). Media ownership and public service news: How strong are institutional logics? *The International Journal of Press/Politics, 23,* 275–298.

Benson, R., Powers, M., & Neff, T. (2017). Public media autonomy and accountability: Best and worst policy practices in 12 leading democracies. *International Journal of Communication, 11,* 1–22.

Boczkowski, P. J. (2010). *News at work: Imitation in an age of information abundance.* University of Chicago.

Bonin, G. A. (2016). Organizational factors influencing journalists' use of user-generated content: A case of Canadian radio newsrooms. *The Radio Journal, 14,* 109–122.

Breed, W. (1955). Social control in the newsroom: A functional analysis. *Social Forces, 33,* 326–335.

Bucher, H.-J., & Schumacher, P. (2008). Konstante Innovationen [Constant innovation]. In B. Pörksen, W. Loosen, & A. Scholl (Eds.), *Paradoxien des Journalismus [Paradoxes in journalism]* (pp. 477–501). Wiesbaden: VS Verlag für Sozialwissenschaften.

Curran, J., Salovaara-Moring, I., Cohen, S., & Iyengar, S. (2010). Crime, foreigners and hard news: A cross-national comparison of reporting and public perception. *Journalism, 11,* 3–19.

D'Alessio, D., & Allen, M. (2000). Media bias in presidential elections: A meta-analysis. *Journal of Communication, 50,* 133–156.

Dimitrov, R. (2014). Do social media spell the end of journalism as a profession? *Global Media Journal, 8,* 1–16.

Djankov, S., McLiesh, C., Nenova, T., & Shleifer, A. (2003). Who owns the media? *Journal of Law and Economics, XLVI,* 341–381.

Domingo, D., & Paterson, C. (2011). *Making online news, volume 2: Newsroom ethnographies in the second decade of internet journalism.* New York: Peter Lang.

Dunaway, J. L. (2008). Markets, ownership, and the quality of campaign news coverage. *The Journal of Politics, 70,* 1193–1202.

Dunaway, J. L., Davis, N. T., Padgett, J., & Scholl, R. M. (2015). Objectivity and information bias in campaign news. *Journal of Communication, 65,* 770–792.

Dunaway, J. L., & Lawrence, R. G. (2015). What predicts the game frame? Media ownership, electoral context, and campaign news. *Political Communication, 32,* 43–60.

Eberl, J.-M., Boomgarden, H. G., & Wagner, M. (2015). One bias fits all? Three types of media bias and their effects on party preferences. *Communication Research, 44,* 1125–1148.

Eisinger, R. M., Veentra, L. R., & Koehn, J. P. (2007). What media bias? Conservative and liberal labeling in major U.S. newspapers. *The International Journal of Press/Politics, 12,* 17–36.

Elejalde, E., Ferres, L., & Herder, E. (2018). On the nature of real and perceived bias in the mainstream media. *PLoS ONE, 13,* 1–28.

Fenton, N. (2010). News in the digital age. In S. Allan (Ed.), *The Routledge companion to news and journalism* (pp. 557–567). London: Routledge.

Ferrucci, P. (2015). Primary differences: How market orientation can influence content. *Journal of Media Practice, 16*, 195–210.

Ferrucci, P. (2018). It is in the numbers: How market orientation impacts journalists' use of news metrics. *Journalism*. Advance online publication. doi:10.1177/1464884918807056

García-Avilés, J. A., Kaltenbrunner, A., & Meier, K. (2014). Media convergence revisited: Lessons learned on newsroom integration in Austria, Germany and Spain. *Journalism Practice, 8*, 573–584.

García-Avilés, J. A., Meier, K., Kaltenbrunner, A., Carvajal, M., & Kraus, D. (2009). Newsroom integration in Austria, Spain and Germany: Models of media convergence. *Journalism Practice, 3*, 285–303.

Gentzkow, M., & Shapiro, J. M. (2010). What drives media slant? Evidence from U.S. daily newspapers. *Econometrica, 78*, 35–71.

Hamilton, J. (2004). *All the news that's fit to sell: How the market transforms information into news*. Princeton, NJ: Princeton University Press.

Hanitzsch, T., & Berganza, R. (2012). Explaining journalists' trust in public institutions across 20 countries: Media freedom, corruption, and ownership matter most. *Journal of Communication, 62*, 794–814.

Hanitzsch, T., & Mellado, C. (2011). What shapes the news around the world? How journalists in eighteen countries perceive influences on their work. *The International Journal of Press/Politics, 16*, 404–426.

Hanusch, F. (2017). Web analytics and the functional differentiation of journalism cultures: Individual, organizational and platform-specific influences on newswork. *Information, Communication & Society, 20*, 1571–1586.

Haselmayer, M., Wagner, M., & Meyer, T. M. (2017). Partisan bias in message selection: Media gatekeeping of party press releases. *Political Communication, 34*, 367–384.

Henkel, I., Thurman, N., & Deffner, V. (2019). Comparing journalism cultures in Britain and Germany: Confrontation, contextualization, conformity. *Journalism Studies*. Advance online publication. doi:10.1080/1461670X.2018.1551067

Jackob, N., Schultz, T., Jakobs, I., Ziegele, M., Quiring, O., & Schemer, C. (2019). Medienvertrauen im Zeitalter der Polarisierung [Media trust in times of polarization]. *Media Perspektiven, 5*, 210–220.

Kovach, B., & Rosenstiel, T. (2007). *The elements of journalism: What news people should know and the public should expect* (2nd ed.). New York: Three Rivers Press.

McLachlan, S., & Golding, P. (2000). Tabloidization in the British press: A quantitative investigation into changes in British newspapers, 1952–1997. In C. Sparks & J. Tulloch (Eds.), *Tabloid tales: Global debates over media standards* (pp. 76–90). Lanham, MD: Rowman and Littlefield.

Mellado, C. (2015). Professional roles in news content: Six dimensions of journalistic role performance. *Journalism Studies, 16*, 596–614.

Mellado, C., Humanes, M. A., & Márquez-Ramírez, M. (2018). The influence of journalistic role performance on objective reporting: A comparative study of Chilean, Mexican, and Spanish news. *The International Communication Gazette, 80*, 250–272.

Mellado, C., & van Dalen, A. (2014). Between rhetoric and practice. *Journalism Studies, 15*, 859–878.

Menke, M., Kinnebrock, S., Kretzschmar, S., Aichberger, I., Broersma, M., Hummel, R., . . Salaverría, R. (2016). Convergence culture in European newsrooms, *Journalism Studies*. Advance online publication. doi:10.1080/14616 70X.2016.1232175

Meyer, P. (2004). The influence model and newspaper business. *Newspaper Research Journal, 25*, 66–83.

Mothes, C., Knobloch-Westerwick, S., & Pearson, G. (2019). The PFAD-HEC model: Impacts of news attributes and use motivations on selective news exposure. *Communication Theory, 29*, 251–271.

Picard, R. G., & van Weezel, A. (2008). Capital and control: Consequences of different forms of newspaper ownership. *The International Journal on Media Management, 10*, 22–31.

Reese, S. D., & Shoemaker, P. J. (2016). A media sociology for the networked public sphere: The hierarchy of influences model. *Mass Communication and Society, 19*, 389–410.

Reich, Z., & Hanitzsch, T. (2013). Determinants of journalists' professional autonomy: Individual and national level factors matter more than organizational ones. *Mass Communication and Society, 16*, 133–156.

Reinemann, C., Stanyer, J., Scherr, S., & Legnante, G. (2011). Hard and soft news: A review of concepts, operationalizations and key findings. *Journalism, 13*, 1–19.

Rosenstiel, T., & Mitchell, A. (2004). The impact of investing in newsroom resources. *Newspaper Research Journal, 25*, 84–97.

Shoemaker, P., & Reese, S. (2013). *Mediating the message in the 21st century: A media sociology perspective*. New York: Routledge.

Singer, J. B. (2007). Contested autonomy. Professional and popular claims on journalistic norms. *Journalism Studies, 8*, 79–95.

Thurman, N., & Fletcher, R. (2019). Has digital distribution rejuvenated readership? *Journalism Studies, 20*, 542–562.

Underwood, D., & Stamm, K. (1992). Balancing business with journalism: Newsroom policies at 12 west coast newspapers. *Journalism & Mass Communication Quarterly, 69*, 301–317.

Usher, N. (2014). *Making news at the New York Times*. Ann Arbor, MI: University of Michigan Press.

Waisbord, S. (2013). *Reinventing professionalism: Journalism and news in global perspective*. Cambridge: Polity Press.

Wyss, V. (2003). Journalistische Qualität und Qualitätsmanagement [Journalistic quality and quality management]. In H.-J. Bucher & K.-D. Altmeppen (Eds.), *Qualität im Journalismus [Journalistic quality]* (pp. 129–146). Wiesbaden: Westdeutscher Verlag.

11 Journalistic Role Performance

A Societal-Level Approach

Agnieszka Stępińska, Gabriella Szabó, Mireya Márquez-Ramírez, Svetlana Pasti, and Nikos Panagiotou

Although decisions about which events will be covered and how journalists will write about them are made in newsrooms, it is worth going beyond the individual and organizational features of the press to study the societal-level environment in which roles are performed. Depending on the characteristics of that environment, news professionals may have more or less agency in regard to conducting investigations into improprieties. They may also have more or less interest in addressing the audience as spectators, representing citizens' questions and demands, or helping the public solve everyday problems. Moreover, they may combine several of these roles.

A societal-level approach to the study of journalistic role performance provides an opportunity to analyze macro-structural dimensions and their indicators alongside the relationship between the media system and political, economic, and social systems. Such a broad perspective includes numerous external factors that influence journalistic performance.

To identify these factors, we draw on comparative media systems research, which has a long tradition in journalism and media studies that dates back to *Four Theories of the Press* by Siebert, Peterson, and Schramm (1956).

However, we must consider the limitations of this strategy. First, we note that the main difference between media system studies and research on journalistic practice is the object of study. In the former, the journalistic profession is part of a more general concept of the system, while in the latter, it is the subject of analysis. In other words, from the media system perspective, journalistic role performance is one element of media system characteristics, while from the journalism studies perspective, the outcomes of journalistic work (news) are affected by the features of the media system as well as political, economic, and social ones.

Second, if we want to "borrow" a set of societal factors that may affect journalistic performance from the perspective of contemporary media system research, we must start by reviewing previous studies to identify the main aspects of the media system and the social system. While Siebert et al. (1956) focused on the relationships between the political regime and media systems, recent approaches use more categories to describe media systems (dimensions and indicators). Most of these studies have expanded our knowledge of the "usual suspects," such as political factors (political regime, freedom of speech, state control of the media, or political parallelism). This includes the level of autonomy enjoyed by journalists (press freedom), cultural values, and economic pressure on the media sphere (Blumer & Gurevitch, 1995; Brüggemann, Engesser, Büchel, Humprecht, & Castro, 2014; Dobek-Ostrowska, 2015; Hallin & Mancini, 2004, 2012; Mellado & Lagos, 2013; Meyen, 2018; Peruško, Vozab, & Čuvalo, 2013). Other scholars have added religion (Couldry, 2005; Engesser & Franzetti, 2011; Norris, 2009) and culture (Hayashi & Kopper, 2014) as categories of comparison that could have a decisive impact on media systems.

We note that most comparative studies that have applied this media system framework to factors affecting journalism have been conducted in the U.S. and other Western democracies (Aalberg, van Aelst, & Curran, 2010; Brüggemann et al., 2014; Albæk, van Dalen, Jebril, & de Vreese, 2014; Esser, 2008; Esser & Umbricht, 2013; Curran, Iyanger, Brink Lund, & Salovaara-Moring, 2009). Studies on professional roles that incorporate a broader range of regions are still quite rare and mostly limited to the evaluative level (Hanitzsch, Hanusch, Ramaprasad, & De Beer, 2011, 2019; Weaver & Willnat, 2012). Only a few studies cover specific regions such as Central and Eastern Europe (e.g., Dobek-Ostrowska, 2015; Peruško et al., 2013), Latin America (e.g., Guerrero & Márquez-Ramirez, 2014; Mellado & Lagos, 2013), Africa (Lohner, Banjac, & Nevela, 2016), and Asia (Hayashi & Kopper, 2014). We should thus consider the fact that the categories derived from centuries of Western-centrism cannot be easily applied to other countries and cannot fully explain journalistic cultures worldwide (Mellado et al., 2017; Gunarante, 2010; Mattoni & Ceccobelli, 2018).

Our previous studies on professional roles have revealed patterns of hybridity in journalistic cultures across countries with different traditions and political regimes (e.g., Mellado et al., 2017; Márquez-Ramirez et al., 2020), all of which we deconstruct and analyze in an in-depth manner in this book. Our analyses show that the practice of journalism must go beyond specific media system typologies to analyze the extent and ways in which societal-level and macro dimensions affect the performance of certain roles. We acknowledge that certain roles are more strongly connected to sociopolitical structures, whereas other roles might be more connected to market structures.

This chapter is guided by the following research question: *How do societal factors affect newspaper journalistic role performance across 18 countries?* We follow previous media studies by paying attention to political and economic factors that shape journalism across countries. We also avoid assumptions about regional similarities. Instead of employing a "classic" media system approach, we study relationships between types of journalistic role performance and measurements, describing select aspects of the political and economic conditions that contribute to the media environment.

Measuring Societal-Level Predictors of Journalistic Role Performance

In regard to potential societal-level effects, we look for metrics that could be used to generate a meaningful description and comparison that recognizes the nested structure of our data. This chapter relies on several sources. As described elsewhere in this book, professional roles (e.g., interventionist, watchdog, loyal-facilitator, infotainment, civic, service) were measured in print news stories from national desk sections of popular and elite publications in the countries analyzed. We used external databases to collect data on the legal, political, and economic environment indicators and focused on the following criteria: 1) the indicators covered all 18 sampled countries from 2012 to 2015, and 2) the data was collected using a reliable, trustworthy, and transparent methodology. Specifically, we used evidence from Freedom in the World indices published by Freedom House (FH), the Heritage Foundation (HF), the Economist Intelligence Unit (EIU), and the Varieties of Democracy Project (V-Dem). These secondary data were then turned into ten societal-level variables to estimate their impact on journalistic role performance.

We arranged the ten societal-level variables into two groups. The first contains the *media*-specific or *close context* metrics. We collected measurements of social factors related to journalists' activities and media content production. In drawing from influences research (Shoemaker & Reese, 2013), we acknowledge that media law and regulation, editorial independence from political influence, and the structural dimensions of media ownership shape journalists' work realities. To evaluate the impact of the media-specific legal, political, and economic aspects, we focused on three variables: (1) Freedom of the Press (FoP) legal environment, (2) FoP political environment, and (3) FoP economic environment. These three variables are sub-categories of the FH FoP Index and measure press freedom and editorial independence in a given country.

Specifically, the FH *FoP legal environment* category (FHLegalEnviroment) examines laws and regulations that could influence media content and the extent to which they are used to support or restrict the media. This composite variable assesses the impact of legal and constitutional guarantees on freedom of expression and aspects of security legislation, the penal code, and other statutes; penalties for libel and defamation; freedom of information legislation; the independence of the judiciary and regulatory bodies; and registration requirements for media outlets and journalists. The scores range from 0 to 30, where 0 indicates the most freedom and 30 the least.[1] Journalists in countries with the lowest scores can freely cover societal issues with only minor constitutional and legal restrictions. High scores point to serious regulatory limitations.

The FH *FoP political environment* category (FHPoliticalEnviroment) measures political control over news content. It covers editorial independence of state-run and privately owned media, access to information, official and self-censorship, media vibrancy, news diversity, the ability to cover the news freely, and intimidation of journalists, including detention and imprisonment, attacks, and threats. The scores range from 0 to 40, where 0 indicates the most freedom and 40 the least.[2] In other words, lower scores indicate more journalistic autonomy, while the higher scores indicate that political entities have more authority over journalism. Journalists in countries with high scores in this category may risk their job, freedom, and even their life; while in countries with low scores, journalists may cover political actors' performance without experiencing any political pressure.

The FH *FoP Freedom of Press economic environment* category (FHEconomicEnvironment) assesses media ownership, transparency, and concentration of ownership, the costs of establishing media, impediments to news production and distribution, the selective withholding of advertising or subsidies by the state or other actors, the impact of corruption and bribery on content, and the extent to which a country's economic situation impacts the development and sustainability of the media. Scores range from 0 to 30, where 0 indicates the most freedom and 30 the least.[3] Higher scores suggest that media organizations are economically very vulnerable, and that journalistic work and media content production depend on media owners. Concentration of media ownership may also produce higher scores, which indicate less journalistic freedom from economic constraints. Scores closer to 0 suggest a greater level of journalistic independence from economic powers.

The second group contains the *media environment's specific* or *broad context* metrics. Here, we measure social factors broadly related to journalists' activities and content production. These variables do not describe the media system, but the social system, specifically the political and economic one. Several features of these subsystems can be regarded as influential components of role performance. Specifically, our study introduces the following broad context factors: (4) quality of democracy, (5–7) principles of democracy, (8) political rights, (9) civil liberties, and (10) economic/market freedom.

For *quality of democracy*, we use the *Democracy Index* (DemIndex) generated by the EIU, a composite variable of political culture. We used the mean value for 2012 to 2015, and scores of 0 to 10. Scores below 4 indicate that the regime is authoritarian and that political pluralism is extremely limited or degraded. Scores of 4–6 indicate a hybrid regime with more pressure on political opposition, non-independent judiciaries, widespread corruption, and weak rule of law. Scores of 6–8 are assigned to flawed democracies in which elections are fair and free, and civil liberties respected, but media freedom infringement and suppression of political opposition are prevalent. A country that is assigned a score above 8 is a full democracy with pluralism, high levels of civil liberties, and respect for fundamental political freedoms.[4]

For *principles of democracy*, we focus on the deliberative, liberal, and participatory approaches measured by the VoD (V-Dem indices). The *Deliberative Democracy Index* (5) assesses how decisions are reached in a polity. A deliberative process is one in which public reasoning focused on the common good motivates political decisions. This stands in contrast with emotional appeals, solidary attachments, parochial interests, and coercion.[5] *The Liberal Democracy Index* (6) measures whether the democracy emphasizes protecting individual and minority rights against the tyranny of the state and the majority. It also evaluates constitutionally protected civil liberties, strong rule of law, an independent judiciary, and effective checks and balances that, together, limit the exercise of executive power.[6] *The Participatory Democracy Index* (7) collects data on active participation by citizens. This index evaluates the engagement of civil society organizations, direct democracy, and subnational elected bodies. The scale of all three V-Dem indices runs from low (0) to high (1).[7]

We also include (8) the FH *Political Rights* (FHPoliticalRights) and (9) the FH *Civil Liberties* (FHCivilLiberties) ratings. A country is assigned one rating for political rights and one for civil liberties. Each is given a score of 1 to 7, with 1 representing the greatest degree of freedom and 7 the most limited. Countries with a rating of 1 have a wide range of political rights, including free and fair elections. A 2 signals weaker political rights and more corruption. Countries with ratings of 3, 4, or 5 either moderately protect almost all political rights or strongly protect some while neglecting others. Countries with a rating of 6 have restricted political rights and are ruled by authoritarian regimes. Those with a rating of 7 have severe government oppression, often in combination with civil war, extreme violence, or rule by regional warlords.[8]

Finally, (10) HF's *Economic Freedom Index* (EcoFreedom) was used to investigate the impact of economic circumstances on journalistic role performance. EcoFreedom is based on 12 quantitative and qualitative factors grouped into four categories of economic freedom: rule of law, government size, regulatory efficiency, and open markets. Scores range from 0 to 100, where 100 represents the freest and 0 the least free in terms of the economic environment.[9]

Drawing on primary and secondary data sources and close-context and broad-context variables, we determined how available societal-level factors predict the presence of different journalistic roles. We used a two-step analytical procedure to test for influential predictors of journalistic performance for the six roles. First, we ran Pearson correlation tests to identify relationships between role performance and the societal-level variables. Second, multilevel models were separately conducted for each role with variables. For the sake of coherence with Chapters 9 and 10, we use the same analytical procedure. Our multilevel models work on three levels: news articles, media organizations, and countries. This chapter does not examine the organization level (for organizational effects, see Chapter 10) or individual news-story-level (see Chapter 9). However, we include media organizations to determine whether the estimated effects are stable in different types of media outlets if the selected societal-level factors are influential. With the aid of multilevel modeling, we shed light on the impacts of predictors and variance between newspapers and countries. We include the random intercepts of the two higher levels (newspaper and country) in all models, while societal-level predictors were considered as fixed effects.

Given that our analysis works with a great variety of societal factors, our goal was to identify those that hold explanatory power over journalistic role performance at a statistically significant level given the possibilities available.

Standard (i.e., Pearson correlation coefficients) and more sophisticated (i.e., multilevel modeling) analytical tools allowed us to narrow down the variables in both groups, excluding factors that do not seem to be connected or influential. While Pearson correlation coefficients were estimated for all variables, the multilevel models were only conducted with factors that showed a significant relationship with role performance and did not exhibit collinearity problems (VIF<10, see Hair, Anderson, Tatham, & Black, 1995).

Results

Close and Broad Context Factors Influencing Role Performance: Correlation Analysis

Pearson coefficients results show a statistically significant positive or negative linear relationship among almost all three *close-context* variables (sub-categories of the FH Press Freedom Index, namely Political Environment, Legal Environment, and Economic Environment) and all six professional roles (see Table 11.1). Given that the FH Legal Environment, Political Environment, and Economic Environment factors are composite variables (i.e., created by combining individual indicators into a single variable), we should be careful about the interpretation, because different explanations can be valid simultaneously.

Table 11.1 Linear Correlations Between Close-Context Societal Variables and Journalistic Role Performance Across Countries

Journalistic role performance	Variable	R
Interventionist	FHLegalEnvir	−.012**
	FHPoliticalEnvir	−.037**
	FHEconomicEnvir	.022**
Watchdog	*FHLegalEnvir*	*−.116**
	FHPoliticalEnvir	−.035**
	FHEconomicEnvir	−.099**
Loyal	*FHLegalEnvir*	*.226**
	FHPoliticalEnvir	*.221**
	FHEconomicEnvir	*.253**
Infotainment	FHLegalEnvir	−.022**
	FHPoliticalEnvir	−.022**
	FHEconomicEnvir	−.008**
Service	FHLegalEnvir	−.030**
	FHPoliticalEnvir	−.017**
	FHEconomicEnvir	−.019**
Civic	FHLegalEnvir	−.033**
	FHPoliticalEnvir	−.038**
	FHEconomicEnvir	−.007

** Correlation is significant at the 0.01 level (2-tailed). N = 33,640.

First, we traced a negative significant relationship between political and legal environments and the interventionist role. In contexts with more political control over news content (r. =-.037, p< .01), and more laws and regulations that could influence media content (r.=-.012, p< .01), the print press shows a lower level of interventionism. At the same time, the print press performs the interventionist role significantly more in countries with more economic pressure on journalists (r= .022, p< .01).

Our data also suggest that less economic freedom of the media correlates with a low presence of the watchdog roles and vice versa (r = -.099, p< .01). This aligns with the Organization for Security and Co-operation in Europe report on the impact of media concentration on professional journalism. It states that cross-ownership of non-media-related companies in publishing houses prevents journalists from serving as watchdogs for the business sector (Dohnanyi, 2003, pp. 36–42), perhaps because journalists are expected to reshift their efforts towards producing market-driven content. Similarly, the legal environment may be connected to the watchdog role. Less constitutional and legal protection of media freedom correlates to more limited performance of this role (r = -.116, p< .01).

On the other hand, correlations between the FH Legal Environment (r= .226, p<.01), the Political Environment (r= .221, p< .01), the Economic

Environment (r= .253, p<.01), and the loyal-facilitator role show a significant and positive relationship. We thus argue that a higher presence of the loyal-facilitator role tends to be found in social contexts with higher levels of legal, political, and economic controls over the media.

However, due to the composite nature of FH Political, Legal, and Economic environment variables, we cannot reach a conclusion about which of the issues that constitute each of these sub-dimensions actually impacts journalistic performance.

In regard to infotainment, service, and civic roles, we found statistically significant, though very weak, correlations. The exception was the correlation between the Economic Environment and the civic role, which was statistically insignificant (r=-.007, p=. 219). Therefore, we cannot claim our specific media close-context variables (FH Political, Legal, and Economic) have a significant relationship with the performance of these three roles.

In relation to *broad context* factors and performance of all six journalistic roles (see Table 11.2), Pearson's correlations show a statistically significant negative linear relationship between the Democracy Index (r=-.033, p< .01) and the performance of the interventionist role. This leads us to a preliminary conclusion that journalists in more authoritarian countries exhibit a more interventionist role. That supports the findings presented in Chapter 5 that show the mean value of a presence of interventionist indicators was the highest among non-democratic countries, followed by advanced democracies and then transitional ones. However, as noted in Chapter 5, these are style-related indicators of interventionism that follow an interpretation that can align with the interests of those in power. These are mainly predominantly present in the news in non-democratic regimes.

We also traced a correlation between a level of interventionism and the Economic Freedom Index (r=-.16, p< .01). Given that a higher score signals less state interference in the economy, these data show that the interventionist role is less prevalent in countries with limited interference of those in power into the general market. Though very weak, higher performance of the interventionist role is positively correlated with higher levels on the Participatory Democracy Index (r= .024, p< .01). This shows that journalistic voices tend to be more present in contexts with more active citizen participation in political processes (both electoral and non-electoral).

All factors related to conditions of democracy are significantly correlated with watchdog role performance. Specifically, this role is positively correlated with the Deliberative (r= .157, p< .01), Liberal (r=. 155, p<. 01), and Participatory Democracy (r=. 151, p< .01) Indexes, as well as the Democracy Index (r=.127, p<.01). It is negatively correlated with the FH Political Rights (r=-.169, p< .01) and FH Civil Liberties (r=-.133, p<. 01) Indexes.[10] This shows that the watchdog role is more present in

Table 11.2 Linear Correlations Between Broad-Context Societal Variables and Journalistic Role Performance Across Countries

Journalistic role performances	Variables	r
Interventionist	Democracy Index	−.033**
	EcoFreedom	−.16**
	VDEM Delib. Dem. Index	−.018**
	VDEM Lib. Dem. Index	.004
	VDEM Particip. Dem. index	.024**
	FH Political Rights	.008
	FH Civil Liberties	−.009
Watchdog	*Democracy Index*	.127**
	EcoFreedom	−.062**
	VDEM Delib. Dem. index	.157**
	VDEM Lib. Dem. Index	.155**
	VDEM Particip. Dem. index	.151**
	FH Political Rights	−.169**
	FH Civil Liberties	−.133**
Loyal	*Democracy Index*	−.176**
	EcoFreedom	−.254**
	VDEM Delib. Dem. index	−.186**
	VDEM Lib. Dem. Index	−.188**
	VDEM Particip. Dem. index	−.173**
	FH Political Rights	.190**
	FH Civil Liberties	.216**
Infotainment	Democracy Index	.16**
	EcoFreedom	.010
	VDEM Delib. Dem. Index	.024**
	VDEM Lib. Dem. Index	.033**
	VDEM Particip. Dem. index	.017**
	FH Political Rights	−.042**
	FH Civil Liberties	−.047**
Service	Democracy Index	.034**
	EcoFreedom	−.035**
	VDEM Delib. Dem. Index	.041**
	VDEM Lib. Dem. Index	.047**
	VDEM Particip. Dem. index	.046**
	FH Political Rights	−.066**
	FH Civil Liberties	−.044**
Civic	Democracy Index	.055**
	EcoFreedom	−.077**
	VDEM Delib. Dem. Index	.068**
	VDEM Lib. Dem. Index	.061**
	VDEM Particip. Dem. index	.063**
	FH Political Rights	−.070**
	FH Civil Liberties	−.043**

** Correlation is significant at the 0.01 level (2-tailed). N= 33640

social contexts with higher levels of citizen engagement and political freedom or, in other words, regime type is strongly connected to the capacity to scrutinize powerholders.

But there is more to the role. The performance of the watchdog role is negatively correlated ($r=-.0.62$, $p< .01$) with the level of economic freedom. In case of the HF Economic Freedom Index, lower scores indicate more state control of the economy. This means that watchdog role performance is higher in countries with more market regulations and vice versa.

A negative correlation can be found between loyal-facilitator role performance and economic freedom ($r=-.25$, $p< .01$). Again, since lower scores indicate repression of the economy, we interpret such findings as follows: the less economic freedom, the more prevalent the loyal-facilitator role. However, our tests cannot show which components of HF's Economic Freedom Index are important for the loyal-facilitator role. As it is a composite variable, certain dimension of the index might be more relevant for the performance of some roles. We suggest that the implementation of the rule of law principle has more to do with journalistic roles than government size or the separation of monetary and fiscal policies. Namely, a general negation of the rule of law principle might lead journalists to avoid confrontations with people in power.

There is a positive relationship between the FH Civil Liberties ratings and the loyal-facilitator approach ($r= .216$, $p< .01$). High scores represent serious violations of individual and collective civil rights. Greater protection of civil liberties thus correlates with a low level of performance of the loyal-facilitator role. The evidence indicates that when civil liberties (that is, freedom of expression, assembly, association, education, and religion) are less guaranteed in a country, loyal-facilitator journalism is more likely to blossom.

We also note that the service role significantly correlates with all variables describing political systems and economic freedom. Positive connections were found between service role performance and the Democracy Index ($r=. 034$, $p< .01$), and all three types of the V-Dem democracy principles (Deliberative: $r=. 041$, $p< .01$; Liberal: $r=.047$, $p<.01$; Participatory: $r=.046$, $p<.01$). We also identified negative correlations between the service role and FH Political Rights ($r=. -066$, $p< .01$) and FH Civil Liberties ($r=-.044$, $p< .01$). There is a negative correlation between the service role and market freedom ($r=. -0.35$, $p< .01$), though these associations are rather weak, suggesting societal factors are less connected to the performance of this role.

The civic role presents a similar pattern. While positive connections were found between the presence of the civic role and the Democracy Index ($r=. 055$, $p< .01$) and all three V-Dem democracy principles (Deliberative: $r=. 068$, $p< .01$; Liberal: $r=. 061$, $p<. 01$; Participatory: $r=.063$, $p<.01$), there were negative correlations between the civic role and FH

Political Rights (r=-.070, p<.01) and FH Civil Liberties (r=-.043, p<.01). There was a negative correlation between the service role and market freedom (r=-.0.77, p<.01). Again, the level of association is rather low, so the results must be interpreted with caution.

The findings on service and civic roles in Chapter 7 suggest that journalists in advanced and transitional democratic systems perform the civic role more than journalists in non-democratic countries. Civic role presence is also greater in countries with more state market regulations. This implies that regulatory measures like consumer protections and antitrust laws might create a social climate in which journalism is thought to encourage participation and involvement in community life.

The infotainment role was the only one that positively correlated to HF Economy Index (r=. 010; p< .05), meaning that the media and journalists try to entertain and relax the audience more in the countries where there is a higher level of business, labor, and monetary freedom and a more open market overall. Infotainment role performance followed the same pattern as other roles in regard to the audience for other broad context factors.

Finally, positive connections were found between the civic role and the Democracy Index (r= .55; p< .01) and all three types of the V-Dem democracy principles (Deliberative: r=. 024, p< .01; Liberal: r=. 033, p< .01; Participatory: r=. 017, p< .01). We found negative correlations between the civic role and the FH Political Rights (r=-.042, p< .01) and the FH Civil Liberties (r=-.047, p< .01). This means that processes in deliberative and participatory settings and respect for political and civil liberties in a society might be associated with the performance of the civic role.

Close and Broad Context Factors Influencing Role Performance: Multilevel Models

Next, we used multilevel modeling to gain more in-depth knowledge of the association between societal-factors and role performance, controlling for organizational factors.

We checked collinearity to determine which variables would be included in our multilevel models. Serious collinearity issues (VIF > 10) were found in the VDEM Deliberative Democracy Index, VDEM Liberal Democracy Index, VDEM Participatory Democracy Index, FH Political Rights, and FH Civil Liberties variables, so we excluded all of them from the multilevel modeling.

FH Legal Environment (VIF = 9,529949), FH Political Environment (VIF = 6,127348) and FH Economic Environment (VIF = 9,769286) metrics—as close context variables —and the Democracy Index (VIF = 1,688661) and Economic Freedom Index (VIF = 1,688661)—as broad context variables—passed the collinearity tests. In view of this, we ran our multilevel modeling testing for the influence of these five societal-level factors.

We will start with findings that show the influence of *close context* societal factors on role performance. First, the FH Legal Environment (b= .005, p< .05), FH Political Environment (b= .004, p< .01), and FH Economic Environment (b= .007, p<. 01) variables predict loyal-facilitator role performance, though they do not seem to be able to predict the interventionist, watchdog, service, infotainment, and civic roles (see Table 11.3 and Table 11.4).

Again, bear in mind that FH Legal Environment, Political Environment, and Economic Environment factors are composite variables. In the case of the political environment, the loyal-facilitator role may be triggered by censorship or self-censoring. This may also be shaped by limited availability of reporters who are willing to cover the news freely, or by fear of being harassed or imprisoned.

The same holds true for the legal environment. Frequent violations of freedom of expression or more rigorous media registration requirements may activate the loyal-facilitator role. Concerning the economic environment, we may consider the impact of more frequent bribery on media content or high levels of media ownership concentration. It is plausible that journalists limit what they report or how they cover certain issues when a small number of companies control the media market to avoid offending the political and economic interest of media owners and their advertisers or sponsors. This could create a rewards system that glorifies unconditional journalistic loyalty to owners' interests. Such centralization of ownership might contribute to the instrumentalization of journalism, the emergence of the biased media, and structural obstacles to journalistic independence.

If we zoom in on variance within levels (e.g., country and newspaper) in the case of loyal-facilitator role, estimates of covariance parameters show that the contrast between countries and newspapers can be explained by the different legal, political, and economic environment (b $_{\text{intercept country}}$ = .003, p< .01; b $_{\text{intercept newspaper}}$ = .000; p< .01) around the media. Chapter 10 demonstrates that the organizational background of the newspaper matters in that state-run newspapers exhibit significantly higher performance of the loyal-facilitator role.

Further analyzing the loyal-facilitator role across countries, we observed that a higher level of performance of this role is the result of excessive political control over news content in Cuba (M$_{\text{Loyal-facilitator}}$=.3386, M$_{\text{FHPoliticalEnvironment}}$=35,0000, coefficient of variation, or CoV=77%), Malaysia (M$_{\text{Loyal-facilitator}}$=.1133, M$_{\text{FHPoliticalEnvironment}}$=33,0000, CoV=113%), and Russia (M$_{\text{Loyal-facilitator}}$=.0524, M$_{\text{FHPoliticalEnvironment}}$=32,0000, CoV=220%).

Similarly, the media's lack of economic freedom explains the higher level of performance of the loyal-facilitator role in Cuba (M$_{\text{Loyal-facilitator}}$=.3386, M$_{\text{FHEconomicEnvironment}}$=28,0000, CoV=77.4%) and

Table 11.3 Societal-Level Effects on Journalistic Role Performance: Interventionist, Watchdog, and Loyal-Facilitator

	Interventionist			Watchdog			Loyal-Facilitator		
	$b\ (SE_b)$	p	95%CI	$b\ (SE_b)$	p	95%CI	$b\ (SE_b)$	p	95%CI
Fixed Effects									
Close-context variables									
Intercept	.227	.000	.170; .285	.075	.001	.039; .111	-.038	.280	-.086; .027
FHLegalEnvironment	-.004	.380	-.016; .006	-.003	.227	-.010; .003	.005	.004**	.002; .009
FHPoliticalEnvironment	-.004	.174	-.011; .002	.003	.112	-.001; .008	.004	.009**	-.001; .007
FHEconomicEnvironment	-.011	.065	.000; .024	-.002	.543	-.010; .005	.007	.001**	.003; .011
Covariance Parameters (ID)									
Residual	.041	.001	.040; .041	.010	.001	.010; .011	.007	.001	.006; .007
Intercept Newspaper	.001	.103	.000; .005	.001	.020	.000; .002	.003	.040	.001; .005
Intercept Country	.003	.001	.002; .006	.001	.001	.000; .001	.000	.001	.000; .001
2LL	-11610.324			-56079.309			-71077.387		
AIC (df)	-11596.321			-56065.309			-71063.387		
BIC (df)	-11537.357			-56006.345			-71004.423		
Fixed Effects									
Broad-context variables									
Intercept	.234	.120	-.067; .537	.118	.125	-.035; .273	.217	.115	-.058; .498
DemIndex	-.011	.552	-.098; .027	.010	.291	-.009; .029	.003	.825	-.031; .038
EcoFreedom	.000	.504	-.001; .003	-.001	.034**	.003; .001	-.003	.018**	-.0060; .0066
Covariance Parameters (ID)									
Residual	.041	.001	.040; .041	.010	.001	.010; .011	.007	.001	.006; .007
Intercept Newspaper	.002	.057	.008; .006	.001	.025	.000; .001	.002	.004	.001; .005
Intercept Country	.003	.001	.002; .006	.001	.001	.000; .001	.001	.001	.0002; .0005
2LL	-11606.531			-56082.701			-71077.459		
AIC (df)	-11592.531			-56068.701			-71063.459		
BIC (df)	-11533.567			-56009.736			-71004.495		

Table 11.4 Societal-Level Effects on Journalistic Role Performance: Infotainment, Civic, and Service

	Infotainment			Civic			Service		
	$b\ (SE_b)$	p	95%CI	$b\ (SE_b)$	p	95%CI	$b\ (SE_b)$	p	95%CI
Fixed Effects									
Close-context variables									
Intercept	.078	.001	.044; .111	.033	.042	.001; .065	.037	.001	.017; .057
FHLegalEnvironment	.000	.882	-.006; .007	-.004	.155	-.010; .001	-.000	.882	-.004; .003
FHPoliticalEnvironment	.000	.912	-.004; .003	.004	.046**	.000; .008	-.000	.825	-.002; .002
FHEconomicEnvironment	.001	.647	-.009; .005	.000	.995	-.007; .007	.000	.822	-.003; .004
Covariance Parameters (ID)									
Residual	.013	.000	.013; .014	.012	.000	.0120; .0124	.011	.001	.011; .012
Intercept Newspaper	.000	.347	.000; .002	.000	.028	.000; .001	.000	.079	.0000; .0006
Intercept Country	.002	.001	.001; .003	.000	.001	.000; .001	.000	.001	.0003; .0007
2LL	-48020.239			-52293.917			-53548.345		
AIC (df)	-48006.239			-52279.917			-53534.345		
BIC (df)	-47947.275			-52220.953			-53475.380		
Fixed Effects									
Broad-context variables									
Intercept	-.079	.275	-.228; .068	.118	.125	-.035; .273	.217	.115	-.058; .498
DemIndex	.008	.350	-.010; .027	.010	.291	-.009; .029	.003	.825	-.031; .038
EcoFreedom	.000	.182	.000; .002	-.001	.034**	.003; .001	-.003	.018**	-.0060; .0066
Covariance Parameters (ID)									
Residual	.013	.001	.013; .014	.012	.001	.012; .012	.011	.001	.011; .012
Intercept Newspaper	.000	.632	.000; .008	.000	.032	.000; .001	.000	.264	.0001; .0005
Intercept Country	.002	.001	.001; .003	.000	.001	.000; .001	.000	.001	.0003; .0007
2LL	-48022.921			-52296.575			-53552.821		
AIC (df)	-48008.921			-52282.575			-53538.821		
BIC (df)	-47949.957			-52223.610			-53479.856		

Russia ($M_{\text{Loyal-facilitator}}$=.0524, $M_{\text{FHEconomicEnvironment}}$=24,0000, CoV=220%). The restrictive legal environment has a significant impact on the performance of loyal-facilitator role in Cuba ($M_{\text{Loyal-facilitator}}$=.3386, $M_{\text{FHLegalEnvironment}}$=29,0000, CoV=77.4%), Russia ($M_{\text{Loyal-facilitator}}$=.0524, $M_{\text{FHLegalEnvironment}}$=25,0000, CoV=220%), and Malaysia ($M_{\text{Loyal-facilitator}}$=.1133, $M_{\text{FHLegalEnvironment}}$=25,0000, CoV=113.9%). Our analyses show that close context variables have a significant though somewhat weak effect on loyal-facilitator role performance in Germany, Ireland, Spain, Switzerland, and the U.S. From this perspective, the relative unpopularity of the loyal-facilitator role resonates with the greater political, legal, and economic autonomy of the media.

We find the results for close context variables noteworthy for the civic role. Somewhat similar to our linear correlation results, multilevel analyses show a significant effect of the FH Political Environment index on the performance of this role (b= .004, p<.05). Both analyses suggest that journalists are more likely to behave as carriers of the civic role if the media enjoy more freedom from governmental or political influences. To evaluate variance within levels (e.g., country and newspaper), we considered covariance parameter estimates, which yielded significant differences. The variances are high among countries and newspapers ($b_{\text{intercept country}}$ = .000, p< .01; $b_{\text{intercept newspaper}}$ = .000; p< .05) for the civic role. Chapter 10 confirms that newspapers' political leanings impact the civic role performance. We found that left-leaning, more liberal newspapers perform this role more than centrist newspapers (b = .027, p<.05).

Our investigation of the effects of *broad context variables* found that HF Economic Freedom is somewhat influential in the loyal-facilitator (b= -.003, p<. 01), watchdog (b= -.001, p< .01), and civil roles (b= -.001, p< .05). Linking this back to the linear correlations, the data suggest that liberal market economies increase the prevalence of loyal-facilitator role. We also found that less economic freedom contributes to the prevalence of watchdog journalism. It is difficult to comprehend this without a deeper analysis of the relationship between the free market economy and the freedom of expression principle country by country. The country and newspaper-level differences can be explained by the general freedom of the economic sector ($b_{\text{intercept country}}$ = .003, p<. 01; $b_{\text{intercept newspaper}}$ = .000; p< .01). Chapter 10 notes that ownership type makes a difference in watchdog role performance. State-run newspapers exhibited significantly lower performance of the watchdog role (b = -.047, p<. 05) than privately owned newspapers.

From the perspective of economic freedom, civic role performance exhibits the same patterns as the watchdog role. By connecting these two roles, this chapter suggests that the mechanisms that control the free market through strong unions, large public sectors, and substantial state ownership encourage journalists to monitor government decision-making processes, corporate fraud, illegal activity, and immorality and encourage the audience to get involved in their community.

Though linear correlation tests indicate that there are correlations between the interventionist role and close/broad context variables, multilevel analysis failed to prove significant effects. Likewise, extremely weak linear correlations were identified between the infotainment and service roles and societal-level factors, and we did not find evidence to such relationships controlling for the organizational level.

Conclusion

This chapter looked at the influence of societal contexts on role performance (Blumer, McLeod, & Rosengren, 1992; Esser & Pfetsch, 2004) by broadening variables and dimensions beyond existing media systems theory (Hallin & Mancini, 2004, 2012, 2017; Brüggemann et al., 2014).

The analysis of relationships between societal variables and journalistic roles revealed that the explanatory power of political and socio-economic factors is neither uniform nor straightforward, as it varied across roles. Our study showed that more political and public service-oriented roles are significantly influenced by societal-level factors. Specifically, we found that political and socio-economic context are significant predictors of the loyal-facilitator role and, to some extent, the civic and watchdog roles.

At the simple correlations level, our analyses detected significant connections between societal-level factors and interventionist, infotainment, and service role performance.

The findings on linear correlations between the interventionist role and freedom of the press in a given economic environment show that the journalistic voice has a greater presence in contexts with more economic pressure on media outlets. This is consistent with the higher presence of style-related indicators (mostly the use of adjectives) in the market-oriented (popular) press as compared to the elite press across our sample (see Chapter 5). This is a nuanced relation not normally acknowledged in media systems literature.

Also, linear correlation analyses show that more opportunities for public deliberation and citizen participation are associated with a higher tendency of journalism to monitor the political actors' performance and give the public a voice. The same can be said of the infotainment role, which tends to be performed more in contexts in which journalists and the media have more freedom, and where the principles of democracy are more visible.

Interestingly, the impact of different democracy principles—such as deliberation and participation—on role performance seems weaker than expected. When controlling for the organizational level, the relationship between these factors and journalistic performance is only significant for the loyal-facilitator, civic, and watchdog roles, thus corroborating the multi-factorial nature of role performance.

Press freedom factors are also telling. Our analyses show that better political, legal, and economic circumstances are positively associated with the watchdog and civic roles, and negatively associated with loyal-facilitator and interventionist roles. Multilevel modeling supports the influence of those factors with the loyal-facilitator and civic roles. As theoretically expected, the loyal-facilitator role, which might be manifested by positive feelings about the country or those in power, is higher in countries with less press freedom and more limitations on civil liberties (freedom of speech, religion, assembly, or association).

The emergence of the civic role is impacted by the media's freedom from governmental intervention. A higher level of independence creates a media environment in which journalists advocate for active citizenship and public dialogue.

The level of democracy development matters when it comes to the political functions of journalism such as the loyal-facilitator role. Specifically, one can trace a higher level of support for the country or political actors in power in countries with a lower democracy index, suggesting that authoritarianism and press loyalism are, in fact, strongly linked.

While this is the case for simple correlations between the democracy index and the watchdog role (with a higher democracy index there is a higher tendency to monitor the political, economic, and social elite), the association between the two disappears when controlling for organizational level.

Indeed, considering overall economic freedom leads us to a revealing scenario. We found that liberal market economies increase the prevalence of the loyal-facilitator role and slightly decrease the performance of the watchdog role. This initially contradictory evidence can be explained by a deeper analysis of the measures used by HF to calculate its Economic Freedom Index. Our analyses show that in some contexts, freedom of the press and the Democracy Index do not go hand-in-hand with state-level interventionism in the market because the state may govern the media market differently than the general market in some countries. Between 2012 and 2015, only a few countries from our sample that ranked very high on the Democracy Index or the FH Index received equally high scores on HF Economic Freedom Index Ranking. The U.S., Switzerland, and Ireland appeared at the top of the Economic Freedom Index Ranking (2019), as well as the Economist Unit Democracy Index ranking (2013) and The FH Freedom Press Index ranking (2012, 2013, 2014, 2015).

By contrast, Hong Kong, which is considered a flawed democracy and partly free in terms of the press freedom, was ranked the freest market in the HF Economic Freedom Index Ranking.

Considering that liberal market economies decrease the performance of the watchdog role, it is understandable why Hong Kong, but also

Switzerland, Ireland, and Chile, exhibit a very marginal level of watchdog role performance overall—just as low as Cuba and China (see Chapter 6).

While our study shows the relevant influence that well-known societal-level factors have on the performance of the loyal-facilitator role, and to some extent on the watchdog and civic roles, it lacks explanatory power for the other three roles. This demonstrates that organizational- and story-level factors seem to be more associated with the performance of interventionism, service, and infotainment roles. With these findings in mind, we are able to better interpret the assumptions of media-system research in the future, with roles associated to power elites and to the public sphere more strongly interrelated to societal factors. Also, this leads us to question the extent to which the available measures of the societal-level factor truly reflect the specificities of national journalistic culture traits (Powers & Vera-Zembrano, 2018). There is a need for even more sophisticated, innovative, and revised indexing mechanisms to fully elucidate the nuances of the differences between societies.

Notes

1 See https://freedomhouse.org/report/freedom-press-2013/methodology.
2 See https://freedomhouse.org/report/freedom-press-2013/methodology.
3 See https://freedomhouse.org/report/freedom-press-2013/methodology.
4 See www.eiu.com/public/topical_report.aspx?campaignid=Democracy0814.
5 See www.v-dem.net/en/analysis/VariableGraph/.
6 See www.v-dem.net/en/analysis/VariableGraph.
7 See www.v-dem.net/en/analysis/VariableGraph/.
8 See https://freedomhouse.org/sites/default/files/FIW%202013%20Booklet. pdf.
9 See www.heritage.org/index/about.
10 FH Political Rights and FH Civil Liberties are scored from 1 to 7, with 1 representing the most freedom and 7 the least.

References

Aalberg, T., van Aelst, P., & Curran, J. (2010). Media systems and the political information environment: A cross-national comparison. *The International Journal of Press/Politics, 15*(3), 255–271.

Albæk, E., van Dalen, A., Jebril, N., & de Vreese, C. H. (2014). *Political journalism in comparative perspective.* New York: Cambridge University Press.

Blumer, J.G., & Gurevitch, M. (1995). *The crisis of public communication.* London: Routledge.

Blumer, J. G., McLeod, J. M., & Rosengren, K. E. (1992). An introduction to comparative communication research. In J. G. Blumer, J. M. McLeod, & K. E. Rosengren (Eds.), *Comparatively speaking: Communication and culture across space and time.* London: Sage Publishing.

Brüggemann, M., Engesser, S., Büchel, F., Humprecht, E., & Castro, L. (2014). Hallin and Mancini revisited: Our empirical types of Western media systems. *Journal of Communication, 64*(6), 1037–1065.

Couldry, N. (2005). Comparing media systems: Three models of media and politics. *Political Studies Review*, 3, 304–306.

Curran, J., Iyanger, S., Brink Lund, A., & Salovaara-Moring, I. (2009). Media system, public knowledge and democracy: A comparative study. *European Journal of Communication*, 24(1), 5–26.

Dobek-Ostrowska, B. (2015). 25 years after communism: Four models of media and politics in Central and Eastern Europe. In B. Dobek-Ostrowska & M. Głowacki (Eds.), *Democracy and media in Central and Eastern Europe 25 years on* (pp. 11–46). Frankfurt am Main: Peter Lang Edition.

Dohnanyi, J. (2003). *The impact of media concentration on professional journalism. Organization for security and co-operation in Europe (OSCE)*. Retrieved from www.osce.org/fom/13870?download=true

Economist Unit (2013). *Democracy index 2013. Democracy in limbo. A report from The Economist Intelligence Unit*. Retrieved from https://thepeoples-convention.org/wp-content/uploads/2015/04/TheEconomist-DemocracyIndex2013.pdf

Engesser, S., & Franzetti, A. (2011). Media systems and political systems: Dimensions of comparison. *International Communication Gazette*, 73(4), 273–301.

Esser, F. (2008). Dimensions of political news cultures: Sound bite and image bite in France, Germany, Great Britain, and the United States. *The International Journal of Press/Politics*, 13(4), 401–428.

Esser, F., & Pfetsch, B. (Eds.). (2004). *Comparing political communication theories, cases, and challenges*. Cambridge: Cambridge University Press.

Esser, F., & Umbricht, A. (2013). Competing models of journalism? Political affairs coverage in US, British, German, Swiss, French, and Italian newspapers. *Journalism*, 14(8), 989–1007.

FH (2012). *Breakthroughs and pushback in the Middle East. Selected data from FH's annual press index*. Retrieved from https://freedomhouse.org/sites/default/files/Booklet%20for%20Website.pdf

FH (2013). *Middle East volatility amid global decline. Selected data from FH's annual press index*. Retrieved from https://freedomhouse.org/sites/default/files/FOTP%202013%20Booklet%20Final%20Complete%20-%20Web.pdf

FH (2014). *Freedom in the world 2014*. Retrieved from https://freedomhouse.org/sites/default/files/FIW2014%20Booklet.pdf

FH (2015). *Freedom in the world 2014*. Retrieved from https://freedomhouse.org/sites/default/files/01152015_FIW_2015_final.pdf

Guerrero, M., & Márquez-Ramirez, M. (Eds.). (2014). *Media systems and communication politics in Latin America*. London: Palgrave Macmillan.

Gunarante, S. (2010). De-Westernizing communication/social research: Opportunities and limitations. *Media, Culture & Society*, 32(3), 473–500.

Hair, J. F. Jr., Anderson, R. E., Tatham, R. L., & Black, W. C. (1995). *Multivariate data analysis* (3rd ed.). New York: Macmillan.

Hallin, D., & Mancini, P. (2004). *Comparing media systems: Three models of media and politics*. Cambridge: Cambridge University Press.

Hallin, D., & Mancini, P. (Eds.). (2012). *Comparing media systems beyond the western world*. Cambridge: Cambridge University Press.

Hallin, D., & Mancini, P. (2017). Ten years after comparing media systems: What have we learned? *Political Communication*, 34(2), 155–171.

Hanitzsch, T., Hanusch, F., Ramaprasad, J., & De Beer, A. S. (Eds.). (2019). *Worlds of journalism: Journalistic cultures around the globe.* New York: Columbia University Press.

Hanitzsch, T., & Mellado, C. (2011). What shapes the news around the world? How journalists in eighteen countries perceive influences on their work, *The International Journal of Press/Politics, 16*(3), 404–426.

Hayashi, K., & Kopper, G. G. (2014). Multi-layer research design for analyses of journalism and media systems in the global age: Test case Japan. *Media, Culture & Society, 36*(8), 1134–1150.

Heritage Foundation (2019). *HF economic freedom index rankings.* Retrieved from www.heritage.org/index/

Lohner, J. L., Banjac, S., & Nevela, I. (2016). *Mapping structural conditions of journalism in Egypt, Kenya, Serbia and South Africa.* The Working Papers in the MeCoDEM series. Retrieved from www.semanticscholar.org/paper/Mapping-structural-conditions-of-journalism-in-andLohnerBanjac/8478d016e64bcc74a17325eb3c18d604c3d0e951#references

Márquez-Ramirez, M., Mellado, C., Humanes, M. L., Amado, A., Beck, D., Davydov, S., . . Wang, H. (2020). Detached or interventionist? Comparing the performance of watchdog journalism in transitional, advanced and non-democratic countries. *International Journal of Press/Politics, 25*(1), 53–75.

Mattoni, A., & Ceccobelli, D. (2018). Comparing hybrid media systems in the digital age: A theoretical framework for analysis. *European Journal of Communication, 33*, 540–557.

Mellado, C., Hellmueller, L., Márquez-Ramírez, M., Humanes, M. L., Sparks, C., Stępińska, A., . . Wang, H. (2017). The hybridization of journalistic cultures: A comparative study of journalistic role performance. *Journal of Communication, 67*(6), 944–967.

Mellado, C., & Lagos, C. (2013). Redefining comparative analyses of media systems from the perspective of new democracies. *Communication & Society, 26*(4), 1–24.

Meyen, M. (2018). Journalists' autonomy around the globe: A typology of 46 mass media systems. *Global Media Journal, German Edition, 8*(1).

Norris, P. (2009). Comparative political communications: Common frameworks or Babelian confusion? *Government and Opposition, 44*(3), 321–340.

Peruško, Z., Vozab, D., & Čuvalo, A. (2013). Audience as a sources of agency in media system: Post-socialist Europe in comparative perspective. *Mediálni Studia, 2.*

Powers, M., & Vera-Zembrano, S. (2018). The universal and the contextual of media systems: Research design, epistemology, and the production of comparative knowledge. *International Journal of Press/Politics, 23*(2), 143–160.

Shoemaker, P., & Reese, S. (2013). *Mediating the message in the 21st century: A media sociology perspective.* New York: Routledge.

Siebert, F. S., Peterson, T., & Schramm, W. (1956). *Four theories of the press: The authoritarian, libertarian, social responsibility, and Soviet communist concepts of what the press should be and do.* Urbana, IL: University of Illinois Press.

Weaver, D. H., & Willnat, L. (Eds.). (2012). *The global journalist in the 21st century: News people around the world.* New York: Routledge.

12 Beyond Journalistic Norms
Empirical Lessons on Role Performance in the News

Claudia Mellado, Mireya Márquez-Ramírez, María Luisa Humanes, Cornelia Mothes, Adriana Amado, Sergey Davydov, Jacques Mick, Dasniel Olivera, Nikos S. Panagiotou, Svetlana Pasti, Patric Raemy, Sergio Roses, Anna-Maria Schielicke, Henry Silke, Agnieszka Stępińska, Gabriella Szabó, and Edson Tandoc Jr.

News events with global appeal such as the COVID-19 pandemic, terrorist attacks, mass shootings, plane crashes, and earthquakes are flagship examples of journalistic role performance in action. But so are more ordinary developments like G20 summits, presidential speeches, parliamentary sessions, council meetings, daily crime news, judicial processes, protests, and industry reports. All kinds of news stories and story angles can, at some point or under certain circumstances, serve as exemplars of how the interventionist, loyal-facilitator, watchdog, civic, service, and infotainment roles not only manifest in practice, but also co-exist and interact across and within cultures, topics, types of newspapers, and even single news stories.

In this book, we analyzed how professional journalism roles materialize in print news in different organizational, institutional, and social settings, examining journalistic practice under the umbrella offered by the multidimensional concept of role performance. We have made a case for the ever-changing, fluid, and dynamic nature of journalistic roles, which are activated and deactivated by certain triggers, events, and circumstances, showing the extent to which news stories in a given country exhibit indicators of one or more of them.

In doing so, we have gone beyond the expectations of journalistic norms to locate our work at the heart of journalism and media practices. Normative roles might be firmly anchored in journalists' mindsets as guiding ideals and aspirations that give meaning to the profession, but journalistic practice is by no means static and does not depend on individuals' will alone. Our efforts have unraveled the complex nature of such dynamic practices to account for journalistic role performance in news content, allowing us to more fully understand the issues at stake when discussing similarities and differences in journalistic cultures around the world.

General Conclusions: Transcending Norms and Looking Into Role Performance

We began this book from the position that journalists' missions and the performance of journalistic roles can take many forms. Indeed, one of the main contributions of this volume is that it shifts the focus from the construct of professional roles as static and binary classifications of ideals and taken-for-granted behaviors to that of professional roles as socially constructed, non-mutually exclusive, and comprised of both ideals and meaningful practices. This approach can better explain journalistic roles across and within professional cultures beyond the Western countries that have traditionally been studied in existing literature.

By drawing on a more diverse sample of countries, including transitional democracies and non-democracies across the world, and on a broad sample of news items beyond front page news, we can paint a much clearer picture of the issues and conditions that cause the press performance of certain countries to move along or further away from others in both expected and unexpected ways. As we have argued throughout this book, unlike normative values that tend to be assumed as somewhat fixed and stable, the reporting practices that lead to role performance are constantly mutating and can be mediated by multiple influences and local contexts.

While the presumption in traditional research on journalistic role conception is that norms tend to dictate actions, our study demonstrates that there are much more complicated interactions between these two variables and that they often influence each other.

The erosion and increasing porosity of the professional, material, and occupational boundaries of a profession once considered the jurisdiction of a few experts (Carlson & Lewis, 2015; Waisbord, 2013) is not solely a consequence of the digital age. Our book shows that boundary permeability has always been an inherent aspect of news production, reporting styles, and storytelling overall, with certain events and contexts triggering the blending and hybridization of roles, role sub-dimensions, and role indicators. Indeed, by looking at how journalistic roles interact with each other in the news, the circumstances that prompt such interactions, and the resulting hybridization of roles, we have found a great deal of boundary permeability. New pressures and contexts are making professional roles even more flexible and permeable, and they are almost always dependent on contingent factors and events, from the rescue of people in danger to impeachment hearings, from global pandemics to everyday news.

The authors of this book use role performance research to demonstrate that it is possible to study the performative level of journalistic culture beyond journalistic norms. This new way of analyzing journalistic cultures moves past idealizations and perfect representations of typologies to grapple with questions about variations in professional practices, revealing the forces that can guide this change over time.

The study of practice cannot be fully understood outside of a meaningful context (Vos, 2017; Anderson, 2020). Our project reflects a commitment to that premise and a renewed focus on the different meanings that the performance of professional roles, their combinations, and the gaps and relationships between ideals and practices acquire for the practice of journalism in different parts of the world.

This is not, of course, an attempt to disarticulate the normative discourses at the heart of the profession. Journalists' efforts to oil the wheels of society, develop communities, entertain and serve the public, and hold the powerful accountable are stronger than ever (Rusbridger, 2018, p. ix; Schudson, 2018). Nevertheless, this book invites us to think outside of the limited space that the normative world gives us in order to analyze a more detailed layer of journalistic practices and routines as observed in news content and to understand the validity of the discreet categories and classifications normally used to explain a profession that is consistently challenged across spaces and time. It is clear to us that the sometimes narrow focus of existing research instruments—and, more importantly, the issues that we choose not to research because of the limitations imposed by theoretically pigeon-holed norms—prevent us from engaging in analyses of the multiple and unexpected functions that the profession is fulfilling in contemporary society (Schudson, 2018; Skinner, Gasher, & Compton, 2001; Zelizer, 1993, 2015).

More than ever, when traditional assumptions about the nature of professional roles and news practices are being questioned, it is crucial to create spaces of dialogue between idealizations and practices, and to deeply analyze the different layers that comprise journalistic cultures, where both norms and practices need to face their own limitations to explain each other. Moreover, we suggest that new ways of thinking about comparative studies in journalism are attainable, aware of the great deal of work to be done.

While our book title and research endeavor might initially seem to go against fixed journalistic norms and categories, one of our aims has been, in fact, to make a normative contribution. To the extent that we can discuss the practices of the profession and how they relate to the norms that bring journalists together as members of a profession, it is possible to reach a greater understanding about how both rules and practices are constantly changing.

That is the perspective adopted in this book. By suggesting theoretical and methodological models that can be used to study role performance, developing instruments for content and survey analysis to be applied in different countries, and proposing a theoretical and empirical operationalization of roles, we hope to have made a significant contribution to the study of journalistic roles.

First, we have not only analyzed six professional roles that manifest themselves in news content in different journalistic domains. We also disaggregated them into individual indicators and into analytical sub-dimensions that illustrate the nuances, orientations, and intensities of professional roles so that role performance can be theorized, measured, and compared. This allowed us to more accurately pinpoint how certain roles are manifested in news content and interact with one another by reflecting the specific practices and narratives that comprise journalistic work. Since journalistic norms and ideals are normally taken as a given, previous research had not paid sufficient attention to the actual operationalization of roles in news content or the multiple ways professional roles can actually be traced back to practice and content. It is our hope that this contribution will pave the way for future developments in journalistic role performance studies.

Second, we have contested and challenged assumptions about the "type of journalism" that prevails in specific political, economic, and geographical contexts, as only a few media systems prominently exhibit certain expected roles, and only do so with respect to specific role sub-dimensions or indicators. Most of the journalism that is performed in countries around the world is, in fact, hybrid.

Third, we highlighted the usefulness and prevalence of roles that are normally either stigmatized or left out of the normative literature despite the fact that they are common in news content, as is the case of the infotainment and loyal-facilitator roles. Again, the manifestation of and interaction between indicators and sub-dimensions of role performance have painted a much more accurate picture of the frequent circumstances that trigger their use, especially when interacting with other roles or with specific topics. We have departed from Western perspectives that hold that some "good" roles as more attuned to the idea of quality journalism and therefore deserve more scholarly attention in news content, marginalizing roles that are considered more instrumental to elites, commercialism, or consumerism. News production and the functions of journalism are not only shaped by public service but also impacted by market-driven economies in which media systems operate and by for-profi t enterprises. Leaving these roles aside would be naïve and would ignore the growing infl uence of audiences on media content. Likewise, we have left aside perspectives that deem the interventionist role to be less indicative of factual, objective news. As our study shows, the interventionist role is indeed transversal to the other roles.

Fourth, since there is a general consensus regarding the inevitable discrepancies between ideals and performance, we made a serious effort to disentangle, measure, and compare the width of this link across roles. We accounted for the multiple ways in which certain roles are more difficult to perform than others, as the norms-practice gap is deeper when performing certain functions in specific contexts or circumstances.

Fifth, we have shown how role performance varies and materializes across different countries, news organizations, and types of stories, accounting for the social, organizational, and reporting-level factors that explain the prevalence of roles. Our analyses of roles in the news go beyond front pages, headlines, and the single-topic focus that tends to prevail in content analysis literature. We embraced a perspective that accounted for a broad universe of thematic stories in order to elicit a more realistic and comprehensive picture of journalistic practices behind everyday, ordinary news.

Finally, we have adopted a more holistic, horizontal approach in which roles go hand-in-hand and serve each other in practice. We have found this perspective to be more useful for understanding the extent to which professional norms prevail and are interiorized in daily reporting practices in different contexts, and can co-exist with the current practice of journalism in a way that strengthens the profession.

Unraveling Journalistic Role Performance

Our book began with the observation that journalistic roles and their characteristics are often performed simultaneously due to the fact that multiple missions and news values are accomplished and displayed as events unfold on a daily basis. The chapters that comprise this book have shown that when performing their roles on behalf of their news organizations, journalists interact with different forms of power, colleagues, and audiences, and have to "set the scene" of their performance in what can be very challenging contexts. We have addressed the link between professional or normative ideals and journalistic practices, explaining the gap between role conceptions, perceived role enactment, and journalistic performance.

Overall, our results show that, apart from the primary function of disseminating the news, there is no single prevailing model of journalistic performance around the world. Nor is there a particular societal or organizational setting that can ensure perfect models to guarantee the full performance—i.e., the overall presence of all role indicators—of each individual role, as it is impossible to classify journalism in discreet categories. Indeed, the situational and evolving nature of journalistic roles seems to be pushing us towards pluralistic conclusions, helping us to understand how and why journalism behaves in certain ways at certain times and in certain contexts.

With these overall conclusions in mind, each of the empirical chapters of this book provides detailed research findings, addressing global topics from in-depth perspectives. This allows us to understand the complex

230 Claudia Mellado et al.

nature of journalistic cultures across and within countries, with professional cultures displaying types of journalism that rarely resemble traditional ideals of the profession.

Focusing on different domains and professional roles, Chapter 4 showed that the variation of role performance across countries cannot always be attributed solely to countries with the same type of media system, political regime, geographic region, or cultural tradition. Role performance also varies depending on historical moments, journalistic traditions, and the nature of the news itself. Generally, countries that have both not been theorized and those that have been widely theorized, such as non-Western and Western countries, respectively, show different levels of hybridization in the performance of journalistic roles. For these reasons, we believe that existing media systems theory, while holding valuable predictive power at the structural, macro level of the media and their links to other variables (Brüggemann, Engesser, Büchel, Humprecht, & Castro, 2014), is not always the best fit when it comes to explaining and predicting role performance at the practice and routine levels of analysis, specially for certain roles (see next section). Media systems theory tends to link contrasting reporting traditions with systemic or market-level factors (Hallin & Mancini, 2004). Our book pinpoints the specific roles and sub-dimensions in which macro variables hold a greater predictive power, but also addresses the multi-factorial nature of role performance, yielding richer, more detailed, and even unexpected results.

For example, Chapter 4 shows that news in Polarized Pluralist countries exhibit a great deal of interventionism, as expected, but that the liberal U.S. press tops them all. Similarly, for the watchdog role, unexpectedly, newspapers from Polarized Pluralist systems lead the pack; while for the civic role, it is the U.S. and Greece, two countries with little in common at the media-system level. The greatest presence of the infotainment and service roles is found in a very heterogeneous group of countries, with nothing at the media-system level clearly triggering their performance. Only Cuba, by far, meets expectations with relation to the loyal-facilitator role, which turned out to be considerably higher than in the rest of participating countries. Our results are thus important for understanding how different levels of performance of the six roles in the print press are scattered across a diverse group of countries and political regimes, suggesting that there is no fixed grouping of countries around known media systems constructs.

With respect to role co-occurrence, we found a significant correlation between the interventionist and watchdog roles, but only in contexts closer to the Polarized Pluralist model (Hallin & Mancini, 2012). Another unexpected finding is that authoritarian regimes present a strong negative correlation between the interventionist and loyal-facilitator roles, meaning that the use of the journalistic voice is not always channeled towards propagandist aims. We might expect interventionism to go hand-in-hand with infotainment, but that only tends to happen in very different countries, and decidedly not in East Asian news. Meanwhile, the service and interventionist roles co-occur only in the print press of two countries, while a strong interrelation between the civic and interventionist roles is found in some established and transitional democracies, perhaps reflecting the social movements going on there at the time.

Another key finding is that, just as normative theories would expect, democratic roles such as the watchdog and civic are highly interrelated, but surprisingly not in liberal, established democracies where they were first theorized. This coupling is instead found in emerging democracies and even in a non-democracy, suggesting that when there are weak institutions or rule of law, the empowerment of citizens may go hand in hand with the ongoing scrutiny of political elites. Hence, the interplay between certain roles does not appear to correspond to regime-type expectations. With a handful of unrelated cases exhibiting different role combinations, it is clear that changing sociopolitical contexts, rather than systemic characteristics, drive role hybridization.

To what extent are these general results, then, boosted by the particular characteristics of the roles? In disentangling these results more closely, Chapter 5 focused on the interventionist role and indicators such as interpretations, opinions, calls for action, the use of evaluative adjectives, and the use of the first person in the news and their variations. We examined the extent to which journalists are detached reporters or sources of explanations and demands. We also addressed the distinction between *content-related* and *style-related* indicators of the active stance of the journalistic voice. Overall, the study showed an important performance of the interventionist role in newspapers around the world, especially in the U.S., a country that has been the hallmark of factuality and detachment. However, we also determined that style-related interventionism is common in censorship-prone transitional democracies in East Asia, while content-related interventionism is higher in both (post) communist societies and advanced democracies. These results invite future theoretical discussion on the disaggregated analytical sub-dimensions of this role, which is sometimes understood in rather abstract ways. Most importantly, we found that the performance of the interventionist role and its indicators was not limited to partisan media cultures, non-democratic countries, or autonomous media systems and transcends macro-level variables.

If we take into account the theories that link journalistic autonomy with liberal media systems, our results fail to corroborate such assumptions. Professional autonomy does not necessarily lead to more interventionism, while the lack of autonomy does not necessarily prevent interventionism, as journalists may be more interventionist in their reporting because they are more autonomous, because they are defending specific causes or because there is a tradition of political parallelism (partisan press). We also found no significant difference between the popular press and the elite press in the overall sample with regard to the presence of the three content elements that comprise the interventionist role—opinion, interpretation, and call for action. In other words, even when it appears counterintuitive, tabloid news does not necessarily exhibit a more prominent voice. The biggest differences in how the popular and elite press address the interventionist role tend to be more a matter of style than substance.

In terms of the relationship between journalists and those in power, the watchdog role has a significantly higher presence than the loyal-facilitator role in the news overall, meaning that at least in the explicit content they produce, journalists are keener to scrutinize political and economic elites than they are to serve them. Hence, even if official sources primarily drive the news, this does not necessarily translate into support for elites or their actions. Chapter 6 provided a more nuanced discussion of journalists' relationship with established powers by disaggregating roles into analytical sub-dimensions, proposing the *detached* and *interventionist* approaches for the case of the watchdog role and an *elite-supporting* and *nation-supporting* approaches for the case of the loyal-facilitator role.

We discovered that both forms of watchdog reporting are performed across countries, but that the detached orientation towards monitoring, such as questioning and criticism of third parties rather than journalists' own voice, is preferred globally except for Polarized Pluralist media systems and countries undergoing political change or crisis, which display both watchdog orientations. The press in some liberal democracies preferred the most detached variation, owing perhaps to their tradition to factuality and objectivity, and non-democracies generally had low levels of both orientations. This was, however, also true in some transitional and established democracies.

Moreover, the interventionist variation of the watchdog role in which journalists use their own voice to scrutinize elites was found to be more stable across topics than the highly variable detached approach. This means that print journalists who manage to get their voices heard in news content are able to do so across different topics, whereas the detached orientation is more dependent on the type of issue at stake. We also found that both right- and left-leaning newspapers engage in detached monitoring, but that when it comes to being openly interventionist in their scrutiny, it is right-leaning papers who, at the time of data collection, had more incentives to be antagonistic, indicating that scrutiny can indeed be triggered by partisanship and not by public service alone.

Regarding to the loyal-facilitator role, we found that its elite-supporting orientation is significantly more present than its nation-supporting orientation in the news. However, the gap between the two is smaller than the gap between the two sub-dimensions of the watchdog role, suggesting this is a more stable role overall, although the performance of both orientations is practically null in most countries, except in Cuba or Malaysia. The slightly higher presence of the elite-supporting approach varied across countries, with vast differences between non-democratic and democratic states, whereas the nation-supporting orientation is more scattered across different types of countries. This means that certain forms of nationalism and patriotism are context-driven rather than regime-driven. Moreover, media's political leaning has a significant impact on the elite-supporting orientation of this role, corroborating the partisan nature of sycophantic news coverage in certain news outlets.

We found several patterns of role hybridization, but we could highlight that in countries with state control and political instrumentalization, greater support for elites or the nation means lower levels of detached watchdog reporting. In contrast, in liberal and transitional democracies, role sub-dimensions at the domain of power relations are decisively independent from one another at the country level, except for Greece, where all of them correlate, suggesting crisis-driven hybridization between different forms of monitoring and of loyalism. Moreover, specific news topics such as courts, defense and national security, protests and demonstration, police and crime, elections, and economy actually trigger various forms of hybridization, but only in certain countries, especially those experiencing political turbulence.

With respect to the audience approach domain, Chapters 4 and 7 showed that the civic role, and especially the infotainment role, have a higher global presence than the service role, meaning that the national desks of newspapers may have a lot to learn from their sister "soft" news desks in terms of engaging with everyday audiences' needs. Our results show that the infotainment role is spread out across diverse types of newspapers, topics, and cultural contexts, whereas the civic role can be highly prominent in dissimilar media systems such as the U.S. or Greece, perhaps owing to not only specific moments in time, such as crisis or elections, but also their political culture and presence of grassroots organizations. Chapter 7 specifically analyzed how these three roles, their sub-dimensions, and their characteristics materialize in the print press across countries.

We proposed two analytical sub-dimensions of the civic role, which correspond to a more deliberate approach to the promotion and defense of citizen activities (civic-advocate) and to guidance of citizens (civic-educator). The analysis of these two sub-dimensions showed two groups that include countries with different journalistic traditions from different geographical locations, yielding a first layer of hybridization: group heterogeneity with respect to audiences. However, we did find a greater performance of the advocate approach in transitional democracies than in advanced democracies and non-democratic countries, suggesting that future theorizations of civic journalism should analyze the role's advocacy elements in unstable democracies with more marginalized voices.

Meanwhile, no clear grouping patterns were observed for the educational approach, which suggests the context-driven nature of this role orientation, as it is more frequently manifested in countries needing societal change. We also found that most national newspapers implement the infotainment and service roles mainly through a single indicator: the use of personalization in the case of infotainment, and the impact on everyday life in the case of the service role. As such, they show specific aspects of journalistic narrative and function, tying journalistic cultures together regardless of regime type. However, stand-alone national exceptions were found, such as Chile and the Philippines, where a more consumer-oriented journalism dominates, and Mexico, where sensationalism prevails over other infotainment elements.

Our data also showed a significant co-occurrence of the infotainment and civic roles in the U.S., as well as a significant hybridization of the three roles in Spain and Mexico—countries that were experiencing massive protests at the time the data was collected. Moreover, the activation of at least one combination of roles occurs across all topics, and is mainly observed in elite newspapers across the world, revealing another pattern of topic-driven hybridization.

Predictors of Role Performance

Having discussed how the performance of different role sub-dimensions varies across countries, topics, and political leanings, it became clear that some roles might be more difficult to materialize in practice, and that factors such as the structure of the social system, the organizational level, or the nature of the issues or events covered and reported on also affects the extent to which particular roles are performed (Shoemaker & Reese, 2013).

Chapter 8 analyzed the extent to which journalists are able to maintain their role ideals and endorse the practices leading to the performance of these roles. To address these questions, we examined the link between role conception and role performance both as a gap and as a relationship. We also included journalists' perceived role enactment as a potential intersection between normative ideals and institutional practice. Our analyses revealed that the largest discrepancies are found in public service-oriented roles such as the watchdog and civic roles. This means that, with many political interests and forms of power at stake, journalists have a harder time executing roles that are intertwined with the political realm and the public sphere, such as vigilance or citizen empowerment.

The comparatively smallest gaps occurred with roles that allow individual, political, and economic influences to affect news coverage to a greater degree (i.e., interventionist, loyal-facilitator, infotainment). Our findings thus suggest that journalists more easily recognize and even implement roles that aim to influence the public in one way or the other, and in which they face fewer structural obstacles. Given that public information tends to be more sensitive with its potential to affect those in power and elected officials, we can expect an increasing number of external factors—on top of newsroom restrictions—to come together to limit opportunities to fully perform the watchdog and civic roles. The rest of roles are less harmful in that respect.

This is also reflected in the analyses of the link as a relationship instead of a gap. Whereas the performance of the interventionist, loyal-facilitator, infotainment, and service roles were—to different levels—significantly related to journalists' role conception and perceived role enactment, the watchdog and civic roles showed no substantial association between normative ideals and perceived role enactment with actual news performance.

Our data revealed that while press performance and normative journalistic standards might vary widely from country to country when measured separately, journalistic cultures yield similar gaps between journalists' ideals and their media organizations' performance, with all countries presenting similarly evident gaps. This applies in particular for roles that are directly linked to the media system, the political system, and the public, such as the civic and watchdog roles. Our results also show that the extent to which journalists' role conceptions match their perceived role enactment and the extent to which both match actual role performance differ significantly across countries. This was especially true for public influence-oriented roles such as the interventionist and loyal-facilitator roles. We could thus argue that hybridization is more prominent overall with respect to role performance, but less prominent for the ideals-practice gaps.

In Chapter 9, we learned that story-level characteristics are significantly related to journalistic role performance and that news topic, news sourcing, and geographic focus influence particular journalistic roles. For example, we found that the performance of the watchdog role is more likely in state-related topics such as government issues, political campaigns, and police and court stories, while economy, transportation, and health topics are more associated with the service role. We also found that sourcing patterns are related to role performance: the use of civil society and individual citizens as sources seems to foster the performance of the civic role. Finally, in terms of geographic focus, the more local a story is, the more likely it is to exhibit the loyal-facilitator role. In contrast, as the story becomes decoupled from a local perspective, the more likely it is to exhibit service, infotainment, and civic roles. Hence, these findings could be interpreted as empirical evidence of the routine-level influence on journalistic role performance and support perspectives suggest that roles are in many ways context-driven (Mellado, Hellmueller, & Donsbach, 2017; Mellado, 2019).

Through this lens, news-story-level factors might act more as moderators between journalists' intentions and actual role performance. Based on our argument that news-story-level factors are reflections of news routines, we can state that routine-level influences matter significantly in accounting for how the performance of certain roles manifests in news content. While there are some variations, our results show that differences between news topics, sourcing, and geographic focus tend to be similar across news outlets in different organizations and countries.

While Chapter 9 focused on the news-story level and its impact on role performance, Chapter 10 examined whether and how attributes of news organizations are reflected in specific professional role performances. The data revealed that business principles were generally more influential than the journalistic and technological principles applied in print media.

Our analyses of the effects of business principles showed that—not surprisingly—elite newspapers were less likely to use infotainment in their news coverage. However, no other roles were affected by newspapers' audience orientation. This suggests that growing economic pressures from the audience market in today's high-choice environments may not automatically lead to a general transformation of journalism. Rather, they contribute to an adjustment of roles that can easily be adapted to the needs of particular audiences, revealing a great deal of potential hybridization of professional roles at the organizational level. We also found, rather expectedly, that state-owned newspapers were significantly less likely to perform the watchdog role and substantially more likely to perform the loyal-facilitator role than private and corporate newspaper companies. Given that all other roles remained unaffected by state-ownership, this finding illustrates how state-owned newspapers manage to suppress news coverage that may be critical of the government, supporting compliance of loyal-facilitators and keeping critical-analytical reflection by watchdogs in check.

Journalistic principles were found to be slightly less influential than business principles, which also contain political principles. This reflects the process by which newspaper organizations are increasingly becoming businesses. However, the effects of this process may have serious implications for the future of newspaper journalism. Our findings suggest that newsrooms that commit to ethical standards via editorial guidelines appear to be less exposed to political and economic influences. This means that they are insulated from influences that may harm journalists' professional autonomy. More specifically, we found that newspapers that have implemented ethical guidelines were both less likely to cover the news in a non-critical, government-favorable way, and less amenable to turning the news into service products. Furthermore, our analyses showed that left-leaning, more liberal outlets seem to succeed in maintaining journalists' public service-oriented roles, though this comes at the expense of a primarily neutral and detached reporting style.

Finally, Chapter 11 identified sources of influence on journalistic role performance at the societal level. Our study showed that more political and public service-oriented roles, such as the civic and watchdog, and especially the loyal-facilitator, were significantly influenced by societal-level factors. Specifically, better political and legal circumstances were positively associated with the prevalence of the watchdog and civic roles, while both elements have a negative relationship with the loyal-facilitator and interventionist roles.

However, we also found that liberal market economies not only increase the performance of the loyal-facilitator role, but also slightly decrease the performance of the watchdog role. These findings mirror the complexity of the contexts in which the media have been operating. In some countries, journalists may benefit from high democratic standards and press freedom (despite some control over the market) that allows them to monitor those in power and serve as a moderator for expressing citizen demands. In others, economic freedom does not guarantee more space for the monitoring role when democracy is weak.

Although moderated by the organizational level, our study also revealed the following tendency: the more democratic a political regime is and the more freedom journalists have, the more eager they are to perform different roles (except for the loyal-facilitator). In this regard, journalists serve purposes that go beyond protecting citizens from the government's wrongdoings and providing a forum for public debate. They also entertain the audience and provide advice.

In sum, our findings show that although the most frequently performed roles in everyday news are the infotainment and civic roles, and to some extent the watchdog role, with a transversal presence of the interventionist role at different levels, the manifestation of journalistic roles are subject to changes due to the fluid context of the news-making processes. We determined that societal-level factors are relevant for understanding the forces that render specific types of performances of the most political roles. In that respect, media systems theory is useful for predicting the presence of roles related to the public sphere—revealing that news media reflect or are shaped by society and politics much more than news media actively shape society and politics—but not necessarily for other roles.

We also found that organizational settings are key for interpreting how journalism relates to those in power, how it approaches the audience, how different journalistic voices are included in the news, and how different routinized practices significantly predict the performance of professional roles at the story level.

Overall, our analyses have revealed that the strongest discrepancies between the ideals and practice of the profession tend to be concentrated globally on public service-oriented roles. Different patterns and levels of journalistic cultures' hybridity emerge, with some roles and their subdimensions interacting with each other more in certain countries, and some aspects of journalistic cultures remaining more stable with respect to other issues.

While the findings reported in this book show the reality of just one period in the history of journalism (2012–2015), they illuminate the various approaches that can be used to analyze the performance and co-occurrence of professional practice across time and space.

The results of this book thus go against interpretations of the performative side of journalistic cultures as only commanded by normative perspectives that do not apply in everyday practice. It is important to bear in mind that, unlike studies that focus on the structure of the media, role performance analysis examines the practice of journalism, which, as we saw throughout this book, is much more complex and dynamic than media system categories alone. The closer analysis of role sub-dimensions and indicators, as well as their interplay, has revealed the extent to which media system theory holds true when incorporating organizational- and content-level elements in shaping reporting practices and narratives.

Lessons Learned and Limitations: Looking to the Future of JRP

This book is the result of several years of work by dozens of scholars, research assistants, and colleagues interested in going beyond journalistic norms and broadening the scope of journalism studies by including the theoretically and empirically rich dimension of role performance in the analysis of journalistic cultures.

Collaborative work is an endeavor that needs to be encouraged and critically addressed. We experienced numerous challenges during our journey of writing this book and completing the overall research project. Nevertheless, when we look back at our first day of work on it, we find that walking this path together has been profoundly worthwhile. Although researchers' to-do lists are often endless, our team members generously devoted their time and efforts to writing their respective chapters. The results show how journalists perform their work from different angles and in different areas, and the various chapters manage to maintain a dialogue with one another, creating what we think is a coherent and valuable volume.

Our project was designed to overcome some of the challenges related to international comparative research on journalistic cultures, such as the lack of standardized measures, the theorization of professional roles as a socially constructed practices, and the inclusion of countries not normally theorized in the journalistic roles literature specifically, and in comparative news-content literature in general. For example, our analytical models contain variables and indicators that can be measured at the evaluative and performative levels of journalistic cultures (role conceptions, perceived role enactment, and role performance).

This has proven the feasibility of comparable data collection in several countries, triangulating content analyses and surveys (van Dalen, de Vreese, & Albæk, 2017). In isolation, each instrument favors specific findings: content analysis allows for the comparison of role performance models in each country, while the survey facilitates the mapping of differences in how journalists perceive professional functions and practices, as well as the level of agreement between what journalists find important to their work as news professionals and what they feel they can actually enact in their work. Therefore, the combination of content analysis and surveys allowed us to measure the link between ideals and reported behaviors and actual journalistic practices.

Though comparative research has included several non-Western countries in their samples, we believe that our theorization and operationalization of journalistic roles in the JRP Project more accurately portrays what journalism looks like in different countries and regions. We have moved away from the long-questioned idea that journalism is based on universally recognized and practiced standards, or that journalistic cultures are characterized by the endorsement of roles that are antagonistic and mutually exclusive.

While our project is pioneering in that it empirically unfolds the layers of journalistic professional roles around the world, it also reveals the many theoretical and methodological challenges and limitations that are inherent to international comparative research on journalism, as experienced by other scholars who previously engaged in this endeavor (Benson, 2013; Hanitzsch, Hanusch, Ramaprasad, & De-Beer et al., 2019; Hanitzsch et al., 2011; Reinemann, Stanyer, Aalberg, Esser, & de Vreese, 2019; Weaver & Willnat, 2012). Indeed, we grappled with difficulties and blind spots, some of which led to the same criticism addressed towards other comparative journalism studies, and we acknowledge that some limitations can be attributed to our study design.

Table 12.1 summarizes the major challenges that we faced in this comparative project, as well as the actions taken to address them and the limitations of the project's achievements.

In acknowledging our limitations, this study has posed even more new challenges that can serve as a roadmap for future scholarship. Our results invite scholars to consider the complexity of the factors that influence journalistic cultures and to develop new ways of analyzing role performance. They invite us to think not only about how journalists approach those in power and the public, but also about the impact of the audience on current journalistic practices. Although we did not analyze role performance with respect to audience expectations, perceptions, or behaviors, our data reveal that the civic role was performed more prominently in contexts with more active participation in the public space at the time the sample was collected. It would be important, in that sense, to determine whether the results for the performance of the civic role change in countries during massive protests and social movements, or if the performance of the loyal-facilitator role increases as a strategy of unity and defense of national values after global health crises.

Table 12.1 Challenges, Actions, and Limitations Faced by the JRP Project

Challenges	Actions	Limitations
Measuring role performance cross-nationally	Combining several reporting practices as indicators to measure underlying role dimensions.	Some measures are culturally bounded.
Measuring role ideals in different epistemological spaces	Design of new measures: Because normative and abstract statements can have dissimilar meanings across cultures and even within the same newsrooms, role conceptions were measured with indicators at the same level of abstraction (practical statements) as the indicators of the content analysis.	Risk that journalists answered survey questions in a socially desirable way, trying to reconcile normative ideals with actual behaviors that may contradict these ideals, or out of fear of consequences imposed on them by their superiors when answering in a "non-compliant" way (even if the survey was confidential).
Measurement (functional) equivalence	**Concepts:** Testing professional roles' dimensionality (factor analysis and factorial invariance).	Some measurements are culturally bounded. Partial measurement invariance across countries.
	Methods: Three-step strategy to test for Intercoder Reliability. • Pre-test completed by principal investigators across countries • Pre-tests completed by coders within countries • Post-test conducted within countries	Measure of absence/presence instead of the intensity of presence of each role indicator as a trade-off for gaining external validity while losing in-depth information.
	Language: Translation and back-translation of both codebook (content analysis) and questionnaire (survey).	
Implication of the level of analysis used	Multilevel analysis techniques.	Small N for survey samples.

Challenges	Actions	Limitations
Sampling issues: Countries	Efforts to include representative countries from different continents, various media systems, and different political systems. Eighteen countries from Western and Eastern Europe, Latin American, Asia, and the United States were included in the study.	Country representation restricted to some continents. Several countries and media systems are not represented.
Sampling issues: Survey	Surveys with journalists who produced news articles/work in news media organizations sampled.	Slow response rate.
Sampling Issues: Content analysis	Representative sample of print news stories.	Media systems are much broader, including multimedia and audiovisual dynamics, and possess interaction elements that are nonexistent in print.
Money issue	Different resources secured by researchers from the countries involved in the project.	Lack of central funding.
Implementation of the study: Technical issues, procedural issues, logistic issues	Training: Local researchers arrive at the same understanding of measures. Supervision of national teams.	Different levels of national investigators' expertise working on international projects. Existence of within-country constraints.
Societal-level indicators	Use of available and reliable societal level indexes.	Lack of enough reliable international indexes of societal variables outside the Western world. Risk of cultural bounding in the indexes used.

It would be also crucial to study the relationship between digitalization and new audiences' demands for a blend of classic elements of journalism, such as the civic and watchdog roles and more vivid storytelling. In fact, our analysis of journalistic performance in newspapers from 18 countries shows that even the most traditional media are influenced by the digital ecosystem, with elements such as personalization, citizen participation, and personal assistance emerging as common journalistic practices in traditional national desk news. Future work might also consider studying audience and journalistic performance together as key for understanding the extent to which initiatives such as citizens' leaks are reflected in the performance of the watchdog function in countries that present contrasting features.

Our project demonstrated that focusing on national print media systems was necessary and useful as a first stage of the analysis of professional roles in the news. However, we understand that our decision to focus on print media is a major limitation of the first wave of our project, as the results may reflect the specific culture of print journalism and reporting. In view of this, the work that lies ahead involves broadening the scope beyond newspapers and macro politics. Media systems include multimedia and audiovisual dynamics, and elements of interaction that do not exist in print news, and thus reveal different ways in which journalistic roles can be performed.

At the same time, we agree that journalism is much broader than the world of politics and social affairs. The biggest chunk of the news diet that people consume around the world—such as sports or celebrity journalism—does not come from these specific beats and tends to be understudied due to the stigma (Costera Meijer, 2003) that suggests that "soft news" are far from being "good" journalism (Thussu, 2007; Franklin, Hamer, Hanna, Kinsey, & Richardson, 2005).

Our results clearly show how several standard assumptions and old norms that deal with static and monolithic functions of journalism are no longer valid and are not being reflected in reality. Indeed, discreet categories such as elite or popular media, political regimes, and "hard" and "soft" news no longer seem to fully fit the analysis of media and journalists when the profession is analyzed as a socially constructed ritual. In this sense, we strongly believe that expanding the scope of how we study the journalistic field can open up many new paths.

To be effective in the difficult task of re-enchanting both its audience and its own members, journalism must engage in a serious and honest process of "re-fusion" (Alexander, 2004) between the norms and beliefs that hold the profession together and their everyday practice. As Schudson (2018, p. 194) has suggested, journalism must maintain an optimism of spirit, but this must be paired with a realism of assessment.

References

Alexander, J. C. (2004). Cultural pragmatics: Social performance between ritual and strategy. *Sociological Theory*, 22(4), 527–573.

Anderson, C. W. (2020). Practice, interpretation, and meaning in today's digital media ecosystem. *Journalism & Mass Communication Quarterly*, 97(2), 342–359.

Benson, R. (2013). *Shaping immigration news: A French-American comparison.* Cambridge: Cambridge University Press.

Brüggemann, M., Engesser, S., Büchel, F., Humprecht, E., & Castro, L. (2014). Hallin and Mancini revisited: Our empirical types of Western media systems. *Journal of Communication, 64*(6), 1037–1065.

Carlson, M., & Lewis, S. C. (Eds.). (2015). *Boundaries of journalism: Professionalism, practices, and participation.* New York: Routledge.

Costera Meijer, I. (2003). What is quality television news? A plea for extending the professional repertoire of newsmakers. *Journalism Studies, 4,* 15–29.

Franklin, B., Hamer, M., Hanna, M., Kinsey, M., & Richardson, J. (2005). *Key concepts in journalism studies.* London: Sage.

Hallin, D., & Mancini, P. (2004). *Comparing media systems. Three models of media and politics.* Cambridge: Cambridge University Press.

Hallin, D., & Mancini, P. (2012). *Comparing media systems beyond the Western world.* Cambridge: Cambridge University Press.

Hanitzsch, T., Hanusch, F., Mellado, C., Anikina, M., Berganza, R., Cangoz, I., . . . Moreira, S. (2011). Mapping journalism cultures across nations: A comparative study of 18 countries. *Journalism Studies, 12*(3), 273–293.

Hanitzsch, T., Hanusch, F., Ramaprasad, J., & De-Beer, A. S. (Eds.). (2019). *Worlds of journalism: Journalistic cultures around the globe.* New York: Columbia University Press.

Mellado, C. (2019). Journalists' professional roles and role performance. In *Oxford research encyclopedia of communication.* Oxford: Oxford University. doi:10.1093/acrefore/9780190228613.013.832

Mellado, C., Hellmueller, L., & Donsbach, W. (2017). *Journalistic role performance: Concepts, contexts and methods.* New York: Routledge.

Reinemann, C., Stanyer, J., Aalberg, T., Esser, F., & de Vreese, C. H. (Eds.). (2019). *Communicating populism: Comparing actor perceptions, media coverage, and effects on citizens in Europe.* New York: Routledge.

Rusbridger, A. (2018). *Breaking news: The remaking of journalism and why it matters now.* Edinburgh: Canongate.

Schudson, M. (2018). *Why journalism still matters.* Cambridge: Polity Press.

Shoemaker, P. J., & Reese, S. (2013). *Mediating the message in the 21st century: A media sociology perspective.* New York: Routledge.

Skinner, D., Gasher, M. J., & Compton, J. (2001). Putting theory to practice: A critical approach to journalism studies. *Journalism, 2*(3), 341–360.

Thussu, D. (Ed.). (2007). *Media on the move: Global flow and contra-flow.* London: Routledge.

van Dalen, A., de Vreese, C. H., & Albæk, E. (2017). Mixed quantitative methods approach to journalistic role performance research. In C. Mellado, L. Hellmueller, & W. Donsbach (Eds.), *Journalistic role performance: Concepts, contexts, and methods* (pp. 189–205). New York: Routledge.

Vos, T. (2017). Historical perspectives on journalistic roles. In C. Mellado, L. Hellmueller, & W. Donsbach (Eds.), *Journalistic role performance. Concepts, contexts, and methods* (pp. 59–77). New York: Routledge.

Waisbord, S. (2013). *Reinventing professionalism: Journalism and news in global perspective.* Cambridge: Polity Press.

Weaver, D., & Willnat, L. (Eds.). (2012). *The global journalist in the 21st century*. New York: Routledge.

Zelizer, B. (1993). Journalists as interpretive communities. *Critical Studies in Mass Communication, 10*, 219–237.

Zelizer, B. (2015). Terms of choice: Uncertainty, journalism, and crisis. *Journal of Communication, 65*(5), 888–908.

Appendices

Appendix 1
JRP Codebook for the Analysis of Newspapers News

Introduction

This codebook was designed to help you in the process of coding the content of news stories (i.e., the unit of analysis is the *news story*). Specifically, it will be used to quantitatively analyze the diversity of journalistic role performances adopted by the print media around the globe, as well as other specific variables of interest for this project.

A news story will be understood as a group of continuous verbal/textual and, if relevant, visual elements that refer to the same topic. The coding of the news stories selected for this project is divided into four sections:

1. General Information of the News Story

In the first section, the basic information of each news story should be identified. Coding instructions for the first section of variables are found under "General Information of the News Story."

2. Story Characteristics

The second section analyzes the characteristics of the news story. Coding instructions for this section are mapped out under "Story Characteristics."

3. Sources and Reporting Methods

The third section of the codebook analyzes the sources and actors present in the news story. Coding instructions for this section are found under "Sources and Reporting Methods."

4. Journalistic Role Performance

This section of the codebook analyzes the presence of different professional roles in the news. Coding instructions for this section are found under "Journalistic Role Performance."

Within each section, each variable is defined based on the conceptual framework used by this project. You should refer to these definitions and only these definitions when coding each news story. You may know of other definitions of some of the variables measured here, but they do not apply to this project.

Each news story should be coded based on the following instructions.

General Instructions

Your task here is to read each news story, code each variable in numerical order, and enter the data in the corresponding SPSS template provided. The data for each case (story) will be entered on a separate row in the template.

In each of the following sections you will find the list of variables and their definitions. You first need to familiarize yourself with each variable and its definition. Do this by reading the list of variables several times. If you feel there is something you do not understand, you should ask the Principal Investigator of your country for help.

Remember that there may be definitions that you may not be very familiar with, so it is important that you pay close attention and do not hesitate to ask for help if needed.

Along with the definitions, you will find specific instructions on how to code each variable as well as some examples. If no specific instructions are mentioned with a measured variable, follow these basic instructions:

1. Read the full news story.
2. Read the news story a second time. This time, pay attention to the absence/presence or intensity of the various attributes/characteristics. Please note: These characteristics may be found in words, sentences, images, etc. This is why you must fully understand and internalize the meaning of each variable in order to correctly code the absence/presence or intensity of the attributes/characteristics that are being measured.
3. As you determine the absence/presence or intensity of the measured variables, enter the correct option on the relevant row.
4. For each case (story), you are expected to enter a code for all the variables. Cells must not be left empty.

Measurements: Variables and Coding

PART I. GENERAL INFORMATION OF THE NEWS STORY

Coder ID

ID assigned to the person coding the content of the news story (in each country, IDs should run from 1 thru n).

Story ID

Story identification number (in each country, story ID should run from 1 thru n).

Country

Country of origin. All the countries will receive codes from 1 thru n.

Outlet

Refers to the name of the newspaper in which the news story was produced.

1= (Principal investigators in each country define name of newspaper).
2= (Principal investigators in each country define name of newspaper).
3= (Principal investigators in each country define name of newspaper).
4= (Principal investigators in each country define name of newspaper).
5= (Principal investigators in each country define name of newspaper).

Item Date

Refers to the news item's date of publication.
Year: Corresponds to the year that the news story was published.
Month: Corresponds to the month that the news story was published.

1= January
2= February
3= March
4= April
5= May
6= June
7= July
8= August
9= September

10= October
11= November
12= December

V05c Day: Corresponds to the day of the week that the news story was published.

1= Monday
2= Tuesday
3= Wednesday
4= Thursday
5= Friday
6= Saturday
7= Sunday

Production

AUTHOR

Corresponds to *who* signs the produced information. This information is generally located at the beginning or end of a news story.

1= Reporter/Internal staff (Designates a story that has been reported by one or more internal staff, with or without a byline, if they are individualized.)
2= Combo wire/staff
3= Correspondent (The journalist contributes to the news media from a distant—national or foreign—location, and the news story explicitly names the journalist as such.)
4 = Wire
5= Other media (The author of the news story is the media outlet which provide the news story.)

JOURNALIST NAME

Corresponds to the name of the first author who signs the news story (only if the author is coded as Reporter/Internal staff or Correspondent in the previous question).

If the item is written by a combination of wire/staff, news wire, or if it is signed with initials, by an editorial board, or no name is provided, write 99. If the news story has been written by more than one journalist/staff member, write the name of the first author.

JOURNALIST GENDER

Corresponds to the author's gender.
0= Female
1= Male
99= When no name of a journalist is provided or WIRE

Story Type

It corresponds to the type of news story being coded.

1= Brief. A short story providing information of contingent events. It has up to three paragraphs, and does not usually include subtitles.
2= Article/News Report. This is the most frequent type of story and reports on what happened (who, how, when, and where). It also usually includes sources. It contains more than three paragraphs, and may include subheads and photos.
3= Feature/Chronicle. This kind of news story tends to be similar in length to a reportage. To be coded in this category, the news story must describe individual experiences and testimonials by the author as a witness to one or more events, or use literary language that corresponds to fiction (dialogues, hyperboles, setting descriptions, characterization of people, among others).
4= Reportage. A news story that is usually longer in length than a regular article. This type of news story includes reporting of facts, but also includes in-depth analysis of recent events that have already been covered by the media and did not necessarily happen the day before the news story is published. Reportage usually includes several sources, as well as contextual information, which are considered part of the report.

Image

This refers to the presence/absence of images within the news story.

0= No
1= Yes

Image/Text

This refers to the predominance of images (photographs, graphs, info graphs, maps, etc.) versus text or vice-versa in the news story (measured in terms of space). The coder should evaluate the quantitative relationship. When in doubt, the relationship should be coded as balanced.

1= Predominance of images
2= Balanced relationship between images and texts
3= Predominance of text
4= Just text

PART II. STORY CHARACTERISTICS

Main Topic

This corresponds to the main topic of the story.

You should read the news story from start to finish, paying special attention to the story's central theme. The main topic often appears in the headline of the story and tends to take up the most space. However, you must base your coding on the entire story, as some elements do not appear at the outset. You should indicate the story's main topic according to the following list of categories.

1= Government/Legislatures. The story deals with formal and institutionalized power, including legislation, declarations by heads of state, ministers, MPs, civil servants, local government employees, etc. International relations, state visits, activities and/or declarations from members of parliament, and judicial power (institutional or employee activities and/or declarations) are also included.

It is important to keep in mind that all news stories that refer to specific and sectorial topics such as health, housing, education, etc., will be considered within this category when they are associated to public policies promoted by the government/state.

Example:

"Senate voted in favor of death penalty."

2= Campaigns/Elections/Politics. Stories about elections/campaigns for government at local, state and national levels, and stories focused primarily on the actions of political parties in general (regardless a context of political campaign).

Examples:

"Exit polls 2012: How the U.S. vote has shifted."
"Liberal HQ warns against hubris as Labor wipeout is not assured."

3= Police and Crime. Stories about violent crime (including terrorism), white-collar crime, corruption, statistical data on crime, public safety, and prisons.

Examples:

"Police arrested five of the suspects in Rome."
"Man dies after police-involved shooting in Madrid."

4= Court. Stories about the inner workings of the court system, such as the appointment of judges, specific criminal or civil trials, as well as stories about injunctions and the workings of the court/legal system (at all levels).

Examples:

"Supreme Court challenges gay marriage in Brazil."

"*Nebraska attorney general seeks to revoke license of only nurse at abortion clinic.*"

5= Defense/Military/National Security. Information related to military/ armed forces policies and actions, as well as national/international defense, considering protective actions, exterior threats, and wars.
Examples:

"*Minimal negative impact: Hamid Karzai's view of our Afghanistan role.*"
"*Defense weighs suitability of Triton U.S. drone program for maritime.*"

6= Economy and Business. All non-legislative activities related to businesses, such as business and personal finance. Microeconomics (prices of goods and services, salaries, benefits and incomes, among others) and macroeconomics (total national production, sectorial production, employment and unemployment, balance of payments, inflation, etc.) are included within this topic.
Examples:

"*Push on corporate tax rules goes global.*"
"*Tata Steel reports loss in its fourth quarter on Europe weakness.*"

7= Education. Refers to ALL primary, secondary, and post-secondary education, whether public or private. It refers to information about education management and education practices, as well as processes and instruments of measuring, results, curriculum, etc. It also includes extra-curricular activities (debate, drama, service clubs, etc.) that are explicitly connected with schools.
Examples:

"*Jagadguru Kripalu Parishat Education gets Rajiv Gandhi Global Excellence Award.*"
"*Montgomery middle school students see their films on the big screen.*"

8= Energy, Environment, Climate, and Weather.
Refers to all ecological or human-environment topics, such as the care and conservation of the environment and their agents (i.e., plants, minerals, and animals), and the risks and problems that they face (global warming, pollution of all types, etc.).
It considers matters related to the impact of energy sources and their mechanisms of exploitation and distribution (renewable, non-renewable clean and polluting energy sources, such as fuel, electricity, geothermal heat, etc.).

Examples:

"Gujarat-based unit to work for environment conservation."
"Kosovo brown bears Ari and Arina released into sanctuary after a decade held captive in a cage."
"A new study shows solar batteries have become 300 percent more efficient in the last five years."

9= Transportation. Information related to mechanisms, management, operation, and impact of all means of transportation (air, sea, land, public, and private).
Examples:

"Beltway drivers passing trick turns ramps into high-speed slalom."
"MARC trains will begin running on weekends."

10= Housing, Infrastructure, and Public Works. Information on state policy, planning, and construction of housing and infrastructure, including roads, highways, bridges, tunnels, trains, airports, irrigation reservoirs, river defenses, rain water collectors, telecommunications, neighborhood land integration, etc.
Examples:

"Airports in China Hew to an Unswerving Flight Path."

11= Accidents and Natural Disasters. Information on accidents provoked by man (air, sea, land or rail accidents, explosions, fires, etc.), as well as natural disasters such as earthquakes, tsunamis, mudslides, river overflows, and storms, among others.
Examples:

"Earthquake with a magnitude of 7.3 strikes Japan in same region devastated by earthquake and tsunami in 2011."
"Car chased by Prince George's police hits school bus in D.C."

12= Health. Refers to stories on the health care system, public health, and diseases/prevention. Health care system relates to stories that are focused on the integrity of the health care system in general, such as insurance, medical training, medical care in general, etc. It also deals with stories of pandemics, epidemics, etc., that focus on the impact of health conditions on groups of people.
Examples:

"Corporate clinics on notice for profit fix."
"Shake-up looms for doctors in the bush."

"Hospitals treat more than 200, including dozens of children, after tornado hits Oklahoma."

13= Religion and Churches. Information related to the spiritual development of individuals and the general population, considering the activities of institutions that administer faith (churches, for example), as well as debates on society's beliefs, values, and morality.
Example:

"Cardinals pick Bergoglio, who will be Pope Francis."

14= Human Rights. This refers to information on freedoms and claims on elemental goods that include everybody, simply because they are human beings, guaranteeing a decent life. It refers to civil (for example life, safety, and the freedom of speech), political (voting and being elected), and social and cultural (housing and health) rights.
Examples:

"Life in the UAE: 'We expect anything from the authorities—we are afraid of everything.' Two of the 94 people on trial in the UAE talk to Amnesty International about the state of freedom of expression in the country."

15= Demonstrations and Protests. Situations, facts, and actions depicting social conflict between two or more actors in society, for different reasons. It considers matters associated to demonstrations, marches, protests, strikes, occupations, and other forms of demonstrating social disputes, independent of the matter at hand.
Example:

"Chile student protest resumes as 100,000 people march."

16= Social Issues. Matters of class and inequality, human rights, poverty, development, migration, immigration refugees, racial and ethnic tensions, gender and sexual orientation issues, among others, all of them addressed from a macro perspective rather than just one specific case.
Examples:

"Poverty is growing twice as fast in the suburbs as in cities."
"Life in the UAE: 'We expect anything from the authorities—we are afraid of everything.' Two of the 94 people on trial in the UAE talk to Amnesty International about the state of freedom of expression in the country."

17= Others. Stories that do not clearly fit in any of the previous categories.

Geographic Frame. This variable concerns the location where the news story takes place.

1 = Local. Story focuses on the metropolitan area within which the media outlet publishes.
2 = Non-local/National. Story focuses on either a region outside of the media source's metropolitan area or the nation as a whole.
3 = International. Story takes place in a different country.
99 = Don't Know/Can't Tell.

PART III. SOURCES AND REPORTING METHODS

Sources

In order for someone to be coded as a source, it is necessary that sentences, phrases, facts, or quotes be attributed to them.

Number of Sources

This refers to the total number of sources quoted in the story. If an organization or a person is quoted, count it as one. If the same source is quoted two times, it is considered as one source. You should code the total number of sources.

Document Sources

Are documents included as sources in the news story?
0= No
1= Yes

Human Sources

Are human sources included in the news story?
0= No
1= Yes

Source Type

This is about the source's role(s) within the news story. You should code the absence or presence of each type of source. Note that an individual or organization may have more than one role; however, the role should be coded within the context of the specific news story.

STATE SOURCE

This refers to people who work administering the national, regional/ provincial, or municipal government, as well as political transnational organizations. This category contains a wide array of government divisions and employees including bureaucrats, administrators, representatives, executives, etc., who participate in governmental activities.
0= No
1= Yes

POLITICAL PARTY SOURCE

This refers to political associations or members of these associations.
0= No
1= Yes

BUSINESS OR COMPANY SOURCE

This refers to actors from the commercial sector as well as trade groups. It includes representatives from associations from the corporate sector, companies (public or private), and specific businessmen, or their employees, who are consulted either because of their relevance and specific weight, or as a testimony.
0= No
1= Yes

CIVIL SOCIETY SOURCE

It refers to members of an organized civil society, such as an NGO, union, or similar social organization, other than the state and business world. The source must speak in their capacity as a representative of their institution or group.

Please note that *this type of source* can be perceived and interpreted differently in various cultures. You should use it as it would be considered in your culture.
0= No
1= Yes

CITIZEN SOURCE

This includes people as individual sources of information, and not in representation of anyone, as in the previous categories. This category contains regular citizens. These sources are defined as those who are speaking for themselves. This might also include citizen bloggers and regular YouTubers.
0= No
1= Yes

MEDIA SOURCE

This refers to communication media outlets or to members that speak in representation of them, or professional journalists, other than the author of the news story.

If a politician, sports figure, citizen, celebrity, and the like use social media to communicate with their audience and the news story quotes that post, it SHOULD **NOT** be considered a media source.

Instead, if the news story quotes the post of another media outlet, or another professional journalist, it should be considered a **YES**.
0= No
1= Yes

ANONYMOUS SOURCE

This refers to unidentified sources, sources whose identity (name) or position within the respective organization is not mentioned, and sources who are explicitly referred to as anonymous.
0= No
1= Yes

OTHER SOURCE

This includes sources that cannot be assigned to any of the categories listed previously.
0= No
1= Yes

Balance: Diversity of Sources and Points of View

Does the news story present diverse sources and a diversity of sources' points of view about a particular issue?

1= Absence of sources and/or points of view
   The topic of the news story does not include sources.
2= Unilateral coverage
   The news story only includes one source, or only sources and perspectives from one side.
3 =Presence of different sources and points of view within the story
   The news story includes different sources and points of view.

Expert Source Use

Does the news story include an expert source? This refers to informative sources that are consulted as specialists in their specific area.
0= No
1= Yes

Verifiable Evidence/Hard Data

Does the article include factual information and/or verifiable data? Verifiable data correspond to figures and facts; in other words, it is information that can be verified by a third party that does not correspond to either the author's or the sources' subjective thoughts, feelings, or opinion.

0= Less factual and verifiable information than non-verifiable information
1= Balance between verifiable and non-verifiable information
2= More factual and verifiable information than non-verifiable information
3= Only factual or verifiable information

Conditional Use

Within the news story, does the journalist use verbs in the conditional form? (i.e., It would be. . .)
0= No
1= Yes

Argumentation

Does the journalist use reasoning or logic to prove or support a proposal, or to convince the reader of what (s)he affirms or denies ("since," "due to," etc., tend to be used)? Argumentation challenges, refutes, or reaffirms facts or events through discursive reasoning.

1= Arguments are not used
2= There is one argument
3= There are two arguments
4 = There are more than two arguments
   Examples:

> "*It has often been claimed that if the paper used by every student were collected and rendered into paper pulp that society could reuse, about 5 million trees would be saved each year. However, this kind of recycling could be unnecessary, since the country maintains enough forests to ensure an uninterrupted supply of paper.*"

PART IV. JOURNALISTIC ROLE PERFORMANCE

This section provides instructions for coding indicators associated with the performance of different journalistic roles. Six professional roles are measured by this project: the watchdog, loyal-facilitator, service, civic, infotainment, and interventionist.

Next, the performance of each of these roles in the news will be described in detail so you will be able to understand the content we are looking for. In each case, the presence or absence of different indicators on reporting styles and narrative schemes in the news story will be measured.

As a coder, you need to be clear that the different roles are not mutually exclusive, and that a news story may present attributes/characteristics of multiple roles at the same time; that is, professional roles can overlap in practice.

Interventionist Role

The interventionist role refers to a kind of journalism where the journalist has an explicit voice in the story, and sometimes acts as advocate for individuals or groups in society. In this sense, a greater level of participation by the journalist implies higher levels of interventionism, and vice versa.

JOURNALIST'S POINT OF VIEW

Within the news story, does the journalist/author *explicitly* provide his/her point of view or judgment as an expression of approval or disapproval, indicating what side (s)he is on or what her/his position is?

Journalist's point of view IS NOT limited to political conflicts; rather, it can include taking a side in other types of topics or taking a specific side related to any event. Journalists may also position themselves as advocates or defenders of a group with defined interests.

0= No
1= Yes

Textual example:

> "*The Guantanamo Bay prison is a deeply un-American disgrace. It needs to be closed rapidly.*"

INTERPRETATION

Within the story, does the journalist explain the causes, meanings, and/or possible consequences of certain facts/actions? Performing an interpretative reporting style can be understood as something opposed to a descriptive, fact-based style. Nevertheless, interpretation is not the same as a point of view or opinion since it deals with the explanation of a fact, without necessarily making a value judgment.

0= No
1= Yes

Example:

> *"The announcement could have two effects: First, the government could rid itself of a historically complex negotiation, focusing it on the parliament. However, it could also tear apart the party strategy to close transition, which intended to negotiate a complete package directly with the presidency, including reforms and human rights topics."*

CALL FOR ACTION

Does the journalist **propose or demand changes** as to how a determined action—in any situation and level of life—is being carried out by a group or individual? Basically, is the journalist proposing a way of reacting to a situation or calling for a resolution of a conflict? Is the journalist **calling the audience to action, proposing to behave in a certain way?**
0= No
1= Yes
Examples:

> *"The inhabitants of the city waiting for someone to take responsibility for having built their houses in a landfill. It's time that someone responds."*

QUALIFYING ADJECTIVES

Does the journalist **use qualifying adjectives?** (Adjectives used by sources do not count here.) A qualifying adjective is a word that ascribes to a noun the value of an attribute of that noun (e.g., an intelligent woman or a crazy man).
0= No
1= Yes
Examples:

> *"A heated discussion took place yesterday at the meeting of the Christian Democratic Representatives."*
> *"... dozens of people, for the most part women of humble aspect ..."*

FIRST PERSON

Does the journalist **use first person within the story** (I, we, me, my, our)? The use of first person could include being a witness of a story, appropriating an action, or giving an opinion.
0 = No
1 = Yes

Examples:

"*Many of us are understandably afraid of the way our food is produced, but exaggeration doesn't make our case stronger.*"

0= No
1= Yes

Watchdog Role

The watchdog role seeks to protect the public interest and to hold various elites in power accountable, serving as a "fourth estate." Journalism performance closer to the watchdog role entails being a custodian of conscience, making visible facts hidden by those in power (for example, cases of inefficiency, bad administration, corruption, fraud, the blocking of law projects, harassment and/or misinformation, among others).

What defines the watchdog role is not the journalist's political/ideological stance, but rather the function of questioning, criticizing, or denouncing institutions and individuals that form part of different elites with the objective of maximizing governmental or other institutional transparency and efficiency.

- Political elites include those who have formal and institutional power through different powers of the state, the government, and those who control the political parties and coalitions.
- Economic elites refer to individuals who control the main economic activities, including representatives of business guilds, large companies, and corporations, as well as domestics.
  Organized civil society elites include NGOs, unions, and other organizations not associated with the state or the business world.
- Transnational organizations refer to political or economic organizations whose decisions and actions influence various countries, such as the EU, the UN, or IMF.

INFORMATION ON JUDICIAL OR ADMINISTRATIVE PROCESSES

Does the story include information on **judicial/administrative processes against** individuals or groups of power?
0= No
1= Yes
Examples:

"*The Supreme Court confirmed the sentence for tax fraud and swindle against three civil servants of the Ministry of Health. The ruling affects . . .*"

"Stephen Joseph of San Francisco has sued Kraft foods for putting trans-fat in the company's Oreo cookies. Joseph is asking for an injunction to order Kraft to stop selling Oreos to children."

DOUBTING: JOURNALIST'S EVALUATION

By means of statements or expressions, does the journalist **express doubt about the validity or truthfulness** of what individuals or groups in power say or do? It is always about to whom the doubt is directed.

0= No
1= Yes, government/state
2= Yes, political parties
3= Yes, business/economic elite
4= Yes, civil society (church, unions, etc.)
5= Yes, transnational organizations (IMF, UN, etc.)
6= Yes, more than one (Which?)
    Examples:

> *"The Minister of Education has insisted that he did not profit from his involvement in the University of Phoenix. . . . According to his statements, prior to taking office on March 11, 2010, he divested his shareholdings in the three commercial partnerships that linked him to the private university. However, it is suspicious, to say the least, that up till today, he has not rendered account of his involvement in the aforementioned societies."*

> *"The real estate broker insists he is innocent. However, since the beginning of the trial, testimonies against him have nothing but piled up."*

DOUBTING: OTHER

By means of statements or expression does the news story include **doubt by someone other than the journalist about the validity or truthfulness** of what individuals or groups in power say or do? It is always about to whom the doubt is directed.

0= No
1= Yes, government/state
2= Yes, political parties
3= Yes, economic/business elite
4= Yes, civil society (church, unions, etc.)
5= Yes, transnational organizations
6= Yes, more than one (Which?)

    Examples:

> *". . . (these) members of parliament agree that the police should make the number of complaints about the institution transparent, in*

regards to both wiretapping members of the government as well as in terms of procedural errors or abuse of power. They pointed out that all questioning affecting the institution should be resolved swiftly."

CRITICISM: JOURNALIST'S EVALUATION

Does the news story include any assertion or reference from the journalist in which (s)he **judges or condemns** what individuals or groups in power say or do? Generally, the criticism contains an adverb or an adjective. It is always about to whom the criticism is directed.

0= No
1= Yes, government/state
2= Yes, political parties
3= Yes, economic/business elite
4= Yes, civil society (church, unions, etc.)
5= Yes, transnational organizations
6= Yes, more than one (Which?)
   Examples:

"The shameful behavior of the church in regards to the cases of pedophilia has affected the credibility of the Christian faith among people."

CRITICISM: OTHER

Does the news story include any assertion or reference from someone **other than the journalist,** in which (s)he **judges or condemns** what individuals or groups in power say or do? Generally, the criticism contains an adverb or an adjective. It is always about to whom the criticism is directed.

0= No
1= Yes, government/state
2= Yes, political parties
3= Yes, economic/business elite
4= Yes, civil society (church, unions etc.)
5= Yes, transnational organizations.
6= Yes, more than one (Which?)
   Examples:

Andrea Tantaros commented, "It's the Chicago way. [Obama] said he would change D.C. and the way they do business. Boy, has he ever."

Does the news story include an assertion or reference from the journalist in which s(he) **accuses or makes evident something hidden**, not only illegal, but also irregular or inconvenient concerning individuals or groups of power? This may include, for example, cases of poor administration, corruption, abuses, scandals, fraud, harassment, political blocking to legal initiatives, or misinformation, among others.

It is always about to whom the denouncement is directed.

0= No
1= Yes, government/state
2= Yes, political parties
3= Yes, economic/business elite
4= Yes, civil society (church, unions, etc.)
5= Yes, transnational organizations
6= Yes, more than one (Which?)
   Examples:

> "*An investigation carried out by this newspaper revealed the mismanagement of public funds in school subsidies. . . .* "

UNCOVERING: OTHER

Does the news story include **quotes and/or testimonies from people other than the journalist that account for, accuse, or make evident something hidden, not only illegal, but also irregular or inconvenient,** concerning individuals or groups of power? This may include, for example, cases of poor administration, corruption, abuses, scandals, fraud, harassment, political blocking to legal initiatives, or misinformation, among others?

It is always about to whom the denouncement is directed.

0= No
1= Yes, government/state
2= Yes, political parties
3= Yes, economic/business elite
4= Yes, civil society (church, unions, etc.)
5= Yes, transnational organizations
6= Yes, more than one (Which?)
   Examples:

> "*The list of Berlusconi's convictions is long: bribing officials, tax fraud, illegal financing of political parties. But the divorced Italian leader has managed to dodge the justice system's axe again and again.*"

EXTERNAL INVESTIGATION

Is the news story based on investigations that were not carried out by the journalist—such as police, judicial, administrative, specialized/academic research, among others—but that he/she covers extensively?
0= No
1= Yes
   Examples:

> "*A Human Rights Watch investigation determined the systematic violation of human rights against the indigenous peoples of Bolivia.*"

CONFLICT

Does the news story show **conflict or confrontation between the journalist and/or the media outlet where s(he) works and one or more individuals or groups in power?** Does the journalist directly invoke the source, an institution, or an individual from a sphere of power as an opponent? (Personal confrontation, threats or harassment, veto, etc.)
0= No
1= Yes
   Examples:

> "*The president's office denies the access of this media organization to official press conferences, due to upset concerning the interview published last Friday.*"

INVESTIGATIVE REPORTING

Does the journalist report on abuse of power or wrongdoing, etc., based on **his/her extensive inquiry and research** (i.e., independent review of legal documents, public records, or direct observation), beyond reliance on leaks and secondary sources of information? It is the journalist who conducts the investigation.
0= No
1= Yes
   Examples:

> "*A month after the break of one of the biggest financial scandals in the country, we (the newspaper) provide a map to navigate a detailed time sequence where the successive flow of names, partnerships, the purchase and sale of shares, relationships, and apparent coincidences give shape to this gigantic fraud.*"

"We discovered a network of companies with accounts in the Bahamas, with $8.8 million in commissions, intended to favor them in the tender process."

Loyal—Facilitator Role

This role can be materialized in two facets. First, journalists cooperate with those in power and accept the information they provide as credible. In that line, they support the political agenda set by the government, economic, and/or cultural powers, showing loyalty to power, support and defend the government's policies, give a positive image of the established authority and those in power, and support the status quo. Often, they become public relations channels for the transmission of the power elites' messages to the public.

In its second variation, journalists support their nation-state, portraying a positive image of their country, encouraging a sense of belonging, and *strengthening* national prestige.

DEFENSE/SUPPORT INSTITUTIONAL ACTIVITIES

Does the journalist **praise, promote, or defend by an explicit endorsement specific official activities or measures of improvement** carried out by the political or economic powers?
0= No
1= Yes
Examples:

"A noteworthy initiative, where the municipality will implement a toll-free hotline to answer questions from the residents."

DEFENDING/SUPPORTING POLICIES

Does the journalist **praise, promote, or defend, by an explicit endorsement, national, or regional policies** in general, or any one in particular? The journalist needs to manifest his/her defense or support by explicit statements.
0= No
1= Yes
Examples:

"Michelle Bachelet's administration will be remembered for having boosted the most relevant pension reform in the history of the private savings pension system."

POSITIVE IMAGE OF THE POLITICAL ELITE

Does the story present a **positive image of the political elite?** For example, does the journalist favorably stress or highlight leadership or management skills, as well as personal characteristics, of political leaders? This type of support tends to use positive adjectives when referring to these actors (at the individual or at the organizational level). Note that this item is explicitly about enhancing an image, not just approval of the individual's actions or positions.

0= No
1= Yes
   Examples:

   "*In the official visit around Europe, the president ennobled national politics.*"

POSITIVE IMAGE OF THE ECONOMIC ELITE

Does the story present a **positive image of the economic elite?** For example, does the journalist favorably stress or highlight leadership or management skills, as well as personal characteristics, of economic leaders? This type of support tends to use positive adjectives when referring to these actors (at the individual or at the organizational level).

Note that this item is explicitly about enhancing an image, not just approval of the individual's actions or positions.

0= No
1= Yes
   Examples:

   "*The president of ABE's good managing and lobbying capabilities helped diminish the upset of the business sector.*"

PROGRESS/SUCCESS

Does the journalist **emphasize that their own country is progressing** and doing better than before in any relevant dimension? In order for this characteristic to be present, the news story should not only be based on a specific or isolated situation, it should consider a relatively prolonged period of time, and/or emphasize the topic as a process, where changes and progress are documented or predicted.

0= No
1= Yes

Examples:

> "*Poverty has decreased regularly since 1990 until this date: nowa-days, there are less poor people than ever before in the history of Poland.*"

COMPARISON TO OTHER COUNTRIES

Does the journalist emphasize **the country's advances and triumphs in comparison to other countries?**
0= No
1= Yes
    Examples:

> "*The national political class has shown proof of its managing capa-bilities in comparison to their peers from the region.*"
> "*The economic elite has shown proof of integrity in comparison to other European countries.*"

NATIONAL TRIUMPHS

Are individuals or groups who have triumphed in the country or abroad explicitly highlighted within the news story? It is not just that the person is named or pictured; the person must be framed as a representative of the country.
0= No
1= Yes
    Examples:

> "*. . . Wimbledon champion and Swiss tennis star Roger Federer was presented with a prize cow on Tuesday as part of a homecoming celebration at the Swiss Open in Gstaad.*"
> *A picture shows the German football team holding a trophy at the World Cup.*

PROMOTION OF THE COUNTRY'S IMAGE

Does the news story **highlight activities or actions organized with the objective of promoting the country's image?** Note that the story should largely be about the activity or action.
0= No
1= Yes

Examples:

> *"3D images will promote Hungary on the TVs and stores of more than 50 countries."*

PATRIOTISM

Does the news story include **statements made by the journalist that positively value being from a specific nation?** Different from the promotion of the country's image indicator (which is about activities organized by others and covered by the journalist), here, it is the journalist who is the one that values his/her own country.

0= No
1= Yes
    Examples:

> *"Hospitability towards immigrants is a well-known feature of Australians."*

Service Role

This role combines the rights and self-interests of the audience, creating a client-professional relationship between the journalist and the public. As an answer to the growing complexity of modernity, this model of role performance provides helpful information, knowledge, and advice about goods and services that audiences can apply in their day-to-day lives.

Journalism that prioritizes this role provides help, tips, guidance, and information about the management of day-to-day life and individual problems (*news you can use*).

The focus here is on directly helping the audience (rather than indirectly helping; e.g., a story that seeks to root out wrongdoing might indirectly help the audience, but personal help is not the focus of the story).

IMPACT ON EVERYDAY LIFE

Does the news story refer to **the consequences or meanings that certain facts or events have for people's everyday personal lives?**

For example, a news story on climate change in which the journalist stresses that society will have to change the way it produces energy (social relevance) would not fall into this category, while a news story on the same topic which emphasizes that people will have to pay more for electricity every month would be coded as "yes." Likewise, if there is a news story saying that the price of gas will rise tomorrow, it does not qualify as "yes" since what is reported is just the news. It is not just that

the gas is getting more expensive, **it is what the journalist says about that.**
What would qualify as a "yes" would be if the journalist indicates, for
example, that because of this rise, people will have less money to spend
on other things, or that this will increase the prices of public transportation as well, making it more expensive for people to travel around the
city or to go on holidays, etc.

Stories in which the journalist, besides denouncing the bad service
given by ordinary individuals, focuses on the consequences that this has
on a person's personal life, must be also considered here.

0= No
1= Yes
Examples:

> "*How does the European economic crisis impact the work of farmers?*"
> "*Electricity rates will increase starting Monday. For the typical mid-
> dle class family of four, that means that you will be paying $10,000
> more out of your pocket.*"

TIPS AND ADVICE (GRIEVANCES)

Does the news story give *tips* **or practical advice** to manage everyday
problems that **audiences have with others or their environment?** For
example, how to face noisy neighbors, how to handle wrongful charges,
etc. Although it is not a necessary condition, the stories that have these
characteristics tend to include an expert source, different from the journalist's, which tries to help solve the problem.

Images can also illustrate the journalist's or the expert's tips and advice.
0= No
1= Yes
Examples:

> "*Disturbing noises are most common, and although it is hard to prevent,
> there are several ways to deal with an unwanted neighbor. In order to
> not come across any surprises, it is advisable to investigate what the
> neighbors and the neighborhood is like prior to buying a property.*"
> "*Keys to detect abuses in the charges made by commercial companies.*"

TIPS AND ADVICE (INDIVIDUAL RISKS)

Does the news story provide *tips* **or practical advice to solve personal
problems** that the audience could potentially face every day? For example, how to exercise and eat well in order to stay healthy, how to be a
smart buyer and save money, how to invest and assure savings and a safe
retirement, etc.?

Stories that have these characteristics tend to include an expert's advice, different from the journalist's, which tries to help solve problems in their everyday life. Images can also illustrate the journalist's or the expert's tips and advice.

0= No
1= Yes
  Examples:

> "*Be smart and start exercising today.*"
> "*Historic day at the Stock Exchange: the experts advise how to win.*"
> "*In order to begin your vacation stress-free, your vehicle inspection must be up-to-date, your spare tire in good condition, and you should have a toolkit and a first-aid kit.*"

INFORMATION/CONSUMER ADVICE

Does the news story inform the reader about **the latest trends in products and services in the market,** or **help them distinguish between products of different qualities** based on a third-party perspective, a study, or a review (the last one could be by the journalist too)?

0= No
1= Yes
  Examples:

> "*New Drug May Help Some Asthmatics, Study Finds.*"
> "*After one year on the market, coffee capsules have become popular among consumers. Around $400 pesos are paid for each cup of coffee made at home.*"
> *Two pictures shown side-by-side depict the effects of two detergents on a dirty shirt. Viewers are left to decide which detergent got the shirt the cleanest.*

Infotainment Role

The *infotainment role* of journalism uses different stylistics, narrative, and/or visual discourses in order to entertain and thrill the public. Here, journalism borrows from the conventions of entertainment genres (e.g., action movies, TV dramas, suspense novels) by using storytelling devices and establishing characters and setting. The logic here is to shock the audience's moral and aesthetic sensibilities. This type of journalism addresses the public as spectator, where the audience's relaxation and emotional experiences become the center of attention.

PERSONALIZATION

Does the news story provide **specific information regarding one or more persons and their different intellectual, physical, mental, social characteristics** (i.e., competence, leadership, appearance, capacity), or personal background (where they worked, studied, their name, marital status, etc.)? Simply providing the name or/and position of a person or a picture of a person is not enough to be included in this category.

Differently, a report that includes multiple visuals of the same subject can be an indicator of personalization.

0= No
1= Yes

Examples:

> "*The murderer—better known as MJ—is 34 years old, a married industrial engineer who works in the northern region of the country. The day of the trial, he arrived dejected, in dirty clothes and did not want to comment.*"

> "*Mr. Garcetti now becomes the first Jewish mayor of the city. He is the son of Gil Garcetti, a former district attorney. The grandson of Mexican immigrants who trace their roots to Italy, Mr. Garcetti speaks Spanish and used it frequently during the campaign.*"

PRIVATE LIFE

Does the news story refer to the **private life of one or more individuals?** Private life includes those aspects of a person's life that do not correspond to areas of public interest and/or do not belong to the public sphere context, and that *people normally prefer* to maintain in their personal sphere. Examples include a story on the president of the country as a father, or a famous businessman's youth and past. Other examples could be related to hobbies, affairs and love life, past, or vacations, among others.

If a news story makes general reference to the family of a person in a public context (for example, "the man accused of murder attended to the court with his wife" or "the president was sworn in on May 15, accompanied by his children"), it should not be considered as private life. Instead, if the news story makes reference to the family of a person in a personal context (for example, a picture taken by a paparazzi showing a sports figure on his/her holidays alone or with his/her wife, husband, children, lover, etc., or a news referring to the personal life of the family of someone, should be considered as private life).

Nevertheless, please note that the notion of privacy can be interpreted differently in various cultures. You should use it as it would be considered in your culture.

0= No
1= Yes
Examples:

> "*The minister states that his wife has tried to improve her wardrobe choices in order to meet the protocol requirements.*"
> "*The senator has been separated from her husband for months now.*"

SENSATIONALISM

Does the news story include the **use of style elements or descriptions in the story that highlight or emphasize the** *unusual, incredible, and spectacular?*
The tools used to introduce sensationalism in a story can be found in textual elements such as *metaphors, exaggeration, the use of dramatic superlative adjectives,* and storytelling devices that heighten suspense. Image elements for sensationalism include: the *use of distorted or fake images or the use of exaggerated images, for example.*
The difference with a simple description is illustrated in the following examples: "the barbarian crime" should be coded as sensationalist, while "a colorful ceremony" or "the distinguished president" should not.

0= No
1= Yes
Examples:

> "*The 'hard' stance of the porn movie industry on the use of condoms. They threatened to dump California if actors are forced to wrap it up.*"
> "Richard Brown is the 'Superman' of the patients. *The Mayor began a campaign to lower the prices of medicines for complex diseases.*"

EMOTIONS

Does the news story make explicit references to feelings or emotions? Elements typically included within this category are general descriptions of different emotions and the author's own emotional state, such as being anxious, angry, sad, confident, embarrassed, happy, disgusted, scared, and euphoric, among others.
Does the news story make **explicit references to or include feelings or emotions through textual, sound, or image elements?** Research literature defines six basic emotions: anger, disgust, fear, happiness, sadness, and

surprise. In news texts, these can be exhibited either by the journalist describing the emotional state of people and/or by presenting images that display the people in such emotional states.

Images may often portray an emotion experienced by individuals in the story. Typical images in this category include people crying, yelling, expressing anger or desperation, roaring with laughter, etc.

Coding for the presence of emotions requires a moderate to high level of expression, thus a simple smile, for example, would not count as significant emotion.

0= No
1= Yes
   Examples:

> "*Yesterday, this former coal worker was coming back home happy, eager to hug his family and to begin a new stage of his life.*"
> "*Woman whose child was stolen suffered 22 hours of deep anguish, pain, and uncertainty.*"

MORBIDITY

Does the news story exacerbate the audience's attention through textual or image elements, describing or **portraying acts of violence, crime, extreme poverty, or sex scenes/scandal in the news, or of the subjects *in concrete detail*?**

The notion of morbidity can be perceived and interpreted differently in various cultures. You should use it as it would be considered in your culture.

0= No
1= Yes
   Examples:

> "*Deranged, he got her off the car at a deserted path, where he began to beat and ultimately strangle her, choking her with his bare hands, using all of his strength until he finally killed her.*"

Pictures of cadavers and dying people after a terrorist attack.

Civic Role

The *civic role* focuses on the connection between journalism, the citizenry, and public life. Journalistic performance that reflects these ideas encourage the public to get involved in public debate and to participate in social, political, and cultural life. The space given to sources without social empowerment who demand recognition or reinstatement of a right is an important aspect of this role. This role does not assume that it is the journalist who can create an improved community via their own resources; rather, the emphasis is on supporting the citizens' efforts to do so.

The performance of this role allows people to do their jobs as citizens in a broad sense. That is, this role focuses not only on educating citizens for participating in electoral processes, civil protests, as well as participation, affiliation, and support of political parties, but also on helping them to make sense of their own communities and on how they can be affected by different political decisions (heritage, city planning, population health, impact on environment, speed limit regulations, etc.).

CITIZEN REACTIONS

Does the news story include the **vision/reaction of regular or organized citizens on a topic or event,** showing how they perceive or are affected by political decisions? Quotes or references by citizens may be included.
0= No
1= Yes
   Examples:

> "*David Swanson, a Charlottesville native who was one of the organizers, said a group numbering in the hundreds had gathered on open walkways that face the building's atrium on the third, fifth, and seventh floors. He said they chanted, 'How do you fix the deficit? End the wars! Tax the rich!'*"
> "*The president of the students' federation, Camila Vallejo, said that Minister Joaquin Lavin's proposals (regarding the education crisis and the university model) will be analyzed by the students . . . 'There are points which fail, not all is in there, but there is an answer, which was what we were expecting.'*"

CITIZEN DEMAND

Does the news story include **regular or organized citizens' demands or proposals** on how different political decisions should be handled? Citizens may be included via direct or indirect quotes, or references made of them.
0= No
1= Yes
   Examples:

> "*The neighbors ask for public works in exchange for having the jail put close to their houses. They want work such as paving and installment of sewage systems to be done.*"

A news story about a prisoner on a hunger strike who is demanding better living conditions is accompanied by a photo of the emaciated man.

CREDIBILITY OF CITIZENS

Does the news story include information, such as the journalist's own statements, the opinion of another source, or the citation of evidence that enhances the **credibility of what the citizens perceive, denounce, or demand?**
0= No
1= Yes
   Examples:

> *"The spokesman for the residents has led the activities of people who demand to take part in the municipality's master plan. That is why he knows what he is talking about. The residents know that the state of the area can cause damage to the environment and they have been consistent in the arguments presented to local authorities."*

The news includes a graph showing that a citizen's labor claims are backed by the last five years of economic data.

LOCAL IMPACT

Does the news story mention or depict the **impact of certain political decisions on local geographical locations or settings?** Local geographically defined communities may include towns, provinces, or villages, among others.
0= No
1= Yes
   Examples:

> *"A group of neighbors from Santa Barbara filed an injunction to restrain the municipality from setting up a dumping site near a pond in the vicinity."*

A graphic shows the drop in violent crime, for each of the city's neighborhoods, following the introduction of a new community-based policing policy.

EDUCATING ON DUTIES AND RIGHTS

Does the news story **inform people on their duties and rights as citizens** (economic, social, and/or political)? For example, when the government gives a subsidy and the news story informs where to go, or how to justify voter absenteeism.

0= No
1= Yes
   Examples:

> "*If you are a woman, head of your household, and your income is in the $1,000–$2,500 range, you must fill out your social report in order to get the housing subsidy.*"
> *A map shows the boundaries of the various wards or precincts of the city, indicating where citizens for each precinct should go to vote.*

CONTEXTUAL BACKGROUND INFORMATION

Does the news story provide political, economic, or social **background information in order to make decisions as citizens** (to participate in elections, affiliation and support of political parties, participate in protests, to make sense of how their communities can be affected by political decisions, etc.)?

Background information can be distinguished from current facts. It involves more specificity in terms of the information provided, contributing with essential **political, economic, or social-level context to the facts that are being reported.** It includes explaining actors' and sources' positions or decisions (e.g., how they have previously behaved), the reasons behind demonstrations, or the objectives of citizen groups, etc.

0= No
1= Yes
   Examples:

> "*Initially, only the 24 Peronist pact senators were expected to vote in favor of the initiative, plus two former Supreme Court ministers. However, yesterday, two more senators who have traditionally had a tougher stance in favor of the death penalty joined the initiative.*"

CITIZEN QUESTIONS

Does the news story include **inquiries from common people for politicians or those who are in power?** Citizens may be included via quotes, or references made of them.

0= No
1= Yes
   Examples:

> "*The president of the Almind Resident's Association confronted the mayor about the dumping site over which their houses were built: "What solution can you give us?"*"

INFORMATION ON CITIZEN ACTIVITIES

Within the news story, does the journalist give **information about citizen acts, such as campaigns, collective actions, commemorations, demonstrations, and protests?** Normally, this type of story includes information on where and when these activities occurred, and can also explain the importance of these acts for the community.

0= No
1= Yes
   Examples:

> *"The resident's association of the locality of Tolus organized a symbolic act for August 20 at 11 am, in which trees will be planted all along the route in which the new metro line will pass."*

The news reports on a cycling event organized by an ecological civil society group and it shows a map with the route for the event.

SUPPORT OF CITIZEN MOVEMENTS

Does the story include information, such as the journalist's own statements, the opinion of sources, or the citation of evidence that **support the objectives of an organization or citizen movement, and/or position the organization as a positive example to follow?**

0= No
1= Yes
   Examples:

> *"The residents' associations showed the ability to represent the legitimate demands of the residents of the area, to which the municipality was forced to listen and accept them."*

The news includes a series of pictures depicting how an ecological citizen group's annual clean-up effort has improved the quality of a creek running through their neighborhood.

Appendix 2
JRP Survey on Journalistic Roles

Thank you for agreeing to take part in this survey.

The questionnaire contains several types of questions. Please use the mouse or keyboard to indicate *(or please tell me what is the – in the case of PIs conducting a face-to-face interview or using a self-administered questionnaire mode)* the option of your choice.

(**FOR ONLINE SURVEY**) Finally, click the "Submit" button to send your answers to us.

Below is a list of specific journalistic practices that can be followed when reporting a news story. Please read the instructions to answer the questions:

— Please read the statements in the left-hand column and answer the question in the middle column based on how much importance you ascribe to each of these practices as a journalist. Please use the 5-point scale where *1 is "not important at all," 2 is "not very important," 3 is "somewhat important," 4 is "quite important," and 5 is "extremely important."*

— Then, in the right-hand column, please rate the statements based on what you can actually do in your work. Specifically, we would like to know how common these practices are in the stories you get published. Please use the 5-point scale where *1 is "not common at all," 2 is "not common," 3 is "sometimes," 4 is "quite common," and 5 is "extremely common."*

	How much importance do you give to each of these professional practices as a journalist?					How common are these practices in the news stories you get published?				
	1 Not important at all	2 Not very important	3 Somewhat important	4 Quite important	5 Extremely important	1 Not common at all	2 Not very common	3 Sometimes	4 Quite common	5 Extremely common
Questioning what powerful individuals or groups say or do										
Providing your opinion on the facts/issues you are reporting										
Including new voices of the citizen's group or organizations										
Featuring one or more individuals and their personal, intellectual, physical, and/or social characteristics										
Indicating how a particular event or action might influence the lives of ordinary people										
Formulating your own proposals regarding the development or solution to issues or events.										
Accusing powerful individuals or groups of holding back important information										
Expressing positive feelings about being from your own country										
Encouraging the public to behave in a specific way regarding different events or issues										
Including explicit references to emotions of people involved in an event										
Presenting official activities and/or national or regional policies in a positive light										

(Continued)

	How much importance do you give to each of these professional practices as a journalist?					How common are these practices in the news stories you get published?				
	1 Not important at all	2 Not very important	3 Somewhat important	4 Quite important	5 Extremely important	1 Not common at all	2 Not very common	3 Sometimes	4 Quite common	5 Extremely common
Including information on judicial or administrative processes regarding powerful individuals or groups										
Informing people on their economic, social, and/or political duties and rights as citizens										
Giving tips and practical guidance to the public to deal with everyday life problems. For example, how to deal with noisy neighbors, how to protect oneself in cases of natural disasters and so on										
Exposing conflicts between the journalist/media and powerful individuals or groups										
Using evaluative terms about events or persons in your news reporting										
Providing information on abuses of power or wrongdoing based on extensive inquiry and your own research, rather than simply relying on secondary sources										
Favorably stressing and highlighting the leadership or management skills of institutional powers and leaders										
Stressing the political, social, and economic achievements of your own country										
Explaining the causes, meaning or consequences of specific events or issues										
Championing the achievement of individuals or groups that belong to your own country or locality										

(Continued)

(Continued)

	How much importance do you give to each of these professional practices as a journalist?					How common are these practices in the news stories you get published?				
	1 Not important at all	2 Not very important	3 Somewhat important	4 Quite important	5 Extremely important	1 Not common at all	2 Not very common	3 Sometimes	4 Quite common	5 Extremely common
Quoting sources that question, criticize or accuse powerful groups or individuals of wrongdoing										
Providing information about products/services in the news*										
Including details of private life of people being covered in the news										
Judging what powerful individuals or groups say or do through your own subjective assertions										
Presenting background information and context for citizens regarding specific political events in the news										
Emphasizing unusual, spectacular or unexpected aspects of an event/issue by the use of stylistic elements or descriptions such as dramatic adjectives, and/or metaphors in the news										
Mentioning the impact of political decisions beyond the capital and/or the main cities										
Including very concrete details when describing acts of violence, crime, sex scenes, or similar events in the news you are covering										
Giving a positive evaluation of a social organization or citizens' movement in the news										
Including different ideological, political, religious, ethnic and/or cultural perspectives in a news story										

* This statement remained in our scales when measuring perceived role enactment but not when measuring role conception.

** The statements in bold demonstrated goodness of fit in our models. As such, these are the indicators that remained in our scales. The others were not included because they did not present a decent goodness of fit with our data at the comparative level.

Below you will find a list of statements about possible functions of journalism in society. Please tell us how much importance you give to those functions and how common they are in the news stories you write.

— Please read the statements in the left-hand column and answer the question in the middle column based on *how important are for you each of these functions as a journalist*. Please use the 5-point scale where *1 is "not important at all," 2 is "not very important," 3 is "somewhat important," 4 is "quite important," and 5 is "extremely important."*

— Then, in the right-hand column, please rate the statements based on what you can actually do in your work. Specifically, *we would like to ask you to tell us* how common these things are in the news stories you get published. Please use the 5-point scale where *1 is "not common at all," 2 is "not common," 3 is "sometimes," 4 is "quite common," and 5 is "extremely common."*

	How much importance do you give to each of these functions as a journalist?					How common are these things in the news stories you get published?				
	1 Not important at all	2 Not very important	3 Somewhat important	4 Quite important	5 Extremely important	1 Not common at all	2 Not very common	3 Sometimes	4 Quite common	5 Extremely common
To monitor and scrutinize political leaders										
To provide analysis of current affairs										
To champion national values										
To provide advice and direction in matters of daily life										
To provide information people need to make political decisions										
To influence public opinion										
To support national development										
To advocate a particular point of view										
To provide entertainment and relaxation										
To influence public policy decisions										
To educate the audience										
To be a detached observer										
To motivate people to participate in political activity										
To monitor business										
To support government policy										
To provide the audience with the information that is most interesting										
To surveil civic society										
To convey a positive image of political leaders										
Let people express their views										
To provide the kind of news that attracts the largest audience										
To promote tolerance and cultural diversity										
To convey a positive image of economic leaders										
To advocate for social change										

** The statements in bold demonstrated goodness of fit in our models. As such, these are the indicators that remained in our scales. The others were not included because they did not present a decent goodness of fit with our data at the comparative level.

In this section, you will find another list of statements about your work. Please tell us to what extent these statements apply to your daily practice. *Please follow the 5-point scale where 1 is "never," 2 is "seldom," 3 is "sometimes," 4 is "often," and 5 is "always."*

	Never	Seldom	Sometimes	Often	Always
When I have a good idea about a topic that I consider important, I always get it covered	1	2	3	4	5
I have quite or a lot of freedom to select the news/stories on which I will work on	1	2	3	4	5
I have quite or a lot of freedom to decide which aspects of a news/story I should emphasize	1	2	3	4	5
My work does not tend to be edited by others	1	2	3	4	5

In your view, how important are the following aspects in the news you write?

	Not important at all	Not very important	Somewhat important	Quite important	Extremely important
Presence of different sources and points of view	1	2	3	4	5
Usage of hard facts and verifiable data	1	2	3	4	5
Quotes from sources	1	2	3	4	5
Starting a story with facts before opinion	1	2	3	4	5
Using of reasoning or logic within the news item to prove or show a proposal	1	2	3	4	5
Using conditional expressions	1	2	3	4	5

This final set of questions will be used to make some general statistical comparisons within the study. None of it will be used to identify you or anyone else participating in the study.

In your daily work, do you work on:

1. a specific beat
2. different beats

Which beat do you work on?

. . . .

How many news items do you normally write in a regular week?

. . . .

What is your current position in your newsroom?

1   Editor
2. Reporter
3. Trainee
4. Other (specify)

What is your current employment status?

1. Full-time
2. Part-time
3. Freelancer
4. Other (specify): . . . .

How many years have you been working as a journalist?

. . . .

How many years have you been working for your news organization?

. . . .

Gender

1. Male
2. Female

What is your age?

What is your level of education?

1. Did not complete high school
2. Some university studies, but no degree
3. Bachelor's degree or equivalent
4. Master's degree or equivalent
5. Ph.D.

(If your answer is 3, 4, or 5) What was your major?

. . . .

In political matters, people talk of "the left," "the right," and the "center." On a scale where 0 is left, 10 is right, and 5 is center, where would you place yourself?

0	1	2	3	4	5	6	7	8	9	10

Thank you!

Appendix 3

Journalistic Role Performance Domains and Roles: Models Fit (CFA)

Domain/ Level	Role performance*	Role conception**	Perceived role enactment***
Journalistic Voice	χ2 = 415.530, p < .001; RMSEA = .038 (90% confidence interval [CI] = .035, .041); CFI= .978; TLI=.963	χ2 = 65.876, p < .001; RMSEA = .049 (90% confidence interval [CI] = .031, .060); CFI=.929; TLI=.865	χ2 = 59.734, p < .001; RMSEA = .044 (90% confidence interval [CI] = .030, .054); CFI=.942; TLI=.879
Power Relations	χ2 = 5132.104, p < .001; RMSEA = .029 (90% confidence interval [CI] = .028, .033), CFI = .921, TLI = .927	χ2 = 329.823, p < .001; RMSEA = .017 (90% confidence interval [CI] = .009, .020); CFI = .938; TLI = .898	χ2 = 345.227, p < .001; RMSEA = .023 (90% confidence interval [CI] = .016, .031); CFI = .911; TLI = .863
Audience Approach	χ2= 3204.178, p < .001; RMSEA = .020 (90% confidence interval [CI] = .020, .023); CFI = .976; TLI = .968	χ2 = 426.957, p < .001; RMSEA = .011 (90% confidence interval [CI] = .010, .020); CFI = .975, TLI = .914	χ2 = 435.356, p < .001; RMSEA = .013 (90% confidence interval [CI] = .011, .021); CFI = .963, TLI = .912

Root Mean Square Error of Approximation (RMSEA)
Comparative fit index (CFI)
Tucker—Lewis index (TLI)
* The goodness of fit was calculated for the 18-countries full dataset of news content
** The goodness of fit was calculated for the 9-countries full survey dataset
*** The goodness of fit was calculated for the 9-countries full survey dataset

Index

Note: Page numbers in *italics* indicate figures; page numbers in **bold** indicate tables.

advanced democracies interventionist role in **93**, 99
Argentina 46; analytical sub-dimensions of civic role in **132**, *133*, *134*; audience approach 74, *75*; audience approach roles *75*; correlation between journalistic roles in **76**; detached orientation of watchdog role **109**, *111*, *112*; elite-supporting orientation of loyal-facilitator role **114**, *116*, *117*; infotainment role performance **135**, *136*; interventionist orientation of watchdog role **110**, *111*, *112*; interventionist role **70**, *72*; interventionist role in **90**, *92*, 98–99; interventionist role in popular and elite press **95**; nation-supporting orientation of loyal-facilitator role **115**, *116*, *117*; newspaper, audience orientation and news items **48**; news topics, sources and geographic focus **176**; performance of journalistic roles in **71**; power relation roles *72*, *74*; role performances in **81**; service role performance **138**, *139*
audience approach: business principles 193; civic role 35, 126–127; country variance in 73–75, *75*; domains and roles **288**; hybridization of roles within 139–140, 142; infotainment role 35, 127–128; journalistic roles 37, *38*; organizational effects 194, 195, 197, 198; professional culture

of journalism in 125–126; role domain 35–36, 233–234; service role 35–36, 128–129; situational and contextual influence on role influence 129–130

Biden, Joe 4
Brazil 46; analytical sub-dimensions of civic role in **132**, *133*, *134*; audience approach*75*; audience approach roles *75*; correlation between journalistic roles in **76**; detached orientation of watchdog role **109**, *111*, *112*; elite-supporting orientation of loyal-facilitator role **114**, *116*, *117*; infotainment role performance **135**, *136*; interventionist orientation of watchdog role **110**, *111*, *112*; interventionist role **70**, *72*; interventionist role in **90**, *92*; interventionist role in popular and elite press **95**; nation-supporting orientation of loyal-facilitator role **115**, *116*, *117*; newspaper, audience orientation and items **48**; news topics, sources and geographic focus **176**; performance of journalistic roles in **71**; power relation roles *72*, *74*; service role performance **138**, *139*

Chile 46; analytical sub-dimensions of civic role in **132**, *133*, *134*; audience approach 74, *75*; audience approach roles *75*;

correlation between journalistic roles in **76**; detached orientation of watchdog role **109**, *111, 112*; elite-supporting orientation of loyal-facilitator role **114**, *116, 117*; infotainment role performance **135**, *136*; interventionist orientation of watchdog role **110**, *111*, *112*; interventionist role **70**, *72*; interventionist role in **90**, *92*; interventionist role in popular and elite press **95**; miners trapped underground **4**, **6**, **36**, **149**; multiple roles in **77**; nation-supporting orientation of loyal-facilitator role **115**, *116, 117*; newspaper, audience orientation and news items **48**; news topics, sources and geographic focus **176**; power relation roles **73**, *74*; service role performance **138**, *139*

China **46**, **61**; analytical sub-dimensions of civic role in **132**, *133, 134*; audience approach **74**, **75**; audience approach roles *75*; correlation between journalistic roles in **76**; detached orientation of watchdog role **109**, *111, 112*; elite-supporting orientation of loyal-facilitator role **114**, *116, 117*; infotainment role performance **135**, *136*; interventionist orientation of watchdog role **110**, *111*, *112*; interventionist role **70**, *72*; interventionist role in **90**, *92*; interventionist role in popular and elite press **95**; multiple roles in **77**; nation-supporting orientation of loyal-facilitator role **115**, *116, 117*; newspaper, audience orientation and news items **48**; news topics, sources and geographic focus **176**; performance of journalistic roles in **71**; power relation roles **73**, *74*; role performances in **80**, **81**; service role performance **138**, *139*

civic role: advocate and educator orientations **140–141**; analytical sub-dimensions and indicators in **132**, *133, 134*; approaches to, in news **130–133**; audience approach **35**, *38, 39*, **126–127**; audience approach by country *75*; business principles and **191**; conception-performance perception-performance and conception-perception gaps *155*; correlations between societal variables and performance **213**, **214–215**; country differences in conception-performance perception-performance and conception-perception gaps *157*; country variance in journalistic role **73–75**, *75*; news topics **177**, **178**; organizational effects **194**, **195**, **197**, **198**; performance in news by country **71**; relationship between conception, enactment and performance **161**; social-level effects on role performance **218**; societal variables **211**; story-level effects on role performance **179–181**; survey items and coding indicators **53**

civil rights **27**, **214**

clientelism **12**

Communist Party, journalists in Cuba **105**

comparative: content analyses **189**; data **15**; media system **25**, **205**; research **3**, **9–11**, **16**, **34**, **59–61**, **150**, **238–239**; role conceptions **68**; sampling of countries **47**, **48–49**;

comparative studies **59**, **100**, **206**; journalism and journalistic roles **9–12**, **227**; journalistic interventionism **88–89**;

confirmatory factor analyses (CFAs) **59**

consumerism **9**

content analysis **8**, **10**, **46**, **61**, **238–239**; measurements **51–52**, **55**; role performance indicators **53–55**, **57**, **59**, **150**, **154**; sample units (media outlets) **47–50**, **241**; units of analysis **50–51**

COVID–19 pandemic **5**, **6**, **36**, **130**, **225**

Cuba **46**, **61**; analytical sub-dimensions of civic role in **132**, *133, 134*; audience approach **74**; audience approach roles *75*; correlation between journalistic roles in **76**; detached orientation of watchdog role **109**, *111, 112*; elite-supporting orientation of

loyal-facilitator role **114**, *116*, *117*; infotainment role performance **135**, *136*; interventionist orientation of watchdog role **110**, *111*, *112*; interventionist role 70, 72; interventionist role in *90*, *92*; interventionist role in popular and elite press **95**; journalists in Havana 105; loyal-facilitator role 73; multiple roles in 77, 78; nation-supporting orientation of loyal-facilitator role **115**, *116*, *117*; newspaper, audience orientation and items **48**; news topics, sources and geographic focus 174–175; performance of journalistic roles in **71**; power relation roles 73, *74*; role performances in 79, 81; service role performance **138**, *139*
cultural pragmatism 31–33

Deliberative Democracy Index 209, 215
democracy: principles of 209; quality of 208–209
Democracy Index (DemIndex) 208–209, **213**, 215
Democratic Corporatist model: interventionist role in 98; media system 10–11, 47
development journalism 103
dynamic interactionism 31, 32

EcoFreedom 209, **213**
Economic Freedom Index, Heritage Foundation (HF) 209, 212, 214, 219, 221
Economist Intelligence Unit (EIU) 207
Ecuador, news topics, sources and geographic focus **176**
elite press: audience orientation 193, 199; indicators of interventionism 94, **94**, **95**, 220; popular and 99–100, 137, 142, 220, 231–232; service role 137
European media systems 10–11

factor analysis **240**
factorial invariance **240**
Four Theories of the Press (Siebert, Peterson and Schramm) 205
Fox News 4

Freedom House (FH) 207–208; Economic Environment 215–216, **217**, **218**; FH Civil Liberties 209, 213, 215, 222n10; FH Political Rights 209, **213**, 215, 222n10; Freedom Press Index 221, 222n1–3; Legal Environment 215–216, **217**, **218**; Political Environment 215–216, **217**, **218**; societal variables **211**
functional role theory 31

gap(s) 7, 17, 154; conception-perception *155*, *156*, *157*, *158*, 159, 162; conception-performance 154–155, *155*, *156*, *157*, *158*, 162, 163; ideals and practices 30, 37, 47, 147–149, 151, 227–229; link as a 149, 154–159, 234–235; normative-practice 80; perception-performance *155*, *156*–159, *156*, *157*, *158*, 162, 163
Germany 46; analytical sub-dimensions of civic role in **132**, *133*, *134*; audience approach 74, 75; audience approach roles *75*; correlation between journalistic roles in **76**; detached orientation of watchdog role **109**, *111*, *112*; elite-supporting orientation of loyal-facilitator role **114**, *116*, *117*; infotainment role performance **135**, *136*; interventionist orientation of watchdog role **110**, *111*, *112*; interventionist role 72; interventionist role in *90*, *92*; interventionist role in popular and elite press **95**; multiple roles in 77; nation-supporting orientation of loyal-facilitator role **115**, *116*, *117*; newspaper, audience orientation and news items **48**; news topics, sources and geographic focus 174–175; performance of journalistic roles in **71**; power relation roles 72, *74*; response rate 56; role performances in 80, 81; service role performance **138**, *139*
Greece 46; analytical sub-dimensions of civic role in **132**, *133*, *134*; audience approach roles *75*; correlation between journalistic roles in **76**; detached orientation

of watchdog role **109**, *111, 112*; elite-supporting orientation of loyal-facilitator role **114**, *116, 117*; infotainment role performance **135**, *136*; interventionist orientation of watchdog role **110**, *111, 112*; interventionist role 70; interventionist role in *90, 92*; interventionist role in popular and elite press 95; nation-supporting orientation of loyal-facilitator role **115**, *116, 117*; newspaper, audience orientation and news items **48**; news topics, sources and geographic focus **174–175**; performance of journalistic roles in 71; power relation roles 72, 73, *74*; role performances in 80; service role performance **138**, *139*

Heritage Foundation (HF) 207, 209; Economic Freedom Index 209, 212, 214, 219, 221

Hong Kong 46; analytical sub-dimensions of civic role in **132**, *133, 134*; audience approach 74, 75; audience approach roles *75*; correlation between journalistic roles in **76**; detached orientation of watchdog role **109**, *111, 112*; elite-supporting orientation of loyal-facilitator role **114**, *116, 117*; infotainment role performance **135**, *136*; interventionist orientation of watchdog role **110**, *111, 112*; interventionist role 70, *72*; interventionist role in *90, 92*; interventionist role in popular and elite press 95; multiple roles in 77; nation-supporting orientation of loyal-facilitator role **115**, *116, 117*; newspaper, audience orientation and news items **48**; news topics, sources and geographic focus **176**; performance of journalistic roles in 71; power relation roles 73, *74*; response rate 56; role performances in 80; service role performance **138**, *139*

Hungary 46; analytical sub-dimensions of civic role in **132**, *133, 134*; audience approach 74, 75; audience approach roles *75*;

correlation between journalistic roles in **76**; detached orientation of watchdog role **109**, *111, 112*; elite-supporting orientation of loyal-facilitator role **114**, *116, 117*; infotainment role performance **135**, *136*; interventionist orientation of watchdog role **110**, *111, 112*; interventionist role 70, 72; interventionist role in *90, 92*; interventionist role in popular and elite press 95; multiple roles in 77; nation-supporting orientation of loyal-facilitator role **115**, *116, 117*; newspaper, audience orientation and news items **48**; news topics, sources and geographic focus **174–175**; performance of journalistic roles in **71**; power relation roles 72, *74*; role performances in 80; service role performance **138**, *139*

hybridization 7, 108, 130; of audience approach domain 129, 139–140; of civic and infotainment 140, 234; of civic and service roles 129; of infotainment and interventionist 136; of infotainment and service 130, 139; of journalistic cultures 37, 68–69, 78–81, 89, 118–120, 206, 230, 237; news and power 118–120; professional roles 11, 14, 16–18, 40, 75, 126, 129, 226, 231, 233, 235–236; role and sub-role 121, 142; sensitizing concept 40

ideals 24, 28; democratic role 195; of developmental journalism 86, 98 institutional behavior and 162; journalistic norms and 228; loyal-facilitator 187; news practices and 162–163, 193; normative 7, 27, 150, 159, 162, 229, 234–235, **240**; practice and 30, 37, 47, 147–149, 151, 227–229; of professional journalism 3, 7, 28, 160, 163, 168, 225–226, 229–230; roles as 10, 27–29, 46, 160, 168, **240**; service-oriented 162, 237; studying link between rhetoric and practice 148–149; *see also* gap(s)

infotainment role: audience approach 35, *38, 39*, 127–128;

audience approach by country 75; business principles and 190, 191; characteristics of 141; conception-performance perception-performance and conception-perception gaps *155*; correlations between societal variables and performance 213, 215; country differences in conception-performance perception-performance and conception-perception gaps *158*; country variance in journalistic role 73–75, *75*; elements of performance across news topics *136*; indicators of 135; news topics 177, 178; organizational effects 194, 195, *197*, 198; performance in news by country 71; performance of 134, **135**, 136, *136*; relationship between conception, enactment and performance **161**; social-level effects on role performance 218; societal variables **211**; story-level effects on role performance 179–181; survey items and coding indicators 54–55

Institutional Review Board (IRB) 58

interactionism 31, 32, 33

international research, processes for articulating 60–62

Internet: digital media 49, 77; digital technologies 22, 27, 100; journalistic media and 186–187; technology changes 22–23. 125

interpretative community 33

interventionism: call for action 88, 92–93; content-determined 88, 91; interpretation 88; journalistic autonomy 231–232; offering opinion 88; point of view 88, 92–93; research questions 89; style-determined 88, 91

interventionist role: conception-performance, perception-performance, conception-perception gaps *155*; content-related indicators of *90*, *92*; correlations between societal variables and performance 211, 212, **213**; country differences in conception-performance, perception-performance,

conception-perception gaps *156*; country variance in 70, 72; distribution of indicators measuring performance of 89–93; as elite-supporting 119; increase in 87–88; indicators of 231; journalistic voice 34; journalistic voice by country 72; as nation-supporting 119; news sources 178; news topics 177; organizational effects 194, **196**, 198; performance in different types of news stories 95–96, *96*; performance in journalism 97–100; performance in news by country 71; Polarized Pluralist model 98, 230; presence across different news topics 96–97, *97*; presence in different media types 94, **94**, 95; presence in types of political regimes 93, *93*–94; relationship between conception, enactment and performance **161**; social-level effects on role performance 217; societal variables **211**; story-level effects on role performance 179–181; study of 86–87; style-related indicators of *90*, *92*; survey items and coding indicators **54**

Ireland 46; analytical sub-dimensions of civic role in **132**, *133*, *134*; audience approach 74, 75; audience approach roles *75*; correlation between journalistic roles in **76**; detached orientation of watchdog role 109, *111*, *112*; elite-supporting orientation of loyal-facilitator role 114, *116*, *117*; infotainment role performance 135, *136*; interventionist orientation of watchdog role 110, *111*, *112*; interventionist role 72; interventionist role in *90*, *92*; interventionist role in popular and elite press 95; nation-supporting orientation of loyal-facilitator role 115, *116*, *117*; newspaper, audience orientation and news items 48; news topics, sources and geographic focus 176; performance of journalistic roles in **71**; power relation roles 73, *74*; service role performance 138, *139*

journalism: assumptions about
type of 228; changes in 22–24;
comparative studies on 9–12;
independence principle 187–189;
interpretive and opinion-based
85–86; invention of 8; neutral and
participant 86; performance 23;
performance of interventionist role
in 97–100; role performance as
research area 12–14; roles as ideals
27–29; roles as norms 25–27; roles
as performance 29–31; roles of
24–31
journalist(s): acting as experts 86;
analytical strategy 59; comparative
studies of journalism and roles
9–12; conceptual models of roles
33–37; measurements of 56–59;
role conception 28; roles as
dimensions and sub-dimensions
37–40; roles of 3–4, 6; sampling of
55–56; survey of 55–59
journalistic cultures: co-occurrence
of roles across countries
76–78; country variance in
role performance 67–68, **71**;
hybridization of 68–69, 78–81;
research questions of 69
journalistic interventionism, indicators
of 88–89
journalistic professionalism, Western
model of 8, 10, 11
journalistic role performance:
concept of 7; coupling news-
story-level factors and 168–172;
domains and roles 288; exploring
ideals and practice 147–148,
160, 162–163; imperfect match
between concept, enactment and
149–154; linking conception and
perception as relationship 159–160,
161; link of ideals and practice
as a gap 154–159, 234–235;
measuring societal-level predictors
of 207–210; multilevel models
influencing 215–216, 219–220;
perceived role enactment-role
performance gaps 156–159;
predictors of 234–238; research
questions 153; role conception-
perceived role enactment gaps 159;
role conception–role performance
gaps 154–155; societal-level

approach and 205–207, 220–222;
studying link between rhetoric and
practices 148–149; transcending
norms and looking into 226–229;
unraveling 229–234; *see also*
news-story-level approach;
organizational-level approach;
societal-level approach
Journalistic Role Performance
(JRP) project 7–9, 15, 16, 18;
challenges, actions and limitations
240–241; content analysis
47–55; future of JRP 238–239,
241–242; JRP Codebook for the
Analysis of Newspapers News
247–279; measurements 51–52,
55, 56–59, 62n3; processes for
articulating international research
60–62; sample units (media
outlets) 47–50, **48–49**; sampling
of countries 47; six roles of 52;
social-level and external indicators
59–60; survey items and coding
indicators **53–54**; survey of
journalists 55–59; three-stage
research project 46–47; unit of
analysis 50–51
journalistic voice 37, *38*; acting as
advocates in society 87; advocate-
neutral 86; definitions of two
types 85; domains and roles
288; interventionist role 70, 72;
journalistic roles 37, *38*, *39*; in
media 85; passive-active 86; role
domain 34
JRP Codebook for the Analysis of
Newspapers News 247–279; civic
role 275–279; general information
of news story 249–251; general
instructions 248; infotainment
role 272–275; interventionist
role 260–262; journalistic role
performance 259–279; loyal-
facilitator role 267–270; service
role 270–272; sources and
reporting methods 256–259; story
characteristics 251–256; watchdog
role 262–267
JRP Survey on Journalistic Roles 18,
46, 52, 280–287; actions **240–241**;
challenges **240–241**; lessons learned
238–239, 241–242; limitations
240–241; *see also* survey

Liberal Democracy Index 209, 215
Liberal media system 11, 47
literary journalism 99
loyal-facilitator role: business
    principles and 190–191;
    conception-performance
    perception-performance and
    conception-perception gaps *155*;
    correlations between societal
    variables and performance 212,
    213, 214; country differences
    in conception-performance,
    perception-performance,
    conception-perception gaps *157*;
    country variance in journalistic
    role 72–73, *74*; elite-supporting
    orientation across countries 114,
    116, *117*, 232–233; hybridization
    patterns in roles 120–122; nation-
    supporting orientation across
    countries 115, *116*, *117*; news
    sources 178; news topics 177;
    organizational effects 194, 195,
    196, 198; performance in news by
    country 71; power relations 35, *38*,
    39; power relations by country *74*;
    relationship between conception,
    enactment and performance 161;
    role of 103–104; role performances
    approaches of, in news 113,
    116–118; social-level effects on role
    performance 217; societal variables
    211; story-level effects on role
    performance 179–181; supporting
    elites and the nation 106–108;
    survey items and coding indicators
    54; watchdogs as ally with 119;
    watchdog *vs* 107

Malaysia 46; analytical sub-
    dimensions of civic role in 132,
    133, *134*; audience approach *74*,
    75; audience approach roles *75*;
    correlation between journalistic
    roles in *76*; detached orientation
    of watchdog role 109, *111*, *112*;
    elite-supporting orientation of
    loyal-facilitator role 114, *116*, *117*;
    infotainment role performance 135,
    136; interventionist orientation
    of watchdog role 110, *111*,
    112; interventionist role 70, *72*;
    interventionist role in *90*, *92*;

interventionist role in popular and
    elite press 95; multiple roles in 77,
    78; nation-supporting orientation of
    loyal-facilitator role 115, *116*, *117*;
    newspaper, audience orientation
    and items 49; news topics, sources
    and geographic focus 176;
    performance of journalistic roles
    in 71; power relation roles 73, *74*;
    service role performance 138, *139*
media coverage: Chilean mine
    accident 4, 6; COVID-19 pandemic
    5, 6; political polarization in
    186–187
media interventionism, concept of 106
media ownership 47, 60, 195, 196,
    197, 207, 208, 216; business
    principles 190, 193; corporate 191,
    193, 196, 199; cross- 211; owners
    23, 208, 216; private 191; 193,
    196, state 191, 196, 197, 198, 199,
    219, 236
media systems 8, 9–13, 68–69, 195,
    205–208, 220, 222; Democratic
    Corporatist 98; European 10;
    hybrid 11, 79; Liberal 11, 70;
    Mediterranean 86; non-Western
    60; Polarized Pluralist 11, 86, 98;
    sampling *241*; theory 25, 220, 230,
    238; Western models 47, 60
media types, interventionist role by
    different 94, *94*, *95*, 99
Mexico 46; analytical sub-
    dimensions of civic role in 132,
    133, *134*; audience approach *74*,
    75; audience approach roles *75*;
    correlation between journalistic
    roles in *76*; detached orientation
    of watchdog role 109, *111*, *112*;
    elite-supporting orientation of
    loyal-facilitator role 114, *116*, *117*;
    infotainment role performance 135,
    136; interventionist orientation
    of watchdog role 110, *111*,
    112; interventionist role 70, *72*;
    interventionist role in *90*, *92*;
    interventionist role in popular and
    elite press 95; multiple roles in 77,
    78; nation-supporting orientation of
    loyal-facilitator role 115, *116*, *117*;
    newspaper, audience orientation
    and items 49; news topics, sources
    and geographic focus 174–175;

performance of journalistic roles in 71; power relation roles 72, 74; service role performance **138**, *139*

narrative journalism 99
newsroom: business practices and culture 193–194; changing practices 191–192; press freedom factors 221; strengthening journalistic principles 200
news stories: coverage 9; global appeal 225; hard news 8–9, 11, 32, 137, 168; hybridization of journalistic roles 118–120; interventionist role by different 95–96, **96**; role performance and 228–229; soft news 8, 11, 32, 127, 168, 189, 191, 233, 242
news-story-level approach: analytical strategy 172–173; coupling role performance and 168–172; effects on journalistic role performance **179–181**; geographic focus 171–172, **175**, **176**; journalistic performance and 167–168, 173, 177–178, 182–183, 235–236; news sources 170–171, **175**, **176**; news topics 169–170, **174**, **176**; topics, sources and geographic focus by country **174–176**
news topics: advocate and educational sub-dimension of civic role *133*, *134*; elements of infotainment role performance *136*; elements of service role performance *139*; interventionist role across different 96–97, **97**, 119; performance of infotainment role 134, 136
non-democratic regimes, interventionist role in **93**, 99
non-Western: countries 12, 230, 239; journalism 80, 86, 98; media systems 60, 128; region/worlds 11, 68
norms roles as 25–27

objectivity, concept of 8
Olympic Games, Rio 104
organizational-level approach: audience-orientated journalistic roles 194, 195, **197**, 198; business principles of 189–191, 199–200, 236; changing newsroom practices

191–192; civic roles 194, 195, **197**, 198; infotainment roles 194, 195, **197**, 198; interventionist role performance 194, **196**, 198; journalistic independence 187–189, 199, 236; loyal-facilitators role 194, 195, **196**, 198; measures of principles 192–194; service roles 194, 195, **197**, 198; technological principles 191–192, 201; watchdogs role 194, 195, **196**, 198
organizational sociology 37

Participatory Democracy Index 209, 215
patriotism **54**, 62n3; Cuban journalism 73; loyal-facilitator role 270; nationalism and 121, 233; nation-supporting sub-dimension 107, **115**, 118
perceived enactment 30, 56, 58, 149–150, 154, 156, 158–159
performance: concept of 23, 32; roles as 29–31; *see also* journalistic role performance
Philippines 46; analytical sub-dimensions of civic role in **132**, *133*, *134*; audience approach 74, 75; audience approach roles *75*; correlation between journalistic roles in **76**; detached orientation of watchdog role **109**, *111*, *112*; elite-supporting orientation of loyal-facilitator role **114**, *116*, *117*; infotainment role performance 135, *136*; interventionist orientation of watchdog role **110**, *111*, *112*; interventionist role 70, 72; interventionist role in *90*, *92*; interventionist role in popular and elite press **95**; multiple roles in **77**; nation-supporting orientation of loyal-facilitator role **115**, *116*, *117*; newspaper, audience orientation and news items 49; news topics, sources and geographic focus **176**; performance of journalistic roles in **71**; power relation roles 73, **74**; service role performance **138**, *139*
Poland 46; analytical sub-dimensions of civic role in **132**, *133*, *134*; audience approach 74; audience

approach roles 75; correlation between journalistic roles in 76; detached orientation of watchdog role 109, *111*, *112*; elite-supporting orientation of loyal-facilitator role 114, *116*, *117*; infotainment role performance 135, *136*; interventionist orientation of watchdog role 110, *111*, *112*; interventionist role 70, 72; interventionist role in 90, 92; interventionist role in popular and elite press 95; multiple roles in 77; nation-supporting orientation of loyal-facilitator role 115, *116*, *117*; newspaper, audience orientation and news items 49; news topics, sources and geographic focus 174–175; performance of journalistic roles in 71; power relation roles 72, 74; role performances in 80; service role performance 138, *139*
Polarized Pluralist model 80, 90; interventionist role in 98, 230; media system 11, 47; in Mediterranean media systems 86–87
political parallelism 12
political regimes: indicators of interventionist role by type of 93, 93–94, 99; journalists monitoring elites 105
popular press: audience orientation 99, 193, 199; elite and 99–100, 137, 142, 220, 231–232; indicators of interventionism 94, **94**, **95**, 220; infotainment role 35, 127, 134, 142; service role 137
power relations: business principles and 189–191; detachment and interventionism for monitoring elites 105–106, 232; domains and roles 288; hybridization of journalistic roles in news 118–120; journalism independence and 187–189; journalistic roles 37, *38*, *39*; loyal-facilitators 35, *38*, *39*, 72–73, *74*, 103–104, 120–122; organizational effects 194, 195, 196, 198; political leaning and 193; role domain 35; supporting elites and nation 106–108, 232;

watchdogs 35, *38*, *39*, 72–73, *74*, 103, 120–122
press *see* elite press; popular press
professional roles 3, 6, 7–8, 11, 13–18, 46, 126; civic role 73–75, *75*; conceptions among journalists 86; conceptual models of journalistic 33–37; construct of 23–25, 33, 226, 238; correlations between roles 76; hybridization of 129, 206, 226, 236; as ideals 27–29; infotainment role 73–75, *75*; intersection of roles 37–40; interventionist role 70, 71, 72; measurements 51, 56–57, 240; as norms 25–27; as paradigm divide of 31–33; performance 29–31, 89, 167, 200, 207, 227, 236–237; performing multiple roles 76–78, 228; service role 73–75, *75*; term 50; watchdog and loyal-facilitator roles 72–73, *74*
professionalism 8, 10, 24, 81, 87, 150

reporter voice 85
research role performance as emerging area 12–14
role interaction 10, 11
role performance, concept of 13
roles: audience approach 35–36; conceptual models of journalistic 33–37; as dimensions and sub-dimensions 37–40; as ideals 27–29; intersection of 37–40; of journalism 24–31; journalistic voice 34; as norms 25–27; paradigm divide of 31–33; as performance 29–31; power relations 35; term 24
Rousseff, Dilma 104
Russia 46; analytical sub-dimensions of civic role in 132, *133*, *134*; audience approach 74; audience approach roles 75; correlation between journalistic roles in 76; detached orientation of watchdog role 109, *111*, *112*; elite-supporting orientation of loyal-facilitator role 114, *116*, *117*; infotainment role performance 135, *136*; interventionist orientation of watchdog role 110, *111*, *112*; interventionist role 70, 72; interventionist role in 90, 92;

interventionist role in popular and elite press 95; multiple roles in 77; nation-supporting orientation of loyal-facilitator role 115, *116, 117*; newspaper, audience orientation and news items 49; news topics, sources and geographic focus 174–175; performance of journalistic roles in 71; power relation roles 74; role performances in 80; service role performance 138, *139*

service role: audience approach 35–36, *38, 39*, 128–129; audience approach by country 75; business principles and 190, 191; comparing indicators across news topics 141–142; conception-performance, perception-performance, conception-perception gaps *155*; correlations between societal variables and performance 213, 214–215; country differences in conception-performance, perception-performance, conception-perception gaps *158*; country variance in journalistic role 73–75, *75*; elements of performance across news topics 137, *139*; indicators of 137, **138**; news sources 178; organizational effects 194, 195, **197**, 198; performance in news by country 71; performance of 137, **138**, *139*; relationship between conception, enactment and performance 161; role indicators 52, **138**; social-level effects on role performance 218; societal variables 211; story-level effects on role performance 179–181; survey items and coding indicators 55
socialization process 26, 152, 167
social media 8, 33, 56, 163, 167, 171
societal-level approach: correlation analysis of factors influencing role performance 210–212, 213, 214–215; effects on journalistic role performance 217, 218; FoP (Freedom of Press) economic environment category 207, 208; FoP legal environment category 207–208; FoP political

environment category 207, 208; Freedom House (FH) 207, 209; Freedom in the World indices 207; Heritage Foundation (HF) 207, 209; journalistic role performance 205–207, 220–222, 236–237; measurement predictors of journalistic role performance 207–210; multilevel models influencing role performance 215–216, 219–220; principles of democracy 209; quality of democracy 208–209
Spain 46; analytical sub-dimensions of civic role in 132, *133, 134*; audience approach 74; audience approach roles *75*; correlation between journalistic roles in **76**; detached orientation of watchdog role 109, *111, 112*; elite-supporting orientation of loyal-facilitator role 114, *116, 117*; infotainment role performance 135, *136*; interventionist orientation of watchdog role 110, *111, 112*; interventionist role 72; interventionist role in 90, *92*; interventionist role in popular and elite press 95; multiple roles in 77, 78; nation-supporting orientation of loyal-facilitator role 115, *116, 117*; newspaper, audience orientation and news items 49; news topics, sources and geographic focus 174–175; performance of journalistic roles in 71; power relation roles 72, 73, *74*; role performances in 80; service role performance 138, *139*
survey 8, 10, 46–47; analytical strategy 59, 227, 238–239; items and coding indicators in 53, **54–55**; of journalists 55–59, 61, 150, **240–241**; JRP Survey on Journalistic Roles 280–287; measurements 56–59; sampling 55–56
Switzerland 46; analytical sub-dimensions of civic role in 132, *133, 134*; audience approach 75; audience approach roles *75*; correlation between journalistic roles in **76**; detached orientation

of watchdog role 109, *111*, *112*; elite-supporting orientation of loyal-facilitator role 114, *116*, *117*; infotainment role performance 135, *136*; interventionist orientation of watchdog role 110, *111*, *112*; interventionist role 72; interventionist role in 90, 92; interventionist role in popular and elite press 95; nation-supporting orientation of loyal-facilitator role 115, *116*, *117*; newspaper, audience orientation and news items 49; news topics, sources and geographic focus 174–175; performance of journalistic roles in 71; power relation roles 73, 74; role performances in 80, 81; service role performance 138, *139*
symbolic interactionism 31, 32

transitional democracies interventionist role in 93, 99
Trump, Donald 4, 6

United States 46; analytical sub-dimensions of civic role in 132, *133*, *134*; audience approach 75; audience approach roles 75; correlation between journalistic roles in 76; detached orientation of watchdog role 109, *111*, *112*; elite-supporting orientation of loyal-facilitator role 114, *116*, *117*; infotainment role performance 135, *136*; interventionist orientation of watchdog role 110, *111*, *112*; interventionist role 70, 72; interventionist role in 90, 92, 98–99; interventionist role in popular and elite press 95; multiple roles in 77; nation-supporting orientation of loyal-facilitator role 115, *116*, *117*; newspaper, audience orientation and news items 49; news topics, sources and geographic focus 176; performance of journalistic roles in 71; power relation roles 72, 74; service role performance 138, *139*
U.S. Congress, Trump's impeachment 4, 6

Varieties of Democracy Project (V-Dem) 207, 213
Vietnam War 27, 127

war on terrorism 105
watchdog role: business principles and 190–191; conception-performance, perception-performance, conception-perception gaps *155*; correlations between societal variables and performance 211, 212, 213, 214; country differences in conception-performance, perception-performance, conception-perception gaps *156*; country variance in journalistic role 72–73, 74; detached orientation of role across countries 109, *111*; hybridization patterns in roles 120–122; interventionist orientation of role across countries 110, *111*; loyal-facilitator as ally with 119; loyal-facilitators *vs* 107; in monitoring elites 105–106, 232; news sources 178; news topics 177; organizational effects 194, 195, 196, 198; performance in news by country 71; power relations 35, *38*, *39*; power relations by country 74; relationship between conception, enactment and performance 161; reporting 9, 106; role as 34, 103; role performances approaches of, in news 108, 111–113; scrutiny of detached orientation 120; social-level effects on role performance 217; societal variables 211; story-level effects on role performance 179–181; survey items and coding indicators 53; variations across news topics *112*
Watergate scandal 27, 106, 127
Western European journalism 98
Western models: of journalism 80–81, 228; of professionalism 8, 10, 11, 150
Western countries/world 11, 60, 72, 226, 230; democracies 11, 60, 106, 206; media systems 47, 60, 68
World Cup 104